CRIMINAL LAW REFORM NOW VOLUME 2

If you could change one part of the criminal law, what would it be? Following the success of the first volume, the same question is put to a new selection of leading academics and practitioners.

The first eight chapters of the collection present their responses in the form of legal reform proposals, with topics ranging across criminal law, criminal justice and evidence – including corporate liability, consent to bodily harms, prostitution, domestic abuse, economic crimes, defendant anonymity, appeal court structures and the procedures of the Criminal Cases Review Commission.

Each chapter is followed by a comment from a different author, providing an additional expert view on each proposal. Finally, the last two chapters broaden the debate to discuss criminal law reform in general, from the challenges of decriminalisation to exploring the systemic dynamics of centralisation, austerity and politicisation. The collection highlights and explores the current reform debates that matter most to legal experts, with each chapter making a positive case for change.

Criminal Law Reform Now

Proposals and Critique
Volume 2

Edited by
Melissa Bone
JJ Child
and
Jonathan Rogers

•HART•
OXFORD • LONDON • NEW YORK • NEW DELHI • SYDNEY

HART PUBLISHING

Bloomsbury Publishing Plc

Kemp House, Chawley Park, Cumnor Hill, Oxford, OX2 9PH, UK

1385 Broadway, New York, NY 10018, USA

29 Earlsfort Terrace, Dublin 2, Ireland

HART PUBLISHING, the Hart/Stag logo, BLOOMSBURY and the Diana logo are trademarks of Bloomsbury Publishing Plc

First published in Great Britain 2024

A catalogue record for this book is available from the British Library.

A catalogue record for this book is available from the Library of Congress.

ISBN: HB: 978-1-50995-918-1
ePDF: 978-1-50995-920-4
ePub: 978-1-50995-919-8

Typeset by Compuscript Ltd, Shannon

PREFACE

In March 2021, the Law Commission launched a public consultation on its 14th programme of law reform. Our criteria for choosing programme projects, previously agreed with the Lord Chancellor, are related to their impact, suitability, support, urgency, and the need to achieve a balanced portfolio of projects. In the context of the criminal law, the impact might be modernisation to respond to technological advances, for example our recent projects on modernising communications, protection of official data and intimate image abuse offences, which will also improve access to justice for victims and ensure that defendants' right to freedom of expression is protected. We also asked consultees specifically about potential projects on technological advances and procedural efficiency in the criminal courts, and search, production and seizure of electronic material. Or the impact might be economic, for instance the predicted £250 million savings over ten years of the Sentencing Code, which will also improve the efficiency and simplicity of the law and make it more transparent. Or the greatest impact might be in relation to fairness: our recent project on confiscation of the proceeds of crime after conviction aimed to make the law fairer and thereby more efficient. Making more realistic confiscation orders would ensure fairness to the defendant, who is more likely to be able to satisfy an order which more accurately reflects their benefit from crime. In our current project on evidence in sexual offences prosecutions, we aim to prevent rape myths from influencing trials, better protect complainants' privacy, ensure complainants are treated humanely and that defendants are tried fairly. Several consultees raised the perceived unfairness of the single justice procedure discussed by Stephen Wooler in his chapter.

We received around 500 responses to the consultation, covering nearly 200 possibilities for law reform. In April 2022 and again in February 2023, we decided to extend the timetable for finalising the programme:

> We have concluded that now is not the time to set in stone a list of projects which will determine a significant percentage of our work over the next four to five years and beyond. We are concerned that to do so will reduce our capacity to respond flexibly to law reform needs arising in the near future.

Nonetheless, some projects we considered for inclusion in the 14th programme have already been referred to us by government departments and work on them has commenced. The first is a holistic review of contempt of court which was one of the projects we suggested as part of the consultation and was well-supported, particularly by judges. That project involves a more general review and codification of the law than our previous work on contempt, and will also consider the extension of a contempt jurisdiction to first instance tribunals and the utility of the distinction between criminal and civil contempt.

Another project we suggested as part of the 14th programme consultation was either a technical or more substantive review of the law governing criminal appeals. The government asked us to take on the broader project, which is examining, among other issues, the two possible reforms considered by Paul Jarvis in his chapter: consolidating the three different ways for the defendant to challenge decisions made in the magistrates' court; and expanding the scope for the prosecution to appeal an acquittal beyond the current provision for acquittals tainted by an offence against the administration of justice and the limited so-called 'double jeopardy' appeals. (The latter provision for prosecution appeals implemented Law Commission recommendations that had been prompted by the Macpherson Report into the murder of Stephen Lawrence.) That project is also considering potential reform of the powers of the Criminal Cases Review Commission (CCRC), which Lucy Welsh discusses in her chapter. In particular, we are examining whether the test used by the CCRC to refer cases to the appellate court should be reformed. Currently that test requires the CCRC to decide whether there is a 'real possibility' that the conviction will not be upheld. One of the possible reforms is advocated by Welsh: changing the test to whether 'there might (reasonably) have been a miscarriage of justice meaning that the conviction might be unsafe.'

Finally, we have recently been asked to take on a project on defences to homicide in the context of domestic abuse as part of the government's response to the Clare Wade domestic homicide review. Although the chapter by Vanessa Bettinson, Vanessa Munro and Nicola Wake focuses on compulsion-based defences which have less salience in the context of victims of domestic abuse who kill their abusers, multiple consultees suggested both that and other aspects of work on victims who become defendants as potential 14th programme projects. In relation to compulsion-based defences in particular, the Howard League for Penal Reform argued in its consultation response that the current defences of duress and compulsion fail the most vulnerable and exploited defendants and should be reformed to afford 'those who have felt compelled to act a meaningful opportunity to avoid being criminalised.'

Although the impetus for this collection was the consultation on the Law Commission's 14th programme, the collection rightly includes proposals for law reform that may not be suitable for the Commission. As our Chair has said, 'Our law reform programme will not include subjects where the relevant considerations are shaped primarily by political judgements (for example, abortion, capital punishment, decriminalisation of drug use) or issues of established Government policy such as taxation.' The chapters on the decriminalisation of prostitution by Tanya Palmer, anonymity for suspects prior to charge by Joe Purshore and modernising and simplifying tax evasion offences by Samantha Bourton arguably fall within this category, as did the conference presentation by Alex Stevens, Niamh Eastwood and Kirstie Douse on the decriminalisation of drug possession, to which Doug Husak responds in his chapter. (Although a decriminalisation project could become suitable for the Commission if the politically sensitive decision to decriminalise were taken by Government or Parliament, and the Commission was asked to design a regulatory regime, for example.) These proposals may nonetheless be of interest to government departments and Parliamentarians, in the same way as reforms too small to form a Law Commission project might be, such as the reform to the time limit on prosecutions for underage sexual intercourse in the Sexual Offences Act 1956 proposed by Jonathan Rogers in the CLRNN collection prompted by the Law Commission's consultation on its 13th programme of law reform. One could imagine such a reform being taken forward by a government department without the involvement of the Commission, or perhaps becoming a Private Member's Bill, just as more political proposals might find their way into a manifesto or King's Speech.

In contrast, the chapter by Daniel Bansal and Tracey Elliott on consent to bodily harm falls squarely within the realm of possible Law Commission projects, following on from earlier Law Commission work on consent in the criminal law in the mid-1990s, which was never completed. Inclusion in a programme of law reform requires the agreement of the Lord Chancellor. In addition, and as is the case whether a project is included in a programme or is an individual reference, Ministerial support from the department with policy responsibility for the relevant area of law is required. As our Chair said at the launch of the consultation on the 14th programme:

> If Government does not intend to see the law reformed, and there is no realistic prospect of any recommendations we make becoming law, then there is no reason for the Law Commission to embark upon a law reform project.

In their chapter, Jeremy Horder and Gabriele Watts consider an issue which partially arose in our project on corporate criminal liability which resulted in an options paper published in 2022, two options of which, a corporate offence of failure to prevent fraud and reform of the identification doctrine are currently before Parliament in the Economic Crime and Corporate Transparency Bill. The Commission did not consider Horder and Watts' proposal for liability for senior managers for crimes committed by those who are under their management authority (whether direct attribution or liability for failure to prevent such crimes) because such liability is neither corporate nor contingent on corporate criminal liability, so it fell outside of our project's scope.

The Commission – and in particular the criminal law team and I – are grateful for the enthusiasm with which the Criminal Law Reform Now Network has responded to our consultations on the 13th and 14th programmes of law reform and the high quality of presentations, chapters and responses that their two conferences have produced. Our door is always open to ideas for new projects, whether a new programme is on the horizon or not. Ideas can be submitted via a dedicated page on our website.

Professor Penney Lewis
Commissioner for Criminal Law
September 2023

CONTENTS

LIST OF CONTRIBUTORS

Paramjit Ahluwalia is a Barrister at 1 Pump Court Chambers. She has been named by *the Observer* (culture) in January 2019 as a 'new talent: rising star' in relation to her work 'representing society's most vulnerable, fighting human trafficking, modern day slavery and immigration crime.' She is the contributing author to the chapter on Modern Slavery and Immigration Offences in the leading Criminal Practitioner Text *Blackstone's Criminal Practice*. Paramjit published a popular blog 'Protecting domestic abuse survivors who offend' with *The Law Society Gazette* and *Criminal Law Reform Now Network* website.

Daniel Bansal is an Associate Professor of Law at the University of Leicester, UK. Daniel's teaching and research interests predominantly lie in the theory and doctrine of criminal law.

Vanessa Bettinson is a Professor of Criminal Law and Criminal Justice, Leicester De Montfort Law School, UK. Vanessa's research currently focuses on criminal justice and human rights responses to domestic violence and/or abuse. In particular, she is currently interested in comparative legal responses to coercive control.

Melissa Bone is an Associate Professor Leicester Law School, University of Leicester, and Criminal Law Reform Now Network Committee Member, UK. Melissa's research explores the values and opinions of people who use drugs on policy reform, the legal landscape of cannabis social clubs throughout Europe, cannabis activism and medical cannabis laws in the UK.

Sam Bourton is a Senior Lecturer in Law at the University of the West of England, UK. Sam's research interests lie in the law of financial crime, particularly, the law relating to tax evasion and money laundering. Sam is currently writing a monograph for Routledge, which examines the law and enforcement policies pertaining to tax evasion in the UK and US. Sam has published her research in several journals, including the *Criminal Law Review* and *Journal of Business Law*.

John Child is a Professor of Criminal Law at the University of Birmingham; Co-Director of the University of Birmingham Centre for Crime, Justice and Policing; Co-Director of the Criminal Law Reform Now Network. John's research interests centre on criminal law theory and doctrine, where he has published widely. John is a co-author of two leading criminal law textbooks: *Smith, Hogan and Ormerod's Essentials of Criminal Law* and *Simester and Sullivan's Criminal Law*.

Alison Cronin is a Principal Academic in Law, Bournemouth University, UK. Called to the Bar by the Honourable Society of the Inner Temple in 2004, Alison researches corporate crime and history and law.

John Curtis is a Barrister and In-House Counsel at the Criminal Cases Review Commission, UK. The Criminal Cases Review Commission (CCRC) is the statutory body responsible for investigating alleged miscarriages of justice in England, Wales, and Northern Ireland. It was established by section 8 of the Criminal Appeal Act of 1995 and began work on 31 March 1997. John is leading on the CCRC's response to the Law Commission's review of criminal appeals and contributed to the chapter on the CCRC in *Taylor on Criminal Appeals* (3rd edition).

Michelle Madden Dempsey is Harold Reuschlein Scholar Chair and Professor of Law, Villanova University Charles Widger School of Law, USA. Michelle writes in the areas of criminal law, feminist legal theory, and jurisprudence. She has served as Chair of the American Association of Law School's Section on Scholarship and Section on Jurisprudence, and was elected to the American Law Institute in 2015. Her book, *Prosecuting Domestic Violence: A Philosophical Analysis*, was awarded second prize in the UK's Society of Legal Scholars Peter Birks Award for Outstanding Legal Scholarship.

Matthew Dyson is Professor of Civil and Criminal Law, Tutorial Fellow of Corpus Christi College, Faculty of Law, University of Oxford; Global Professor of Law, London Law Programme at the University of Notre Dame in England; Associate Member of 6KBW College Hill. Matt specialises in criminal law, tort law, and the relationship between the two. His work is often historical and comparative, a recent example being *Explaining Tort and Crime*.

Tracey Elliott is a Lecturer in Health Care Law, University of Leicester, UK. Tracey was called to the Bar and practised from 4 Paper Buildings and 9–12 Bell Yard, specialising in criminal litigation and advisory work and acting for both prosecution and defence, before joining Leicester Law School in 2012. She remains a (non-practising) door tenant at Foundry Chambers. Tracey has published widely on the criminal law, and is a co-author of *Clarkson & Keating: Criminal Law*.

Jonathan Fisher KC is a practising Barrister at Red Lion Chambers London and Visiting Professor in Practice at LSE, UK, where he teaches Financial Crime. Between 1991 and 2003, he was Standing Counsel (Criminal) to the Commissioners of Inland Revenue at the Central Criminal Court and London Crown Courts. He is Editor Emeritus of *Lloyds Law Reports Financial Crime*.

Jeremy Horder is a Professor of Criminal Law, London School of Economics, UK. From 2005-2010, Jeremy was a Law Commissioner for England and Wales, with responsibility for criminal law reform. His research interests focus on history, philosophy and politics of English criminal law, and criminal law reform. More particularly, homicide, bribery and corruption, and the intersection of criminal law and other forms of sanction.

Douglas Husak is a Distinguished Professor of Philosophy and Law, Rutgers University, USA. Doug's primary research projects are in the intersection of moral philosophy and criminal law, with a special interest in drug policy. His most important publications are *Drugs and Rights*; *Overcriminalization*; and *Philosophy of Criminal Law: Selected Essays.*

Paul Jarvis is a Barrister; Criminal Law Reform Now Network Committee Member, UK. Paul is a barrister in private practice at 6KBW College Hill. He is also Treasury Counsel at the Central Criminal Court, appointed by the Attorney General to handle the most complex prosecution cases in the country. He has previously worked with the Criminal Team at the Law Commission. He is a contributor to *Blackstones' Criminal Practice* and *Millington and Sutherland Williams on the Proceeds of Crime*. He has written articles for the *Criminal Law Review, Archbold Review, Blackstone's Quarterly* and the Max Planck Institute for Foreign and International Criminal Law in Freiburg.

Vanessa E Munro is a Professor of Law at University of Warwick, UK. With funding from the ESRC, Nuffield Foundation, Scottish Government and British Academy, Vanessa has conducted extensive research with colleagues into law and policy responses to sexual violence, focusing particularly on criminal justice and asylum decision-making, and with a prominent interest in juror and lay participants. She has worked closely with third sector NGOs and policy-makers to amplify the social impact of her research. Recent projects have also included research on the implementation of coercive control offences, and the causal intersections between domestic abuse and suicide.

Tanya Palmer is a Senior Lecturer in Law, University of Sussex, UK and Co-Director of the Sussex Centre for Gender Studies. Tanya's research is primarily concerned with the legal regulation of sexual encounters, particularly through the criminal law, and with the intersection of sexual and domestic abuse. Her upcoming monograph draws together doctrinal, theoretical and empirical research to critique current legal constructions of sex and sexual violation and to develop a new model of sexual offending based around a concept of 'freedom to negotiate'.

Joe Purshouse is a Senior Lecturer in Criminal Law and Justice, University of Sheffield, UK. Joe's research focuses on how advances in technology shape criminal procedure and evidence law and practice in several contexts. Joe has published several evaluations of the police use of facial recognition technology, and evaluating English law's response to the emergence of online child sex abuse activists (commonly known as paedophile hunters). His PhD research examined the extent to which the privacy interests of those subject to the criminal process are recognised and afforded adequate protection in England and Wales. Joe has published in leading law journals, including the *Modern Law Review*, *Public Law*, *Criminal Law Review*, and the *Journal of Law and Society*.

Paul Roberts is Professor of Criminal Jurisprudence, University of Nottingham School of Law, UK, and Adjunct Professor of Law, China University of Political Science and Law (CUPL), Beijing. He researches and teaches in the areas of criminal procedure and evidence, forensic science, criminal justice and legal theory, including comparative, international and philosophical perspectives. Recent publications include *Roberts and Zuckerman's Criminal Evidence*, 3rd edn (OUP, 2022); Roberts and Stockdale (eds), *Forensic Science Evidence and Expert Witness Testimony* (Edward Elgar, 2018); and Hunter, Roberts, Young and Dixon (eds), *The Integrity of Criminal Process* (Hart, 2016).

Jonathan Rogers is Associate Professor in Criminal Justice at the University of Cambridge and a Fellow at Fitzwilliam College; Co-Director of the Criminal Law Reform Now Network, UK. Jonathan's research interests cover a range of fields, from substantive criminal law to procedure and evidence, with special interests in prosecutorial decision-making, abuse of process and human rights.

Monica Stevenson is a barrister at the Chambers of 25 Bedford Row. She has a criminal defence practice and been instructed in a range of allegations, including serious violence, historic sexual offences and cases involving modern slavery and human trafficking. Monica has written for a variety of publications, including the *New Law Journal* and *Criminal Justice Quarterly*. She is an Advocacy Trainer (Middle Temple), accredited training facilitator for vulnerable witnesses, and Panel Member of *The Bar Tribunals & Adjudication Service.*

Miles Trent is a Senior Case Review Manager at the Criminal Cases Review Commission, UK. Criminal Cases Review Commission (CCRC) is the statutory body responsible for investigating alleged miscarriages of justice in England, Wales, and Northern Ireland. It was established by section 8 of the Criminal Appeal Act of 1995 and began work on 31 March 1997. Miles is one of the CCRC's most experienced case reviewers and has worked on some of its largest and most complex cases. In recent years he has taken a leading role in the CCRC's review of the Post Office Horizon group of cases. Miles was called to the bar in 2002.

Nicola Wake is a Professor of Law, University of Northumbria, UK. Nicola is Director of Equality, Diversity and Inclusion for Law at Northumbria University and Honorary Subject Sections Secretary for the Society of Legal Scholars. Nicola has published widely on mental condition defences, holds several editorial positions, and has secured funding from prestigious providers.

Gabriele Watts is a Barrister, Lincoln's Inn, UK. Gabriele accepts a broad range of instructions covering both defence and prosecution work, in the Youth Court, Magistrates Court and Crown Court. Gabriele previously worked at the Serious Fraud Office (SFO) for two years. During this time, she assisted on cases involving serious and complex fraud, as well as international bribery and corruption spanning multiple jurisdictions. Gabriele also worked for the Office of General Counsel. Gabriele now writes in the area of white-collar crime, and she is a Fellow of the International Academy of Financial Crime Litigators. She also lectures at the London School of Economics and Political Science on the financial crime course.

Ronald Weitzer is a Professor of Sociology, George Washington University, Washington DC, USA. Ron is a criminologist, and much of his research has investigated police-minority relations in the United States and in other nations (including Northern Ireland and South Africa). He is also an expert on the sex industry, with particular expertise on American policies and law enforcement on prostitution and sex trafficking. His most recent book is *Sex Tourism in Thailand: Inside Asia's Premier Erotic Playground*.

Lucy Welsh is a Reader in Criminal Justice, University of Sussex, UK. Lucy has a long-standing interest in all aspects of criminal law and justice, and is lead author of the 5th edition of *Sanders and Young's Criminal Justice*. Lucy has completed funded research projects which have examined the impact of legal aid cuts on expert witnesses, and on criminal appeal/post-appeal cases. In October 2023, she began a third funded project about applicants' experiences of the (post)appeal process. Lucy is a solicitor and spent 10 years practicing criminal defence before joining academia.

Stephen Wooler is a Barrister; Criminal Law Reform Now Network Committee Member, UK. Following practice at the criminal and common law bar, Stephen joined the office of the Director of Public Prosecutions in 1973, rising to become Assistant Director of Public Prosecutions in 1982. He was seconded to the Law Officers' Department in 1983 and was instrumental in establishing first the Crown Prosecution Service and then the Serious Fraud Office. In 1987 he became Chief Crown Prosecutor in London before a returning to the Law Officers' Department as Deputy Legal Secretary where he served until 1999 when he became HM Chief Inspector of the Crown Prosecution Service. He was made a Companion of the Order of the Bath in the Queen's Birthday Honours 2005.

Introduction: Criminal Law Reform Now in 2024

MELISSA BONE, JJ CHILD AND JONATHAN ROGERS*

This is the second volume of essays on criminal law reform collected under the banner 'Criminal Law Reform Now'. Following the pattern of the first volume, this volume was preceded by a live event during which a selection of writers, both academic and from legal practice, made their proposals and received feedback. Also in common with the first event, each proposer was paired with a suitable commentator, and the event was timed to coincide with the Law Commission's latest call for proposals for statutory reform. Unlike the first event, being online, it was freely accessible to all those who were interested, and we thank all those who did 'attend' and give their comments. It is likely that we will wish to follow this new format in the future. Readers of the first volume might also notice that there is a partly new editing team to this volume.

These last two differences reflect more significant changes since the first event in 2016. Shortly afterwards, the Criminal Law Reform Now Network (CLRN Network) was founded as a freely accessible network for anyone interested in criminal law reform.[1] Its membership includes many practitioners and policy makers besides academics. It has published two reports, one on computer misuse,[2] and one on deceptions which induce sexual activity;[3] and it is in the process of writing reports on private prosecutions and systemic responses to controlled drugs. The CLRN Network has also recently entered into a memorandum of understanding with the Law Commission, the first of its type, in pursuance of which it will contribute to scoping a possible project on extradition and international co-operation. As a now established reform network, so it is that this present volume is edited by three of the committee members. We invite interested readers to look at our website,[4] our other published papers and blog entries.

* Dr Melissa Bone, University of Leicester; Professor John Child, University of Birmingham; Dr Jonathan Rogers, University of Cambridge and Fitzwilliam College. Our continued thanks to all the authors who have contributed to this volume, and for the authors of the previous volume for updating us on their progress in reform (discussed in this chapter).

[1] We are grateful to have received funding from an AHRC Network Grant (AH/RO13160/2).

[2] Criminal Law Reform Now Network, *Reforming the Computer Misuse Act 1990* (CLRNN1, 2020).

[3] Criminal Law Reform Now Network, *Reforming the Relationship between Sexual Consent, Deception and Mistake* (CLRNN3, 2023).

[4] www.clrnn.co.uk. We are also present on LinkedIn; Twitter/X; and YouTube.

To readers of the first volume, the aim of this second will be quite familiar. It is to provoke discussions about concrete law reform proposals, and this includes consideration not only of their merits but also the best routes for achieving them. We feature here eight proposals, with each proposal chapter followed by commentary from an invited author. The aim of the commentator on each proposal is, as before, to widen the scope for discussion and not necessarily to agree or disagree. Although the contributions at the live event in 2021 were timed to coincide with the Law Commission's Fourteenth Programme, when writing the final chapters in this volume, authors have been encouraged to consider all different routes to reform even where this is not likely to include a future Law Commission project. As with the first volume, the collection concludes with two stand-alone chapters considering broader issues of criminal law reform.

1. Topics Discussed in the New Volume

Paul Jarvis starts with two proposals concerning rights of criminal appeals in **Chapter One**. The first proposal is to simplify appeals by defendants convicted in the magistrates' courts. Jarvis would abolish an automatic rehearing in the Crown Court, and he would require appellants to seek leave to appeal to the Crown Court with reasons for supposing the conviction is unsafe, as is required when appealing from convictions in the Crown Court. There would be no other direct route of appeal from the magistrates' court for the defendant. The Crown Court could quash the conviction, and possibly remit the case to the magistrates where appropriate. Jarvis' second proposal is to allow, with safeguards, a prosecution right of appeal following acquittal by jury where that jury had been incorrectly directed and might have returned a verdict of guilty had it been properly directed. Jarvis points to parallels with other Commonwealth jurisdictions here. Underlying both proposals is the supposed triumph of principle over historical anomaly; if we trust magistrates to try cases fairly, rightly or not, why do we allow a number of amorphous and generous routes of appeal to defendants convicted by them? Further, if we allow prosecutors to seek review from acquittals in magistrates' courts where the law has been misapplied, why do we not allow them the same with regard to judicial misdirections in Crown Court trials?

Undoubtedly there is no shortage of apparent anomalies between appeals from magistrates' courts and appeals from Crown Courts in particular. Commentator Professor Paul Roberts, however, urges us not to cast aside our traditions quite so readily. There certainly are reasons to be more concerned about the quality of justice in many magistrates' courts, even if they are less strong when a district judge sits instead of three lay magistrates. Roberts notes too that we have not traditionally spoken of 'unsafe acquittals' in the way that we have spoken of 'unsafe convictions', and that a certain asymmetry between the rights of the prosecution and the accused has become accepted.

We might add that there would surely have been considerable public concern if the 'Colston Four' – Jarvis' chosen example – *had* faced a retrial after their jury acquitted them of criminal damage.[5] As it was, there were concerns, albeit misplaced, that the decision by the Attorney-General simply to refer to the Court of Appeal a point of law arising from a judicial direction to the jury was politically motivated. This is not to say that all reforms to the rule against double jeopardy should be resisted on the basis of fear, or perception, of state oppression, but these are surely factors to be considered. They did not hold back the reforms in Part 10 of the Criminal Justice Act 2003, which are still relatively uncontentious (Roberts' objections notwithstanding); but that is surely precisely because 'new and compelling evidence' must be found in such cases.

There is clearly some appetite for reform in this area. At the time of writing, the Law Commission has sought responses from the public on both matters,[6] and we await the responses with interest.

In **Chapter Two**, Dr Tanya Palmer makes three related proposals concerning prostitution; to decriminalise soliciting in the street by sex workers,[7] to decriminalise the brothel keeping offences,[8] and to decriminalise kerb crawling, or soliciting in the street by would-be clients.[9]

There are two common threads between these proposals. One is that all three offences operate so as to endanger sex workers, who for various reasons are not able to work from home by themselves. This is arguably as true of the offence against soliciting by the sex worker (who needs to make a very quick decision whether to accept an unknown client, before attracting the attention of the police) as it is when it is the client who takes the risk of committing the offence; again the client will not want to wait while the sex worker assesses the risks that he might pose (nor will he want to give his true name and personal details). Palmer explains that 'sex workers need clients' money more than clients "need" (or rather, want) sex. Thus the burdens of criminalisation are simply passed from the client to the sex worker, who must take steps to absorb additional risk on the clients' behalf.'

The other common thread is that the criminalisation of all activities might be defended by reference to perceived public nuisance, and so reformers must suggest ways to minimise such effects and to argue that they are outweighed by

[5] For readers unaware of the context, the so-called 'Colston Four' were tried for damaging the statute of Edward Colston (who profited from the slave trade that was active in his time) during the 'Black Lives Matter' protests in the summer of 2020. The Home Secretary of the day had immediately condemned the widely publicised act.

[6] The Law Commission published an 'Issues Paper' on 27 July 2023. The second question for consultees asks: 'Is there a need to reform the processes by which decisions of magistrates' courts in criminal cases can be appealed or otherwise reviewed?', with a follow up question 'Should a leave requirement be introduced in respect of appeals from the magistrates' court to the Crown Court?' (paras 3.49–3.50). Its fourteenth question is 'Do you have any views on the circumstances in which an acquittal might be quashed … ?' (para 7.60).

[7] Street Offences Act 1959, s 1 (as amended).

[8] Sexual Offences Act 1956, ss 33–36 (as amended).

[9] Sexual Offences Act 1985, ss 1–2 (as amended).

safety concerns. Palmer does not underestimate these difficulties and refers to the potential problem of Public Spaces Protection Orders by which local councils may prohibit certain (otherwise lawful) activities and which may be enforced by fixed penalty notices. Commentator Professor Ronald Weitzer observes that considerable regulation would be likely to follow decriminalisation, and by implication that self-regulation of sex work would be most unlikely. As much as sex work might be regarded by some as a profession, its past characterisation as a vice is likely to continue to attract laws designed to deter bad actors from controlling local markets.

It is easy to agree with much of what is said in these chapters. One observation may be that timing is not in favour of the proposal. Powers of local authorities to make provisions against anti-social behaviour have now been with us for so long that, as Palmer anticipates, the arguments for permitting sex workers to ply their work safely have to be won at local level as well as national level. Further, if different areas adopt different approaches, it might be that areas with more tolerant regimes will prove to attract sex workers from other areas, in which case attitudes may change even in the more 'progressive' areas. A related observation is that campaigners surely have a disproportionately large amount to do as it is, without having also to suggest suitable regulations, eg concerning premises where sex may legally be sold, following decriminalisation. Palmer discusses the broadly positive experiences in Aotearoa New Zealand, but although the Prostitution Reform Act of 2003 passed as a Private Member's Bill, it is noteworthy that three parties to the coalition government of 1999–2002 all had decriminalisation on their own party manifestos. Even then, the narrow passing of the Bill was reported to still have come as a surprise. One might anticipate that winning public and political support in this country will need to precede the changes in the law which Palmer seeks, and the likely regulation that would need to follow. As Palmer anticipates, this in turn may involve some agreement (perhaps hitherto missing in this jurisdiction) as to whether the primary aim is to dissuade persons from sex work, or to enable them to work safely (and in so doing to reduce incidents of violence and abuse and to encourage reporting of those incidents which do occur).

In **Chapter Three**, Professor Jeremy Horder and Gabriele Watts focus their proposals on the potential individual liability of senior corporate managers for crimes committed by their employees. The future shape of corporate liability has been under a particular spotlight recently, with the Economic Crime and Corporate Transparency Bill (when enacted) creating a new corporate offence of failure to prevent economic crime and, just as significantly, expanding the scope of the identification doctrine to engage corporate wrongdoing further down the executive ladder. However, despite this attention, the potential individual liability of corporate managers – alongside, or independent of corporate liability – has remained somewhat obscure. Individual liability is often possible where a senior manager 'consents to' or 'connives' at the corporate offence, but as Horder and Watts observe, despite the growing prevalence of such offences, requiring a corporate offence as a threshold for individual liability means that prosecution via this route will remain extremely restricted.

Horder and Watts recommend the expansion of individual liability for corporate managers principally by decoupling consent or connivance offences from corporate liability. In this manner – beyond existing routes in complicity – corporate managers would be guilty of an offence where they consented to or connived at offences committed by the corporation *or* by individual employees committed for the intended benefit of the company. The expansion of liability here is justified with reference to broader theories of complicity. However, on a similar basis, Horder and Watts contend that consent or connivance liability (as with complicity more generally) should not be applied where D is merely negligent of offences committed by others; and they therefore recommend the narrowing of consent or connivance offences where negligence is currently permitted.

There is clear merit in the headline proposal to expand individual corporate manager liability, lifting a form of corporate veil to ensure individual managers are criminally accountable for serious crimes committed within their authority. However, as Dr Cronin explores in her response, whether such an expansion can be justified *within* current theories of complicity is more questionable; or whether, as she suggests, an alternative justification should be identified. So too for individual corporate negligence, where Cronin highlights an alternative basis, this time to suggest that negligence may – in some cases at least – be an appropriate basis for liability. The proposals (and debate) here are extremely useful, and it is hoped that the potential for the individual liability of corporate managers gains more prominence in debates about the future of corporate liability.

Professors Vanessa Bettinson, Vanessa Munro and Nicola Wake propose to create a new defence for victims of domestic abuse in **Chapter Four**. Their concern is that the constraints of the common law defence of duress by threats make it unsuited where a victim of abuse is threatened by their abuser into committing offences, even when the threshold of a (reasonable) belief in a threat of serious injury or death is met. Where duress is in issue, courts are likely to put too much emphasis on apparent opportunities for the victim to have dissociated from the abuser; contrary to the hopes expressed by Baroness Hale in *Hasan*[10] in 2005. Nor might the possible lack of immediacy of the threat be sympathetically received; it may still too easily be thought that the victim had time to contact the police instead of committing the offence in question. In this case the victim may be badly judged if she had never contacted the police, but also if she had done so, on previous occasions – showing thereby that she was capable of appealing for help.

Their solution is a bespoke defence, which arises where D was a victim of the offence of abusive behaviour (by which they refer to domestic abuse within section 1 of the Domestic Abuse Act 2021), where that offence would appear to have been committed to undermine D's sense of independence in various

[10] [2005] 4 All ER 685, [2005] UKHL 22.

(specified) ways, and as a result of which D did not have a 'fair opportunity' to avoid the offence committed.

Quite probably many will agree with the authors, and with commentator Paramjit Ahluwalia, that the common law defences are inapt to protect many sufferers of domestic abuse. Indeed, the default position generally is for common law defences to be narrow and to leave hard cases to prosecutorial discretion. It is perhaps disappointing that the government was inclined to rely on the availability of duress when it rejected the creation of a (differently designed) defence during the passing of the Domestic Abuse Bill 2021. But whether the differences between that model, proposed by the Prison Reform Trust, and the model proposed here by Bettinson, Munro and Wake are such as to make a big difference is hard to say. If it is thought that prosecutors and magistrates (for it is worth bearing in mind that many offences caused as a result of domestic abuse may be tried by magistrates) are slow to understand the very difficult circumstances suffered by victims of domestic abuse when duress is relied on, then one wonders whether this will also blight any attempt to establish a defence based on 'a fair opportunity to avoid committing an offence'. Ahluwalia adds that in many cases of domestic abuse, further factors such as alcohol and drug consumption arise. For example, a magistrate might think that if only D 'had got herself clean', then that too might have given her a fairer 'opportunity' not to offend. To what extent such other difficulties have arisen independently of the abuse, and to what extent they operate independently from it, is likely to be an additional complication, and perhaps one reason why the question of 'fair opportunity' has never been embraced by the courts as much as by some writers.

It should be added that campaigners in this area might have done more to resist the abolition of the common law defence of marital coercion in 2014.[11] It would likely have been better to point to the potential positive sides of that defence (in terms of assisting those subject to domestic abuse) and to urge for appropriate amendments to it (including widening it to all abusive domestic partnerships) rather than to allow it to die, only to try to recover that ground in a new format several years later. To be sure, when governments are pressed or tempted into hurried action, the opposition needs to be especially well organised. Here and elsewhere, we see that the would-be law reformer must constantly be alert to raise their concerns at every opportunity.

In **Chapter Five**, Dr Lucy Welsh makes proposals to reform the way in which the Criminal Cases Review Commission (CCRC) decides whether to refer cases to the Court of Appeal. As readers will know, the CCRC is tasked with making referrals where it considers that there is a 'real possibility' that the Court of Appeal will allow the appeal.[12] There is necessarily a predictive element here. It is not

[11] Anti-Social Behaviour, Crime and Policing Act 2014, s 177. Bettinson, Munro and Wake note that Professor Susan Edwards did raise a contemporaneous objection.

[12] Criminal Appeal Act 1995, s 13 (1)(a).

necessary for the accused already to have appealed directly under the usual route for lodging appeals; but in these so-called 'no appeal' cases, the CCRC must also consider that there are 'exceptional grounds'[13] for them to justify making the reference themselves (and the increasingly likely explanation that the defendant cannot access legal aid to lodge an effective appeal is, sadly but unsurprisingly, insufficient). Welsh suggests that the test for referral should be whether there might reasonably be thought to be a miscarriage of justice (but such as would enable the Court of Appeal to quash the conviction), and that the process for determining 'exceptional circumstances' should be clarified.

Welsh's preference for a test of reasonably supposing a miscarriage of justice to have occurred is mainly based on the removal of a predictive element, at the risk of accepting a lower 'success rate' of referrals. Commentators from the CCRC, John Curtis and Miles Trent, doubt whether this would make significant difference to case outcomes, however. It is a similar picture concerning the merits in setting out more clearly what might count as 'exceptional circumstances', and it is interesting to read Curtis and Miles on the efforts of the CCRC to educate prisoners on what are, and are not, good reasons to approach the CCRC before seeking leave to appeal in their own right.

The CCRC referral test will be reviewed by the Law Commission as part of its new project on criminal appeals.[14] But CCRC reform must surely be discussed with reference to two other factors. First, it is no secret that the CCRC has been the victim of several successive cuts to its resources.[15] We would not want amendments to their terms of reference to obstruct the urgent need for significantly greater resources, for it is hard to see how any legal reform could be an adequate substitute for this. The second question, which Welsh touches upon, is their secondary relationship to the Court of Appeal. It is reasonable to contend that the Commission should risk a lower success rate for the sake of bringing more arguable cases, as Welsh urges. But perhaps there are those who consider that its proper relationship is precisely a secondary one.

In this latter context, consider the situation when the CCRC might refer a (very strong) case to the Court of Appeal for which the Court of Appeal, left to its own devices, would nonetheless have declined to give leave to appeal. This used to arise where the common law applied at the time of trial is later understood more generously for the defendant, who has almost inevitably appealed after the 28 day-limit for seeking leave to appeal because only then has the relevant legal development occurred. The Court of Appeal has always nonetheless declined to

[13] Criminal Appeal Act 1995, s 13 (2).

[14] The Law Commission (n 6), asks a fifth question 'Is there evidence that the referral test used by the Criminal Cases Review Commission when considering whether to refer an appeal hinders the correction of miscarriages of justice?'.

[15] See, eg, the criticism of Glyn Maddocks KC, reported as saying 'You've got part-time commissioners, a part-time chair … Every one of them is working from home. They have an office, which I've been to, which is only manned for meetings … The wheels are coming off': *The Guardian* (26 August 2023).

give leave to appeal out of time unless there would be a 'substantial injustice' were it not to hear the case. In 2007 the CCRC referred an 'out of time' case which depended on subsequent judicial development of the law,[16] which the Court would have preferred not to hear and in respect of which it criticised the CCRC for the referral.[17] There swiftly followed a statutory amendment to permit the Court of Appeal to dismiss an appeal in such cases,[18] thus effectively mandating the CCRC to have regard to the Court's own practice in this respect, as it does in all others.

But arguably, there is a difference between second-guessing whether an appeal would succeed, and deciding whether it is just to refer a case which is very likely to succeed. Some might think that the latter decision is well suited to the opinion of an independent non-judicial body, and which is not seen to be concerned primarily with the (admittedly) heavy demands on the Court of Appeal. The statutory amendment which prohibits this is perhaps a cause for regret, the long-term effect of which has been to institutionalise the CCRC's subservient role to the Court of Appeal. Meanwhile there can be little doubting the wide dissatisfaction with which the Court of Appeal's hard-line stance in interpreting 'substantial miscarriage of justice' has applied in cases of convictions arising from the discredited 'joint enterprise' doctrine.[19]

But this unfortunate episode means that two powerful obstacles stand in the way of reforms to CCRC practice; politicians need to be convinced of the merits of investing more resources, while senior lawyers and judges[20] themselves need to be convinced that the body deserves greater independence (and likely the two are in some way connected).

Dr Daniel Bansal and Dr Tracey Elliott return to the vexed subject of consent to bodily harm in **Chapter Six**. They suggest that the categories of exceptions which currently apply when the rule in *Brown*[21] is engaged should be abolished and replaced with a statutory 'public interest' defence which applies whenever harm that was less than 'serious disabling injury' was caused, assuming factual consent. Further, where serious disabling injury *was* caused, intentionally or recklessly, there should only be a defence where 'there is a regulatory framework encapsulating

[16] *R v Cottrell* [2007] EWCA Crim 2016.

[17] ibid, [58], in the process disapproving *R (DRCP) v Criminal Cases Review Commission* [2007] 1 Cr App R 395, which had held that 'the independent Commission was under no obligation to have regard to, still less to implement, a practice of the CACD which operates at a stage with which the Commission is not concerned'.

[18] Criminal Justice and Immigration Act 2008, s 42 inserted a new s 16C into the Criminal Appeal Act 1968 entitled 'Power to dismiss certain appeals following references by the CCRC'.

[19] The Law Commission (n 6), highlights the issue and asks its eleventh question 'Is there evidence that the application of the "substantial injustice" test to appeals brought out-of-time on the basis of a change in the law hinders the correction of miscarriages of justice?' (para 6.83). However, although it notes the saga following *Cottrell*, it does not raise the possibility of returning to the CCRC its former power to determine the question for itself when deciding whether to refer such a case.

[20] Members of the senior judiciary itself called for the amendment which became Criminal Justice and Immigration Act 2008, s 42: *Hansard* (HL), 21 April 2008, vol 700, cols 1284–1286.

[21] [1993] UKHL 19; [1994] 1 AC 212.

the circumstances in which the harm occurs' (applicable, for example, to medical procedures and sports). They would supplement this with presumptions of non-consent where the defendant acted in 'an abusive capacity'.

Bansal and Elliott note the recent passing of section 71 of the Domestic Abuse Act 2021, which effectively codifies the rule in *Brown* (as well as the distinction drawn in *Dica*[22]), and rightly bemoan that it was passed with no effective consultation among those who practice BDSM and who do not cause serious injury.[23] That the provision should have passed in the face of so much earlier academic and other literature does make one wonder whether yet more academic criticism is likely to have an effect. This appears rather to be an area in which simple messages go far, and where legal campaigners, who feel required to provide overriding structures which deal with all potential cases, risk being sidelined. Commentator Professor Michelle Dempsey takes up the issue of whether 'abuse' and 'non-consent' are conflated and whether the defendant should have to disprove both, if there is evidence of abuse presented by the prosecution. (It is then another question when there might be said to be evidence of abuse in the first place, if there is no more evidence than the nature of the injury itself.)

Part of the problem in suggesting a simplified reform, we suggest, arises from the familiarity of language. We are familiar with the terms 'actual bodily harm' and 'grievous bodily harm', and it is notable that section 71 of the Domestic Abuse Act makes use of them; even the proviso that the act be done 'for sexual gratification' echoes many like qualifications to offences found in the Sexual Offences Act 2003. It is more difficult for the reformers who consider that a presumptive line must be drawn in some other, new, place to make their case; and all the more so if they wish to provide for defences in appropriate cases. To have to deal with 'serious disabling injury', the 'public interest', a 'regulatory framework', and presumptions of non-consent arising from 'abuse' would surely to inject several unfamiliar concepts which are likely thereby to meet considerable opposition.

Whether it is possible to realise the (undoubtedly laudable) aims of Bansal and Elliott in a simpler, more familiar way, and to tie them with serious injustices that have already occurred (as the 'We Can't Consent to This' campaign undoubtedly did) would seem to be key to worthwhile reform in this area. The paradox is that while academic writers have much to contribute to understanding this area of law, where many cases seem to turn on fine distinctions, nonetheless too much sophistication and too little attention to the urgency of real-life injustices may fall short when it comes to reform. It might, in the end, be no coincidence that the Law Commission too has not returned to this fraught area since the 1990s.[24]

[22] [2004] EWCA Crim 1103.

[23] We (CLRNN) wrote about this on our blog page while the Bill was still in progress: 'Abolition of the 'Rough Sex' Defence: Hurried legislation and Missed Opportunities': www.clrnn.co.uk/blog/?page=7.

[24] Law Commission, *Consent and Offences Against the Person* (Consultation No 134, 1994); Law Commission, *Consent in the Criminal Law* (Consultation No 139, 1995).

In **Chapter Seven**, Dr Sam Bourton asks whether it is time for the next seminal economic crime statute; a question that her respondent (Jonathan Fisher KC) answers in the negative. The debate between the two experts provides a fascinating insight into the legal issues, as well as the often contrasting perspectives of academic and practicing lawyers.

Bourton focuses on tax evasion offences, criticising the current regime as a 'patchwork of offences, causing duplicity and redundancy'; as well as on what she describes as the 'overuse of broad common law offences'. On the first issue, Bourton sets out a plethora of complex overlapping statutory offences, highlighting inconsistencies in their structure, their mens rea/culpability requirements, and the potential availability (and construction) of defences. The problem here is one of unnecessary complexity, affecting both prosecutors and in particular those attempting to understand and stay within the law; as well as the potential for critical points of uncertainty and/or unfairness (ie, points of over or under inclusivity) being obfuscated. The second issue relates to the first, in that when faced with such statutory complexity prosecutors are typically opting instead to pursue broad overlapping common law offences of cheating the public revenue and conspiracy to defraud. Bourton – like many before her[25] – is critical of such offences, and she presents the potential for a new statutory regime as a route to their abolition.

Fisher is more sympathetic to the current law, presenting the current mix of offences in terms of a useful toolbox for prosecutors: 'retaining focused statutory offences … affords the prosecution options in less serious cases where specific taxes have been evaded but the weight of the common law offence or more general fraud offences is not required.' He also takes on Bourton's vision for a new economic crime statute, which she sketches principally from a comparison with US law. As Bourton states, 'the UK should consider enacting a US-style system of tax evasion offences, which apply to a range of taxes and clearly distinguish culpable actions from omissions.' Fisher suggests that the advantages of a US-style approach – and particularly the use of 'wilfulness' in evasion as opposed to the English concept of 'dishonesty' – is far from self-evident. We should all agree with the pursuit of legal certainty, but it is important not to simply substitute one set of uncertain concepts for another; particularly where such substitution sidelines decades of jurisprudence.

The debate is well balanced, and many will agree with Bourton that the current mix of offences is in need of rationalisation; not least in light of increased enforcement of these laws since 2010. The key will be the nature and extent of such rationalisation, and it may be that a body such as the Law Commission is best placed to take the reform project forward, engaging with experts from both academic and practitioner perspectives.

In **Chapter Eight**, Dr Joe Purshouse presents a simple and attractive idea: to provide by statute that a person who has been investigated by the police or other

[25] Including the Law Commission: *Fraud* (LC No 276, 2002) 57.

state agents, but not yet charged, nor already dealt with by way of an out of court disposal, should have a presumptive immunity from being identified as a subject of investigation. This should not affect the conduct of the police and the media too far. It is largely consistent with longstanding practice, and since the successful suit brought by Sir Cliff Richard against the BBC,[26] and other subsequent cases, rather close to the position reached by the courts when asked to apply Article 8 ECHR.

But there are reasons to urge legislation. For a start, new criminal offences cannot be created by invoking the Human Rights Act 1998,[27] and Purshouse proposes that there should be a new offence which might be committed by anyone who publishes any material which breaches the restriction on publication. Liability would be strict, except in so far as one who might be regarded as a publisher reasonably did not suspect that the publication contained the material in question. The effect of criminal liability might be both that the media will not be tempted to publish the arrest of well-known figures and simply to risk having to pay damages, and that social media users might be deterred from publicising arrests of which they become aware. Purshouse recommends too that identification may be permitted 'in the interests of justice' on application to the magistrates' court. But it should not normally suffice that the police and prosecution simply hope that publicity will cause more complainants, currently unknown, to lodge their own complaints (and this could, of course, still happen *after* the defendant has been charged). At the same time, the media might still publish reasons to be suspicious of a person not yet charged; for the criminal prohibition would only bite where there is a revelation that the person (uncharged) is being investigated by the authorities.

There are certainly details to be further considered. Seen through the lens of enforcing privacy rights, the proposal may seem to be well founded but there is likely to be some concern regarding the resulting respective spheres of criminal and civil liability. If it is only remediable in defamation for a person to suggest that another has in fact committed a crime, should it then be an offence merely to identify a person as one who has been arrested by the police for a crime (without any suggestion that he is necessarily guilty)? Determining the respective roles of criminal and civil liability will assist on other points of detail too; for example, commentators Monica Stevenson and Professor Matt Dyson advert to the situation where a user of social media wrongly identifies someone as having been the subject of arrest (in which case, no true confidential information about the named person is revealed).

Purshouse does acknowledge that such a proposal might in any event be politically contentious. Picking fights with the media often comes at a cost in the UK, and pretexts can certainly be found for either of the main political parties to declare that it does not favour the proposal. But it is also possible for (further)

[26] *Sir Cliff Richard v The British Broadcasting Corporation, The Chief Constable of South Yorkshire Police* [2018] EWHC 1837 (Ch).

[27] Human Rights Act 1998, s 7(8).

cases concerning sympathetic and determined public figures to carry their own momentum for reform.

The volume concludes with two chapters on the politics of law reform. In **Chapter Nine** Professor Doug Husak does so from the particular perspective of reform to the laws concerning drugs. At our Conference in 2021, a proposal simply to decriminalise drug possession and use (but retaining penalties for possession of controlled drugs with intent to supply) was made by Professor Alex Stevens, Niamh Eastwood and Kirstie Douse. Professor Husak, a veteran of such campaigns in the USA, expressed his views then and does so in more detail in this volume. Husak emphasises, inter alia, the need to be accurate and balanced when making factual assertions or projections (such as concerning the impact of decriminalisation on future drug use) and to offer as much detail as one can about experiences in jurisdictions where such reforms have already taken place. These warnings can be generalised to many other reform proposals. It is easy for academics to assume that experiences in other jurisdictions are of limited value, because so many other factors, including local cultures and history, may affect the outcomes of any reform, not to mention that the outcomes will themselves be likely contested in the short-term. This notwithstanding, we should expect it to be one of the first questions which politicians might ask. (An example of this may be found in Dr Palmer's discussion of the reforms relating to prostitution in Aotearoa, New Zealand).

We also note that Husak reports that in private, arguments made from the perspective of rights of users, whose lives might be affected disproportionately by arrests and prosecutions, are heard with some interest. It is easy to assume from much political rhetoric that such matters are of little importance to politicians, but this may to infer too much from public rhetoric. Private conversations may be altogether different. Maximum objectivity with facts (and the limitations to any forecasts) together with emphasis on injustice may be effective in private, even though in public any reform might still be presented in terms of cost savings rather than in ending injustice.

For our own part (CLRN Network), as we take forward a new project on 'Reforming systemic responses to controlled drugs', we have taken the decision to set to one side the question of decriminalisation. Law reform is often about timing, and we are not currently convinced that either major political party is ready to stand on this platform. Rather, in our project (led by co-editor Dr Melissa Bone) we will engage with a range of associated systematic issues, such as the availability of controlled drugs for medical purposes, offender diversion regimes, and sentencing. In each case, we are seeking reforms to protect vulnerable drug-users within the current system, identified with lower culpability.

Finally, in **Chapter Ten**, Stephen Wooler CBE presents an overview of how the criminal justice system has been managed over the last 50 years. Some, though likely not all, of his observations will be familiar to many. There is the by-passing of local justice as the magistracy has declined, that prosecution policy is centralised within the CPS, and local authorities are divested of responsibility for managing offenders on probation; and then the consequences of reduced resources for all nationally managed services (leading to such questionable innovations as the Single Justice Procedure). It is illuminating to see the historical patterns behind these developments. Wooler also notes an increased tendency for ministers to interfere with decisions and to react to media pressure, but still there is no single minister with overall responsibility for the criminal justice system.

Indeed, to take further this last point, it is not obvious nowadays where the would-be law reformer must go – to the Home Office, Ministry of Justice, or perhaps some other department altogether with a special interest?[28] The lack of any central 'ownership' of criminal justice, let alone criminal law reform,[29] is an obvious recipe for inconsistency and it may mean that proposals are viewed from one angle only, and not in respect of the interests of other stakeholders; or conversely that proposals made in one area of the law, thoughtfully made by relevant analogy with other areas of the criminal law, might not get the hearing which they merit. Readers may notice for themselves the application of many of these themes to some of the proposals in this volume. The hurry to abolish the defence of marital coercion, without considering whether the defence could be adapted to give better protection to those who suffer domestic abuse, is one example of a one-sided approach to an issue; another example might be the hurry to codify the effect of the highly controversial decision regarding consent to sado-masochistic activity in *Brown*. Both moves provide considerable obstacles to those who now try to undo the damage. This is to say nothing of the perhaps obvious political obstacles (magnified by a predominantly right-wing media) to any liberal reforms in the areas of prostitution and drug use. We might fear too that, by contrast, interest in the appeal system is lacking in political interest, and that the diversity of views concerning, inter alia, appeals from magistrates' courts (exemplified in this volume) will stultify any interest in reform even though it had been proposed for the sake of promoting integrity within the system.

2. Revisiting the Proposals in the First Volume

It is important to maintain a sense of practical realism when engaging with reform debates. It is better to be aware of the obstacles to reform, and for campaigners to engage with them (ie, rather than to ignore or bypass them). Reflecting further on obstacles to reform prompted us to revisit the proposals made in our first volume. We invited the authors to let us know of any relevant developments that have happened since publication in 2019, either in England and Wales or elsewhere. We

[28] In some respects, it was always thus. See J Lee, '"Not time to make a change"? Reviewing the Rhetoric of Law Reform' in *Current Legal Problems* 76 (2023) 1–43 at 11.

[29] See J Chalmers, '"Frenzied law-making": over-criminalisation by numbers' (2014) 67 *Current Legal Problems* 483–502.

should say at once that immediate impact was never to be a measure of success; the most profound of changes may, for a variety of reasons, take a considerable time – and so what follows is, at most, an interim progress report.

In some cases, the political appetite for reform was never likely to be forthcoming in the short term, as in the case for abolishing the restrictions on the right to silence when questioned as a suspect by the police,[30] and the proposal to abandon a general inchoate form of attempted crime in favour of a series of specific targeted preparatory offences.[31] Nor has any move to liberalise the law on assisted suicide[32] been successful; as one of the current editors once wrote, at the political level in the UK, 'tomorrow is always the right time to consider euthanasia.'[33] Sadly too, no progress has been made in England and Wales to raise the age of criminal responsibility;[34] though we are encouraged to see the age of criminal responsibility in Scotland recently raised to 12 years,[35] and ongoing debates about reform in Wales.[36]

Progress has been made in other areas considered in the first volume, though again the lesson is one of perseverance for the would-be reformer. The proposals made in the first volume concerning confiscation orders,[37] for example, have gained some traction, and were considered by the Law Commission which subsequently conducted its own project.[38] At the time of writing, the Commission is working with the Office of Parliamentary Counsel to produce a draft bill setting out its preferred reform. The proposal to revisit the structure of homicide offences, including a form of vehicular manslaughter,[39] remains an issue of debate in England and Wales; it should be remembered that this was a major Law Commission project as recently as 2006.[40] Elsewhere, the Scottish Law Commission are currently

[30] H Quirk, 'The Case for Restoring the Right of Silence' in JJ Child and A Duff (eds), *Criminal Law Reform Now* (Hart, 2019) 253–69.

[31] S Eldar, 'Reforming the Law of Criminal Attempts: Take Two' in JJ Child and A Duff (eds), *Criminal Law Reform Now* (Hart, 2019) 75–91.

[32] A Sanders, 'The CPS, Policy-Making and Assisted Dying: Towards a Freedom Approach' in JJ Child and A Duff (eds), *Criminal Law Reform Now* (Hart, 2019) 133–54.

[33] J Rogers, 'The New Homicide Ladder' (2007) *New Law Journal* 157.

[34] H Keating, 'How should the Criminal law Respond to the "Special Status" of Children?' in JJ Child and A Duff (eds), *Criminal Law Reform Now* (Hart, 2019) 165–83.

[35] The Age of Criminal Responsibility (Scotland) Act 2019, amending the Criminal Procedure (Scotland) Act 1995, s 41.

[36] It should be noted that the Welsh Assembly does now have some powers to pass legislation concerning the substantive criminal law, and they have commissioned research in this area (including from Professor Keating). Sch 7B, para 4(3)(a) to the Government of Wales Act 2006 (as amended), however, currently precludes the Welsh Assembly from passing any laws concerning the age of criminal responsibility.

[37] M Levi, 'Reflections on Proceeds of Crime: A New Code for Confiscation?' in JJ Child and A Duff (eds). *Criminal Law Reform Now* (Hart, 2019) 1–24.

[38] Law Commission, Confiscation of the Proceeds of Crime after Conviction: A Final Report (LC No 410, 2022).

[39] S Kyd, 'Done to Death? Reform of Homicide Law' in JJ Child and A Duff (eds). *Criminal Law Reform Now* (Hart, 2019) 101–23.

[40] Law Commission, *Murder, Manslaughter and Infanticide* (LC304, 2006).

undertaking a systematic analysis of homicide offences with a view to reform;[41] and we note reform (with a similar structure to that recommended by Professor Kyd) in Israel.[42]

We have also seen movement on other topics discussed in the first volume, showing useful trends in the direction of the reforms recommended. This is true of civil preventive orders,[43] a topic that has remained of interest to successive governments.[44] We also now see an increasing focus on the trauma victims experience within the justice system.[45] The Domestic Abuse Act was passed in 2021 which, alongside other measures, creates the role of Domestic Abuse Commissioner who has statutory powers to raise public awareness and hold both agencies and government to account. There have also been significant developments in relation to special measures, with provision now extending the witnesses eligible for assistance 'on grounds of fear or distress about testifying' to automatically include 'any offence where it is alleged that the behaviour of the accused amounted to domestic abuse within the meaning of the Domestic Abuse Act 2021.'[46] Further, section 65 of the Domestic Abuse Act prohibits parties from cross-examining each other in both family and civil court proceedings where there is evidence of abuse. This is a welcome measure as it not only shows that the government has recognised that perpetrators often use the court process as a means of extending their abuse, but also indicates that there is emerging recognition of the traumatic nature of domestic violence and abuse, since the prohibition was introduced in part due to recognition that victims were being retraumatised by their experiences in court.

Finally, the proposal by current co-editor Dr Jonathan Rogers,[47] to abolish the time limit of one year that is attached to the offence of underage sexual intercourse in section 6 of the Sexual Offences Act 1956, did get so far as being considered by the House of Lords as a proposed amendment at the Committee stage of the Police, Crime, Sentencing and Courts Bill 2021. Readers may recall that this time limit, which still applies to sexual intercourse with a girl between 13 and 16 where the act occurred before 1 May 2004, can cause immense problems in dealing with serious historic sexual offending which nonetheless falls short of rape. The proposal simply to abolish the time limit, so that suitable historic cases can be prosecuted

[41] See updates on the Scottish Law Commission website: scotlawcom.gov.uk.

[42] The Penal Law Amendment (No137) came into force in 2019, creating several new categories of offences causing death.

[43] S Shute, 'Rationalising Civil Preventive Orders: Opportunities for Reform' in JJ Child and A Duff (eds), *Criminal Law Reform Now* (Hart, 2019) 37–66.

[44] We have seen a rapid expansion of civil orders in the last decade, covering areas such as sexual offence prevention, economic crime prevention, and so on.

[45] C Bishop, 'Safe and Effective Courtroom Procedure for Domestic Violence Complainant-Witnesses' in JJ Child and A Duff (eds), *Criminal Law Reform Now* (Hart, 2019) 223–42.

[46] Youth Justice and Criminal Evidence Act 1999, s 17(4A)(c), as amended by the Domestic Abuse Act 2021, s 62.

[47] J Rogers, 'The Time Limit on Prosecutions for Underage Sexual Intercourse in the Sexual Offences Act 1956: a Continuing Problem' in JJ Child and A Duff (eds), *Criminal Law Reform Now* (Hart, 2019) 193–213.

under section 6 of the Sexual Offences Act 1956, was tabled by Baroness Alicia Kennedy. The arguments as set out in this first volume were referred to and quoted by Baroness Kennedy and by Baroness Brinton.[48] The proposal received widespread support from the floor of the House, including from Baroness Shami Chakrabarti and Lord Pannick, the latter of whom observed that trial judges would still retain the ability to stop trials for abuse of process where the passage of time affected the evidence so as to make the trial unfair.[49]

However, the government objected to the amendment on the basis that it might be incompatible with the rights of the defendant under Article 7 ECHR, who would necessarily be tried some considerable time after the former time limit had elapsed. There was some recent Strasbourg authority to the effect that the expiry of time limits might engage Article 7 ECHR as well as changes to the substantive law and penalties,[50] and it was thought that there might then be an important difference between extensions to (or abolition of) time limits made at a time when prospective defendants could still be prosecuted under the existing time limit, and abolition of time limits after they have expired in all affected cases. Dr Rogers and Baroness Kennedy were invited to (and did) have further conversations with Lord Wolfson (then Parliamentary Under-Secretary of State for Justice) and his legal advisers. Whilst Lord Wolfson acknowledged that the time limit problem is real and rightly a subject for the Ministry's attention, the view remained that there was too great a risk of the proposal being found incompatible with Article 7 ECHR. The proposed amendment was then withdrawn at the next reading of the Bill.[51]

From the overall experience of the last of these proposals, we offer four general observations for would-be reformers. First, it is necessary to keep the issue in the public eye whenever an opportunity presents itself. In this case, Baroness Kennedy was alerted to the problem by a letter by Rogers published in the *Guardian* following another historic injustice.[52] But generally, a team of reformers is more likely to ensure the necessary publicity than an individual researcher. Second, in law reform, timing is everything. Had this proposal been considered at an earlier time (and it was worthy of consideration ever since the decision in *J* in 2004) then the same objection could not have been raised, except very speculatively, in the absence of authority concerning the application of Article 7 ECHR to time limits. Third, inevitably law reform is regarded in terms of risks as well as merits by government. The merits of reform were not in question here, but the risk of a convicted person

[48] *Hansard*, 22 Nov 2021 (HL) vol 816 at col 619, 620–21.

[49] *Hansard*, 22 Nov 2021 (HL) vol 816 at col 627.

[50] *Antia and Khupenia v Georgia*, no. 7523/10, 18 June 2020. However, this was a case where the domestic courts had simply disregarded a time limit currently still in force.

[51] *Hansard*, 12 Jan 2022 (HL) vol 817 at col 1145. It should be said that, shortly afterwards, the European Court of Human Rights expanded its jurisprudence on Article 7 ECHR, now giving the opinion that a state cannot legislate so as to enable a prosecution in respect of which a time limit has elapsed to be revived. See the Advisory Opinion given by the Grand Chamber in response to the Armenian Court of Cassation, P16-2021-001, 26 April 2022.

[52] *The Guardian* (9 August 2019).

taking a case against the government to Strasbourg under Article 7 ECHR was thought to be substantial. Fourth, it was significant that the converse possibility (that a victim of underage sexual intercourse before 1 May 2004 might bring a case against the government in relation to insufficient legal protection against sexual abuse, under Article 8 of the ECHR) had not in fact happened, and this notwithstanding regular opportunities for victims to bring such an action since 2004. Statutory reform comes much more easily when there is a sense of urgency, and it is regrettable that it had proved to be so difficult to make many relevant practitioners even aware of the time limit,[53] let alone of the means for challenging it.

Time will tell what fortunes lie ahead of the various reforms in this second volume. But we hope that readers are convinced of the importance of activism in promoting law reform, and that both academics and practitioners have an important role in developing greater understanding of the mechanics and pitfalls of criminal law reform. We hope to have the opportunity to say more about this in a third volume of *Criminal Law Reform Now*.

[53] See the first volume on the widespread ignorance of the time limit. The CPS has never publicised the problem and continues to surprise complainants when it applies it in individual cases. In 2021 Rogers heard from a practitioner who advises victims of abuse in launching civil proceedings against their abusers, often out of time. This lawyer too had only just learned of the problem when the CPS had discontinued a case affecting one of his clients.

1

Two Proposed Reforms to the Present System of Criminal Appeals

PAUL JARVIS*

The present system of appeals in criminal cases in England and Wales has grown piecemeal over the course of centuries.[1] It now offers a variety of asymmetrical rights of appeal to the prosecution and defence against both final and interlocutory decisions arrived at in the magistrates' court and in the Crown Court. No systematic overview of the operation of the appellate system in all criminal cases has ever been undertaken; but in July 2022, the government asked the Law Commission to review the law relating to criminal appeals. The Law Commission aims to publish a consultation paper by late 2023, which will invite views on some provisional proposals for reform. The Law Commission's terms of reference show just how extensive this review could be. The stated purpose of the review is for the Law Commission to:[2]

> … consider the need for reform with a view to ensuring that the courts have powers that enable the effective, efficient and appropriate resolution of appeals. The review will be particularly concerned with inconsistencies, uncertainties and gaps in the law.

The terms of reference then list 12 areas that the review will focus on, although the list is said not to be exhaustive. The first six concern appeals against conviction and sentence in the Court of Appeal (Criminal Division) (the CACD), the seventh concerns the powers of the CACD to deal with appeals relating to findings of unfitness to plead, the eighth and ninth concern appeals against conviction and sentence from the magistrates' court to the Crown Court, the tenth concerns CCRC referrals to the CACD and the eleventh focusses on the law concerning the retention and disclosure of evidence with respect to appeals. The twelfth invites consideration of whether the various rights of appeal 'which are currently spread across a number of statutes' should be consolidated in order to make the law 'clearer and more consistent'. The page on the Law Commission's website that

* Barrister, 6KBW; Committee Member for the Criminal Law Reform Now Network.

[1] See, generally, R Pattenden, *English Criminal Appeals 1844–1994* (OUP, 1998).

[2] Law Commission, *Criminal Appeals – Law Commission Review – Terms of Reference* (2023).

is reserved for this review[3] reveals only a few tantalising details about what the Commission's principal areas of focus will be, but they are likely to include the effectiveness of the 'safety' test, as applied by the CACD, as a means to overturn miscarriages of justice and whether permitting defendants several routes by which to challenge convictions returned against them in the magistrates' court is an efficient use of court resources.

This chapter explores two possible reforms to the law concerning criminal appeals, one of which (reduction in avenues of appeal from the magistrates' court) is foreshadowed in the terms of reference for the Law Commission's review, and the other of which (introducing limited avenues for appeals against acquittals in the Crown Court) is not. The chapter seeks to argue that both of these reforms are desirable in practice and justifiable in principle, and that they should be taken forward by the Law Commission as part of its review.

1. Appeals from the Magistrates' Court to the Crown Court

Where a defendant has been convicted of a criminal offence in the magistrates' court there are three ways in which he can seek to set aside that conviction in another court. The first is that he can seek to judicially review the decision of the magistrates to convict him on the basis, perhaps, that there was some irregularity in the procedure adopted by the court on its way to returning that conviction.[4] The second is that he can invite the magistrates to state a case for the decision of the High Court where, for example, the defendant contends that the conviction is based upon an erroneous view of the law taken by the court.[5] The third is that he can appeal to the Crown Court pursuant to what is now section 108 of the Magistrates' Court Act 1980.[6] Unlike judicial review and case stated, there is no need for the defendant to be able to identify any flaw in the decision of the magistrates in order for him to be able to exercise this particular right of appeal.

If the convicted defendant's appeal to the Crown Court is unsuccessful, he may be able to bring a claim for judicial review against the decision of the Crown Court to convict him, or he may be able to appeal to the High Court under the aforementioned case stated procedure.[7] Even if the convicted defendant does *not* seek

[3] See www.lawcom.gov.uk/law-commission-to-undertake-review-of-the-appeals-system/.
[4] Senior Courts Act 1981, ss 29 and 29A.
[5] Magistrates' Court Act 1980, ss 111, 112 and 114.
[6] The same right existed under the Magistrates' Court Act 1952, s 83, which was repealed and replaced by the 1980 Act. At that time, an appeal would have been to the courts of Quarter Sessions. The Crown Court was established by Part II of the Courts Act 1971 whereupon the jurisdiction of the Quarter Sessions was transferred to the Crown Court. The jurisdiction of the Crown Court was restated by the Senior Courts Act 1981, s 45(2)(a), which refers explicitly to the appellate function of the Crown Court.
[7] Senior Courts Act 1981, s 28.

to appeal his conviction to the Crown Court, he can still appeal his sentence to the Crown Court.[8] Again, there is no requirement for him to point to some error in the approach taken by the magistrates' court to the sentencing exercise before he is entitled to pursue such an appeal.

The number of appeals to the High Court by way of case stated is very small, and insignificant by comparison with the number of appeals to the Crown Court from magistrates' courts. For each of the years 2018, 2019 and 2020 there were 62, 39 and 33 appeals by case stated respectively received from magistrates' courts, and 10, 16 and 7 such appeals from the Crown Court. By contrast, in 2020 there were 2,377 sentence appeals and 2,130 conviction appeals from the magistrates' courts to the Crown Court. In 2021, the statistics show that there were a total of 6,345 appeals from the magistrates' court to the Crown Court (against conviction and/or sentence), and in 2022 that same figure was 6,153.[9]

A number of features about appeals against conviction and sentence from the magistrates' court to the Crown Court can be noted here. The first is that under section 108 of the 1980 Act, a defendant can appeal to the Crown Court against his conviction only if he pleaded not guilty but was convicted by the court following a trial. If he entered an unequivocal guilty plea he cannot challenge his conviction in the Crown Court, but he can appeal against any subsequent sentence he received having pleaded guilty. The second is that the procedure for appealing to the Crown Court is governed by Part 34 of the Criminal Procedure Rules (the CrimPR). A defendant must serve an appeal notice not more than 15 business days after the decision he seeks to appeal against, whether it be his conviction, his sentence, or both. That time limit can be extended by the Crown Court. Importantly, the appeal notice must summarise the issues, and, where the defendant intends to appeal against his conviction, set out as much information as possible about the course of the trial in the magistrates' court. There is no requirement in statute or in the CrimPR for the defendant to identify a ground of appeal.

A third feature is that an appeal against conviction in the Crown Court takes the form of a re-hearing of the case. The Crown Court is not bound by any rulings that may have been made in the lower court, and nor are the parties bound to call the same evidence that they called before the magistrates' court. Essentially, the appeal takes the form of a re-trial. The fourth is that under section 74(1) of the Senior Courts Act 1981, at the hearing of the appeal against conviction the Crown Court shall comprise (i) one justice of the High Court, one judge of the Crown Court or one Recorder, and (ii) between two and four justices of the peace, also known as lay magistrates. A judge alone may conduct any pre-appeal hearings to avoid the need to draft in lay magistrates to deal with simple case management issues. The fifth is that upon the determination of an appeal, the Crown Court has the powers set out in section 48 of the Senior Courts Act 1981. The Crown Court may 'confirm, reverse or vary' the decision that is being appealed against, or

[8] Magistrates' Courts Act 1980, s 108.
[9] See www.gov.uk/government/statistics/criminal-court-statistics-quarterly-october-to-december-2022.

remit the case to the magistrates' court with its opinion on the issue that is being appealed against or make any order that the magistrates' court would have had the power to make. This means the Crown Court can sentence the defendant more heavily than the magistrates' court did, provided that it does not exceed the maximum sentence that was available to the lower court.

What is the justification for granting defendants who have been convicted and/or sentenced in the magistrates' court an automatic opportunity to seek to overturn those decisions in the hope of achieving a more favourable outcome? In his *Review of the Criminal Courts of England and Wales*,[10] Sir Robin Auld reflected in Chapter 12 on the nature of appeals from the magistrates' court to the Crown Court. He opined that,[11]

> The right of appeal from magistrates' courts by way of rehearing must have its origins in a general lack of confidence in the impartiality and competence of the old 'police courts', mostly manned by local worthies with little knowledge of the law, little or no training and not obliged, unless required to state a case, to explain their decisions.

Sir Robin drew a distinction between those 'local worthies' and modern, well-trained District Judges and lay magistrates. District Judges are, of course, legally qualified whereas lay magistrates are not, but they nonetheless receive assistance from a legally qualified court clerk. With those observations in mind, Sir Robin wrote – '... it is hard to see what is left of the original justification for permitting another tribunal, even one presided over by a judge, to re-hear the case'. As Sir Robin appreciated, the existence of the defendant's automatic right of appeal to the Crown Court does not depend upon the identity of the judicial office-holder who made the decision that the defendant now complains about. It follows that even where a defendant is convicted after trial by the Chief Magistrate – the most senior District Judge in the country – he can appeal that conviction to the Crown Court where he could be re-tried before a Recorder – a part-time Crown Court judge – and two lay magistrates, who are also part-time judges.

One could be forgiven for asking why, in such a scenario, the decision of a senior and experienced full-time judge should be subject to an appeal to a panel of potentially inexperienced part-time judges, on the application of an aggrieved defendant without any requirement for him to show that the first decision was even arguably unsound? For Sir Robin, the solution was to change the law so that appeals from the magistrates' court to the Crown Court could only be pursued with the permission of the Crown Court.[12] In the same breath he recommended that appeals to the Crown Court should be the *only* route by which a defendant can challenge decisions made by the magistrates' court, thus avoiding the risk of a multiplicity of different challenges before different courts. Moreover, Sir Robin

[10] Review of the Criminal Courts of England and Wales by The Right Honourable Lord Justice Auld, September 2001. The Review can be found here: www.criminal-courts-review.org.uk/auldconts.htm.
[11] Paragraph 17, 617.
[12] Paragraph 30, 621.

inclined to the view that if the Crown Court decides to permit the defendant to pursue his appeal, the appeal itself would not take the form of a re-hearing. Instead, the Crown Court would act like the CACD and decide whether the conviction was unsafe, or the sentence unlawful, wrong in principle, or manifestly excessive.

That recommendation was not taken forward by the Government of the day, but in his *Review of Efficiency in Criminal Proceedings*,[13] Sir Brian Leveson pursued this theme. He observed that '[a]t present, the less serious the alleged offence, the greater the possible rights of appeal'.[14] In his view, that approach was 'disproportionate' and 'no longer justifiable'.[15] He observed that District Judges and lay magistrates are required to produce reasons for their decisions, and if those reasons disclose an error of law or procedural irregularity, then the aggrieved defendant can seek redress in the High Court without the need to be afforded an unfettered right of appeal to the Crown Court. Sir Brian noted that the exercise of that right by the defendant could require all of the prosecution's witnesses to attend court to give evidence for a second time, in circumstances where there was no complaint about the course of the first trial save in respect of the outcome. For these reasons he too recommended that on an appeal against conviction, the Crown Court should be required to review the decision of the magistrates' court to look for errors that undermine the safety of the conviction, but there should be no re-hearing of the case in the Crown Court. If the Crown Court detected such an error, then it should have the power to remit the case to the magistrates' court for it to be re-tried there.

Sir Brian agreed with Sir Robin that it would make little sense in these circumstances for the defendant to have available to him, in addition, a challenge to the High Court, either by a claim for judicial review or an appeal by way of case stated, and so if the Crown Court was to adopt the function of a court of appeal in the mould of the CACD then those other avenues of challenge should be closed off. Sir Brian did recognise that a countervailing consideration against his proposal was that the written decisions of lay magistrates in particular would come under greater scrutiny than before, and that this would place an increased burden on them, and on their legal advisors, to produce more detailed rulings. Inevitably, that would take more time within a system that is meant to deliver justice swiftly.

Professor Peter Hungerford-Welch has also made the point that appeals by way of case stated would, presumably, still need to be made available to the prosecution and, moreover, that Crown Court cases are rarely reported whereas appeals by way of case stated result in a reasoned judgment from the High Court that could establish a useful precedent in a difficult area of the law.[16] By shoe-horning all defence

[13] Review of Efficiency in Criminal Proceedings by The Right Honourable Sir Brian Leveson, President of the Queen's Bench Division, January 2015. The Review is available here: www.judiciary.uk/wp-content/uploads/2015/01/review-of-efficiency-in-criminal-proceedings-20151.pdf.

[14] Paragraph 324, 84.

[15] ibid.

[16] P Hungerford-Welch, *Criminal Procedure and Sentencing*, 9th edn (Routledge, 2019) 185.

appeals from the magistrates' court into the Crown Court, there is a danger that the ability of the High Court to clarify the law with respect to criminal procedure and evidence, as well as substantive criminal law, will be hindered considerably to the detriment of the parties and the public.

As with Sir Robin's recommendations, Sir Brian's recommendations similarly disappeared into thin air, but interest in reforming this area of criminal procedure did not disappear with them. On 17 March 2022, the Director of Public Prosecutions (the DPP), Max Hill KC, delivered a talk at King's College in London as part of the Future of Legal Practice Series. His talk was entitled 'Criminal justice after COVID-19'.[17] The DPP noted that now, more than ever, court time is at a premium and so it is important to make the most of it. On that subject he asked, rhetorically, whether it was time to make some fundamental changes to aspects of criminal procedure, one of which being a defendant's unfettered right of appeal from the magistrates' court to the Crown Court. He queried whether the existence of this right struck the proper balance between fairness to defendants, and fairness to victims and witnesses, who, after all, may have to endure a second trial months or even years later with all of the stress and anxiety that could bring. The DPP stated that some of these appeals succeeded simply because the prosecution's witnesses refused to come to court to give evidence for a second time, or because they could no longer be traced and warned to attend for a second trial.

Although unsaid, one of the DPP's concerns may have been the potential for defendants to 'game' the system by pursuing a second trial in the Crown Court in the hope that witnesses would not come to court and that the prosecution would be forced to offer no evidence against them. The DPP was keen to stress that defendants convicted in the magistrates' court should enjoy a right of appeal against their convictions, but, without saying so in terms, he favoured the recommendations made by Sir Robin and Sir Brian about how appeals to the Crown Court should be conducted in future:

> But why not adopt a system – like that from the Crown Court, which requires permission to appeal from a judge – which would sift out cases without merit? It would make the system more efficient, and a great deal fairer. And when an application for permission to appeal is granted, why not do as we have long done in the Court of Appeal – decide the appeal based on an accurate record of the trial proceedings, without witnesses having to come to court to give evidence all over again.

As proceedings in the magistrates' court are not recorded, or at least not yet, it is unlikely that there would ever be an entirely accurate record of what took place during the course of a trial. The legal advisor to the magistrates' court might have taken a note of proceedings, but that is no substitute for a transcript of the evidence given by witnesses, or of the submissions made by the parties. Inevitably, that is one further argument against adopting an approach that would require the

[17] See www.cps.gov.uk/cps/news/criminal-justice-after-covid-19-max-hill-qc-director-public-prosecutions.

Crown Court to act as the CACD when faced with appeals against decisions of the magistrates' court. If the defendant complained that his conviction was unsafe because the lay magistrates' refused his application to adduce evidence of the bad character of a prosecution witness, and the note of the submissions of the parties and the decision of the magistrates was of poor quality, how could the Crown Court reach any firm conclusion as to whether the justices had been entitled to reach the decision they did?

Further, even if the justices had *not* been entitled to refuse the application, without a good note of the evidence how would the Crown Court be able to determine whether the defendant's conviction was nevertheless safe? Against this it should be noted that the CACD does not always have available to it transcripts of evidence or submissions or even the judge's summing-up when deciding whether a defendant's conviction is unsafe. This is particularly so in cases that were heard decades earlier, and yet the CACD is still expected to, and does, arrive at an answer to that question in each case.

If Sir Robin Auld was right in 2001 about the reason *why* this particular right of appeal was created in the first place, then there is even more reason to suppose that in 2023 the justification for its continued existence no longer applies. Recently, both Parliament and the higher courts have shown an increased confidence in the ability of the magistrates' court to deliver justice. That confidence has manifested itself in a number of ways. For example, Parliament enacted the Judicial Review and Courts Act 2022 to increase the sentencing powers available to District Judges and magistrates from a maximum of six months' custody to a maximum of 12 months, and the Divisional Court has recognised that the magistrates' court can stay criminal prosecutions in order to protect the integrity of the criminal justice system whereas previously in summary proceedings that function was reserved to the Divisional Court itself.[18] The extension of the powers available to the magistrates' court does not sit comfortably alongside the existence of an unfettered right of appeal against convictions and sentences returned by District Judges and lay magistrates that is predicated on the notion that those judges cannot be trusted to deliver justice the first time around.

In this climate, the arguments put forward by Sir Robin Auld in 2001 and Sir Brian Leveson in 2015, and endorsed by the present DPP in 2022, for reforming avenues of appeal from the magistrates' court, are even more powerful. There is no good reason why a defendant who wants to challenge his conviction or sentence should be able to pick and choose from a menu of options, one of which could result in a re-hearing of his trial months or years after the first one. The defendant should be confined to a single route of challenge in the form of an appeal to the Crown Court with the permission of that court. Any such appeal will be determined *not* by requiring the Crown Court to undertake the exact same exercise that was carried out in the magistrates' court, but by the Crown Court considering

[18] *Mansfield v Director of Public Prosecutions* [2021] EWHC 2938 (Admin); [2022] QB 335.

whether there was a flaw in the approach taken in the court below. If there was, then the Crown Court should be able to set the decision aside and then either make a different decision or remit the case to the magistrates' court for a fresh decision to be made there. If the Crown Court itself falls into error, then either the prosecution or the defence should be able to appeal that decision to the High Court by way of case stated, thus ensuring that the higher courts retain the ability to supervise the exercise by the Crown Court of its appellate functions and, indirectly, the work of the magistrates' court. If the quality of justice delivered in the magistrates' court is no longer second-class, then the restriction of a defendant's rights of appeal in this way will bring parity with the rights of appeal he would have if convicted and sentenced in the Crown Court, will ease the burden on the Crown Court in dealing with re-trials from the magistrates' court, and will give some comfort to victims and witnesses that whether they will have to endure another trial will be a matter for the court and not for the defendant alone.

2. Appeals against Acquittals from the Crown Court

On 28 September 2022, the Court of Appeal handed down its judgment in the case of *Attorney General's Reference (No.1 of 2022)*.[19] The reference followed the acquittal in Bristol of four protestors who were accused of damaging the statue of Edward Colston. The Attorney General sought the opinion of the CACD on three questions of law that arose out of that trial. The first of those questions concerned the trial judge's decision to direct the jury that they could only find the defendants guilty of criminal damage if they were sure that a conviction 'would be a proportionate interference with their rights to freedom of thought and conscience, and to freedom of expression'.[20] That was not the only defence raised by the defendants, but if the jury answered that particular question in the negative then the defendants would have been found not guilty regardless of the force of the other defences. The CACD concluded that whether a conviction for criminal damage would amount to a proportionate interference with a defendant's Convention rights was not a matter for a jury to determine and so that particular 'defence' should not have been left for them to consider.[21] It follows that the jury were misdirected and provided by the judge with a legally impermissible route by which to find the defendants not guilty. Of course, the jury may have acquitted the defendants for other reasons but, equally, the jury may have acquitted the defendants only because they were not sure that their conviction would be a proportionate interference with their Convention rights and, if the latter, then the proper verdict would have been one of guilty. As the case was an Attorney General's reference on a point of law, the conclusions of the CACD have no bearing on the safety of the

[19] [2022] EWCA Crim 1259.
[20] See [15].
[21] At [115].

defendants' acquittals. But, given the nature of the trial judge's error, why should those acquittals not be set aside and a retrial ordered? Why must an unsafe conviction returned in the Crown Court fall but an unsafe acquittal stand, especially when the prosecution can appeal by way of case stated against acquittals returned in the magistrates' court?

The doctrine of autrefois acquit, also known as the double jeopardy rule or *ne bis in idem*, states that no person who has been acquitted of an offence shall be tried again for the same offence. The purpose of the doctrine is to protect defendants from being subject to repeated prosecutions for the same alleged wrongdoing. Although a doctrine of the common law, the principle of autrefois acquit finds form in a number of international instruments too, including the European Convention of Human Rights (ECHR). Article 4(1) of Protocol 7 stipulates that no-one shall be tried or punished again in criminal proceedings under the jurisdiction of the same State 'for an offence for which he has already been finally acquitted … in accordance with the law and penal procedure of that State'.[22] The common law also insists that an acquittal must be final before the doctrine can apply.[23] In the magistrates' court, as the prosecution can appeal to the High Court by way of case stated against an acquittal, a finding of not guilty is not a final acquittal and will not become so until the prosecution decides not to pursue an appeal, or until the High Court dismisses the prosecution's appeal. Article 4(2) of Protocol 7 provides for two exceptions to the doctrine. The first is where 'there is evidence of new or newly discovered facts' since the return of the acquittal, and the second is where 'there has been a fundamental defect in the previous proceedings, which could affect the outcome of the case'. Parliament has made inroads into the doctrine in the last 30 years in reliance on both of these exceptions.

In terms of new or newly discovered facts, Part 10 of the Criminal Justice Act 2003 granted prosecutors the power to seek the permission of the CACD to re-try an acquitted defendant where there is new and compelling evidence of his guilt and where it would be in the public interest for him to be re-tried. These provisions followed a recommendation in the Macpherson report that 'consideration should be given to the Court of Appeal being given power to permit the prosecution after acquittal where fresh and viable evidence is presented'.[24] Sir William reflected on the fact that the doctrine of autrefois acquit would prevent a subsequent prosecution of the defendant for the same offence even where the fresh evidence of his guilt was overwhelming. He wrote:

> Both we and others … have considered, in the context of this case, where the law which absolutely protects those who have been acquitted from any further prosecution for the same or a closely allied offence should prevail. If, even at this late stage, fresh and viable evidence should emerge against any of the three suspects who were acquitted,

[22] The UK has not ratified Protocol 7.

[23] *Connelly v DPP* [1964] AC 1254.

[24] The Stephen Lawrence Inquiry – Report of an Inquiry by Sir William Macpherson of Cluny (1999) Cm 4262, Recommendation 38.

> they could not be tried again however strong the evidence might be. We simply indicate that perhaps in modern conditions such absolute protection may sometimes lead to injustice. Full and appropriate safeguards would be essential. Fresh trials after acquittal would be exceptional. But we indicate that at least the issue deserves debate and reconsideration, perhaps by the Law Commission, or by Parliament.

On 2 July 1999, the Government of the day invited the Law Commission to do just that. The Law Commission published a Consultation Paper in October 1999[25] on the possibility of re-opening acquittals where new evidence has come to light that is probative of the defendant's guilt. Subsequently, the Home Affairs Select Committee of the House of Commons launched its own investigation into the possibility of reform in this area, and it published its report in June 2000.[26] It recommended that there should be a limited exception to the doctrine of autrefois acquit to provide for the possibility of a re-trial on the basis of fresh evidence. The Law Commission published its final report in March 2001.[27] Like the Select Committee, it recommended that the rule against double jeopardy should be subject to an exception in certain cases where new evidence is discovered after an acquittal. In the Law Commission's assessment, this exception should be limited to cases of murder, genocide and reckless killing,[28] and it should only apply where the new evidence is both reliable and compelling, in the sense that it makes the defendant's guilt highly probable. Moreover, the Law Commission stated that a further prosecution should only be commenced if it is in the interests of justice to do so.

Section 75 of what is now the Criminal Justice Act 2003 provides that the powers in Part 10 only apply where the defendant has been convicted of a qualifying offence, which means any offence listed in Part 1 of Schedule 5. That list is much longer than the list contained within the Law Commission's report. It includes genocide, murder, manslaughter, kidnapping, various offences under the Sexual Offences Act 2003, various offences under the Misuse of Drugs Act 1971, and arson. An application by the prosecutor to the CACD for permission to re-try the acquitted defendant in such a case can only be made with the written consent of the DPP.[29] The CACD must grant the application[30] if it is satisfied that there is 'new and compelling evidence against the acquitted person in relation to the qualifying offence'[31] and that 'in all the circumstances it is in the interests of justice for the court to make the order' for a re-trial,[32] having regard to a list of factors set out in the Act. There is no requirement that an application should be brought within a set period of time because, of course, it will not be possible for the prosecution to predict when any new and compelling evidence of guilt will emerge. Importantly,

[25] Law Commission, *Double Jeopardy* (Consultation 156, 1999).
[26] See publications.parliament.uk/pa/cm199900/cmselect/cmhaff/190/19002.htm.
[27] Law Commission, *Double Jeopardy and Prosecution Appeals* (Law Com No 267, 2001).
[28] Page 127.
[29] Section 76(3).
[30] Section 77(1)(a).
[31] Section 78(1).
[32] Section 79(1).

the effect of section 75(3) of the Act is that if the CACD sets aside the acquittal and directs that the defendant be re-tried, and he is acquitted at that re-trial and then further new and compelling evidence of his guilt is found, the prosecution *cannot* seek to have the acquittal set aside a second time. That follows a recommendation from the Law Commission that 'where an acquittal is quashed on grounds of new evidence, and the defendant is acquitted at the re-trial, no application to quash that later acquittal on grounds of new evidence should be permitted'.[33]

In terms of a fundamental defect in the earlier proceedings, sections 54 to 57 of the Criminal Procedure and Investigations Act 1996 created a jurisdiction whereby the prosecution can seek to overturn what is known as a tainted acquittal. Section 54 applies where a person has been acquitted of an offence, and the same person has been convicted of an offence concerned with the administration of justice (such as the common law offence of perverting the course of justice) involving interference with, or the intimidation of, a juror or witness (or potential witness) in any proceedings that concluded in the acquittal. In these circumstances, if it appears to the court before which the person was convicted of the administration of justice offence that there is a real possibility that, but for the interference or intimidation, the person would not have been acquitted of the underlying offence, the court shall certify that it so appears provided it is in the interests of justice to do so. If the court of conviction so certifies, then the prosecution can apply to the High Court for an order quashing the acquittal and the High Court shall make the order if the four conditions in section 55 are met. The conditions are that it appears to the High Court that (i) but for the interference or intimidation it is likely the person would not have been acquitted, (ii) it would not be contrary to the interests of justice to require the acquitted person to be re-tried for the offence, (iii) the acquitted person has had a reasonable opportunity to make written representations to the High Court, and (iv) the conviction for the administration of justice offence will stand. If the High Court quashes the acquittal, then new proceedings can be commenced against the defendant for the offence of which he was acquitted. There is no reported case on the operation of these provisions, but the procedure is governed by Part 27 of the CrimPR. Rule 27.2(2) requires the prosecutor to apply as soon as practical after the defendant's conviction for the administration of justice offence for the court to certify that the safety of the acquittal is fit to be considered by the High Court. That time limit can be extended by the court. If the court at which the conviction was returned so certifies then the procedure for bringing the matter before the High Court is set out in rules 77.6 to 77.15 of the Civil Procedure Rules.

A 'fundamental defect' in the proceedings that leads a judge of the Crown Court to conclude that the jury should be directed to acquit the defendant can also be the subject of an appeal under the provisions of Part 9 of the Criminal Justice Act 2003. This is not an appeal against the acquittal itself, of course, but is a power available

[33] Report, 128.

to the prosecution that can be exercised whenever the judge of the Crown Court makes any ruling in criminal proceedings up to the moment the summing-up commences. As with the powers in Part 10, this reform followed recommendations by the Law Commission after a formal referral from Government. As early as 1999, the Attorney General had identified what he described as an 'imbalance in the system'[34] that meant the prosecution could not seek to correct on appeal adverse decisions such as those staying the proceedings as an abuse of process or directing the jury to return a verdict of not guilty against a defendant. Ought not the prosecution to be able to test those decisions on appeal, the Attorney General asked rhetorically. In so saying, the Attorney General was keen to stress that the imbalance he had identified should not be subject to over-correction thereby leaving the defence at a disadvantage, and nor should the introduction of an 'interlocutory' right of appeal to the prosecution cause undue delays. In the same report that recommended the creation of a power for the prosecution to seek a re-trial following an acquittal, the Law Commission recommended the introduction of a power for the prosecution to appeal rulings 'on potentially terminating matters', to include 'an acquittal arising from a ruling of no case to answer made at the conclusion of the prosecution case'.[35]

The provisions of Part 9 of the 2003 Act contain a number of important safeguards around the use of this power, which the CACD has interpreted strictly since they represent 'a significant shift of rights towards the Crown as against an individual'.[36] Although the Law Commission stated that it should be a power to appeal against an acquittal,[37] in reality the power is confined to appeals against rulings made by a Crown Court judge in the course of a trial on indictment. Where that ruling consists of a decision that there is no case for a defendant to answer, then the judge should *not* invite the jury to find the defendant not guilty because in those circumstances, while the CACD has the power under section 67 to reverse the ruling, it has no power under Part 9 to set aside the acquittal itself. In order to invoke this right of appeal, the prosecution has to take a number of carefully orchestrated steps. Taking them too slowly, or in the wrong order, can deprive the CACD of jurisdiction to determine the appeal. In particular, the prosecution must notify the court of its intention to appeal immediately after the ruling has been handed down, or by the time given by the court for the prosecutor to consider its position has elapsed, and either at the time of doing so, or before doing so, the prosecutor must give what is known as the acquittal agreement, which means that if it abandons the appeal, or if the CACD dismisses the appeal, then the defendant will be entitled to be acquitted of the offence to which the ruling relates. If notice of an intention to appeal is not given promptly, or the acquittal agreement comes too late, then the appeal will fail regardless of its merits.

[34] Tom Sargant Memorial Lecture, 29 November 1999.
[35] Law Com No.267, at 132 and 133.
[36] *Y* [2008] EWCA Crim 10, [19].
[37] Law Com No.267, at page 108, para 7.74, Recommendation 27.

An analysis of these statutory powers that enable the High Court and the CACD to interfere with acquittals, or to overturn rulings that would have resulted in acquittals if left undisturbed, shows how restrictive they can be, and how many safeguards are in place to ensure that the powers are not misused. Those safeguards include:

(a) Restrictions on the types of offences that can be the subject of the power.
(b) Restrictions on the number of times the power can be exercised in respect of the same offence.
(c) Requirements that the power should only be exercised in a limited range of circumstances.
(d) Requirements that the power should only be exercised if it is in the public interest to do so.
(e) Requirements that the power should only be exercised with the consent or approval of the DPP or of a court.
(f) Restrictions on the time available to the prosecution in which to invite the court to exercise the power.
(g) Requirements of strict compliance by the prosecution with certain procedural steps towards the exercise of the power by the court.
(h) Restrictions on the time for the re-institution of proceedings if the court exercises the power in favour of the prosecution.

While Parliament has not yet embraced the possibility of enabling the prosecution to appeal against an acquittal returned by a jury at the conclusion of a trial that power exists elsewhere in the common law world, and is quite common in Continental Europe. For example, in Germany, Section 362 of the Code for Criminal Procedure permits the re-opening of an acquittal in specific circumstances, which include where documents produced at trial for the defendant's benefit turn out to be false, or where witnesses called to give evidence for the defendant did so falsely or in breach of their duty to the court. In Canada, section 676 of the Canadian Criminal Code provides that the Attorney General of a province, or counsel instructed by him, may appeal to the court of appeal against a verdict of acquittal 'on any ground of appeal that involves a question of law alone'. Although section 11h of the Canadian Charter of Rights and Freedoms stipulates that where a person is finally acquitted of an offence he may not be tried for it again, the Supreme Court of Canada has held that section 676 of the Criminal Code does not offend the guarantee against double jeopardy.[38] The Supreme Court of Canada in *R v Graveline*[39] recognised the traditional importance that the courts have placed on acquittals, but observed that since the introduction of what is now section 676

[38] *Morgentaler, Smoling and Scott* [1988] 1 SCR 30, 37 CCC (2d).
[39] [2006] 1 SCR 609.

'acquittals are not necessarily sacrosanct'[40] although the burden on the prosecution to overturn an acquittal remains a heavy one. LeBel J went on to say this:

> It must … be recognised that the appeal function is an important component of a legal system whose purpose is to ensure that the rules of criminal procedure and evidence are properly applied. The accused has a right to a fair trial in accordance with the substantive and procedural rules of criminal law and the principles of the Constitution. The Crown, which represents the state and the public interest in the proper administration of the criminal law, has the same right. It is that right that is protected by the existence of an appeal function, which must be performed with care, but firmly, when the need arises.[41]

In order to succeed on an appeal against an acquittal, the prosecution has to show that the error of law made by the trial judge *might* reasonably be thought to have had a material bearing on the fact of the acquittal. It is not necessary for the prosecution to show that but for the error, the defendant would have been convicted. In *R v Morin*,[42] Sopinka J approached that question in this way:

> An accused who has been acquitted once should not be sent back to be tried again unless it appears that the error at the first trial was such that there is a reasonable degree of certainty that the outcome may well have been affected by it.

This involves a two-step analysis. The first step is to identify whether the trial judge made any legal errors. The second step is to consider whether any legal errors she did make 'were sufficiently material to justify appellate intervention'.[43] Whether an error is 'legal' generally turns on its character rather than on its severity, and so it is not open to an appellate court to translate its strong objections to the trial judge's factual findings into identifiable legal errors unless those findings were perverse. That approach disregards the restraint that the Canadian Parliament chose to place upon the Crown's right to seek to appeal against acquittals. That restraint is also evident in the rule that prevents the prosecution on appeal from putting forward a new legal argument that was not advanced at trial.[44] However, where the prosecutor did not quarrel with the error at trial that does not necessarily prevent an appeal against the acquittal because the public have an obvious interest in ensuring that verdicts are not tainted by a material deficiency.[45] Where the prosecution exercises its right to appeal against an acquittal the defendant is entitled to seek to uphold the acquittal on the alternative basis that the trial judge made errors to the disadvantage of the defence and which, had they not been made, would probably have resulted in an acquittal in any event.[46]

[40] At [27].
[41] Pages 619–620.
[42] [1988] 2 SCR 345, 374.
[43] *George (Barbara)* [2017] 1 SCR 1021, 349 CCC (3d), [14].
[44] *Suarez-Noa* (2017), 350 CCC (3d) 267 (Ont C.A.).
[45] *Barton*, 2019 SCC 33.
[46] *Atlantic Sugar Refineries Co* (1978), 41 CCC (2d) 209 (Que C.A.).

Stepping away from Canada, a number of Caribbean jurisdictions also recognise the ability of the prosecutor to challenge an acquittal. Various specific legislative provisions allow the prosecution to appeal against a directed acquittal, but even where the acquittal has been returned by the jury of its own volition at the conclusion of a trial certain jurisdictions do permit a prosecution appeal with a view to setting such an acquittal aside. For example, section 40A of Chapter 335, West Indies Associated States Supreme Court (Grenada) Act, allows the DPP to appeal to the Court of Appeal against an acquittal in circumstances where the trial judge had given the jury a material misdirection as to law or fact. In Saint Christopher and Nevis, section 42(1) of Chapter 3.11, the Eastern Caribbean Supreme Court (Saint Christopher and Nevis) Act, consolidates the rights of appeal afforded to the DPP against acquittals, and these include where there has been a substantial misdirection of the jury on the law or facts or on a mixed question of law and fact by the trial judge in the course of his summation. Section 42(3) requires the DPP to notify the court orally before it discharges the defendant that he intends to appeal against the acquittal and, oral notice having been given, the DPP then has 14 days in which to file his formal notice of appeal and grounds of appeal. An appeal under section 42 has the effect of suspending the execution of the decision, judgment or other order appealed against. Section 42(6) places a limitation on the categories of offence that can be the subject of an appeal by the DPP. The list of qualifying offences includes murder, treason, manslaughter, robbery, housebreaking, burglary, theft and a range of sexual offences.

In Guyana, the Court of Appeal Act was amended in 2010 to insert a new section 33B that permits the DPP to appeal against a judgment or verdict of acquittal of an accused person in proceedings by indictment in the High Court when the judgment or verdict is the result of, *inter alia*, 'the trial judge's substantial misdirection of the jury in the course of the judge's summation on the law or factors or on a mixed question of law or fact'. In *Hyles v DPP* [2018] CCJ 12, the Caribbean Court of Justice ruled that this provision was compatible with the prohibition on double jeopardy contained in Article 144(5) of the Constitution of Guyana. In doing so the Court pointed out that Article 144(5) should be understood against the background of Article 14(7) of the International Covenant on Civil and Political Rights (the ICCPR) to which Guyana is a signatory. Article 14(7) of the ICCPR states that no person shall be liable to be tried again for an offence for which he has already been finally acquitted in accordance with the law and penal procedure of each country. The Court ruled that the availability of an avenue of appeal against an acquittal means that the acquittal, once returned by the jury, cannot be said to be final and so the existence of a right of appeal cannot breach the rule against double jeopardy. On this analysis, the Court concluded that the prosecution of an appeal against a person who has been acquitted is not a second prosecution of that person for the same offence, but a continuation of, or resumption of, the original prosecution.[47] The Court pointed to a number of examples, including in England

[47] At [40].

and Wales, where inroads into the rule against double jeopardy had been made, and asked itself why these developments had taken place. The Court then answered its own question:[48]

> Certainly, accused persons have, and should have, a guaranteed and fundamental right to protection of the law but they are not the only ones. We are well aware that the principle that all proceedings should at some point come to an end … is important …. We are also aware that the presumption of innocence requires respect for a final judgment once the accused has been acquitted. However, this represents a fragment of the argument. The principal of fairness … equally requires the protection of the rights of other stakeholders in the criminal justice process … It is true that a criminal justice system must be fair and be seen to be fair but above all it must be effective in protecting the rights of all; in fact, a profusely ineffective criminal justice system can hardly ever be fair.

For the Court, the statutory provisions that allow for a right of appeal against an acquittal did not fall foul of the Constitution of Guyana because there are a number of important safeguards in place that regulate the use of that right. They are (i) that an appeal must be brought within a limited time, (ii) the right of appeal is limited to certain serious offences as set out in section 33C, (iii) the grounds of appeal are limited to serious procedural errors or flaws that brought about the acquittal, and (iv) the appellant court has a discretion whether to allow the appeal even if the statutory criteria are made out.

The recognition by the Court in *Hyles* that an effective system of criminal justice requires the protection of the rights of all of the participants in it – which will include not just the defendant, but also victims and the public generally – is important. A power that vests in a prosecutor, acting on behalf of the state, to correct injustice by appealing against an acquittal returned following a material misdirection by the trial judge, should not breach any right a defendant has to retain the benefit of an unsafe acquittal. As Lord Hoffmann put it in *State of Trinidad & Tobago v Boyce*:

> There is nothing particularly unfair or unjust about a statutory rule which enables an appellate court to correct an error of law by which an accused person was wrongly discharged or acquitted and order that the question of his guilt or innocence be properly determined according to law.[49]

In England and Wales, the ability of the prosecutor to correct errors of law that lead to acquittals is severely curtailed. Where a trial judge indicates in advance of his summing-up that he intends to give the jury a particular direction that the prosecutor considers to be wrong in law, the prosecutor could theoretically launch an appeal against that 'ruling' under Part 9 of the Criminal Justice Act 2003 – but in order to do so he would have to concede that in the event the appeal failed the defendant should be acquitted, and that is unlikely to make the prospect of

[48] At [41].
[49] [2006] UKPC 1; [2006] 2 AC 76.

an appeal a welcome one. For example, on a charge of murder, if the trial judge ruled that the partial defence of loss of control should be left to the jury, and that ruling was in error, it would take a brave (or even foolhardy) prosecutor to appeal that ruling because if the appeal fails the defendant would have to be acquitted of murder. The position is different where the challenge is to a successful submission of no case to answer, because if the appeal fails the outcome will be an acquittal regardless. In that scenario the prosecutor has little to lose by appealing against the ruling, but where the prospect of a conviction notwithstanding the proposed erroneous direction is still a realistic possibility, why take the chance of appealing and losing?

Moreover, if the judge misdirects the jury in the course of his summing-up but in circumstances where that misdirection was not foreshadowed before the summing-up commenced, even the possibility of an appeal under Part 9 of the 2003 Act will not be open to the prosecutor. That is because the misdirection is unlikely to be a ruling, but even if it is section 58(13) expressly states that only rulings made before the judge embarks on his summing-up can be the subject of an appeal, and so unless the judge is willing to unwind the misdirection and direct the jury in accordance with the law, that misdirection cannot be challenged by the prosecutor. If the misdirection was to the disadvantage of the defendant and resulted in his conviction, he could appeal that conviction to the CACD; but if the misdirection was to the disadvantage of the prosecution and resulted in the defendant's acquittal, on the present state of the law the prosecution, the victim and the public simply have to live with that outcome. That does not seem fair or just.

That is why Parliament should legislate to afford prosecutors an opportunity to appeal against acquittals that have been returned by a jury. That would not amount to an impermissible trespass on the rule against double jeopardy, but even if Parliament was uneasy about taking that step there are a number of safeguards that could be put in place to ease those concerns. Drawing from the points already made in this chapter by reference to other jurisdictions, and existing prosecution rights of appeal, any right of appeal against an acquittal could (i) relate only to a specified range of offences, (ii) require the prosecution to comply with strict procedural requirements including the time at which notice of appeal is given, (iii) be restricted to cases where there has been a material misdirection of law and where it can be safely inferred that had the error not taken place the trial would not have resulted in an acquittal, and (iv) be subject to the additional judgment of the CACD as to whether it would be in the public interest to interfere with the acquittal and thus require the defendant to be re-tried for the offence. This reform would bring the law of England and Wales closer into line with that in Canada, and a number of Caribbean countries, and ensure that regardless of the jury's verdict in any given case, if it was reached as a result of a material error of law, that error can be put right and another verdict sought on a correct legal basis at a re-trial.

3. Conclusion

The Law Commission has been presented with a significant opportunity to correct some of the injustices that have taken root in the system of criminal appeals as it operates in England and Wales. There are many more ways in which that system could be improved beyond the two discussed in this chapter, but both represent a necessary corrective to an approach that seems to favour the rights of defendants over the rights of prosecutors, victims and the public. The proposals for reform set out in this chapter would be a very good place for the Law Commission to start its important work.

Comment on Chapter 1

Unappealing? How (Not) to Rationalise Criminal Procedure

PAUL ROBERTS*

With the flair of a skilled advocate, Paul Jarvis argues for two structural reforms to the existing system of criminal appeals in England and Wales. First, Jarvis would consolidate multi-track appeals from summary proceedings into a single Crown Court review process; and second, he would empower prosecutors in trials on indictment to challenge 'unsafe acquittals' on points of law. The following commentary, written from an academic perspective, highlights methodological shortcomings in Jarvis' argument, which – I will suggest – fatally compromise his law reform case notwithstanding the (debateable) merits of particular proposals.

1. Learning from History

Criminal adjudication in England and Wales is the product of a long, idiosyncratic and somewhat tortuous institutional history,[1] in which a system of regular criminal appeals did not emerge until as late as April 1908, when the Court of Criminal Appeal (as it then was) came into operation pursuant to the Criminal Appeal Act 1907. Campaigners championed the new appellate court as the solution to miscarriages of justice lacking effective institutional remedy.[2] Almost a century later, criminal appeals were reconsidered by the Runciman Royal Commission,[3] generating the most significant institutional innovation since 1907: the Criminal

* Professor of Criminal Jurisprudence, University of Nottingham, UK.

[1] BL Berger, 'Criminal Appeals as Jury Control: An Anglo-Canadian Historical Perspective on the Rise of Criminal Appeals' (2005) 10 *Canadian Criminal Law Review* 1; LB Orfield, 'History of Criminal Appeal in England' (1936) 1 *Missouri Law Review* 326.

[2] R Pattenden, *English Criminal Appeals, 1844–1994* (OUP, 1996).

[3] Royal Commission on Criminal Justice (Chair: Viscount Runciman), *Report* (HMSO, Cm 2263,1993) Ch 10. Also see Lord Justice Auld, *Review of the Criminal Courts of England and Wales* (TSO, 2001), Ch 12.

Cases Review Commission.[4] There is no harm in the Law Commission now taking another look,[5] albeit whether there is either need or appetite for major overhaul of criminal appeals in England and Wales remains to be seen.

George Santayana famously predicted recurrent failure and disappointment as the price of historical amnesia. On Jarvis' retelling, 'injustices … have taken root in the system of criminal appeals as it operates in England and Wales', inviting remedial treatment as a 'necessary corrective to an approach that seems to favour the rights of defendants over the rights of prosecutors, victims and the public'.[6] One symptom of more diffuse deterioration are 'asymmetrical rights of appeal'.[7] Yet Jarvis' revisionist history is belied by the institutional record. Nothing new or unexpected 'took root'; and the asymmetry he targets is *deliberate* and *principled*. Procedural safeguards favouring the accused serve as bulwarks against the over-weaning power of the state and mitigate risks of wrongful conviction. Only a system of criminal adjudication committed to principled asymmetry could have devised our conventional burden and (steeply asymmetric) standard of proof.[8] Viewed in crudely adversarial terms, procedural safeguards may appear as inconvenient fetters on the prosecution awarding tactical advantages to the accused (just as the employee's health and safety rights are the factory owner's 'red tape' and 'burdens on business'). However, common law prosecutors are simultaneously 'ministers of justice', backed by and representing the state, and accordingly shoulder more burdensome procedural duties than the accused.[9]

The 'right to a fair (criminal) trial' undoubtedly, today, encompasses the interests of all participants in criminal proceedings and the general public interest. *Exclusive* preoccupation with the rights and interests of the accused would be lopsided, and incompatible with both European human rights jurisprudence[10] and domestic procedural law.[11] Nonetheless, any simplistic assumption or implicit appeal to equivalence (*literal* 'equality of arms') should be stoutly resisted. Only the accused is on trial and uniquely in jeopardy, and this framing fact conditions the legitimacy of criminal adjudication, in both reality and perception. Absent legitimacy, penal law is just another coercive mechanism of social hygiene or a convenient tool for eliminating enemies and managing nonconformists. The central institutional design challenge for criminal adjudication lies in striking a legitimate balance between competing, non-fungible interests in the administration of justice.

[4] Criminal Appeal Act 1995, s 8.

[5] Law Commission, *Criminal Appeals* (Issues Paper, 2023).

[6] Jarvis, 36.

[7] Jarvis, 19.

[8] P Roberts, *Roberts and Zuckerman's Criminal Evidence*, 3rd edn (OUP, 2022) Ch 6.

[9] *Lobban* [1995] 1 WLR 877, 887, PC (Lord Steyn); *Preston* [1993] 4 All ER 638, HL.

[10] '[P]rinciples of fair trial also require that in appropriate cases the interests of the defence are balanced against those of witnesses or victims called upon to testify': *Doorson v Netherlands* (1996) 22 EHRR 330, [70]; *Y v Slovenia* (2016) 62 EHRR 3.

[11] '[T]he discretionary power to ensure fairness means fairness to both the defendant and to the prosecution. It is important that the guilty are convicted as well as the innocent acquitted': *Lamont* [2010] EWCA Crim 2144, [19] (Elias LJ). 'A fair trial denotes fairness to both sides. To have taken the course

That the accused has forensic advantages and remedies not available to the prosecution, in and of itself, affords *no reason whatsoever* to adjust the existing balance. Late twentieth century adjustments in criminal appeal rights, including exceptional mechanisms for quashing acquittals[12] and the introduction of prosecution appeals against 'terminating rulings',[13] were controversial.[14] Procedural safeguards against oppressive proceedings and wrongful convictions were integral to these reform packages and might well have been instrumental in securing parliamentarians' votes and the acceptance or acquiescence of practitioners, commentators, campaigners, and the general public. In an astonishing historical inversion, Jarvis insinuates that asymmetrical safeguards now require 'levelling down' to eliminate unanticipated unfairness to the prosecution. Santayana might have winced.

2. Authority and Experience

Taking his lead from the Law Commission's terms of reference, Jarvis' two proposals are presented as rationalist measures to enhance efficiency and eliminate structural anomalies. Efficiency was a leitmotif of official process *Reviews* by Auld and Leveson,[15] and animates the DPP's post-covid plea to ration criminal justice resources. '[N]ow, more than ever', we are admonished, 'court time is at a premium and so it is important to make the most of it'.[16] We must contemplate 'fundamental changes to aspects of criminal procedure', with an eye to eliminating needless duplication and pre-empting 'gaming' by opportunistic defendants. The right to appeal convictions in magistrates' courts by way of full rehearing *ab initio* at the Crown Court is supposedly objectionable on both counts.

Now, the most *efficient* system of criminal adjudication is the one where the police arrest suspects and impose spot-fines or, for more serious offences, frog-march offenders straight to gaol. To be clear, conviction and punishment of the guilty is the agreed aim: errors are never efficient and nobody advocates wrongful convictions of the innocent. Policy debates dispute effective means and relative normative priorities. Efficiency is not an *objective* of criminal adjudication, but rather a constraint on whatever else it is that we want criminal adjudication

sought by the defence in the present case in relation to these two potential witnesses would have been grossly unfair to the Crown': *Khan (Shafiq)* [2010] EWCA Crim 1692, [37].

[12] CJA 2003, ss 75–84.

[13] CJA 2003, Part 9. See R Pattenden, 'Prosecution Appeals Against Judges' Rulings' [2000] *Crim LR* 971.

[14] I was sceptical of double jeopardy reform, and have not materially altered my view over the ensuing two decades, subsequent developments notwithstanding: P Roberts, 'Justice for All? Two Bad Arguments (and Several Good Suggestions) For Resisting Double Jeopardy Reform' (2002) 6 *Evidence & Proof* 197; 'Double Jeopardy Law Reform: A Criminal Justice Commentary' (2002) 65 *Modern Law Review* 393.

[15] L Marsh, 'Leveson's Narrow Pursuit of Justice: Efficiency and Outcomes in the Criminal Process' (2016) 45 *Common Law World Review* 51.

[16] Jarvis, 24.

to achieve.[17] Despotism and oppression achieve their apogee when administered with greatest efficiency. The more pertinent, nuanced, question is, 'How, if at all, can we enhance the efficiency of procedures for rendering legitimate criminal verdicts?'

Jarvis insists that his reform proposals would promote system efficiency whilst simultaneously correcting injustices and protecting rights (including putative 'rights' of prosecutors). Rationalising appeal rights in summary proceedings would almost certainly simplify procedures and probably[18] save money. Enabling prosecutors to appeal against jury acquittals on points of law would, conversely, *increase* delay and expense, since – *ex hypothesi* – these appeals concern currently finalised cases. As Jarvis points out, the new jurisdiction introduced by the Criminal Justice Act 2003 for interlocutory appeals by prosecutors contains a major structural disincentive. A 'stick or twist' precondition was – deliberately – imposed on this novel procedure,[19] which was always envisaged as a last resort for forensic disputes that could not be resolved satisfactorily through astute and context-sensitive exercise of the trial judge's discretion.[20] Jarvis invokes the recent successful Attorney-General's Reference in the Colston Four case[21] as proof that this mechanism is too restrictive.

Since hard cases notoriously make bad law, let us set aside particular controversies[22] and focus instead on structural factors. Whereas Jarvis ostensibly advocates a convenient mechanism to enable prosecutors to have judicial errors corrected, what he is actually proposing is a mechanism for challenging what *prosecutors believe to be* judicial error. Within the current procedural framework, appellate tribunals sometimes uphold the original decision and dismiss the Attorney's application.[23] An expansion in prosecutor appeals on points of law will presumably entail more unsuccessful appeals both in absolute numbers and in relative terms (albeit with unknown and unpredictable ratios). Unsuccessful appeals will impose additional costs on the system, which could be justified only by countervailing benefits. Lacking plausible instrumental efficiency, the reform argument must rest squarely on other normative considerations. Jarvis frames the question rhetorically:

[17] Cf CrimPR Rule 1.1 (efficiency ranking sixth in the specified components of '[t]he overriding objective … that criminal cases be dealt with justly').

[18] Only 'probably', because ripple effects are unpredictable, eg if the diminution in appeal rights incentivised more defendants to elect (vastly more expensive) Crown Court jury trial, any savings on appeals could be gobbled up by increased trial costs.

[19] CJA 2003, ss 58(8) and (12); s 61(3).

[20] For institutional panorama, (still) see R Pattenden, *Judicial Discretion and Criminal Limitation*, 2nd edn (OUP, 1990) esp. 175–212.

[21] Attorney General's Reference (No 1 of 2022) [2022] EWCA Crim 1259.

[22] Cf N White, 'Edward Colston Statue: Race Campaigners Say "Justice Has Been Done" After Four Cleared of Criminal Damage' (*The Independent*, 5 January 2022), quoting one of the acquitted four proclaiming 'We didn't change history; we rectified it'.

[23] Including cases argued to the apex of the appellate pyramid: eg *Sheldrake v DPP*; *Attorney General's Reference (No 4 of 2002)* [2005] 1 AC 264; [2004] UKHL 43; *Looseley*; *Attorney-General's Reference (No 3 of 2000)* [2001] UKHL 53, [2002] 1 Cr App R 360, HL.

> Why must an unsafe conviction returned in the Crown Court fall but an unsafe acquittal stand, especially when the prosecution can appeal by way of case stated against acquittals returned in the magistrates' court?[24]

Observe the play of spurious equivalence in this rhetorical manoeuvre. Whereas 'unsafe conviction' is a term of art in English law,[25] 'unsafe acquittal' is a loaded neologism conveying the unwarranted impression that (arguable) legal errors render acquittals, somehow, 'unsafe', rather than routine implications of legitimate process.

Having cited heavyweight (extra)judicial authority for his proposals, but with no regard to empirical data, Jarvis concludes:

> If the quality of justice delivered in the magistrates' court is no longer second-class, then the restriction of a defendant's rights of appeal [in summary proceedings] … will bring parity with the rights of appeal he would have if convicted and sentenced in the Crown Court, will ease the burden on the Crown Court in dealing with re-trials from the magistrates' court, and will give some comfort to victims and witnesses that whether they will have to endure another trial will be a matter for the court and not for the defendant alone.[26]

This conclusion rests on the flimsy observation that 'both Parliament and the higher courts have shown an increased confidence in the ability of the magistrates' court to deliver justice',[27] coupled with the *Auld Report*'s tendentious speculations on the origins of appeal rights in summary trials. Proposals to upgrade magistrates' courts' sentencing jurisdiction have been circulating for decades,[28] always driven by naked cost-cutting. Justices of the Peace are no longer (predominantly) 'local worthies', but they remain legally unqualified and their so-called 'reasons' for their written decisions are, on my impression, perfunctory and frequently question-begging. Even supposing that parliamentarians and the senior judiciary are now more confident in the quality of magisterial justice than they were, say, twenty or thirty years ago (and I see no actual evidence for that), I am afraid I do not share their optimism.

Empirical data on the current state of summary criminal proceedings paint a bleak picture. Many courthouses have been sold off for development and the lay magistracy has been significantly reduced in size,[29] eroding the meaningfulness of 'local' justice. Progressive erosion of legal aid has left many defendants in the magistrates' courts unrepresented.[30] Qualitative portrayals of summary proceedings

[24] Jarvis, 27.
[25] Criminal Appeal Act 1968, s 2(1) (as amended); *Davis, Rowe* and *Johnson* [2001] 1 Cr App R 8, CA.
[26] Jarvis, 26.
[27] Jarvis, 25.
[28] CJA 2003, s 282 finally came into force on 2 May 2022, pursuant to the Criminal Justice Act 2003 (Commencement No 33) Regulations 2022, SI 2022/500, reg 3.
[29] The lay magistracy has been reduced by half over the last decade, numbering 12,506 in 2021/22: Georgina Sturge, *Court Statistics for England and Wales* (HC Library, 31 Jan 2023) 28.
[30] L Welsh, *Access to Justice in Magistrates' Courts: A Study of Defendant Marginalisation* (Hart, 2022) Ch 5 (estimating that between a fifth and a third of defendants appear unrepresented, and reporting 'a general sense that more defendants appear in court without legal representation' than formerly).

are seldom reassuring. Soubise found that delegation of tasks to police and less-qualified CPS staff coupled with reduced legal aid provision produced routinised bureaucratic case processing in which guilty pleas were the expected norm: '[N]o Crown Prosecutor will have read the case, or made any decision concerning its treatment and disposal .... [C]onvictions are based on a partial account of the facts and could potentially lead to miscarriages of justice'.[31] Along similar lines, Newman reported defence lawyers' cynicism about the prospects of a fair hearing before the magistrates. Occasional adversarial pyrotechnics are merely for show – a bit of theatre by way of client-management – and incidental to the accused's almost inevitable conviction.[32] The Secret Barrister characterises magistrates' courts as 'The Wild West'.[33] To the extent that reported appeals to the High Court by way of case stated afford any additional insight into what sometimes transpires in magistrates' courts, they largely corroborate empirical studies.[34] This is, moreover, an old story. As an experienced defence solicitor memorably confessed to me during a research interview in the early 1990s,[35] 'I can tell you now, the life we lead down in the magistrates' court is not an ideal world in any way, shape or form'. To imagine that the quality of magisterial justice might have significantly *improved* after massive real-terms funding cuts, systematic deskilling and de-professionalisation, and managerialist efficiency drives through 20 years of austerity policies flies in the face of common sense as well as disregarding accumulated empirical data.

Irrespective of the true state of affairs, I am bemused by the proposition that 'the quality of justice delivered in the magistrates' court is no longer second-class'. For I truly hope that it *is* second-class, ie inferior to the standard of justice on offer in full-blown Crown Court jury trials, rather than unacceptably substandard (ignoring, for the sake of specifying ideals, plentiful empirical evidence of substandard practice). If magisterial justice faithfully replicates what the Crown Court can offer, why do we give defendants the opportunity to elect jury trial in either way cases? Why do we not try robberies, rapes and homicides in the magistrates' courts? Why do we *pay for* Crown Court trials, when it would be a lot quicker, easier, simpler and, emphatically, cheaper to run all criminal proceedings as summary justice? The answer is *not* to be found in the limitations of lay justice, because the upper end of summary business is already handled by DJs, and we could, if so desired, create mixed panels of judges and lay magistrates for what are currently indictable

[31] L Soubise, 'Prosecuting in the Magistrates' Courts in a Time of Austerity' [2017] *Crim LR* 847, 856, 848.

[32] D Newman, *Legal Aid Lawyers and the Quest for Justice* (Hart, 2013) 134–39.

[33] The Secret Barrister, *Stories of the Law and How It's Broken* (Picador, 2019) Ch 2 ('if it's the word of a police officer against your client, it's usually game over before you've begun').

[34] Even when a District Judge presides: see *Kotsev v Bulgaria* [2019] 1 WLR 2353, [2018] EWHC 3087; *R (Rathor) v Southampton Magistrates' Court* [2018] EWHC 3278 (Admin); *R (Rankin) v Ipswich Magistrates' Court* [2016] EWHC 2851 (Admin); *Leo Sawrij v North Cumbria Magistrates' Court* [2010] 1 Cr App R 22, [2009] EWHC 2923 (Admin); *R (Flaherty) v City of Westminster Magistrates Court* [2008] EWHC 2589 (Admin).

[35] P Roberts and C Willmore, *The Role of Forensic Science Evidence in Criminal Proceedings* (RCCJ Research Study No 11, London, HMSO, 1993).

offences. The answer is that *nobody really thinks* that summary proceedings are as good as trials on indictment, any more than anybody believes that steerage is the same as first-class – regardless of the fact that all travellers arrive at the same destination (with or without priority disembarkation).

Summary justice is legitimate, when it is, because it is *good enough* relative to the importance of the matters at issue. We have always known that magistrates courts' proceedings are somewhat rough and ready, and focused on substantial justice sometimes at the expense of punctilious legality.[36] It is a question of proportionality and rational allocation of resources in a world of competing priorities and opportunity costs. When confined to relatively minor matters, magistrates courts cannot do great harm. Any injustices they do perpetrate will be *relatively* minor injustices. In its non-pejorative connotation, 'summary justice' demands that level of investigative effort and procedural rectitude appropriate to what is at stake – the forensic jeopardy – for the main protagonists and society at large. Historically, that jeopardy has been confined and ameliorated by at least three notable procedural safeguards: (i) for either way offences, the accused must *choose* summary trial and to that extent render themselves volenti to the known risks; (ii) the maximum penalty on conviction by the magistrates was capped at six months' imprisonment (or 12 months for conviction on multiple counts); and (iii) any aggrieved litigant – prosecutor[37] or defendant[38] – can demand rehearing by way of appeal to a higher court. As Jarvis notes, (ii) is (apparently) going to be doubled,[39] and he wants to dilute (iii) as well. I read this, not as an official vote of confidence in the quality of magisterial justice, but as a penny-pinching challenge to the legitimacy of criminal adjudication in summary proceedings.

The crux of the complaint or suspicion regarding 'summary justice' (in the pejorative sense) has not really changed over the decades: lay magistrates lack legal expertise, and they are prone to become 'case-hardened' and unduly sceptical of (or, according to perspective, less gullible towards) defence arguments, explanations and excuses they have heard a hundred times before.[40] This explains why some defendants elect jury trial, notwithstanding the jeopardy of increased penalty on conviction. They would prefer to be judged by a more diverse and

[36] For example, strict evidentiary doctrine is presumably relaxed in summary trials, partly owing to the absence of a functionally differentiated tribunal: P Darbyshire, 'Previous Misconduct and Magistrates' Courts – Some Tales from the Real World' [1997] *Crim LR* 105; M Wasik, 'Magistrates: Knowledge of Previous Convictions' [1996] *Crim LR* 851.

[37] Prosecutors' rights of appeal to the Crown Court are limited to specified ancillary matters: CrimPR r.34.1(c). Prosecutors' appeals are generally restricted to points of law or jurisdiction under the case stated procedure, and lie to the High Court: MCA 1980, s 111. However, findings of fact can still be challenged on *Wednesbury* grounds, affording some latitude for prosecutors to challenge first instance fact-finding.

[38] MCA 1980, s 108; affording defendants a right to retrial *ab initio* in the Crown Court.

[39] Sentencing Act 2020, s 224(1A), date to be appointed; MCA 1980, s 32 (as amended by the Judicial Review and Courts Act 2022, in force 14 July 2022). But for the latest twist in this convoluted saga, see Sentencing Act 2020 (Magistrates' Court Sentencing Powers) (Amendment) Regulations 2023/298, reg 2 (in force 30 March 2023).

[40] A Sanders, 'Core Values, the Magistracy, and the Auld Report' (2002) 29 *Journal of Law and Society* 324; H Parker, M Sumner and G Jarvis, *Unmasking the Magistrates* (Open UP, 1989).

socially inclusive panel of 12 jurors than by three lay magistrates (or, indeed, by a single DJ), who tend to be drawn from narrower social strata; and in any event cannot rival the combined experience and perspectives of a lay jury of 12. *Pace* Jarvis, valuing broader social experience in common sense factfinding, certainly in terms of bolstering *perceptions* of procedural fairness and possibly also enhancing the accuracy of factual determinations,[41] is not reducible to the disparaging notion that magistrates courts 'cannot be trusted to deliver justice the first time around'.[42]

Jarvis makes passing reference to statistical data on appeals from summary conviction for the years 2018–2022. Combined[43] appeals by case stated never reach three figures annually, which Jarvis judges 'very small, and insignificant'.[44] But that appraisal surely cuts both ways; and an important point of principle is at stake. The rule of law demands that all administrative power should be subject to judicial review to ensure that its exercise is not *ultra vires*. Lacking inherent or original jurisdiction in criminal matters, magistrates' courts have always been treated as administrative tribunals for these purposes. It is already the case that if the defendant – or indeed, the prosecutor – wishes to pursue judicial review via the case stated procedure, the applicant forfeits any concurrent right of appeal to the Crown Court.[45] So, if I read him correctly, Jarvis wants to curtail the rule of law for the sake of 30 or 40 appeals annually. It is by no means assured that this 'reform' would even save judicial resources in the aggregate, since unsuccessful appellants in the Crown Court might *subsequently* proceed by case stated in the High Court. Even supposing that some appeals would be concluded in the Crown Court, the remainder would be elongated at twice the price.

The statistics cited by Jarvis inform us that the Crown Court hears a little over 6,000 appeals annually from magistrates' courts trials.[46] The *meaning* of this number depends on one's point of reference. The Court of Appeal (Criminal Division) deals with approximately half that number of criminal appeal applications from trials on indictment,[47] but these arise from an annual Crown Court case load below 100,000.[48] Magistrates' courts are the workhorses of criminal adjudication, processing some 1.1 million defendants annually.[49] Patently, only

[41] Often these days expressed as worries about 'unconscious bias', but the issue predates modish terminology and should be taken seriously however conceptualised. R Morgan, 'Magistrates: The Future According to Auld' (2002) 29 *Journal of Law and Society* 308.

[42] Jarvis, 25.

[43] Direct appeals from magistrates' courts plus appeals from the Crown Court's appellate jurisdiction.

[44] Jarvis, 21.

[45] Magistrates Courts Act 1980, s 111(4).

[46] Cf Crown Prosecution Service, *Annual Report and Accounts 2022–2023*, (HC 1461, July 2023), 48, reporting 8,650 appeals in 2020–21, rising to 11,034 in 2022–23.

[47] This number has declined from almost 5,000 in 2017–18 to c.3,500 in 2021–22: Judiciary of England and Wales, *A Review of the Year in the Court of Appeal, Criminal Division 2021–22* (2023), Annex F.

[48] Ministry of Justice, *Criminal Court Statistics Quarterly, England and Wales, January to March 2023* (June 2023).

[49] Ministry of Justice, *Criminal Justice Statistics, England and Wales, Year Ending December 2021 (Annual)* (19 May 2022).

a tiny fraction of summary disposals results in appeals to the Crown Court, perhaps in the order of 1 in every 200 cases (half of one per cent). The appeal rate for trials on indictment is six times higher. Recalling that upwards of three quarters of defendants plead guilty without any trial, and of those who contest the charges two thirds are ultimately convicted by the magistrates, the picture that emerges is one of a highly effective system of summary justice in which well over 80% of those proceeded against are convicted. Is this really the place to look for more efficiency savings in the administration of justice? I am reminded of Eric Geddes' infamous electioneering promise that war reparations at Versailles would squeeze Germany like a lemon until the pips squeaked. Another pregnant lesson from history.

3. Forum Shopping in Comparative Law

Comparative law, no less than institutional history, is a treasure trove of shining examples and cautionary tales for would-be law reformers. Gilding his argument with some decorative trinkets, Jarvis notes that Germany permits acquittals to be reopened in certain circumstances, and that Canadian prosecutors may appeal first instance acquittals on points of law. Although the common law prohibition on 'double jeopardy' should not be conflated with the historically distinct civilian doctrine of *ne bis in idem*,[50] there is no *conceptual* difficulty in saying that the prohibition bites only at the point when all regular appeal processes have been exhausted. If authority were needed, Jarvis invokes the jurisprudential titans of the Caribbean Commonwealth,[51] as corroborated by the Privy Council.[52] It is hardly surprising that prosecutor appeals against acquittals are in principle ECHR-compliant, since the standard model of appeal in continental criminal procedure involves re-trial *de novo* and is freely available to any party dissatisfied with the initial ruling. This is the very same model of appeal from summary trial in England and Wales that Jarvis wants to scrap.

Pronounced diversity and idiosyncrasy in domestic legal processes render comparative criminal procedure a fascinating topic for legal study, but a dubious ally in law reform argument. For every comparative supporter cited by Jarvis, an opposing rival could easily be recruited. Canada is an outlier in the common law world in permitting prosecutor appeals against acquittals, a practice intertwined

[50] JE Costa, 'Double Jeopardy and *Non Bis In Idem*: Principles of Fairness' (1998) *UC Davis Journal of International Law and Policy* 181; DS Rudstein, 'Retrying the Acquitted in England, Part I: The Exception to the Rule Against Double Jeopardy for "New and Compelling Evidence"' (2007) 8 *San Diego International Law Journal* 387.

[51] *Hyles v DPP* [2018] CCJ 12 (AJ). Note that the appellants' acquittals were reinstated, because the prosecution could not establish a causal link 'with the required degree of certainty': ibid, [130]; 'CCJ Restores Jury Verdict in Guyana 11-count Murder Trial', *The Gleaner* (Kingston, Jam), 12 May 2018.

[52] *State of Trinidad & Tobago v Boyce* [2006] 2 AC 76, [2006] UKPC 1.

with a distinctive Canadian history involving early[53] institutional adoption of criminal appeals and contemporary use of bench trials for offences that can be tried only by juries in England and Wales. The Canadian practice would be unconstitutional in the United States.[54] Other Anglophone jurisdictions adopt a variety of practices. In South Africa, prosecutors' automatic right of appeal against 'a decision in favour of the accused on any question of law' is confined to magistrates' court trials.[55] There is, however, a reservation procedure in the High Court whereby acquittals can be made conditional on the Appellate Division's resolution of a contested point of law.[56] The Indian Code of Criminal Procedure permits appeals against acquittals on application by *complainants* as well as (with High Court leave) at the instigation of prosecutors.[57] Jury acquittals cannot be appealed in either Northern Ireland or the Republic of Ireland,[58] but are now subject to an exceptional quashing power in cases of 'new and compelling evidence' similar to the English provision.[59]

Investigations in comparative criminal procedure produce surprising – even bizarre – discoveries. In the faraway exotic jurisdiction of Scotland criminal juries have 15 members and decide by simple majority vote.[60] I have never heard anybody suggest that English juries should mimic the Scottish *modus operandi*; though, admittedly, few people south of Berwick may even be aware of such dramatic institutional variation so close to home. Expanded horizons reinforce an important truth about our own procedural traditions. Nobody would consciously *design* a system of criminal adjudication that looks precisely like the one we have today in England and Wales. If we were starting with a blank sheet of paper we would doubtless formulate procedures and practices on more strictly rationalist logical principles. But law reform starts from where we actually are, not from where we would have been in some hypothetical alternative universe. The cultural

[53] By common law standards. In continental legal process, criminal appeals trace an unbroken line via canon law to Roman jurisprudence: PD Marshall, 'A Comparative Analysis of the Right to Appeal' (2011) 22 *Duke Journal of Comparative & International Law* 1.

[54] 'Perhaps the most fundamental rule in the history of double jeopardy jurisprudence has been that "(a) verdict of acquittal … could not be reviewed, on error or otherwise, without putting (a defendant) twice in jeopardy, and thereby violating the Constitution"': *US v Martin Linen Supply Co*, 430 US 564, 571 (1977) (Brennan J, quoting *US v Ball*, 163 US 662, 671 (1896)); *US v Scott*, 437 US 82 (1978). Judgments of acquittal can be quashed in US state and federal prosecutions only where the acquittal is fundamentally defective, as where the defendant bribed the judge and entirely subverted the proceedings: *People of the State of Illinois v Aleman*, 1994 WL 16515305 (Circuit Court of Illinois Trial Order, 12 October 1994).

[55] Criminal Procedure Act 51 of 1977, s 310.

[56] CPA 1977, ss 319, 322(4) and 324.

[57] Code of Criminal Procedure 1976, ss 372 and 378. See *Kodagli (Dead) v State of Karnataka* [2018] INSC 913 (12 October 2018).

[58] G Coffey, 'The Constitutional Status of the Double Jeopardy Principle' (2008) 30 *Dublin University Law Journal* 138.

[59] CJA 2003, s 78.

[60] P Duff, 'The Scottish Criminal Jury: A Very Peculiar Institution' (1999) 62 *Law and Contemporary Problems* 173.

familiarity of already-existing institutionalised criminal practice implies an important methodological lesson: the fact that other jurisdictions do things differently to us, though intellectually fascinating and *potentially* useful in law reform and policymaking, in itself provides *no reason whatsoever* to revise our current criminal trial practice or to depart from our own institutionally-embedded procedural traditions.

French experience affords a particularly salient international comparison. Appeals from trials on indictment are relatively restrictive in France compared with other civilian nations, owing to the French assize court's composition: mixed panels comprised of nine lay jurors and three professional judges.[61] French jurists understood that retrial *de novo* before an appellate bench of three judges would be an entirely different procedural animal to a rerun of the originating *Cour d'assise* jury trial. In recent decades, and influenced by human rights thinking, limited rights of appeal in the most serious criminal cases came to be viewed as anomalous.[62] However, the French solution was the diametric opposite to that proposed by Jarvis: whereas he would abolish full re-hearings on appeal to the Crown Court, the French created a new form of jury trial on appeal in order to preserve the institutional integrity of jury trial at first instance.[63]

The finality of acquittals in the common law tradition is likewise strongly related to the significance of jury trial in our legal system. Strictly speaking, *only* juries are empowered to acquit; magistrates dismiss unfounded charges.[64] Further, jury trial reinforces orality as the preferred mechanism for receiving and testing witness testimony. Albeit few today share Wigmore's extravagant faith in cross-examination as the 'greatest legal engine ever invented for the discovery of truth',[65] critiques of the traditional common law mode of trial barely warrant the inverse conclusion that documentary 'trial on the papers' can be an all-weather substitute for live in-person proceedings. In common law systems appellate tribunals typically exercise a 'review' jurisdiction which does not claim to replicate a first instance criminal trial. As Lord Bingham once put it:

> [T]rial by jury does not mean trial by jury in the first instance and trial by judges of the Court of Appeal in the second. The Court of Appeal is entrusted with a power of review to guard against the possibility of injustice but it is a power to be exercised with caution, mindful that the Court of Appeal is not privy to the jury's deliberations and must not intrude into territory which properly belongs to the jury.[66]

[61] R Munday, 'Jury Trial, Continental Style' (1993) 13 *Legal Studies* 204.

[62] VP Hans and CM Germain, 'The French Jury at a Crossroads' (2011) 86 *Chicago-Kent Law Review* 737.

[63] B McKillop, 'Review of Convictions after Jury Trials: The New French Jury Court of Appeal' (2006) 28 *Sydney Law Review* 343.

[64] Jarvis elides this distinction, by describing magisterial disposals as acquittals. Cf MCA 1980, s 27.

[65] *Wigmore on Evidence* (Chadbourn revision), vol. 5, §1367.

[66] *Pendleton* [2002] 1 WLR 72, [2001] UKHL 66, [17].

Magistrates are not jurors; and one can certainly debate the merits of bench trial by professional judges versus lay adjudication.[67] Still, Jarvis' argument for downgrading full rehearing ab initio in the Crown Court to appellate review of summary trials appears to rest on the contention that this would simplify existing appeal procedures and mirror appeals from trials on indictment.

Are procedural simplicity and neat symmetry enough to justify diluting the rights of the accused (and prosecutors) to appeal from magistrates' courts' determinations? Some commentators argue that requiring reasons for decisions facilitates effective appellate review of fact-finding at first instance.[68] Others dissent.[69] Either way, Jarvis provides no reassurance that, under his proposed system, appeals from magistrates' courts' decisions would not soon lapse into routinised cursory review for blatant error on the face of the record. In the midst of a chronic cost of justice crisis, perhaps this is all the summary justice society can afford. In that case, we should candidly proclaim the economic rationale for change, and then be judged fairly and own its consequences, rather than hiding behind lip-service to more attractive normative ideals.

4. Normative Institutional Reform

The foregoing remarks do not purport to establish that Jarvis' two proposed reforms are definitively misconceived or unwarranted. I have not developed positive normative arguments to justify any particular balancing of priorities in the institutional design and ongoing reform of criminal appeals. Focusing instead on the adequacy of Jarvis' own proffered rationales for his reform package, I identified multiple pressure-points and methodological weaknesses, prominently including: insufficient regard to institutional history and the evolution of existing appeal structures; overreliance on (ostensible) judicial authority to the neglect of empirical information (including appropriately contextualised statistics) on current system performance; and selective *ad hoc* reliance on favourable comparative models. The consummate advocate has failed to persuade the pedantic quibbling academic of the merits of his argument.

As a default methodological principle, I favour an institutionally conservative approach to criminal procedure reform respectful of common law traditions. Our cobbled system of criminal adjudication was a very long time in the making, and

[67] S Doran, JD Jackson and ML Seigel, 'Rethinking Adversariness in Nonjury Criminal Trials' (1995) 23 *American Journal of Criminal Law* 1.

[68] JD Jackson, 'Unbecoming Jurors and Unreasoned Verdicts: Realising Integrity in the Jury Room' in J Hunter, P Roberts, S Young and D Dixon (eds), *The Integrity of Criminal Process* (Hart, 2016); M Coen and J Doak, 'Embedding Explained Jury Verdicts in the English Criminal Trial' (2017) 37 *Legal Studies* 786.

[69] KA Burd and VP Hans, 'Reasoned Verdicts: Oversold?' (2018) 51 *Cornell International Law Journal* 319; A D'Alessio, 'Argentina's Sluggish Journey Toward A Constitutional Criminal Procedure' (2008) 15 *Southwestern Journal of Law & Trade in the Americas* 31.

it seems to function adequately most of the time. This critical standard is self-consciously deflationary: criminal procedure should adopt the least worst solution from a range of generally bad options. Criminal adjudication in England and Wales is far from perfect or beyond improvement. Indeed, recent decades have witnessed major procedural reform, especially in the direction of accommodating the interests of complainants and vulnerable witnesses.[70] Yet the system is complex and multifaceted, thus prone to perverse incentives and unforeseen side-effects from ill-advised tinkering. The burden of persuasion lies squarely with would-be reformers to reassure us that pulling at random threads will not precipitate a more precarious or extensive unravelling of the institutional fabric. Cogent justifications for reforming criminal procedure need to be substantial enough to preserve institutional decency rather than mere fig leaves to spare our blushes.

[70] Roberts (n 8) Ch 10.

2

Decriminalisation of Prostitution

TANYA PALMER*

The existing legislative framework regulating prostitution in England and Wales is piecemeal and lacks a coherent rationale. Whilst neither selling nor paying for sex is in itself illegal, a range of associated activities including soliciting,[1] brothel-keeping,[2] and controlling prostitution,[3] are criminalised. These prohibitions are scattered through a range of statutes introduced at different times and rooted in shifting ideologies variously emphasising morality, the control of disease, the respectability of public space, sexual exploitation and gender equality. There is, therefore, clearly a need to rationalise the law in this area and to ensure that any provisions regulating prostitution share a clear and coherent basis. However, any move to reform inevitably raises normative questions about which direction reform should take, and these questions are hotly contested. Broadly speaking, current calls for reform of prostitution law in England and Wales fall into two categories: the introduction of a 'sex buyer law' to criminalise the purchase of sex, or the full decriminalisation of prostitution.

A full analysis of the different ideological positions underpinning these contrasting reform proposals is beyond the scope of this chapter. However, a brief understanding of the key motivations is instructive. Advocates of the 'sex buyer law' – also known as the 'Nordic Model' or 'Swedish Model' – primarily view sex work as a form of violence against women, which should be abolished. They therefore argue for the criminalisation of 'sex buyers' in the belief that this will 'end demand' for prostitution.[4] This is positioned as part of a multi-pronged strategy

* Dr Tanya Palmer, Senior Lecturer in Law, University of Sussex. My thanks to the editors of this volume Dr Melissa Bone, Prof John Child and Dr Jonathan Rogers for their constructive feedback and their patience; to the participants at the Criminal Law Reform Now Network Conference 2021 who read and commented on the paper on which this chapter is based, particularly Prof Michelle Madden Dempsey and Prof Ronald Weitzer; to the Sussex LPS Writing Group for their companionship during the writing process; and to the many sex workers who have publicly shared their insights into, and experiences of, prostitution laws. The completion of this chapter was supported by a Leverhulme Trust Research Fellowship.

[1] Street Offences Act 1959, s 1 and Sexual Offences Act 2003, s 51A.

[2] Sexual Offences Act 1956, ss 33–36.

[3] Sexual Offences Act 2003, s 53.

[4] 'What is the Nordic Model?' (*Nordic Model Now!*), see www.nordicmodelnow.org.

to eradicate prostitution, alongside the decriminalisation of those who are prostituted, especially 'prostituted women',[5] and the provision of material support to help them exit the sex industry.[6]

By contrast, advocates of decriminalisation (myself included) generally frame the practice of selling sex as 'sex *work*'. To be clear, this framing need not attach any particular normative value to sex work. Sex work need not be empowering, fulfilling, enjoyable, or even non-exploitative to count as work.[7] As a form of labour, it carries risks of harm and exploitation, as do many other types of work.[8] As such, the aim of any regulation of the sex industry should be to reduce this harm and exploitation. That is best achieved through labour law and the strengthening of workers' rights, alongside strengthening the protections of the welfare state for all, rather than through criminal prohibition.[9] This approach is championed by sex worker organisations including the English Collective of Prostitutes[10] and the Sex Worker Advocacy and Resistance Movement,[11] as well as Amnesty International,[12] the World Health Organisation[13] and UNAIDS.[14]

Crucially, both approaches agree that people who sell sex should not be penalised for doing so. They should be protected against harm, violence and exploitation. The disagreement is around how best to achieve that goal. This chapter makes the case for the decriminalisation of prostitution, focusing on the repeal of three key offences. It argues that criminal prohibition – even some offences which appear to be aimed at curbing exploitation by clients and third parties – in practice puts sex workers at increased risk of violence, social isolation and poverty. Sections 1–3 outline three criminal offences – soliciting (by sex workers), brothel-keeping, and soliciting (by clients) respectively – arguing that each of these offences should be repealed. In section 4, I look to Aotearoa New Zealand – the jurisdiction which has come closest to full decriminalisation – to explore how decriminalisation works in

[5] This is the preferred terminology of Nordic Model advocates to refer to women who are paid to engage in sexual activity, emphasising their status as victims of exploitation and highlighting the gendered nature of sex work. See, 'Terminology' (*Nordic Model Now!*) at www.nordicmodelnow.org.

[6] 'What is the Nordic Model' (n 4); M Madden Dempsey, 'Sex Trafficking and Criminalization: In Defense of Feminist Abolitionism' (2010) 158 *University of Pennsylvania Law Review* 1729; C MacKinnon, 'Trafficking, Prostitution and Inequality' (2011) 46 *Harvard Civil Rights – Civil Liberties Law Review* 272.

[7] J Mac and M Smith, *Revolting Prostitutes: The Fight for Sex Workers' Rights* (Verso, 2018) Ch 2.

[8] J O'Connell Davidson, 'Let's go outside: bodies, slaves and worker citizens' (2014) 18 *Citizenship Studies* 516.

[9] K Cruz, 'Unmanageable Work, (Un)liveable Lives: The UK Sex Industry, Labour Rights and the Welfare State' (2013) 22(4) *Social & Legal Studies* 465.

[10] 'Decriminalise Sex Work' (*English Collective of Prostitutes*), see prostitutescollective.net/petition.

[11] 'What We Stand For' (*SWARM: Sex Worker Advocacy and Resistance Movement*), see www.swarm-collective.org/what-we-stand-for.

[12] 'Amnesty International Policy on State Obligations to Respect, Protect and Fulfil the Human Rights of Sex Workers' (POL 30/4062/2016, Amnesty International, 2016).

[13] 'Global HIV, Hepatitis and STIs Programmes: Sex Workers' (*World Health Organisation*), see www.who.int/teams/global-hiv-hepatitis-and-stis-programmes/populations/sex-workers.

[14] Joint United Nations Programme on HIV/AIDS (UNAIDS), *The Gap Report 2014* (UNAIDS / JC2656, 2014).

practice, demonstrating that it has had a net positive effect and highlighting the benefits of adopting a similar model in England and Wales. Recognising that there are likely to be concerns about how the issues of exploitation and public nuisance would be addressed in the context of a decriminalised sex industry, I explore these issues in turn in sections 5 and 6. Here I continue to draw on lessons learned from the Aotearoa New Zealand experience to inform how these concerns could be addressed. Section 7 provides some concluding thoughts on overcoming barriers to the adoption of my proposals.

1. Repeal the Offence of Soliciting (by Sex Workers)

The primary offence directly targeting sex workers themselves is that of 'soliciting for the purposes of prostitution' under section 1 of the Street Offences Act 1959. This section provides that:

> It shall be an offence for a person aged 18 or over (whether male or female) persistently to loiter or solicit in a street or public place for the purpose of prostitution.

This offence was introduced in the wake of the Wolfenden Committee's 1957 Report on Homosexual Offences and Prostitution (though it was preceded by similar offences dating back to the mid-nineteenth century).[15] The Wolfenden Report was underpinned by a liberal understanding of separate public and private spheres; it thus constructed the activities of consenting adults in private as not the state's business.[16] However, activities conducted in public places – such as street prostitution – could be prohibited on the basis that they constituted a public nuisance. The soliciting offence was therefore designed to penalise sex workers themselves – 'common prostitutes' in the language of the Act – for engaging in inappropriate and immoral behaviour *in public*. As introduced, the offence applied only to female sex workers. Male sex work was largely ignored by the Wolfenden Committee or subsumed within its other concern, the regulation of homosexuality.[17]

The soliciting offence has been amended several times this century, reflecting the shifting ideologies and concerns underpinning the regulation of prostitution. The offender can now be female or male,[18] but must be over the age of 18[19] and the term 'common prostitute' has been replaced with 'person'.[20] A requirement of persistence has been added, so that the offence is only made out if the behaviour

[15] Home Office and Scottish Home Department, *Report of the Committee on Homosexual Offences and Prostitution* (Cmnd 247, 1957).

[16] J Weeks, *Sex, Politics and Society: The Regulation of Sexuality Since 1800*, 3rd edn (Pearson, 2012).

[17] H J Self, *Prostitution, Women and Misuse of the Law: The Fallen Daughters of Eve* (Routledge, 2005).

[18] Sexual Offences Act, Sch 1 para 2.

[19] Serious Crime Act 2015, s 68(7).

[20] Policing and Crime Act 2009, s 16(2)(a).

is engaged in more than once within a three-month period.[21] With regard to sentencing, Engagement and Support Orders (ESOs) have been introduced as an alternative to traditional forms of criminal punishment.[22] These changes represent a transition from a logic of penalising sex workers for creating a public nuisance, to a logic of criminalising (adult) sex workers for their own good, which Sanders has termed 'forced welfarism'.[23]

The criminalisation of soliciting is not, in fact, *good* for sex workers.[24] It does not help to alleviate exploitation or violence and can instead increase the risks of these and other harms.[25] Street-based sex-workers take evasive measures to avoid the threat of criminalisation, sacrificing other safety precautions to do so. This can mean, for example, spending less time vetting clients in order to reduce the risk of being caught.[26] It can also mean working in more secluded areas and/or locations that they are less familiar with in order to avoid being detected by the police, or after being moved on by police.[27] Dispersing sex workers from common red light areas can then have a knock-on effect of making it more difficult for them to share information about violent or otherwise problematic clients.[28] While these kinds of safety measures do not offer complete protection, they do go some way to reducing risk and giving sex workers greater control over interactions with clients.[29]

In addition to increasing the risk of harm to street-based sex workers, the criminalisation and policing of soliciting and other aspects of sex work engenders a distrust of the police and the criminal justice system by those workers. This means that when violence does occur, avenues to address it are shut off. Sex workers who are victims of crimes such as rape, assault and robbery are often reluctant to report these offences, fearing they will not be taken seriously.[30] Sex workers also struggle to access support when they are victimised outside of the sex work context – for example by abusive partners – thus the negative impacts of criminalisation

[21] ibid, s 16(2)(b).

[22] ibid, s 17(2).

[23] T Sanders, 'Controlling the "anti-sexual" city: Sexual citizenship and the disciplining of female street sex workers' (2009) 9(4) *Criminology and Criminal Justice* 507.

[24] Home Affairs Committee, *Prostitution* (HC 2016-17, 26).

[25] H Kinnell, *Violence and Sex Work in Britain* (Willan, 2008); T Sanders and R Campbell 'Why hate men who pay for sex? Exploring the shift to "tackling demand" in the UK' in V Munro and M Della Giusta (eds), *Demanding Sex: Critical Reflections of the Regulation of Prostitution* (Ashgate, 2008).

[26] E Sanders-McDonagh and L Neville, 'Service Provision for Street Based Sex Workers' in N Adams, M Brady-Clark, H Michaels, R Wills (eds), *Decriminalisation of Prostitution: The Evidence* (2016); P Grenfell, 'Health Harms of Sex Work Criminalisation' in N Adams et al (2016), *Decriminalisation of Prostitution: the Evidence.*

[27] Kinnell (n 25) Ch 6.

[28] ibid.

[29] ibid.

[30] M Hester, N Mulvihill, A Matolcsi, A Lanau Sanchez and S-J Walker, *The nature and prevalence of prostitution and sex work in England and Wales today* (University of Bristol, 2019); L Connelly, 'Violence Against Sex Workers: A Secondary Analysis of National Ugly Mugs Data 2013–2014' (Leeds Social Science Institute, 2015); L Longstaff, 'Impact of Criminalisation on Women's Safety' in Adams et al (n 26); G Perry, 'Policing of Prostitution' in Adams et al (n 26).

spill over into sex workers' lives outside of work.[31] This lack of protection for sex workers as victims of crime enables violent individuals to weaponise sex workers' reluctance to out themselves to the authorities, in order to attack them with impunity.[32] Fear of criminalisation also impacts sex workers' health and wellbeing beyond acute acts of violence. It makes it harder for sex workers to engage with health services as it disincentivises them from talking frankly about their circumstances and health needs.[33] Moreover, the ongoing stress of potential arrest and identification should be understood as a harm in itself, and clearly contradicts the framing of criminalisation for sex workers' own good.[34]

When sex workers do not manage to evade the police, they can be subject to a range of criminal punishments. As set out above, the offence of soliciting requires that the relevant conduct be 'persistent'. This is evidenced via the use of prostitute's cautions, administered by police when two officers witness an individual who appears to be loitering or soliciting for the purposes of prostitution. Significantly, prostitute's cautions 'differ from ordinary police cautions in that the behaviour leading to a caution may not itself be evidence of a criminal offence and there is no requirement for a person to admit guilt before being given a prostitute's caution.'[35] A person can thus acquire a criminal record for this offence without any proof or admission of guilt.

As noted above, sex workers who are convicted of soliciting can be given an ESO, which requires them to attend three meetings with a court appointed 'supervisor' in order to 'address the causes of the conduct constituting the offence' and 'find ways to cease engaging in such conduct in the future.'[36] Such orders have been welcomed by sex workers and support workers to the extent that they are preferable to more explicitly punitive responses such as fines, which serve only to punish poverty and incentivise continuing with sex work to pay them off.[37] In practice ESOs often consist of the continuation of support from a service the sex worker was already engaged with, and which continues after the order is completed.[38] Thus, they may be relatively benign in cases where they simply formalise a relationship that was already in place. On the more proactively positive side, ESOs can facilitate contact with sex workers who were not previously engaged with support services.[39]

[31] ibid, Hester et al.

[32] ibid; R Bowen, S Redman, K Swindells and T Herrmann, 'Sex Workers Too: Summary of Evidence for VAWG 2020-24 Consultation' (National Ugly Mugs, English Collective of Prostitutes and Umbrella Lane, 2021).

[33] Hester et al (n 30).

[34] Grenfell (n 26).

[35] Crown Prosecution Service, 'Prostitution and Exploitation of Prostitution' (*cps.gov.uk*, 4 January 2019).

[36] Street Offences Act 1959, s 1(2B).

[37] A Carline and J Scoular, 'Saving Fallen Women Now? Critical perspectives on engagement and support orders and their policy of forced welfarism' (2015) 14(1) *Social Policy and Society* 103.

[38] J Scoular and A Carline, 'A critical account of a "creeping neo-abolitionism": Regulating prostitution in England and Wales' (2014) 14(5) *Criminology & Criminal Justice* 608.

[39] Carline and Scoular (n 37).

Ironically however, that lack of previous engagement can be due to the policing of sex workers hindering outreach efforts by displacing sex workers from well-known red light areas.[40] In addition, some sex workers report that since ESOs were introduced, they have had difficulties accessing support if they do not have an ESO.[41] The efficacy of ESOs is limited, as exiting prostitution is a complex and lengthy process unlikely to be achieved after three meetings, as the Home Office itself has acknowledged.[42] A lack of funding for dedicated support services further limits their ability to support women both to stay safe within prostitution and to find alternative employment. Carline and Scoular's research found that sex workers themselves were sometimes held responsible for these limitations of the ESO system. Where women continued to engage in sex work after completing one or two ESOs, this was sometimes viewed as a failure to engage with support, necessitating harsher penalties.[43] This suggests that ESOs themselves provide, 'a mechanism to justify the increased criminalisation of women and the potential to impose a more punitive sanction.'[44]

A more fundamental flaw is that the ESO model individualises the 'problem' of sex work, obscuring the social and structural drivers of prostitution – such as austerity, poverty and discrimination – and the state's responsibility for them.[45] The model is premised on a contradictory framing of street-based sex workers simultaneously as victims who have no choice over selling sex and as agentic offenders who can be deterred through increased criminalisation.[46] For supervisors, this creates a tension between the need to build trust in order to provide effective support, whilst also being cast in an incompatible enforcement role.[47] In summary, the support provided under the guise of ESOs can be beneficial, but it is compromised by being bound up with criminalisation and will only ever have a limited effect if the social and structural forces which push people into prostitution are not addressed.[48]

Despite the introduction of ESOs, a range of punitive sanctions remain available. These can be applied either in the first instance, on breach of an ESO, or after multiple ESOs have been completed. Available disposals include fines, Community Protection Notices and Criminal Behaviour Orders (CBOs). CBOs can be used, for example, to ban a sex worker from the area where she usually solicits. This can have a knock-on effect of pushing her into more dangerous areas and cutting her off from support and outreach services.[49] Whichever disposal is

[40] Scoular and Carline (n 38).
[41] ibid.
[42] Home Office, *Guidance on Section 17 Policing and Crime Act 2009: Engagement and Support Order* (Home Office, 2010).
[43] Carline and Scoular (n 37).
[44] ibid, 107.
[45] ibid.
[46] ibid.
[47] ibid.
[48] ibid.
[49] This has been highlighted by Vera Baird, QC in relation to the previous use of Anti-Social Behaviour Orders to control prostitution. See Home Affairs Committee (n 24) para 56.

used, a criminal record for soliciting can limit employment opportunities, particularly in caring professions working with children or vulnerable adults – sectors in which a high proportion of sex workers have previous employment experience.[50] Following a legal challenge supported by the Centre for Women's Justice, there is now a mechanism to apply for a prostitute's cautions and convictions for soliciting to be filtered from disclosure on both standard and enhanced DBS checks once they are 'spent'.[51] Nevertheless, this presents an additional hurdle for individuals seeking to access mainstream employment and housing, thus further entrapping sex workers within prostitution.[52]

In summary, criminalising soliciting does not benefit sex workers. On the contrary, it exposes them to a significantly increased risk of harm and marginalisation. For this reason, there is a strong consensus among those calling for reform of prostitution laws that the offence of soliciting for the purposes of prostitution should be repealed. The only remaining justification for retaining the offence is public nuisance. This has not been a major part of recent discourse around sex work regulation because of the above consensus, underpinned by a primary concern with protecting people who sell sex on the part of both decriminalisation and Nordic Model advocates. However, a concern with public nuisance does inform the existing legislative framework, acting as a barrier to reforms that would centre sex workers' safety and well-being. As Graham observes, government policies and consultations on sex work in the 2000s focused on protecting 'communities' from the mere presence of sex work, and by implication framed sex work and sex workers as separate from 'the community'.[53] In light of the serious harms of criminalising soliciting by sex workers that I have outlined in this section, I take the position that nuisance concerns are not significant enough to outweigh the case for decriminalisation. Nevertheless, the impact on communities where sex work takes place should be taken seriously. I therefore return to the issue of how public nuisance and community relations can be addressed in a decriminalised context in section 6. My first recommendation then, is:

A. Repeal the offence of soliciting for the purposes of prostitution, Street Offences Act 1959, s 1.

2. Repeal the Brothel-Keeping Offences

A further tranche of offences target (in theory) third parties who profit from the labour of sex workers, and are thus designed to address commercial sexual exploi-

[50] D Taylor, 'Most sex workers have had jobs in health, education or charities – survey' (*The Guardian*, 27 February 2015).

[51] *R. (on the application of QSA) v Secretary of State for the Home Department* [2018] EWHC 407 (admin).

[52] Home Affairs Committee (n 24) paras 55 and 58.

[53] L Graham, 'Governing Sex Work Through Crime: Creating the Context for Violence and Exploitation' (2017) 81(3) *The Journal of Criminal Law* 201.

tation. However, the broad interpretation of these provisions and the enforcement practices they give rise to mean that in practice these laws also penalise and harm sex workers. Those in most urgent need of reform are the brothel-keeping offences under sections 33–36 of the Sexual Offences Act 1956.[54] A premises used by at least two sex workers for the purposes of prostitution qualifies as a 'brothel',[55] thus where two or more sex workers operate from the same premises, they are all potentially liable for brothel-keeping. These offences thus discourage sex workers from working together indoors, despite the fact that working with others is a means of enhancing physical safety, social engagement, sharing advice and saving costs.[56] In addition, the section 34 offence which prohibits a landlord from letting any premises with the knowledge that they are to be used as a brothel, means that where sex workers do work together, they risk eviction if this is discovered by their landlord. Thus, as with soliciting, these offences have an adverse effect on sex workers' safety and wellbeing.

In addition to sex workers, other third parties such as receptionists and security working in brothels can also be subject to liability. One particularly egregious example highlighted by the English Collective of Prostitutes is the case of Christy Norman, a 70-year-old woman working for £6 an hour as a cleaner in a brothel. When a client collapsed, Norman administered CPR and stayed with him until paramedics arrived, while other workers left the premises. She was subsequently convicted of assisting in the management of a brothel, demonstrating the wide interpretation given to this offence.[57]

The brothel-keeping offences, (alongside additional exploitation,[58] trafficking and modern slavery offences[59]) justify a high degree of interference in indoor sex work.[60] As a result, sex workers in brothels live with the 'constant threat' of police raids.[61] Rather than protecting sex workers from exploitation, such raids result in a number of adverse effects including: the confiscation of takings – sometimes a sex worker's entire life savings – under the Proceeds of Crime Act 2002, removal of children from sex workers who are mothers, deportation of migrant sex workers, and the general stress and humiliation of being dragged out of one's place of work, sometimes partially clothed, in view of cameras and crowds.[62]

The rationale for these offences is, in theory, to protect sex workers from exploitative managers. In practice, they have the opposite effect. The criminalisation of brothels means sex workers do not have formal employment rights. As a result, if they are treated poorly by managers, they have limited options beyond

[54] As amended by the Sexual Offences Act 2003 s 55(2).
[55] *Stevens v Christy* [1987] Cr App R 249 (DC).
[56] Hester et al (n 30).
[57] F Mirren, 'If 70-year-old cleaners are convicted of running brothels, the law isn't working' (*The Guardian*, 2 Aug 2017).
[58] Sexual Offences Act 2003, ss 52–53A.
[59] Modern Slavery Act 2015, ss 1–2.
[60] Graham (n 53).
[61] Hester et al (n 30) 20.
[62] Mac and Smith (n 7).

putting up with it or seeking (sex) work elsewhere.[63] The brothel-keeping offences in particular are frequently cited by indoor-based sex workers as the reason they work alone, despite the loneliness and increased risk to their physical safety.[64] They are also a key reason why sex workers do not report violent crime to the police. This disempowers sex workers relative to perpetrators who know that they can attack sex workers with impunity.[65] Fear of criminalisation also discourages brothel-based sex workers from engaging with other state agencies including healthcare and social services.[66] Therefore my second recommendation is:

B. Repeal the brothel-keeping offences contained in the Sexual Offences Act 1956, ss 33–36.

If this proposal is not accepted then, at minimum, these provisions should be reformed to allow up to four sex workers to work together lawfully from shared premises, following the lead of the Aotearoa New Zealand approach discussed in section 4. In section 5 I consider how the issue of exploitation could be addressed in the absence of brothel-keeping laws, via narrower exploitation offences and labour law.

3. Repeal the Offence of Soliciting (by Clients)

Kerb-crawling and 'soliciting of women for the purposes of prostitution' by male clients in public places were criminalised in England and Wales by the Sexual Offences Act 1985, with the offences framed primarily in terms of public nuisance.[67] However, Sweden was the first country to criminalise paying for sex regardless of location or circumstances – ie the Nordic Model – in 1999. The model has since been adopted by five further European jurisdictions (Norway, Iceland, Ireland, Northern Ireland, France) as well as Canada and Israel. It is also endorsed by the European Parliament in the form of a 2014 non-binding resolution drafted by (then) UK MEP Mary Honeyball.[68] The resolution explicitly categorises, 'prostitution and forced prostitution' as 'forms of slavery incompatible with human dignity and fundamental human rights'.[69] This model has not been adopted in England and Wales, despite frequent calls for it to be.[70] Nevertheless, its influence can be seen in recent reforms to prostitution law in this jurisdiction,

[63] J Pitcher, 'Impact of Laws on Indoor-based Sex Workers' Safety and Conditions of Work' in Adams et al (n 26).

[64] Hester et al (n 30); E Klambauer, 'On the edges of the law: Sex workers' legal consciousness in England' (2019) 15 *International Journal of Law in Context* 327; Mac and Smith (n 7); Graham (n 53).

[65] Hester et al (n 30); Klambauer (ibid).

[66] ibid.

[67] Sexual Offences Act 1985, ss 1–2.

[68] European Parliament resolution of 26 February 2014 on sexual exploitation and prostitution and its impact on gender equality (2013/2103(INI)).

[69] ibid, para B.

[70] See, eg, Sexual Exploitation HC Bill (session 2019–21), [228]; Modern Slavery HC Bill (session 2014–15), cl NC6; All-Party Parliamentary Group on Prostitution and the Global Sex Trade (APPG),

which reflect a shifting rationale from controlling the visibility of street prostitution to a primary emphasis on exploitation and ending demand.

At present, soliciting another person in a public place for the purposes of obtaining that person's sexual services as a prostitute is prohibited, regardless of the gender of either party.[71] There is also an offence of paying for sexual services of a person subject to any level of force, threats, coercion or any form of deception,[72] which is rarely used.[73] Rather than extending these offences to adopt a model of blanket criminalisation of clients, I argue that the offence of soliciting by clients should be repealed. This is because these laws cause substantial harm to people who sell sex, whether they do so by choice or due to coercion. As with the offences of soliciting by sex workers and brothel-keeping, they compromise sex workers' safety. Street-based sex workers are pushed to more secluded areas and have to vet clients more quickly to shield them from criminalisation,[74] while indoor workers find it harder to share information about abusive clients when clients are fearful of giving their names.[75] Efforts to protect sex workers by criminalising their clients fundamentally misunderstand the operation of power within these transactions. Sex workers need clients' money more than clients 'need' (or rather, want) sex.[76] Thus the burdens of criminalisation are simply passed from the client to the sex worker, who must take steps to absorb additional risk on the clients' behalf.[77]

To the extent that sex buyer laws succeed in their stated aim of discouraging clients, this decreases sex workers' available income. In the absence of better employment options, this does not incentivise sex workers to exit prostitution but rather to drop prices, engage in riskier sexual acts and become more reliant on managers in order to compete for a decreased pool of clients.[78] There is no evidence that such laws have decreased sex work in Sweden, and no evidence that they would do so here, because the existence of clients is not what drives people to sell sex. It is the costs of basic survival, care of dependants and education, and the lack of better alternative sources of income, particularly for disabled people and trans women, that primarily motivate individuals to engage in sex work.[79] These

'Shifting the Burden: Inquiry to assess the operation of the current legal settlement on prostitution in England and Wales' (March 2014); S Champion, 'Don't legitimise violence against women – adopt the Nordic Model' (*Labour List*, 4 July 2018); R Mason, 'Harriet Harman hits out at Corbyn's support for decriminalised sex work' (*The Guardian*, 4 March 2016); S Rodgers, 'Jess Phillips interview: Factions, feminism and a fighting chance' (*Labour List*, 17 January 2020).

[71] Sexual Offences Act 2003, s 51A.

[72] ibid, s 53A.

[73] Home Affairs Committee (n 24) para 54.

[74] J Levy and P Jakobsson, 'Sweden's abolitionist discourse and law: Effects on the dynamics of Swedish sex work and on the lives of Sweden's sex workers' (2014) 14(5) *Criminology and Criminal Justice* 593.

[75] A Gentleman, 'Sex worker and activist Laura Lee: "It's now far more difficult to stay safe"' (*The Guardian*, 5 Feb 2016).

[76] Hester et al (n 30).

[77] T Mac, 'The Laws that Sex Workers Really Want' in Adams et al (n 26).

[78] ibid; Levy and Jakobsson (n 74).

[79] Hester et al (n 30).

drivers have been exacerbated by an ongoing politics of austerity and current cost of living crisis. I therefore recommend:

C. Repeal the offence of soliciting for the purpose of obtaining sexual services, Sexual Offences Act 2003, s 51A.

4. Decriminalisation in Practice: Lessons from Aotearoa New Zealand

Aotearoa New Zealand's Prostitution Reform Act 2003 (PRA) provides a model for decriminalisation which can provide a starting point for reforming the law in England and Wales. Prior to the passage of the PRA, the position in Aotearoa New Zealand was similar to that in England and Wales – the purchase and sale of sex were not themselves criminalised, but various associated activities were. The PRA repealed offences of soliciting,[80] brothel-keeping, living on earnings of prostitution and procuring for prostitution.[81] It also repealed the Massage Parlours Act 1978, which had been designed to crack down on indoor sex markets, but which had largely pushed sex workers into more dangerous and exploitative working conditions.[82] Nevertheless, while repeal of existing offences was a major strand of the PRA reforms, and Aotearoa New Zealand is often referred to as an example of decriminalisation, the PRA did not fully decriminalise prostitution. The reforms introduced some specific criminal offences as well as other elements of legal regulation specific to the sex industry, explored in sections 5 and 6. Nevertheless, this model should be understood as distinct from models of regulation introduced in, for example, Germany and the Netherlands, on the basis that the New Zealand model is, in Östergren's terms, 'integrative' rather than 'restrictive'.[83] That is, it is an overarching policy framework that seeks 'to integrate the sex work sector into societal, legal and institutional framework[s] in order to protect those selling sex from harm.'[84] This reflects an understanding of commercial sex as a multifaceted, or 'polymorphous' phenomenon,[85] and differs from policies which focus on the restriction or eradication of prostitution.

The integrative approach of the PRA has given rise to three distinct modes of lawful sex work in Aotearoa New Zealand: street-based sex work, private indoor work, and managed brothels. Street-based sex workers lawfully meet

[80] Summary Offences Act 1981, s 26.

[81] Crimes Act 1961, ss 147–149.

[82] *Report of the Prostitution Law Review Committee on the Operation of the Prostitution Reform Act 2003* (New Zealand Government, 2008); P Fitzharris and A Taylor, 'Review of the Prostitution Reform Act' in G Abel, L Fitzgerald, C Healy and A Taylor (eds), *Taking the crime out of sex work: New Zealand sex workers' fight for decriminalisation* (Bristol University Press, 2010).

[83] P Östergren, 'From Zero-Tolerance to Full Integration: Rethinking Prostitution Policies' (DemandAT Working Paper No. 10, June 2017).

[84] ibid, 15.

[85] R Weitzer, 'Sociology of Sex Work' (2009) 35 *Annual Review of Sociology* 213.

clients outdoors, in public spaces, following the repeal of the soliciting offence. The private indoor market is made up of solo sex workers working from homes or hotels, and 'small owner-operated brothels' (SOOBs) consisting of up to four sex workers working from a shared premises, 'where each of those sex workers retains control over his or her individual earnings'.[86] Managed brothels are premises where more than four sex workers work under a manager or operator who determines, to any extent, the terms of their work.[87] Managed brothels are subject to a relatively light touch licensing regime,[88] discussed in section 6, and operators are subject to additional responsibilities in relation to health and safety.[89] These requirements do not apply to SOOBs.[90]

This variety of lawful options grants sex workers greater freedom to choose where and how they work. They may choose to work alone, either indoors or on the streets, due to the relatively high degree of autonomy lone-working affords. In the managed sector, the lower degree of control individual workers have is mitigated by the fact that administration and upfront costs are taken care of, and security may be provided.[91] The creation of SOOBs as a distinct category is particularly significant as these enable sex workers to balance a high degree of autonomy over their working conditions with the safety and companionship of working with others, as well as the ability to share costs and administrative duties. Any reforms to English and Welsh law should ensure that this mode of sex work is a possibility. It should not, however, be the only possibility, and sex workers should be free to choose the mode which best suits them. Evaluation of the PRA indicates the Act has had a minimal effect on movement between these modes, but has benefitted workers in all sectors.[92]

Following the enactment of the PRA, sex workers reported feeling more 'legitimate' with over 90 per cent of respondents in one study stating that they felt they now had legal rights, in particular health and safety and employment rights.[93] This legitimacy has led to improved relations between sex workers and police,[94] as sex workers now feel less harassed by police and are more likely to see them as potential sources of protection;[95] though the extent of this improvement varies

[86] Prostitution Reform Act 2003 (PRA), s 4(1).

[87] PRA, s 5.

[88] PRA ss 34–41.

[89] PRA, s 8.

[90] PRA, s 5(2).

[91] G Abel and M Ludeke, 'Brothels as Sites of Third-Party Exploitation? Decriminalisation and Sex Workers' Employment Rights' (2021) 10(1) *Social Sciences* 3.

[92] *Report of the PLRC* (n 82) 117–19.

[93] ibid, 14 and 44.

[94] L Armstrong, '"I Can Lead the Life That I Want to Lead": Social Harm, Human Needs and the Decriminalisation of Sex Work in Aotearoa/New Zealand' (2021) 18 *Sexuality Research and Social Policy* 941.

[95] L Armstrong, 'From law enforcement to protection? Interactions between sex workers and police in a decriminalized street-based sex industry' (2016) 57(3) *The British Journal of Criminology* 570; G Abel and L Fitzgerald, 'Risk and risk management in sex work post-Prostitution Reform Act: A public health perspective' in Abel et al (n 82).

by area.[96] While this does not necessarily decrease the chances of sex workers experiencing violence, it does at least mean they feel more able to report violence after the fact and feel confident that it will be taken seriously.[97] This effect seems to be most marked in relation to street-based sex workers[98] – perhaps because they experienced the brunt of interactions with police in law enforcement mode prior to decriminalisation.

Removing the fear of prosecution has also shifted the balance of power between sex workers and their clients. Aotearoa New Zealand sex workers report feeling more in control and more able to refuse specific clients or sexual practices.[99] This increased confidence is supported by the material effects of decriminalisation. For example, sex workers can negotiate more explicitly with clients about the terms of their agreement, including which sexual practices they will perform, as they no longer fear being entrapped by undercover police officers.[100] Street-based sex workers can screen clients more effectively and have more control over the location of transactions when clients no longer insist on going to secluded areas to avoid arrest.[101] And those who would do violence can no longer assume that sex workers will be blocked from reporting them by their own fear of prosecution.[102] Similarly, for those in the managed sector, removing the fear of prosecution and instilling an awareness of their rights as workers has decreased their vulnerability to exploitative employment practices, discussed further in section 5.

There are also benefits to sex workers' health and well-being. These include a general sense of relief and validation due to no longer being criminalised,[103] better access to condoms and lubricant which can no longer be interpreted as evidence of a crime,[104] and better access to healthcare and support services.[105] Particularly noteworthy is that some sex workers had access to supported accommodation and a government wage subsidy during the COVID-19 lockdowns.[106] By contrast, UK sex workers struggled to access state support during this period.[107] Fears that decriminalisation would increase the number of people working in the sex industry have not materialised.[108]

[96] E Mossman, 'Brothel operators' and support agencies' experiences of decriminalisation' in Abel et al (n 82).

[97] Fitzharris and Taylor (n 82).

[98] *Report of the PLRC* (n 82) 57.

[99] GM Abel, 'A decade of decriminalization: Sex work "down under" but not underground' (2014) 14(5) *Criminology & Criminal Justice* 580; *Report of the PLRC* (n 82).

[100] Abel and Fitzgerald (n 95).

[101] L Armstrong, 'Screening clients in a decriminalised street-based sex industry: Insights into the experiences of New Zealand sex workers' (2014) 47(2) *Australian & New Zealand Journal of Criminology* 207.

[102] *Report of the PLRC* (n 82).

[103] ibid; Mossman (n 96); Weitzer (n 85).

[104] Mossman (n 96); Abel and Fitzgerald (n 95).

[105] Mossman (n 96); *Report of the PLRC* (n 82).

[106] E Aroney, 'Changing Minds and Changing Laws: How New Zealand Sex Workers and Their Allies Shaped Decriminalisation in New Zealand' (2021) 18(4) *Sexuality Research and Social Policy* 952.

[107] 'Survey of sex workers' access to Covid-19 support in the UK' (*English Collective of Prostitutes*, 16 June 2021).

[108] *Report of the PLRC* (n 82).

Despite these improvements, decriminalisation is, as Mac and Smith make clear, 'no silver bullet'.[109] Sex work in Aotearoa New Zealand continues to carry a stigma.[110] This limits sex workers' willingness to report violent incidents for fear that this will lead to public exposure,[111] and hinders efforts to find alternative work outside of prostitution.[112] There are also reports of increased violence towards and harassment of street-based sex workers, not by clients or managers, but by members of the public as a backlash against the increased visibility and legitimacy of sex work.[113] Nevertheless, the overall picture is that the PRA has been a positive influence on the safety and human rights of sex workers. As an integrative approach to prostitution policy it reduces sex workers' distrust of police, better enabling them to report violence and exploitation of minors. It also empowers sex workers in their interactions with managers and clients, who cannot weaponise sex workers' fear of criminalisation to abuse them with impunity. The Aotearoa New Zealand experience thus supports my proposals to repeal the offences of soliciting (by both sex workers and clients) and brothel-keeping. In sections 5 and 6, I explore how the issues of exploitation and public nuisance could be addressed in a decriminalised (or rather, less criminalised) context, drawing on lessons from Aotearoa New Zealand.

5. Exploitation and Abuse

In section 2 I argued for the repeal of the brothel-keeping offences, but noted that this might raise concerns about how to address the exploitation of sex workers by managers or other third parties. Aotearoa New Zealand addressed this issue through the use of labour law and narrowly defined exploitation offences.

By transforming brothels and other sites of sex work into legitimate workplaces, decriminalisation brings with it a package of positive rights that apply to all employees. These include access to employment tribunals to settle workplace disputes; and application of standard workplace protections such as health and safety, anti-discrimination and sexual harassment law. The PRA also provides for additional protections specific to sex work: refusal to do sex work does not affect benefit entitlements,[114] and the Act is explicit that consent to sex can be withdrawn at any stage.[115] This clarifies that no contract between a sex worker and a manager or client overrides the law of rape, and limits the scope for managers to pressure sex workers to work with specific clients or more often than they wish to.

[109] Mac and Smith (n 7) Ch 8.
[110] Mossman (n 96); Abel (n 99).
[111] Abel and Fitzgerald (n 95).
[112] *Report of the PLRC* (n 82) 77.
[113] ibid, 74; Abel and Fitzgerald (n 95).
[114] PRA, s 18.
[115] PRA, s 17.

As Abel argues, this assemblage of general and specific worker protections has resulted in 'a remarkable shift in the balance of power between workers and brothel operators in the last 10 years.'[116] Indeed, some brothel operators' support for the PRA has waned precisely because they now have less control over sex workers.[117] Sex workers, meanwhile, are more aware of their rights, and more able to move to a different workplace if managers fail to treat them with respect.[118] There have also been cases of sex workers winning cases against managers at the disputes tribunal,[119] and in at least one case, successfully suing a brothel operator for sexual harassment resulting in $25,000 in damages.[120] Sex workers also report that these legal protections give them more power in interactions with clients and that, in a brothel setting, managers are now less likely to side with a client over the worker.[121]

As with the removal of criminal offences, these additional regulations are not a silver bullet. While the overall consensus is that conditions in the managed sector have improved, brothel operators continue to wield considerable influence over the workplace experience.[122] Exploitative management practices still take place, including the use of bonds and fines, pressure to work longer or less flexible hours, or to see more clients per shift, and failure to comply with health and safety requirements.[123] A contributing factor appears to be that most brothel-based sex workers' are classed as independent contractors, which can enable operators to exert a high degree of control over workers while having limited responsibilities towards them.[124] Similar concerns have been raised in relation to other gig-based workers in various jurisdictions, and were the subject of a significant decision of the UK Supreme Court. In *Uber BV v Aslam* it ruled that Uber drivers are 'workers' rather than 'independent contractors', and thus entitled to various rights against the company through which their work is organised.[125] Dancers in strip clubs have also successfully claimed worker status at the UK Employment Tribunal.[126]

[116] Abel (n 99) 585.

[117] Mossman (n 96) 124; *Report of the PLRC* (n 82).

[118] Abel and Ludeke (n 91).

[119] C Bennachie, A Pickering, J Lee, PG Macioti, N Mai, AE Fehrenbacher, C Giametta, H Hoefinger and J Musto, 'Unfinished Decriminalization: The Impact of Section 19 of the Prostitution Reform Act 2003 on Migrant Sex Workers' Rights and Lives in Aotearoa New Zealand' (2021) 10 *Social Sciences* 179.

[120] *DML v Montgomery* [2014] NZHRRT 6, (2014) 11 NZELR 673.

[121] Armstrong, 'I Can Lead the Life That I Want to Lead' (n 94); Abel and Ludeke (n 91); *Report of the PLRC* (n 82).

[122] P Bond, 'The Dunedin Model: Dunedin Sex Worker Experiences Under Decriminalisation in Aotearoa New Zealand' (2021) 18 *Sexuality Research and Social Policy* 968; Abel and Fitzgerald (n 95).

[123] Mossman (n 96); *Report of the PLRC* (n 82); C Zangger, 'For Better or Worse? Decriminalisation, Work Conditions, and Indoor Sex Work in Auckland, New Zealand/Aotearoa' (PhD thesis, University of British Columbia, 2015).

[124] Abel and Ludeke (n 91); *Report of the PLRC* (n 82).

[125] *BV v Aslam* [2021] UKSC 5; [2021] 4 All ER 209.

[126] *Nowak v Chandler Bars Group Ltd* UKET 3200538/2019; and see C Barbagallo and K Cruz, 'Dancers win at work: unionization and *Nowak v Chandler Bars Group Ltd*' (2021) 3 *Studies in Political Economy* 354.

My focus here is on the criminal law, and there is not scope to analyse these employment law issues in detail for implementation in England and Wales. Nevertheless, the Aotearoa New Zealand experience suggests a number of steps that could be taken to enhance sex workers' rights as workers. These include subjecting managed brothels to the UK's standard workplace protections such as the Health and Safety at Work Act 1974; the Equality Act 2010; and the National Minimum Wage. Explicit provision should be made to ensure that refusal to do sex work does not affect entitlement to receive unemployment or other state benefits. Consideration should also be given, in consultation with sex workers and employment law experts, to whether and how to formalise employment relationships in managed brothels, and how best to reduce exploitative practices such as the use of bonds and fines.

Although labour law is now the primary mechanism for protecting sex workers in Aotearoa New Zealand, the PRA also introduced some new criminal offences designed to prevent exploitation. Section 16 of the PRA prohibits inducing or compelling someone to provide commercial sexual services or to hand over their earnings from prostitution. England and Wales currently has offences of 'causing or inciting' and 'controlling' prostitution for gain.[127] At first glance, these look similar in scope and rationale to section 16 of the PRA, however there are important differences.

The English offences are vaguely defined and have been broadly interpreted. 'Controlling prostitution for gain' requires no evidence of coercion and can include administrative activities such as making a website for a sex worker and recording her bookings in a diary, as held in *Massey*.[128] The offence of causing or inciting prostitution for gain is potentially open to a similarly broad interpretation. These 'exploitation' offences thus have the potential to be applied to sex workers who make appointments for each other, as well as 'maids' or receptionists working in brothels. Therefore, in their current form, they would severely limit the impact of decriminalising brothel-keeping.

By contrast, the Aotearoa New Zealand offence is drafted much more narrowly. In place of the ambiguous terms 'causing', 'inciting' and 'controlling', section 16 sets out specific behaviours that constitute 'inducing or compelling' for the purposes of this offence. These include the improper use of power or authority,[129] and the reference to such power arising from 'any occupational or vocational position' would seem to cover both managers and police officers leveraging their status in relation to sex workers.[130] Threats or promises to supply/withhold controlled drugs also amount to unlawful compulsion, effectively making it a crime to use a person's addiction to coerce them into sex work.[131] Also covered is blackmailing a victim by threatening to make disclosures or false accusations of: criminal offences, misconduct that would seriously damage a person's reputation, or unlawfully

[127] Sexual Offences Act 2003, ss 52–53.
[128] *Massey* [2007] EWCA Crim 2664.
[129] PRA, s 16(2)(a).
[130] ibid.
[131] PRA, s 16(2)(d).

being in New Zealand.[132] This makes it a specific legal wrong to weaponise a person's undocumented status in this context. Notably however, no reference is made to threatening to disclose someone's involvement in sex work (given that following the PRA itself this could no longer be classed as either a criminal offence or misconduct), even though such disclosures could still seriously damage a person's reputation. Finally, it is unlawful to threaten to commit a serious criminal offence in order to compel the victim to provide sexual services or hand over their takings.[133] Significantly then, the threshold for what constitutes 'inducing or compelling' under section 16 of the PRA is much higher than the English offence of 'controlling prostitution for gain'.[134] The Aotearoa New Zealand offence carries a relatively high maximum penalty of 14 years imprisonment (double that of the equivalent English offences), appropriate to the high level of coercion required and the fact that, in cases where the defendant succeeds in compelling the victim to engage in sexual activity, the offence overlaps with the crime of rape.

I am generally sceptical about the creation of exploitation offences specific to prostitution, given that offences such as rape and sexual assault already exist to punish coerced sexual activity, and that historically such offences have had the effect of isolating sex workers by criminalising those close to them.[135] Nevertheless, section 16 of the PRA appears to be relatively robust. Moreover, while I argued in section 2 that in the UK such offences have been used as the basis for harmful police raids, section 16 must be read in conjunction with section 30 of the PRA, which sets out strict conditions for police to obtain warrants to enter sex work premises without permission.

There is, however, limited research on the operation of section 16 in practice. It is barely mentioned in the Prostitution Law Reform Committee's five year review of the PRA and it is unclear whether and to what extent the offence has been utilised. Mossman provides some evidence that the use of bonds – whereby a sex worker is required to pay a sum of money to a manager from which fines are deducted for actions such as arriving late or failing to turn up for a shift – has decreased as a result of this provision, but concludes that such exploitative practices by managers do still continue.[136]

Sections 20–23 of the PRA criminalise the 'use of persons aged under 18 in prostitution'. These are very similar to offences under sections 47–51 of the UK Sexual Offences Act 2003, which use the language of 'sexual exploitation of children'. Both jurisdictions make it an offence to obtain the sexual services of under 18s, having paid or promised to pay. And both jurisdictions criminalise assisting

[132] PRA, s 16(2)(c).

[133] PRA, s 16(2)(b).

[134] Notably, Belgium has also recently narrowed its laws on the exploitation of prostitution to ensure that they are not so wide as to prevent sex workers accessing services such as bank accounts and rental accommodation. See: NWSP, 'Sex workers in Belgium celebrate historic vote for Decriminalisation in parliament' (*Global Network of Sex Work Projects*, 25 March 2022).

[135] M Childs, 'Commercial Sex and Criminal Law' in L Bibbings and D Nicolson (eds), *Feminist Perspectives on Criminal Law* (Routledge, 2000).

[136] Mossman (n 96).

or facilitating the prostitution of under 18s, albeit using slightly different terminology. These offences effectively criminalise clients, managers, and potentially other third parties such as receptionists and security for their involvement in underage prostitution. Section 23(2) of the PRA helpfully clarifies that providing legal advice, counselling or healthcare to minors involved in prostitution does not amount to an offence of 'assisting or encouraging'. Amending sections 47–51 of the UK Sexual Offences Act 2003 along similar lines could help to facilitate young people involved in prostitution accessing vital support.

In both jurisdictions the age of consent for (non-commercial) sexual activity is 16 – two years younger than the age at which someone is deemed an adult for the purpose of the commercial sexual exploitation offences. The Aoteroa New Zealand Prostitution Law Review Committee justified this difference on the basis that commercial sex is different to other types of sex. It further highlighted that there are age restrictions on other forms of labour; this restriction is therefore consistent with treating sex work as *work*.[137] However, the Aotearoa New Zealand Sex Workers' Collective (NZPC)[138] has expressed fears that, even while minors selling sex are not criminalised themselves, the criminalisation of their clients may push these vulnerable young people further underground and out of reach of support.[139] In addition, they may be pushed towards more dangerous outdoor sex markets as brothel operators will not risk hiring under-18s.[140] In both jurisdictions however, as with the adult exploitation offences, there is little available evidence about the operation and impact of these offences.

In summary, if soliciting and brothel-keeping were decriminalised in England and Wales, as I recommend, there would still be offences in place which could address the *exploitation* of adults and children in prostitution.[141] However, it is clear that further research is needed on the efficacy of these types of offences. This should include consultation with sex workers. In particular, consideration should be given to whether sections 52–53A of the UK Sexual Offences Act 2003 should be more narrowly defined, in a similar vein to section 16 of the PRA. This is to ensure that sex workers are able to lawfully work with each other and/or with managers, drivers, receptionists and security where they choose to do so.

6. Public Nuisance and Community Relations

I have primarily made the case for the repeal of soliciting and brothel-keeping offences on the basis of protecting sex workers' safety, well-being and rights. What

[137] *Report of the PLRC* (n 82).
[138] This organisation was formerly known as the 'New Zealand Prostitutes Collective' and retains the acronym 'NZPC', see www.nzpc.org.nz.
[139] *Report of the PLRC* (n 82).
[140] Mossman (n 96).
[141] Sexual Offences Act 2003, ss 52–53A and ss 47–51, respectively.

of the impact on the wider communities in which sex work takes place? Research on the relationship between prostitution and the spaces and communities in which it takes place has focused primarily on street-based sex work, and has revealed mixed responses from other local residents and businesses. These include some neutral responses – eg a lack of awareness or concern about the presence of sex work; and even some positive impacts such as increased revenue for local businesses and deterrence of crimes such as burglary due to the visible presence of people on the streets.[142] On the negative side, common concerns include litter (especially condoms and drug paraphernalia), noise, traffic, witnessing transactions and sex acts (especially when children are present), deterring house buyers and customers of local businesses, and being propositioned and harassed by clients and/or sex workers.[143] These issues can have a significant impact on the ways that community members use public space, particularly female residents.[144] In some areas, frustration at a perceived lack of response to these issues from police and other local authorities has given rise to vigilantism. This in turn is experienced more negatively than the presence of sex work by many local residents.[145] However, increased enforcement of soliciting laws (whether against sex workers, clients or both) tends only to displace the problems identified to other local areas, and/or to replace them with the increased threats to sex worker safety identified in section 2.[146] It is clear then, that more sustainable methods of managing relationships between community members – including those involved in sex work and those who aren't – is necessary.

In Aotearoa New Zealand, the PRA did not introduce any new forms of regulation for street-based sex work, leaving this to be regulated through the generic pre-existing process of passing byelaws as well as through more informal mechanisms.[147] Similarly, in England and Wales, existing law already gives local authorities considerable powers to regulate the use of public space through local byelaws and, more concerningly, through Public Spaces Protection Orders (PSPOs).[148] PSPOs can be used to control activities that are not, in and of themselves, unlawful. Brown, for example, demonstrates that they are increasingly used to curtail visible manifestations of poverty such as begging and rough

[142] S Kingston, *Prostitution in the Community: Attitudes, Action and Resistance* (Routledge, 2013); J Pitcher, R Campbell, P Hubbard, M O'Neill and J Scoular, *Living and working in areas of street sex work* (The Policy Press, 2006); K Williams, 'From the oblivious to the vigilante: The views, experiences and responses of residents living in areas of street sex work' in G Letherby, K Williams, P Birch and M E Cain (eds), *Sex as Crime* (Routledge, 2008).

[143] ibid.

[144] Pitcher et al (n 142); Williams (n 142).

[145] Williams (ibid).

[146] M O'Neill and R Campbell, 'Street sex work and local communities: Creating discursive spaces for *genuine* consultation and inclusion' in R Campbell and M O'Neill (eds), *Sex Work Now* (Routledge, 2006).

[147] C Neuwelt-Kearns, T Baker and O Calder-Dawe, 'Informal governance and the spatial management of street-based sex work in Aotearoa New Zealand' (2020) 79 *Political Geography* 102154.

[148] Anti-social Behaviour, Crime and Policing Act 2014, ch 2.

sleeping.[149] PSPOs can be introduced with minimal scrutiny and there is little scope to challenge them in court.[150] They are primarily enforced through fixed penalty notices, again meaning that prosecutorial or judicial scrutiny of their operation is limited.[151] This enforcement can be carried out not just by police but also by a wide range of officials including council officials and private security.[152] Under the Anti-social Behaviour, Crime and Policing Act 2014 injunctions and dispersal orders can also be used to restrict sex workers' activity, and to punish non-compliance.[153]

The existence of these mechanisms has the potential to completely undermine the decriminalisation of soliciting, and even to subject street-based sex workers to greater surveillance and more punitive enforcement than the current criminal law regime.[154] This presents a major challenge to the project of decriminalisation, requiring a two-pronged solution. First, following the repeal of the soliciting offence, considerable organisation and political participation will be needed at the local level to prevent PSPOs being used to recriminalise street sex work. Pitcher et al's work demonstrates the value of 'integrated responses to community concerns … developed with a range of partners, including sex worker support projects' for finding solutions that work for all members of the community.[155] Second, at the national level, the existence of PSPOs as a mechanism for controlling public space in general must be challenged.

With regard to managing the presence of indoor sex work, Aotearoa New Zealand has utilised licensing and local byelaws, with mixed results. Under the PRA, brothel operators are required to hold an operator's certificate.[156] SOOBs are exempt from this requirement (see section 4), and the process of acquiring a certificate is relatively light touch: The only requirements are that the operator is aged over 18, is a citizen of Aotearoa New Zealand, and does not have a record of specific criminal offences that would disqualify them. There have been some concerns expressed – including by operators themselves – that the process is too light touch and that there is a lack of enforcement, compared to liquor licences for example.[157] However, more onerous licensing regimes in other jurisdictions have been shown to create perverse outcomes. In Victoria, Australia, for example, Crofts et al observe that the lack of provision for SOOBs and a reluctance of

[149] KJ Brown, 'The Banishment of the Poor From Public Space: Promoting and Contesting Neo-Liberalisation at the Municipal Level' (2020) 29(4) *Social & Legal Studies* 574.

[150] KJ Brown, 'The hyper-regulation of public space: The use and abuse of Public Spaces Protection Orders in England and Wales' (2017) 37(3) *Legal Studies* 543.

[151] ibid.

[152] ibid.

[153] S Kingston and T Thomas, 'The Anti-social Behaviour, Crime and Policing Act 2014: implications for sex workers and their clients' (2015) 27(5) *Policing and Society* 465.

[154] ibid; L Graham, 'The Human Rights Implications of using Civil Injunctions and Criminal Behaviour Orders Against Sex Workers' (SLSA Annual Conference 2023, Derry, 5 April 2023).

[155] Pitcher et al (n 142) 33.

[156] PRA, s 34.

[157] Mossman (n 96) 131.

local councils to approve brothel licences, coupled with difficulties of enforcement, has ironically resulted in a proliferation of large brothels.[158] Meanwhile in The Netherlands, the legalisation only of licensed forms of sex work, which comes with high costs of compliance, resulted in the creation of a two-tier system:

> The net effect of the new law was a constricted legal sector with better working conditions for a small minority who were also subject to increased regulation and a wider displacement to a larger unregulated illegal sector.[159]

The modest requirements of the PRA licensing regime, coupled with the exemption for SOOBs, limit the proliferation of large commercial brothels and of unlicensed brothels. This is a positive for sex workers and for other members of the local community.

Sections 11–15 of the PRA are designed to minimise public nuisance and offence. Section 11 prohibits the advertisement of commercial sexual services via television and radio broadcasts, newspapers, and public cinemas – though is noticeably silent on online advertising. Sections 12–14 give additional powers to Territorial Authorities to regulate the location of brothels and signage advertising commercial sexual services through local byelaws, and section 15 provides grounds for refusing resource consents for brothels over and above the criteria already set down in generic, pre-existing planning law. These provisions thus create a wide discretion for the regulation of brothels at the local level.

Since the PRA was passed, around a third of territorial authorities have made use of these provisions to limit the operation of brothels within their districts and many are very restrictive.[160] The provisions do not allow for brothels to be restricted on purely moral grounds, and there must be some demonstrable adverse effects.[161] Byelaws which unduly constrain the operation of brothels can be challenged via judicial review, but this is a lengthy and unpredictable process.[162] In practice, public submissions to local regulation processes have been driven by an objection to sex work per se, rather than specific adverse effects of commercial sex premises. As such they reflect the ongoing stigma attached to sex work that does not simply disappear as a result of decriminalisation.[163]

[158] P Crofts, J Maree Maher, S Pickering and J Prior, 'Ambivalent Regulation: The Sexual Services Industries in NSW and Victoria – Sex Work as Work, or as Special Category?' (2012) 23(3) *Current Issues in Criminal Justice* 393; see also, T Crofts and T Summerfield, 'The Licensing of Sex Work in Australia and New Zealand' (2006) 13 *eLAW Journal* 269.

[159] J Scoular, 'What's Law Got To Do With It? How and Why Law Matters in the Regulation of Sex Work' (2010) 37(1) *Journal of Law and Society* 12.

[160] C Warnock and N Wheen, 'Sex Work in New Zealand: The Re-Importation of Moral Majoritarianism in Regulating a Decriminalized Industry' (2012) 24(2) *Canadian Journal of Women and the Law* 414; Bond (n 122).

[161] Local Government Act 2002, ss 145–146.

[162] D Knight, 'The (continuing) regulation of prostitution by local authorities' in Abel et al (n 82).

[163] Warnock and Wheen (n 160) 424.

The businesses most affected by restrictive byelaws are the SOOBs. These tend to be well-suited to residential areas and able to operate relatively discreetly,[164] but are effectively banned when local byelaws restrict brothels to industrial and commercial zones. Ironically, this pushes sex workers into street-based sex work which is both less safe for workers and more likely to be objectionable to other members of the local community, or into the larger managed brothels which have the resources to operate in the permitted areas.[165] This undermines the primary purpose of the PRA and is inconsistent with exempting SOOBs from the licensing regime. As Bond argues, 'a distinct clash [with the PRA] occurs when the bylaws work to restrict the location or signage of brothels to the point where sex work again becomes criminalised.'[166]

What lessons can be learned for England and Wales from this experience? Here, local authorities already have considerable powers to control lawful commercial sex businesses such as strip clubs (known as Sexual Entertainment Venues, or SEVs) and sex shops. Both generic planning law and the specialised licensing regime for SEVs give considerable power to local authorities to 'effectively zone, move and close down SEVs for political or urban policy reasons.'[167] It is difficult to imagine that proposals to repeal the brothel-keeping offences would pass without provision being made for the SEV licensing regime to be extended to brothels. Planning has also been used to prohibit sex work that would otherwise be lawful under the current regime in England and Wales (ie carried out by a lone sex worker in private premises) on the basis that performing commercial sex work in a residential property constitutes a material change of use.[168] The tort of nuisance provides a further route to object to the use of premises for prostitution.[169]

Therefore, even if brothels were decriminalised, there are multiple existing mechanisms available that could be used to severely limit their operation. As in Aotearoa New Zealand, Hubbard notes that it is much easier for larger corporate entities with the resources to employ skilled lawyers to jump through the necessary planning and licensing hoops to lawfully operate SEVs, compared to independent operators.[170] There is then a danger that, following the decriminalisation of brothels in England and Wales, work in large managed brothels would be the primary option for engaging in lawful sex work, with SOOBs existing on paper only. With this in mind, rather than providing additional powers to restrict the operation of brothels post-decriminalisation, it is submitted that an English equivalent to the PRA should explicitly provide for SOOBs to be exempt from both generic planning law and any specialised licensing requirements that would apply to managed

[164] *Report of the PLRC* (n 82).
[165] Warnock and Wheen (n 160) 421, 424.
[166] Bond (n 122).
[167] P Hubbard, 'Law, sex and the city: regulating sexual entertainment venues in England and Wales' (2015) 7(1) *International Journal of Law and the Built Environment* 5, 13.
[168] *E Parchment v Birmingham City Council* T/APP/C/94/P4605/633044.
[169] *Thompson-Schwab v Costaki* [1956] 1 WLR 335.
[170] Hubbard (n 167).

brothels. Legislating for decriminalisation would also provide an opportunity to revisit the efficacy of the existing SEV licensing scheme alongside the question of whether it should be adapted to apply to managed brothels in their newly decriminalised context.

7. Conclusions

Criminalisation harms sex workers. The more vulnerable and structurally disadvantaged an individual sex worker is, the more pronounced that harm will be. For this reason, I have made three recommendations as a first step towards better protecting the safety and wellbeing of sex workers:

A. Repeal the offence of soliciting for the purposes of prostitution, Street Offences Act 1959, s 1.

B. Repeal the brothel-keeping offences contained in the Sexual Offences Act 1956, ss 33–36.

C. Repeal the offence of soliciting for the purpose of obtaining sexual services, Sexual Offences Act 2003, s 51A.

Recommendation A has the greatest chance of being accepted in the foreseeable future. A commitment to decriminalise people selling sex unites both Nordic model and decriminalisation advocates, and has therefore already been called for by individuals and organisations with a range of ideological backgrounds including the World Health Organisation, the English Collective of Prostitutes, Nordic Model Now, and the Terrence Higgins Trust.[171] It is particularly notable that both the Home Affairs Committee (which took a broadly integrative stance) and the All Party Parliamentary Group (APPG) on Prostitution and the Global Sex Trade (which explicitly positions prostitution as a form of violence against women and girls) recommended repealing the offence of soliciting by sex workers.[172] More recently the Sexual Exploitation Bill, a Private Members Bill put forward by Labour MP and Nordic Model supporter Diana Johnson, included provisions to decriminalise selling sex.[173] There is thus a growing consensus on the desirability of repealing the offence of soliciting for the purposes of prostitution. Nevertheless, this proposal is likely to face two key challenges.

First, those who call for the repeal of this soliciting offence as part of a Nordic Model approach would not support a proposed Bill which provided for its repeal alongside provisions to also repeal offences of brothel-keeping and soliciting by buyers. It may perhaps be possible to build consensus around an initial proposal

[171] 'HIV perspective on the 'Nordic' or 'end-demand' model' (National AIDS Trust, Terrence Higgins Trust and The Love Tank, 2020).

[172] Home Affairs Committee (n 24); APPG (n 70).

[173] Sexual Exploitation HC Bill (session 2019–21), [228].

only to decriminalise soliciting by sex workers, and put the other proposals to the side for now. The dangers of this would be that there may be a lack of political appetite for further reforms to prostitution law once the first change is made, and that this staged approach would further add to the fragmented nature of the current legislative framework.

Second, the proposal to decriminalise soliciting by sex workers is likely to face opposition from more conservative forces concerned about the public nuisance of street-based sex work, and its perceived associations with drug use, anti-social behaviour and criminality. Challenging these narratives and recognising sex workers as part of, rather than separate from, their local communities must therefore be a key strategy in countering this strand of opposition. Such a strategy could include engagement with local and national media to challenge problematic representations of sex work. In addition, Participatory Action Research and other collaborative research methodologies can help to facilitate ongoing dialogue between sex workers, agencies, residents and businesses in order to develop community responses to prostitution that reflect the needs and concerns of all stakeholders.[174] In turn such approaches can 'help to challenge dominant discourses and hopefully feed into public policy at local, regional, and national levels.'[175]

Recommendation B, to repeal the brothel-keeping offences is likely to be more challenging than recommendation A. Despite the considerable evidence from Aotearoa New Zealand of the benefits of allowing both SOOBs and managed brothels to operate lawfully, this is likely to be framed by opponents as endorsing exploitation and facilitating human trafficking.[176] It is particularly important here to emphasise the ways in which the Aotearoa New Zealand approach proposed here enables sex workers to work lawfully in a range of different contexts (outdoor, lone indoor work, SOOBs and managed brothels). This is distinct from legalisation models with more restrictive regulations regarding where and how sex work can operate, which can in practice mean the only lawful option is to work in large managed brothels. Given the likely objections, I have suggested an alternative more modest proposal that the existing brothel-keeping offences be reformed to allow independent sex workers to work together from shared premises as in the SOOBs operating under the PRA. Both the Home Affairs Committee and the APPG on Prostitution have recommended this reform.[177]

Recommendation C, to decriminalise soliciting of sex workers by clients is the most controversial of my proposals, as it is in direct opposition to the Nordic Model requirement to criminalise paying for sex. There is a wealth of evidence of

[174] M O'Neill and J Pitcher, 'Sex Work, Communities and Public Policy the UK' in M Hope Ditmore, A Levy and A Willman (eds), *Sex Work Matters: Exploring Money, Power, and Intimacy in the Sex Industry* (Zed Books, 2010).

[175] ibid, 217.

[176] See, eg, All-Party Parliamentary Group on Prostitution and the Global Sex Trade, 'Behind Closed Doors: Organised sexual exploitation in England and Wales' (APPG, 2018).

[177] Home Affairs Committee (n 24); APPG (n 70).

the limitations and dangers of criminalising clients, particularly from countries that have introduced a complete ban on paying for sex such as Sweden[178] and Northern Ireland.[179] Nevertheless, at present the political will to decriminalise clients in England and Wales is lacking. Such a move is unlikely to appeal to most conservatives, while several high-profile feminist Labour MPs have actively called for a complete sex purchase ban.[180]

In those jurisdictions that have moved towards decriminalisation, the most important factor has been the involvement of sex workers in the political process.[181] Prior to passing the PRA, Aotearoa New Zealand had a well-established history of sex worker organising and the NZPC was heavily involved with the development of the Act. This ensured that sex workers' views, knowledge and experience directly informed the law which now governs their work and helped to focus the debate on harm reduction and the human rights of sex workers.[182] This focus facilitated the building of a broad consensus in support of the Act, though the measures still only passed by one vote. Similarly, sex worker activism has been central to the decriminalisation of aspects of sex work in New South Wales, Australia,[183] Belgium,[184] and Victoria, Australia. In Victoria, the Sex Work Decriminalisation Act 2022 was spearheaded by Fiona Patten, then Member of the Victorian Legislative Council and herself a former sex worker.[185] England and Wales has well-established sex worker organisations operating under the umbrella of the UK Network of Sex Work Projects. However, their influence is limited by the lack of MPs willing to align with their goals and this will need to change for these proposals to be realised in full.

[178] Levy and Jakobsson (n 74).

[179] G Ellison, C Ní Dhónaill and E Early, *A Review of the Criminalisation of Paying for Sexual Services in Northern Ireland* (Queen's University Belfast, 2019).

[180] See n 70.

[181] My thanks to Zach Leggett, University of Sunderland, for his insights on this point.

[182] Warnock and Wheen (n 160); L Armstrong and G Abel (eds), *Sex Work and the New Zealand Model: Decriminalisation and Social Change* (Bristol University Press, 2020); G Laverack and A Whipple, 'The sirens' song of empowerment: A case study of health promotion and the New Zealand Prostitutes' Collective' (2010) 17(1) *Global Health Promotion* 33; Aroney (n 106).

[183] E Aroney and P Crofts, 'How Sex Worker Activism Influenced the Decriminalisation of Sex Work in NSW, Australia' (2019) 8(2) *International Journal for Crime, Justice and Social Democracy* 50.

[184] M Scarlett, 'In Conversation With: Utsopi, Belgium' (*European Sex Workers Rights Alliance*, 4 April 2022).

[185] J Buckley, 'Sex Work Has Been Decriminalised in Victoria. Here's What That Means' (*Vice*, 11 February 2022).

Comment on Chapter 2

Prostitution: Decriminalisation or Legalisation?

RONALD WEITZER*

Dr Palmer's essay is an insightful, well-researched analysis of three prostitution laws currently in force in England and Wales: solicitation by sex workers, operating a brothel, and solicitation by customers. She cites research critical of criminalisation and advocates decriminalisation, which is also the position of Amnesty International, Human Rights Watch, the World Health Organisation, and sex worker rights groups around the world. This chapter begins by building on the argument that criminalisation is a failed policy approach, then compares the decriminalisation alternative (Palmer's recommendation) with legalisation, an option that Palmer does not discuss but should be central to any debate on legal reform of prostitution laws.

Decriminalisation removes an offence from the penal code, full stop. Under this *laissez-faire* model, street sellers, for example, would be allowed to operate in any public place, provided that they do not cause a nuisance to others or violate any other law. Similarly, brothels may be allowed, anywhere, as long as they operate in ways that do not compromise public order. Decriminalisation pertains only to the previously illegal behaviour; it has no effect on the status of other crimes such as robbery, assault, and exploitative pimping. Under *legalisation* the act is no longer prohibited, but additional regulations are enacted. Examples include allowing street prostitution only in designated zones, licensing brothels and escort agencies, screening prospective business owners to ensure that they have no criminal record, mandating safe-sex practices or regular STI testing, special 'sin taxes', specific security measures (eg, video monitoring), periodic site visits to erotic businesses by the authorities to ensure compliance with the regulations, and so forth. Decriminalisation, in short, means that an act is no longer prohibited, whereas legalisation involves some kind of regulation, whether minimal or extensive.

* Professor of Sociology, George Washington University, Washington DC.

Prostitution is legal in England and Wales, but only if it involves a single provider working alone and meeting customers at a hotel, the client's residence, or the worker's residence. Escort agencies and independent escorts operate freely. The law prohibits two or more sex workers from operating in the same premises, because that is legally defined as a 'brothel' and brothels are illegal. Street prostitution is prohibited by the offence of 'soliciting for the purpose of prostitution'.

Solicitation arrests declined sharply from 2002/03 to 2022/23: from 2,111 to 301.[1] The decline is even more dramatic when we consider population growth during this time period: from 52 to 60 million in England/Wales. The change is largely the result of significant numbers of sex workers transitioning from street-based to online solicitation, which is much less visible and susceptible to control. Regarding the ban on brothels, Palmer states that 'sex workers in brothels live with the "constant threat" of police raids'. From January 2017 through August 2020, 408 individuals were arrested for brothel-keeping (in England/Wales/Northern Ireland), but only 48 were prosecuted from 2017 to 2019, partly because some of them were simple landlord-tenant cases, not involving two or more sex workers working in the same apartment.[2]

Public opinion in Britain has become more tolerant in recent years. A 2019 poll found that 49 per cent favoured the decriminalisation of brothel-keeping and 44 per cent supported decriminalising street solicitation.[3] But public opinion is not as evenly divided as these figures suggest. Decriminalisation was opposed by only 22 per cent (brothels) and 27 per cent (street soliciting); the remainder selected 'don't know'.

Palmer shows that criminalisation is problematic in multiple ways. It negatively affects sex workers' access to housing, health care, and labour rights, and renders them vulnerable to exploitation and abuse. Managers and customers are also vulnerable insofar as they are compelled to operate in the shadows and are subject to the whims of bad actors. Criminalisation also has the effect of alienating participants from the police and other authorities, and more broadly reinforcing marginalisation and stigmatisation.

An alternative policy is client-only criminalisation, the so-called 'end demand' or 'Nordic model'. Beginning with Sweden in 1999, several other countries have passed laws that 'decriminalise' soliciting by sex workers but increase penalties for customers. The rationale is that outlawing the demand will, over time, shrink the supply. This approach has not been implemented in England and Wales, but it has in Northern Ireland.[4]

[1] Statista, 'Number of Soliciting for Prostitution Offences Recorded in England and Wales from 2002/03 to 2022/23'.

[2] A Phillips, 'Hundreds Arrested For "Running Brothels" as Sex Workers Say It's the Laws That Are Criminal' (*News.Sky.com*, 21 October 2020).

[3] Survation/RightsInfo poll, August 2019.

[4] Human Trafficking and Exploitation (Criminal Justice and Support for Victims) Act (Northern Ireland) 2015, s 15: 'A person (A) commits an offence if A obtains sexual services from a person (B) in exchange for payment'. A conviction is punishable by a fine and/or imprisonment up to six months (for a summary conviction) or one year (conviction on indictment).

The evidence presented by Palmer shows that the end-demand policy does not have the outcomes predicted. Criminalising only one party to a transaction impedes the conduct of the legal party by forcing the latter to act in more clandestine and potentially precarious ways. Evidence from countries that have adopted an end-demand law shows that it exposes both parties to police surveillance; has the effect of rushing furtive transactions and thereby hampering careful screening of customers; makes providers reluctant to report victimisation to the authorities; reduces access to health care, housing, and support services; reinforces the stigma attached to both parties; and negatively affects safety.[5] Nor does this approach significantly reduce the number of sexual transactions. And, as Palmer notes, insofar as such laws succeed in discouraging clients, they decrease workers' income and thus compel them to 'drop prices, engage in riskier sexual acts, and become more reliant on managers in order to compete for a decreased pool of clients'. Finally, the very logic of criminalising only one party in a contractual agreement is fundamentally bizarre. Imagine a law that legalised the sellers of cannabis but criminalised the buyers!

Decriminalisation (of all participants) offers some clear benefits: It eliminates arrests, fines, and incarceration; may increase workers' willingness to report abuse to authorities; paves the way for greater access to health care and social services; and can help reduce stigmatisation insofar as the services rendered are lawful and the businesses operate in conventional ways.[6]

1. Public Soliciting and the Community

The Wolfenden Committee drew a sharp distinction between conduct in public and that which occurs in private. Whereas private conduct has no discernible externalities, the same cannot be said for street prostitution, and Wolfenden advocated decriminalisation only of indoor prostitution. Although the form street prostitution takes varies to some degree by locale and among the actors operating there, it tends to provoke resistance from the local community. Residents and merchants cite a litany of grievances: noise, vehicle traffic, public drug use and sales, sex in public places, disorderly conduct, harassment of local residents, violence and microaggression, and erosion of a community's quality of life and property values.[7]

[5] J Levy and P Jakobsson, 'Sweden's Abolitionist Discourse and Law' (2014) 14 *Criminology & Criminal Justice* 593; S Kohn, *The False Promise of 'End Demand' Laws* (Open Society Foundation, 2017); E Argento et al, 'The Impact of End-Demand Legislation on Sex Workers' Access to Health and Sex Worker-Led Services' (2020) 15 *PLOS ONE* 1; H Le Bail and C Giametta, *What Do Sex Workers Think About the French Prostitution Act?* (Medecins du Monde et al, 2018).

[6] R Weitzer, 'Resistance to Sex Work Stigma' (2018) 21 *Sexualities* 717.

[7] M O'Neill and R Campbell, 'Street Sex Work and Local Communities' in R Campbell and M O'Neill (eds), *Sex Work Now* (Willan, 2006); S Kingston, *Prostitution in the Community* (Routledge, 2014); and C Shdaimah et al, 'Neighborhood Assessment of Prostitution as a Pressing Social Problem and Appropriate Responses' (2014) 25 *Criminal Justice Policy Review* 275.

It is difficult to reduce these problems even in a government-managed street zone. The city of Leeds currently has the only such managed district in Britain, created in 2014. While the health and safety of street sellers have improved, a recent report described ongoing problems, including sex in public, solicitation of residents, fighting, public drug use, and discarded drug paraphernalia. Some residents have asked that 'the zone be moved and that brothels be provided so that activity could take place behind closed doors'.[8] And the street-indoor disparities are replicated in other places where prostitution is allowed. In Queensland, Australia, a government report found that both legal brothels and independent operators had little if any public externalities, whereas street workers 'arouse significant community disquiet'.[9] This explains why some scholars have advocated a 'two-track policy' aligned with Wolfenden, which treats street and indoor prostitution differently precisely because of their differential impacts on the community.[10]

Indoor prostitution is rarely an issue for local residents and merchants insofar as transactions take place in private and are invisible to the public.[11] One exception would be a red-light district that hosts a critical mass of visitors responsible for at least some public disorder, spilling over to residential neighbourhoods nearby. The window-prostitution zones in Amsterdam and Brussels have a fraught relationship with local residents.[12]

Palmer downplays the public disorder often associated with street prostitution, by defining this condition as a mere *nuisance* and concluding that 'nuisance concerns are not significant enough to outweigh the case for decriminalisation'. In fact, the problems cited above cannot be reduced to nuisances: they can have a significant effect on the health and safety of local residents and on their quality of life. Palmer seems to dismiss the grievances as 'perceived associations' made by residents and 'conservative forces' whose narratives deserve to be 'challenged'. The research cited above shows that the syndrome of complaints is widespread and neither imaginary nor a smokescreen for moral concerns.

Palmer also contests the view that pits residents against street sellers, arguing that the latter are 'part of the community'. This is a *variable*, however, as many street sellers operate outside their living area and migrate to the streets where they work. Even with respect to those workers who live where they work, their residential status does not exempt them from behaving orderly in public.

[8] C Hymas, 'Britain's First Red Light District Backfires with Kerb Crawlers Harassing Children, Report Finds' *The Telegraph* (2 February 2021).

[9] Crime and Misconduct Commission, *Regulating Prostitution: An Evaluation of the Prostitution Act 1999, Queensland* (CMC 2004) 45. See also A Schloenhardt and L Cameron, 'Happy Birthday, Brothels! Ten Years of Prostitution Regulation in Queensland' (2009) 29 *Queensland Lawyer* 194.

[10] R Weitzer, 'Prostitution Control in America: Rethinking Public Policy' (1999) 32 *Crime, Law, and Social Change* 83.

[11] Schloenhardt and Cameron (n 9); E Cooper, 'It's Better than Daytime Television: Questioning the Socio-spatial Impacts of Massage Parlors on Residential Communities' (2016) 19 *Sexualities* 547; P Hubbard, 'Noxious Neighbors? Interrogating the Impacts of Sex Premises in Residential Areas' (2013) 45 *Environment and Planning A* 126.

[12] R Weitzer, 'The Social Ecology of Red-Light Districts: A Comparison of Antwerp and Brussels' (2014) 50 *Urban Affairs Review* 702.

If street prostitution is decriminalised, should it be treated by the state in a *laissez-faire* manner? Should it be subjected to zoning restrictions – away from schools, churches, playgrounds? Some dismiss this as a legitimate goal. The government in Victoria, Australia (where legalisation had been in effect since 1994) passed legislation in 2022 that allows prostitution – between 7pm and 6am – near 'a place of worship, hospital, school, education, and care services premises' or 'any other facility or place regularly frequented by children for recreational or cultural activities'. The rationale is that 'separation requirements are discriminatory, reinforce harmful social stigma towards sex workers, and are a barrier to sex work taking place in safe locations'.[13] This may be true to at least some extent in any given city, but it ignores the very purpose of such distancing policies: to minimise friction with the local population and the police by keeping street transactions and erotic businesses discreet.

2. Legalisation

Palmer's chapter does not consider the option of legalisation (the term is mentioned only once, in reference to the Netherlands). Legalisation is generally opposed by sex worker rights groups, either because they misconstrue it or because they seek to be free of all government control.[14] Scholars who study sex work policies vary in whether they consider decriminalisation or legalisation preferable.[15]

In the conventional wisdom, there are two exemplars of a decriminalised system: New Zealand and the state of New South Wales, Australia. Yet neither is an example of pure decriminalisation and are best categorised as *minimalist legalisation*. A country that liberalises its prostitution law almost always engages in a two-step process: removing prostitution offences from the criminal law and then imposing a set of regulations on participants and businesses: decriminalisation → legalisation.[16] Palmer acknowledges that New Zealand is not a case of unfettered

[13] Victoria State Government, *Decriminalising Sex Work*, Discussion paper (2020) 5.

[14] The International Committee for Prostitute's Rights passed a charter in 1985 that called for decriminalisation, insisting that it is 'essential that prostitutes can provide their services under conditions that are absolutely determined by themselves and no one else'. (*World Charter for Prostitutes' Rights*, Amsterdam 1985.) In a survey of 247 sex workers in San Francisco, two-thirds of whom worked on the streets, 80% felt that 'sex workers should determine their own working conditions without being taxed or regulated by government'; a mere 2% felt that sex workers should pay taxes on their earnings; and only 13% agreed that soliciting should be banned near schools, churches, and hospitals. The vast majority felt that street sellers should be allowed to operate anywhere. A Lutnick and D Cohan, 'Criminalisation, Legalisation, or Decriminalisation of Sex Work' (2009) 17 *Reproductive Health Matters* 38.

[15] P Östergren, 'From Zero Tolerance to Full Integration: Rethinking Prostitution Policies' in Z Davy et al (eds), *The Sage Handbook of Global Sexualities* (Sage, 2020); L Shrage, 'Contract Sex: Decriminalisation versus Legalisation' (2022) 5 *Sexuality, Gender & Policy* 8; R Weitzer, 'Criminalisation, Decriminalisation, and Legalisation,' in R Weitzer (ed), *Sex for Sale: Prostitution, Pornography, and Erotic Dancing*, 3rd edn (Routledge, 2023).

[16] ibid.

decriminalisation. There are numerous regulations embedded in the Prostitution Reform Act 2003:

- Owners of sex businesses must obtain an operator's certificate, to be renewed annually. Prospective operators are ineligible if they have been convicted of a drug offence, weapons offence, or serious crime.
- A business with five or more workers is assumed to have a manager, who must be certified. Groups of four or fewer workers require no certification.
- Clients are regulated: the law gives providers the right to refuse clients' requests for a sex act for any reason at any stage of the encounter.
- STI testing is not mandated, but sex workers and clients are required to use condoms for penetrative sex. Failure to do so can result in a fine of up to NZ$1,450 (£713). Since 2005, several individuals have been convicted of removing a condom during sex.[17]
- Advertising is restricted. Sex workers and brothels may not advertise in newspapers, on the radio or television, or on conventional job-listing sites. City councils regulate signage and can prohibit displays that are 'likely to cause nuisance or serious offence to ordinary members of the public using the area' or are 'incompatible with the existing character or use of that area'.
- Government oversight: the authorities periodically monitor sex businesses to ensure health and safety, that no migrants are employed, and that businesses and workers adopt safe-sex practices.[18]

3. Legalisation in Practice

In what follows, I show that *a properly configured regulatory system can benefit those involved in sexual commerce, as well as the wider society* in terms of improved public health and lower criminal justice expenditures. Other vices, like organised gambling and illicit drug markets, have been heavily regulated after they were decriminalised, to facilitate their conversion to conventional businesses. In an occupation where participants remain subject to multiple risks, there remains a need for mechanisms that screen out bad actors (organised crime, abusive or exploitative recruiters and managers) and help to ensure workers' health and

[17] Prostitution Reform Act 2003, Public Act 2003 No. 28. The law requires that 'he or she has taken all reasonable steps to ensure a prophylactic sheath or other appropriate barrier is used if those services involve vaginal, anal, or oral penetration or another activity with a similar or greater risk of acquiring or transmitting sexually transmissible infections' (s 9.1).

[18] 'An inspector may, at any reasonable time, enter premises for the purpose of carrying out an inspection if he or she has reasonable grounds to believe that a business of prostitution is being carried on in the premises' (s 26.1). The inspection may include interviews with personnel, photographs and measurements, or 'seizing and retaining' anything that may be evidence of an offence.

safety. In response to the standard demand of decriminalisation supporters that sex work businesses be treated identically to other businesses, the International Committee for Prostitutes' Rights acknowledges that, 'Existing standard business codes allow abuse of prostitutes. Therefore, special clauses must be included to prevent the abuse and stigmatisation of prostitutes (self-employed and others)'.[19]

Germany legalised prostitution in 2002 and imposed further regulations on the profession in 2016.[20] Reform led to a sharp reduction in the number of officially certified victims and their respective third parties. Whereas in 2000 there were 1,888 certified victims of third-party 'exploitation of prostitutes', the number steadily declined after 2002, to 19 in 2020. For the same time span, the number of victims of pimping/procuring/promotion fell from 1,304 to 146 and of sex trafficking from 1,197 to 201.[21] Official figures also show a parallel decline in the number of suspects prosecuted and convicted for these offences: between 2000 and 2013, convictions for exploitation fell from 153 to 2 and for pimping from 151 to 15.[22] The fact that some individuals are still arrested under these statutes suggests a more nuanced understanding of the ways in which third parties and employers engage with sex workers, compared to the past. Instead of being liable for pimping/promoting prostitution, the law now prohibits conduct that curtails a worker's autonomy by, for instance, dictating the type of services that must be provided, forcing someone to service a particular client, preventing someone from leaving prostitution, or restricting freedom in other ways. Similarly for employers: 'exploitation' is now restricted to keeping someone 'personally or financially dependent' on their business operation.[23]

Queensland, Australia legalised brothels and independent escorts in the 1990s. While the regulations regarding brothel ownership and (very expensive) licensing fees are onerous, forcing some brothel owners to operate illicitly, the overall system has been evaluated positively. A government evaluation of the brothels concluded, 'There is no doubt that licensed brothels provide the safest working environment for sex workers in Queensland. Legal brothels now operating in Queensland provide a sustainable model for a healthy, crime-free, and safe legal licensed brothel industry' and are a 'state of the art model for the sex industry in Australia'. Official corruption and organised crime 'are not of significant concern for the legal prostitution industry in Queensland'.[24]

This evidence from Germany and Queensland shows that legalisation can yield positive outcomes, but the best test of a policy regime is to systematically

[19] This appears to contradict the Committee's previously stated (n 14) opposition to any state involvement.

[20] Prostituiertenschutzgesetz (Prostitute Protection Act), ProstSchG (2016).

[21] J Henning, I Hunecke and G Walentowitz, 'Das Prostituiertenschutzgesetz im Lichte der Kriminalitätsstatistik' (2021) 104 *Monatsschrift für Kriminologie und Strafrechtsreform* 359.

[22] Federal Ministry of the Interior, *Polizei Kriminalstatistik* (Federal Ministry, 2015).

[23] R Weitzer, 'Legal Prostitution: The German and Dutch Models' in E Savona, M Kleiman and F Calderoni (eds), *Dual Markets: Comparative Approaches to Regulation* (Springer, 2017).

[24] Crime and Misconduct Commission (n 9).

compare it with an alternative. In Belgium, a 1948 law repealed existing municipal regulations and prohibited third-party involvement (pimping, brothel-keeping), but not soliciting or engagement in prostitution itself. Some local governments continued to regulate third parties, a form of *de facto legalisation* because operators' involvement was prohibited under federal law. In the cities of Antwerp (late 1990s) and Ghent (2015–2017), officials imposed a rigorous set of extra-legal norms on owners of sex businesses. Brussels represents the alternative practice of *de facto decriminalisation*. There, operators of sex businesses are largely free of any government control. (The red-light district in all three cities contains window-prostitution rooms where women are visible from outside and sell sex inside.) Unlike Antwerp and Ghent, the authorities in Brussels take a *laissez-faire* approach to the zone. Police rarely enter; security cameras are absent; officials conduct no background checks on third-party operators or site visits to monitor working conditions; some visitors harass or attack the window workers, crimes that police tend to ignore; and workers are subject to total control by madams, many of whom are connected to organised-crime networks based in Bulgaria and Romania.[25] In short, the authorities in Brussels do little to combat bad actors, control business operators, or support the window workers.

The red-light districts in Antwerp and Ghent, by contrast, are subject to strict rules governing the owners and managers of window units rented by sex workers, and the workers are periodically interviewed by social workers and health providers to monitor their health and safety and ensure that they are working voluntarily. Security cameras are visible, and the two districts have their own designated health centre, offering free services exclusively to local sex workers. Uniformed and undercover police officers patrol each district.[26] This three-city comparison illustrates the potential advantages of legalisation and serious problems with *laissez-faire* decriminalisation.

Another study compared different regimes in three Australian cities: criminalisation in Perth, Western Australia; decriminalisation in Sydney, New South Wales; and legalisation in Melbourne, Victoria.[27] On almost all measures, *legalisation outperformed both criminalisation and decriminalisation*. Melbourne's brothels featured more security measures, on-site provision of condoms and lubricant, and the highest proportion of brothels awarded a 5-star rating by researchers who visited each site. Only 3 per cent of the decriminalised brothels in Sydney earned a 5-star rating from visiting researchers and 33 per cent of them received a 1-star

[25] M Loopmans and P van den Broeck, 'Global Pressures, Local Measures: The Re-Regulation of Sex Work in the Antwerp Schipperskwartier' (2011) 102 *Tijdschrift voor Economische en Sociale Geografie* 548; S Adeyinka, S Samyn, S Zemni and I Derluyn, *Nigerian and Ghanaian Women Working in the Brussels Red-Light District* (Routledge, 2021); R Weitzer and D Boels, 'Ghent's Red-light District in Comparative Perspective' (2015) 12 *Sexuality Research and Social Policy* 248; Weitzer (n 12).

[26] ibid; Weitzer (n 12).

[27] Perth criminalises all types of prostitution; Sydney decriminalises and does not regulate brothels; Melbourne licenses, inspects, and otherwise regulates brothels.

rating, whereas the figures for Melbourne's legal brothels were 20 per cent and 11 per cent, respectively. (Ratings were based on the presence of supportive staff, cleanliness, lighting, rest areas, and security measures.) Regarding worker safety, 72 per cent of the 229 brothels visited in the legalised system were equipped with room alarms, compared to only 36 per cent of the 201 brothels in the decriminalised system. The former were also more likely to have security cameras and much more likely to provide free condoms and lubricant to the workers.[28] The findings suggest that legalisation can be far preferable to both criminalisation and decriminalisation. I say *can be* because much depends on the *kinds of regulation* associated with a legal regime, a theme I have explored in detail elsewhere.[29]

We cannot generalise from these studies but, coupled with other research,[30] they offer evidence-based comparisons of the three policy models.

4. Conclusion

I agree with Palmer that England and Wales should decriminalise the offences of solicitation by sex workers, operating a brothel, and solicitation by customers. What I have tried to do in the latter half of this essay is to broaden the conversation by noting some additional considerations that have been central in both academic and political circles.

In response to the argument that prostitution should be free of regulation over and above that which governs other enterprises, reliance on standard laws is demonstrably insufficient to protect the health and safety of participants in a vice that is newly decriminalised but remains stigmatised, where workers remain marginalised, and where bad actors continue to prey on participants. Reform of prostitution laws is simply not on the same playing field as legislation that permits same-sex marriage, where there are no externalities that require control. The history of legal reform in casino gambling and cannabis is instructive here: after

[28] C Harcourt et al, 'The Decriminalisation of Prostitution Is Associated with Better Coverage of Health Promotion Programs for Sex Workers' (2010) 34 *Australian and New Zealand Journal of Public Health* 482. Note that the title of the article is *contradicted by the study findings*: the legalised system in Melbourne is rated superior to the decriminalised system in Sydney. The study was conducted prior to the recent reform of Victoria's prostitution law. The Sex Work Decriminalisation Act 2022 repealed four offences: engaging in street prostitution, working while infected with an STI, providing sexual services without a condom, and mandatory three-month STI testing for workers. Provisions regarding licensing of erotic businesses will take effect in late 2023.

[29] Weitzer (n 15); R Weitzer, *Legalising Prostitution: From Illicit Vice to Lawful Business* (New York University Press, 2012).

[30] ibid; A Daalder, *Prostitution in the Netherlands Since the Lifting of the Brothel Ban* (Ministry of Justice, 2007); Y Katsulis, *Sex Work and the City: The Social Geography of Health and Safety in Tijuana, Mexico* (University of Texas Press, 2008); B Sullivan, 'When (Some) Prostitution Is Legal: The Impact of Law Reform on Sex Work in Australia' (2010) 37 *Journal of Law and Society* 85; H Amesberger, L Caixeta, E Greif and B Sauer, 'Austria' in S Jahnsen and H Wagenaar (eds), *Assessing Prostitution Policies in Europe* (Routledge, 2018).

these vices are decriminalised, a host of regulations are typically applied by the state.[31] Why should prostitution be different?

And what *kinds* of regulation can be considered best practices? Screening and licensing business owners, registering workers, zoning street prostitution, health requirements, special business taxes, constraints on advertising in public places or online, official inspections of legal establishments? If brothels were legal in the UK, how should they be regulated? What about escort agencies? Periodic, unannounced site visits by the authorities are common in legal prostitution systems. Finally, we can ask the pragmatic question of political feasibility. It is no accident that *laissez-faire* decriminalisation is rare worldwide. State authorities are much more willing to consider legalisation than unfettered decriminalisation.

[31] For casino gambling, see J Albanese, 'Creating Legal Versus Illegal Gambling Businesses: How Proper Government Regulation Makes a Difference' in Savona et al (n 23).

3

Senior Corporate Managers' Criminal Liability for the Crimes of Employees or Agents

JEREMY HORDER* AND GABRIELE WATTS**

> One of the most effective ways to combat corporate misconduct is by seeking accountability from the individuals who perpetrated the wrongdoing. Such accountability is important for several reasons: it deters future illegal activity, it incentivizes changes in corporate behaviour, it ensures that the proper parties are held responsible for their actions, and it promotes the public's confidence in our justice system.[1]

Many would agree with the views expressed in this passage on the importance of pursuing individual perpetrators of crime in corporate contexts. However, in such contexts, fair and effective law and policy, in relation to the pursuit of individual criminal liability, should not solely be concerned with 'perpetrators' in a narrow sense as primary parties: those committing the conduct element with the fault element (if any). Such an exclusive concern risks overlooking the role of command-and-control relationships between individuals within companies, and hence overlooking the role of people with the normative power to control or influence the individuals who committed the crime. Our concern is with the scope of criminal liability in such cases.

Suppose that fraud has been committed by an employee in order to benefit their company. In such circumstances, the prosecution may seek to charge the individual employee with fraud. However, in English law, the company will not itself be liable for the fraud, in such circumstances, unless one of the more of the directors – or equivalent persons – was also a party to or complicit in the commission of the conduct element with the requisite fault element.[2] This restrictive

* Professor of Criminal Law, London School of Economics.
** Barrister, Lincoln's Inn.

[1] Yates' Memorandum, 'Individual Liability for Corporate Wrongdoing' (2015) 1.

[2] These requirements reflect what is known as the 'identification doctrine': *Tesco v Nattrass* [1971] UKHL 1. As of 2023, 'equivalent persons' include senior managers.

approach to corporate criminal liability for fault-based crimes such as fraud has caused a good deal of controversy.[3] What, though, about the role of individual senior officers within the company? Clearly, in so far as such officers shared in the commission of the crime as primary parties, they have always faced individual liability. However, our focus is on a different kind of involvement by senior corporate officers in the commission of crimes by employees or agents. This is where the senior officers knew about or tolerated the commission of fraud by the employees or agents to benefit the company. In cases where senior officers intentionally offer assistance or encouragement to employees or agents to commit crimes, such officers (and hence the company itself, in accordance with the identification doctrine) may straightforwardly be prosecuted for fraud, if their conduct meets the conditions for complicity in the employees' or agents' crimes.[4] However, the conditions triggering the application of the complicity doctrine are highly stringent. In particular, these conditions do not extend to cases in which senior corporate officers simply know about or tolerate offending by employees or agents under their control, without having intentionally assisted or encouraged the offending. Yet, there is a strong case for saying that knowledge or toleration on the part of senior managers of offending (intended to benefit the company) by employees or agents under their control should itself be a basis for individual criminalisation, quite apart from consideration of the company's liability. Our argument in that respect will be as follows.

Under the current law, senior corporate officers can commonly be held individually liable for serious crimes committed by their company, if they 'consented to' or 'connived' at the commission of the crime by the company. For example, by virtue of section 222 of the Enterprise Act 2002:

> (1) This section applies if the person whose conduct constitutes a domestic infringement … is a body corporate.
> (2) If the conduct takes place with the consent or connivance of a person (an accessory) who has a special relationship with the body corporate, the consent or connivance is also conduct which constitutes the infringement.
> (3) A person has a special relationship with a body corporate if he is—
>
> (a) a controller of the body corporate, or
> (b) a director, manager, secretary or other similar officer of the body corporate or a person purporting to act in such a capacity.

As we will see in due course, in spite of the reference here in section 222 to 'an accessory,' the legal concepts of 'consent' to or 'connivance' at criminal wrongdoing by senior corporate officers are broader than the concepts of 'assisting' and 'encouraging,' as the latter are understood in the modern law of accessories (complicity), and – as we will suggest – rightly so. Nonetheless, the doctrine of

[3] See Law Commission, *Corporate Criminal Liability: An Options Paper* (London, 2022) ch 3; Economic Crime and Corporate Transparency Bill 2023.

[4] See *Jogee* [2016] UKSC 8.

consent-or-connivance, as it applies to individual senior company officers, is itself narrow in a key respect. It applies only when the offence consented to or connived at was committed by *the company itself*. In criminal cases where the 'identification' doctrine applies, that means that the doctrine is in effect applicable only to the conduct of one senior officer (or officers), in consenting or conniving, respecting the conduct of another senior officer (or officers) who committed the offence within the scope of their authority. We argue that it should be made possible to find senior corporate officers individually liable for consenting to or conniving at crimes intended to benefit the company, not only when those crime are committed by the company itself, but also when they are committed by individual employees or agents under the senior officers' supervision and control. Such an extension of liability in principle is warranted, whatever reforms are made to the nature and extent of corporate criminal liability itself.[5] It is warranted by a proper understanding of the permissible limits of complicity in crime, whatever additional benefits may also arise from stiffening the scope and potentially deterrent effect of the criminal law as it applies to serious wrongdoing committed in corporate contexts.

In the next section, and in section 3, we consider the current scope for criminal liability to be imposed on individual company officers in respect of their complicity in corporate wrongdoing. As we will see, such liability is in one respect too narrow, and in another respect too broad. It is too narrow, in that such complicity can only arise, as we said above, in relation to a crime committed by the company itself, and not in relation to a crime committed to benefit the company by an individual employee or agent within the company. It is too broad, in that, in some instances, individual liability arises when wrongdoing by the company is attributable merely to 'neglect' on the part of the company officer, without a requirement for consent or connivance.[6] A prominent example of the latter kind of liability is to be found in section 1255 of the Companies Act 2006:

> Where an offence under this Part committed by a body corporate is proved to have been committed with the consent or connivance of, *or to be attributable to any neglect* on the part of, an officer of the body, or a person purporting to act in any such capacity, he as well as the body corporate is guilty of the offence and liable to be proceeded against and punished accordingly (our emphasis).

This objective (negligence-based) form of individual liability for corporate wrongdoing was to be found in only seven pieces of legislation between 1800 and 1945, but has appeared in no less than 1195 legislative provisions enacted between 1945 and 2023. Drilling down further into the figures for 1945–2023, it is interesting to note that this form of liability appeared in 89 pieces of legislation between 1945 and 1972, but – after the UK's entry into the EU – in 1106 pieces of legislation between 1972 and 2023. Some 485 of those pieces of post 1972 legislation have

[5] On which, see now the Economic Crime and Corporate Transparency Bill 2023.
[6] See discussion in Law Commission (n 3) ch 9.

taken the form of statutory instruments (c. 45 per cent), whereas on only five occasions between 1945 and 1972 was this form of liability created by statutory instrument (c. 6 per cent). Clearly, this form of liability was historically regarded by Parliament as a key element in the parts of EU harmonising legislation designed to hold company directors to account for breaches of community law. This is a massive expansion by any standards, attributable to the rise of a post-war welfarist ideology shaping the contours of the criminal law.[7]

There is certainly a case for saying that, when a crime is committed by someone within the company due to individual 'neglect' on the part of a senior company officer, the company itself should also be regarded as committing the crime. A reform to the basis of corporate economic crime along such lines was one of the aims of the Economic Crime and Corporate Transparency Bill 2023. However, in our view, when an individual senior officer's neglect contributed to corporate criminal wrongdoing, it is not right to say that this establishes the officer's 'complicity' in such wrongdoing. In that respect, we regard as highly contentious the commonplace or automatic inclusion of neglect alongside 'consent and connivance,' as way of establishing a senior officer's derivative liability in respect of an employee or agent's wrongdoing. In some instances, especially those involving stigmatic crimes, it is an unjust anomaly. 'Consent' or 'connivance' may render a senior company officer complicit in a crime, and may hence fully justify criminal liability on that basis, in a way that mere 'neglect' on their part does not. That is so even if, in relation to some non-stigmatic crimes, there might be some instances in which a corporate officer's neglect should lead to individual criminal liability being imposed on that officer.

In section 2, the relevant complicity principles applicable to the corporate wrongdoing context are discussed. As is well-known, the principles of complicity were radically changed – involving a significant narrowing – by the decision of the Supreme Court in *R v Jogee*.[8] The case concerned the law governing the imposition of liability on the alleged accessory, in respect of a perpetrator's crime (Y), when crime Y was committed by the perpetrator in the course of a joint criminal enterprise between the perpetrator and the alleged accessory to commit a different crime (X). The Supreme Court found that there was no justification for holding the accessory liable for crime Y, if the alleged accessory merely *foresaw* that the perpetrator might commit crime Y in the course of committing the agreed crime (crime X). It had to be proved that the alleged accessory *intended* to encourage or assist the perpetrator to commit crime Y (with the fault element, if any), in the course of committing crime X. We suggest that this proposition – the ratio of *Jogee* – may in some contexts prove to be too broad. Suppose that the alleged accessory has in law the power to control and direct the perpetrator's actions

[7] See the discussion in P Ramsay, 'The Responsible Subject as Citizen: Criminal Law, Democracy and the Welfare State' (2006) 69(1) *Modern Law Review* 29.

[8] [2016] UKSC 8.

(an issue considered in section 2 below): a set of circumstances not considered in *Jogee*. In such a case, the alleged accessory's consent to the wrongdoing, or connivance at it – foresight that the perpetrator may engage in wrongdoing, coupled with an unwillingness to do anything to prevent the wrongdoing being committed – provides a sound moral and legal basis for finding the alleged accessory complicit in the wrongdoing committed by the perpetrator. It follows that it is justified to impose derivative criminal liability on senior corporate managers – including those below Board level – when they have consented to or connived at wrongdoing doing by individual employees or agents over whom they exercise control.

1. Officers' Consent, Connivance and Neglect, as Basis for Liability

The proposition that a high-level company officer[9] can be found individually criminally liable either when consenting to or conniving at criminal wrongdoing by their company, or when such corporate wrongdoing is attributable to their neglect, is what can be referred to as a general principle of statute-based offences. We will refer to it as the 'individual accountability' principle. This principle has appeared in well over 1,500 statutes UK-wide: appearing 156 times between 1945 and 1972, but then 1,413 times between 1972 (the year of the European Communities Act) and 2023. It has found a place in a great diversity of legislation creating criminal offences, from theft, fraud and bribery, to the African Horse Sickness Regulations (Northern Ireland) 2013 or the Quality Standards for Green Bananas (England and Wales) Regulations 2012. An analogous basis for liability is also to be found in provisions dealing with individual involvement in fraudulent trading by companies.[10] Section 993(1) of the Companies Act 2006 provides that:

> If any business of a company is carried on with intent to defraud creditors of the company or creditors of any other person, or for any fraudulent purpose, every person who is *knowingly a party* to the carrying on of the business in that manner commits an offence (emphasis added).

In broad terms, the principle of individual accountability has two manifestations. First, in crimes that might be described as *mala in se*, or where stigma otherwise attaches to conviction, the principle is usually restricted to instances in which a company officer 'consented to' or 'connived' at commission of the

[9] See, eg, Health and Safety at Work Act 1974, s 37, which speaks of proceedings against a 'director, manager, secretary or other similar officer'.

[10] For an excellent discussion, see D Foxton QC, 'Accessory Liability and Section 213 Insolvency Act 1986' (2018) 4 *Journal of Business Law* 324.

relevant wrongdoing by their company. For example, by virtue of section 18 of the Theft Act 1968:

> Where an offence committed by a body corporate under 1 of this Act is proved to have been committed with the *consent or connivance* of any director, manager, secretary or other similar officer of the body corporate, or any person who was purporting to act in any such capacity, he as well as the body corporate shall be guilty of that offence, and shall be liable to be proceeded against and punished accordingly (emphasis added).

As indicated above, similar provisions may be found, for example, in section 14 of the Bribery Act 2010 and section 12 of the Fraud Act 2006. The significance of the restriction of the individual accountability principle to instances of consent or connivance, in crimes where stigma attaches to conviction, is that the principle will apply only when the defendant senior company officer had a subjective form of fault. Very broadly – a matter considered in more detail shortly – it must either have been the communicated intention of the officer that the offence should be committed ('consent'), or the officer must have been shown to have willingly stood by whilst the offence went ahead ('connivance').[11]

By contrast, when offences having a more regulatory cast to them are concerned – where no significant stigma attaches to conviction, and securing high levels of compliance is the main goal – liability is usually extended beyond 'consent or connivance.' In such cases, liability is commonly extended to instances in which the wrongdoing was attributable to a senior corporate officer's 'neglect.' Here is an example, in section 157 of the Environmental Protection Act 1990:[12]

> Where an offence under any provision of this Act committed by a body corporate is proved to have been committed with the *consent or connivance of, or to have been attributable to any neglect* on the part of, any director, manager, secretary or other similar officer of the body corporate or a person who was purporting to act in any such capacity, he as well as the body corporate shall be guilty of that offence (emphasis added).

As indicated earlier, similar provisions can be found in many hundreds of UK statutes, including such vitally important pieces of legislation as the Companies Act 2006.[13] In such instances, the individual accountability principle incorporates a basis for liability – neglect – that is wholly objective in character, by way of contrast with liability based on consent or connivance.[14] However, liability on such a basis is also in one way more restricted than liability based on consent or connivance: the commission of the offence must be 'attributable' to the senior corporate officer's neglect, involving proof of a causal link. Proof of such a link is

[11] See the discussion of the meaning of these terms in section 4 below.

[12] There are over 300 UK statutes in the environmental field that use such a provision.

[13] Section 1255, set out above.

[14] See *Wotherspoon v HM Advocate* [1978] JC 74, 78: 'the search must be to discover whether the accused has failed to take some steps to prevent the commission of an offence by the corporation to which he belongs if the taking of those steps ether expressly falls or should be held to fall within the scope of the functions of the office which he holds' (Lord Justice-General).

not necessary in cases of consent or connivance, where – bearing in mind that a senior officer is in a fiduciary relationship with the company – it is the subjective culpability of the officer that does the work of justifying criminal liability in relation to an offence committed by the company.

In one sense, it might seem to accord with settled criminal law doctrine to broaden or narrow the individual accountability principle, depending on the nature of the crime. In other words, it might appear that the reach of the individual accountability principle ought to vary, depending on whether it applies to a crime conviction for which attracts significant stigma, or instead to a non-stigmatic regulatory crime. When stigmatic crimes are in issue, only proof of subjective fault (consent or connivance) will suffice, whereas in the less stigmatic regulatory domain proof that the wrongdoing is attributable to neglect will suffice. However, there are two problems with this approach. First, it is trite law that, across the vast and varied array of criminal offences created by statute, there will inevitably be a large grey area within which it will be unclear or a contested matter whether conviction for a given crime attracts genuine stigma. Accordingly, in such cases, it will also be unclear whether or not the individual accountability principle should embrace liability based on neglect, or be confined to consent or connivance. A possible example is the offence of failure to ensure, so far as is reasonably practicable, the health, safety and welfare at work of all employees.[15] Especially, albeit not solely, when a failure of this kind has led to harm done,[16] a conviction may attract significant stigma; but the individual accountability principle applies in such cases on the basis of consent, connivance, or neglect.[17] There has also been inconsistency in Parliament's approach, that has the potential to lead to significant injustice. An example, highlighted by the Law Commission,[18] is the strict liability offence of taking or distributing indecent photographs of children, contrary to section 1(1) of the Protection of Children Act 1978. It is hard to see how this could count as anything other than a crime conviction for which attracts very significant stigma. Yet, by virtue of section 3 of the 1978 Act, if the taking or distributing of such photographs is done by a company director acting within the scope of their authority (say, taking pictures at a children's party) then other senior company officers will also be liable for that offence if its commission was attributable to their neglect. They will not only incur liability if they consented or connived at the commission of the offence. It is worth citing in full the Law Commission's criticism of this position:

> The offence of taking indecent photographs of children is one that carries very considerable stigma. It is an offence which, following conviction, has applied to it the

[15] Health and Safety at Work Act 1974, s 1.

[16] See, eg, *Chargot* [2008] UKHL 73.

[17] Section 37. See, eg, *Armour v Skeen* [1977] IRLR 310. In this case, the causally significant failure was D's failure to produce a written safety policy for his department, even though the Council had required him to produce one.

[18] Law Commission, *Criminal Liability in Regulatory Contexts* (Consultation 195, 2010) ch 6.

> notification requirements of the Sexual Offences Act 2003 in certain circumstances. It must be highly questionable whether an individual should have on his or her record a conviction for taking indecent photographs of children, and potentially be subject to stigmatising notification requirements, when (a) he or she personally did no such thing, and (b) he or she was wholly unaware that his or her company did any such thing. In our view, section 3 of the Protection of Children Act 1978 involves the use of a measure that is both unjustifiable and disproportionate in the circumstances.[19]

This brings us to the second, more theoretical problem with the bifurcated policy in relation to the scope of the individual accountability principle. English law, in common with many other jurisdictions, severely restricts the scope to impose criminal liability on D, when it is sought to convict D for the free, deliberate and informed act of P in causing some prohibited harm or in creating some prohibited risk. This is so, even when D can in some sense be regarded as having (culpably) contributed to P's decision to act.[20] One set of circumstances in which this is permitted is where D is, in law, complicit in P's conduct. To be found 'complicit' in conduct carries with it an implication of knowledge or awareness on the part of the complicit person. As Lord Goddard CJ put in, in *Johnson v Youden*,[21] 'Before a person can be convicted of aiding and abetting the commission of an offence, he must at least *know* the essential matters which constitute that offence'.[22] Notions of 'consent or connivance' bear a strong family resemblance to the principles of complicity[23] even if, as we will argue below, those notions have distinctive characteristics that reflect the corporate context. A key part of that resemblance is the fact that consent and connivance both imply knowledge or awareness, in relation to an act consented to or connived at. However, liability based on 'neglect' – even when the neglect was causally significant – does not fit into this justificatory story. 'Neglect' clearly carries with it no implication of awareness of the act that constitutes the offence. As a way to promote (regulatory) compliance, it may be justified to impose individual liability based on causally significant neglect by a senior corporate officer, when little or no stigma is attached to conviction.[24] However, if the law seeks to do this through exploiting a version of complicity in crime, as it clearly does when it yokes neglect together with consent or connivance, then the basic principles of complicity ought to be respected and

[19] Law Commission, *Regulatory Contexts*, para 7.43. The Law Commission goes on to contrast the approach in the 1978 Act to the approach in the Public Order Act 1986 to an analogous offence (in drafting terms), where the individual accountability principle is restricted in application to instances of consent or connivance. See now Law Commission, *Corporate Criminal Liability*, ch 9.

[20] *Kennedy (No 2)* [2007] UKHL 38.

[21] [1950] KB 544.

[22] ibid, 546.

[23] For example, just as, in complicity cases, when an allegation of consent or connivance is made against a senior corporate officer, whilst the tribunal of fact must be sure that the predicate offence took place, there is no need for a conviction for that offence to have been obtained: *Dickson and Wright* (1991) 94 Cr App R 7.

[24] Under the Economic Crime and Corporate Transparency Bill 2023, proof of the causally significant neglect of a corporate officer or senior manager, in leading to the commission of an economic crime, would also be a basis for attributing that crime to the company itself.

applied. Historically, it is clear that provisions containing all three bases of liability (consent; connivance; neglect) were regarded as justified by the way in which they sought to make directors *complicit* in the crimes of their company;[25] but it is hard to see how the 'neglect' basis for directorial involvement in the commission of regulatory crime fits into this picture.

When re-visiting this area of law, the Law Commission recommended that the 'neglect' basis for individual directorial liability was the right one for no-fault crimes, with 'consent or connivance' being the right approach for fault-based crimes:

> Our conclusion on this matter is that where director liability is extended to offences requiring proof of intent, knowledge, recklessness or dishonesty, this should be limited to connivance or consent. Director liability on the basis of negligence should be limited to cases where the offence is one of strict liability or negligence (including cases where the offence is one of strict liability subject to a reverse burden).[26]

This approach would leave a director individually liable for a (no-fault) sexual offence, as under the 1978 Act discussed above: a clear injustice. Moreover, attractive though it may be, in point of simplicity, the Law Commission's new approach wrongly ties the basis of individual liability to the nature of the principal offence (fault or no-fault). By contrast, the basis of liability should reflect a complicity-focused justification for liability, based on the subjective fault elements of consent or connivance.[27]

That brings us to the meaning of consent and connivance. In *Huckerby v Elliot*,[28] the Queen's Bench Division approved a definition of consent and connivance by the magistrate, given in the following terms:

> It would seem that where a director consents to the commission of an offence by his company, he is well aware of what is going on and agrees to it. Where he connives at the offence committed by the company he is equally well aware of what is going on but his agreement is tacit, not actively encouraging what happens but letting it continue and saying nothing about it.[29]

Although perhaps not entirely free from ambiguity on the point, this understanding posits a distinction between 'consent' cases, in which D effectively encourages the commission of the offence by 'actively' giving consent to it, and 'connivance' cases in which D stands by and knowingly permits the offence to be committed (or at least turns a 'blind eye' to the occurrence of wrongdoing[30]).

[25] See, eg, the argument of the Solicitor General, in debating the relevant provisions of the Iron and Steel Bill 1949: Hansard, 3 May 1949, vol 464, cc 921.

[26] Law Commission, *Corporate Criminal Liability*, para 9.68.

[27] We return to the issue of company officer neglect in section 6.

[28] [1970] 1 All ER 189.

[29] ibid, at 191 and 194. See also *Attorney-General's Reference (No 1 of 1995)* [1996] 1 WLR 970.

[30] *Chargot Ltd (t/a Contract Services)* [2008] UKHL 73, [8], indicating that the issue is, 'if it was established that the company had committed an offence, he willingly allowed it to do so or knowingly turned a blind eye to it' (Lord Hope). In Hong Kong, the notion of 'connivance' has also been held

Notwithstanding this difference, liability is justified in both cases. For example, Director 1 may seek Director 2's approval to falsify accounts. If Director 2 gives that approval, then that will clearly count as 'consent' to commission of false accounting by Director 1 and hence (*ex hypothesi*) by the company. By contrast, Director 2 may uncover ongoing false accounting on the part of other directors when inspecting the books, but decide to do nothing about it. That will clearly be an instance of 'conniving' at false accounting committed by the company. What we will now do is to set these principles into the broader context of the English law of complicity. We will do so, in order to understand how it may be justified to extend the application of the 'consent or connivance' doctrine to instances in which a director consents or connives at criminal wrongdoing committed by an employee or agent under the director's control.

2. Directorial Complicity and the Power to Control Another's Conduct

In order for D to be complicit in a crime with a fault element committed by P, D must now be shown to have intended to encourage or assist P to act with the fault element.[31] As is well-known, prior to the decision in *Jogee*, a special rule (the 'parasitic joint enterprise' rule) obtained where the alleged complicity on D's part took the form of intentionally participating with P in crime A, in the course or furtherance of which P committed crime B. In such circumstances, D's complicity in crime B could be demonstrated by proof that D foresaw a realistic possibility that crime B might be committed in the course of crime A ('the foresight principle'):

> The liability of [D1] … rests … on his having continued in the joint venture of crime A when he realises (even if he does not desire) that crime B may be committed in the course of it … He has associated himself with a foreseen [crime].[32]

This special rule no longer exists. In cases where D intentionally participates in crime A with P, and P commits crime B in the course or furtherance of crime A, the same rule of liability applies in relation to both crime A and crime B. To be found liable for crime B, D must be shown to have assisted or encouraged P to commit crime B with the intention that P should act with the relevant fault element. The fact that D was already engaged in a criminal enterprise with P (to commit crime A) no longer permits the application of a less demanding set of requirements for D's complicity in crime B.

In *Jogee*, the arguments against the existence of the special rule are mainly legal-historical: that there was no authority for the 'foresight principle' being specially

to include wilful blindness: *MG Mirchandani* [1977] HKLR 52. For a more general understanding that knowledge includes wilful blindness, see *Westminster v Croyalgrange Ltd* [1986] UKHL 9.

[31] *Jogee* [2016] UKSC 8, [90].

[32] *ABCD* [2010] EWCA Crim 1622, [27] (Hughes LJ).

applicable in cases of parasitic joint enterprise.[33] There is relatively little attention paid by the Supreme Court to the policy arguments for and against. However, one argument against the special rule might be the relative arbitrariness of its application. Consider a contrast between the following sets of facts:

> CASE 1: Through his window, D sees P approach V with a concealed knife. D rushes out to assist P in killing V, when P reaches V and brings out the knife, by holding V whilst P stabs V to death.
>
> CASE 2: Through his window, D sees P start an attack on V. D rushes out to assist P in the attack on V by holding V. D knows that P has a knife that P may use with lethal intent. So assisted, P stabs V to death.

In CASE 1, D is not involved in any 'crime A,' in the course of which crime B (the murder of V) is committed, because (*ex hypothesi*) an attempt on V's life has not gone beyond mere preparation when D sets off to assist P to kill V. Accordingly, the issue is (and always was) simply whether D intended to assist P to act with the fault element for murder, by restraining V. By contrast, in CASE 2, there is a 'crime A' in which D becomes jointly involved with P – the initial assault on V – and in the course of which crime B is committed when V is intentionally killed by P. So, the test for D's complicity in the murder is now different: not, 'did D intend to assist P to act with the intent to commit murder?', but 'did D realise that P realistically might act with the intent to commit murder?' Yet, in spite of this important distinction between the fault elements that must be proved against D (the test being, in the latter case, much less favourable to D), what is the significant difference of principle between CASE 1 and CASE 2 that justifies the difference in approach? It is difficult to see what it might be. Moreover, it will sometimes be hard to know, in a case in which the facts are complex and contested, which category the case falls into and hence which fault element the jury should be instructed to apply. Either it should always be enough that encouragement or assistance was given by D with foresight that P might realistically commit a given crime with the fault element, or it should only be enough if encouragement or assistance was given by D with the intention that P act with the fault element for the given crime. There appears to be little or no scope for both kinds of fault to co-exist: hence the Supreme Court decision to opt for the latter (narrower) rule.[34] However, in taking that option, the Supreme Court did not consider the rules and rationale governing the 'consent or connivance' doctrine, and explain how they might fit in to the picture.

The rules governing 'consent or connivance' straddle the two species of complicity. Cases of consent look like a form of complicity that – in most cases – will meet the *Jogee* test. In other words, as suggested earlier, proof of consent will

[33] See, eg, F Stark, 'The Demise of "Parasitic Accessorial Liability": Substantive Judicial Law Reform, Not Common Law Housekeeping' (2016) 75 *Cambridge Law Journal* 550–79.

[34] For a useful discussion of the merits of adopting the former, broader rule, see D Baker, *Reinterpreting Criminal Complicity and Inchoate Participation Offences* (Routledge, 2016).

require proof of knowing encouragement or assistance that is given with intent that the company should act with the fault element for the crime.[35] As Lord Hughes and Lord Toulson put it in *Jogee*:

> [S]econdary liability does not require the existence of an agreement between D1 and D2. Where, however, it exists, such agreement is by its nature a form of encouragement and in most cases will also involve acts of assistance. The long-established principle that where parties agree to carry out a criminal venture, each is liable for acts to which they have expressly or impliedly given their assent is an example of the intention to assist which is inherent in the making of the agreement.[36]

By contrast, cases of connivance look more like the form of complicity (involving application of the foresight rule) formerly applicable only in much-criticised parasitic joint enterprise cases. In *Chan Wing-Siu v R*,[37] Sir Robin Cooke explained this now overruled basis for complicity in the following terms:

> [A] case [may] depend rather on the wider principle whereby a secondary party is criminally liable for acts by the primary offender of a type which the former *foresees but does not necessarily intend*. That there is such a principle is not in doubt. *It turns on contemplation* or, putting the same idea in other words, authorisation, which may be express but is more usually implied. (emphasis supplied)[38]

As we saw in section 3, 'connivance,' whilst being a subjective test of liability for complicity in corporate crime, can nonetheless involve as little subjectivity as turning a 'blind eye' to wrongdoing committed by the company.[39] Does that mean that the continued existence of 'connivance,' as a basis for finding individual company officers complicit in offences committed by their company, has become anomalous in virtue of the overruling of the foresight rule in complicity cases more generally? Far from it. Indeed, the scope for its application – along with consent to wrongdoing – should be extended. To understand why, we need to go back to the analysis of CASES 1 and 2.

The contrast between CASES 1 and 2 shows that the old foresight rule was founded on shifting sands. It was necessary to prove there was a 'joint enterprise' to commit crime A (in the course of which crime B was committed), as a basis for legitimising the application of the foresight rule to determine whether a party to the joint enterprise was complicit in crime B. However, contrary to appearances, this never gave the foresight rule a sufficiently clear and defensible normative foundation, a foundation that could explain exactly when and why a more draconian test for liability – foresight alone – was justified in such cases than would otherwise be justified (in non-joint enterprise cases). So, although it failed to articulate this particular objection to the foresight rule, the Supreme Court was right to

[35] Above (n 22).
[36] *Jogee* UKSC 8, [78].
[37] [1985] AC 168 (PC).
[38] ibid, 175.
[39] *Chargot Ltd (t/a Contract Services)* [2008] UKHL 73, [8].

regard the rule as unsound and unsuited for *general* application, not just as a matter of legal history, but also morally. However, that does not mean that the foresight rule cannot be justified in special moral and legal contexts. In particular, foresight – and *ex hypothesi*, connivance – can be in itself a sound basis for finding someone complicit in a crime when that person had a legal duty or power to control and direct the activities of the person who committed the offence. Under the current law, that is – in effect – what justifies the application of the connivance (foresight) part of the 'consent or connivance' rules to cases in which a director knew of but did nothing about criminal wrongdoing committed by their company. However, the logic of the justification also dictates that these rules can, and perhaps should, be applied to cases in which a director connived at criminal wrongdoing committed not just by the company but by an individual employee (or agent or even subsidiary company) under their control and direction.

3. Wrongdoing in Corporate Contexts: Consent or Connivance

To explore further the suggestion at the end of the last section, a helpful initial focus is the case of *JF Alford Transport*.[40] A transport company's drivers had falsified tachograph records recording the amount of driving they had been doing, contrary to section 99(5) of the Transport Act 1968. The company was charged with and (initially) convicted of the offence, as a complicit party, on the basis that it had known about but done nothing to prevent the drivers' offending. The Court of Appeal was asked to consider whether the company could, in law, be found complicit in the drivers' offences on such a basis. Although it quashed the company's conviction (and those of the company officers) in the light of a misdirection by the trial judge, the Court of Appeal nonetheless said that there could be liability in such circumstances if:

(i) the company knew about the offending,
(ii) the company had the right to control the actions of those engaged in the offending, and
(iii) the company intentionally took no steps to prevent the offending.

Seen in terms of the post-*Jogee* common law elements of complicity, discussed above, the case does not make clear the modern requirement that the omission – taking no steps to prevent or stop offending – would have to be intended to assist or encourage the principal offender, and be accompanied by an intent that the offence itself be committed.[41] However, in the current context, more important is

[40] [1997] EWCA Crim 654.

[41] *Jogee* [2016] UKSC 8. These additional requirements make the so-called 'control principle' in the law of complicity somewhat less controversial than it might otherwise be: see J Horder (ed), *Ashworth's Principles of Criminal Law*, 9th edn (OUP, 2019) 463.

the understanding that when D has in law a power (or *a fortiori*, a duty) to control the actions of employees, D may be found liable for the employees' crimes upon proof that D fulfilled the requisite fault element, even when D made no positive contribution, in terms of conduct element, towards the offending itself. In that respect, *JF Alford* is an important case precisely because it involves the liability of a company for the actions of employees. However, we should note that the 'control' principle, as a basis for establishing liability on the basis of knowledge alone, without an additional requirement of positive conduct to assist or encourage, is well-established. In *Webster*,[42] the question was whether the owner of a car could be found complicit, as a passenger, in dangerous driving on the part of the driver, simply on the basis he – the owner – knew of the circumstances making the driving dangerous and failed to intervene. Although D's conviction in that case was quashed due to a misdirection, the Court held that:

> [T]he prosecution had to prove that [D] knew that [P] was, by virtue of the speed the vehicle was travelling, driving dangerously at a time when there was an opportunity to intervene. It was [D's] failure to take that opportunity and, exercise his right as owner of the vehicle, which would lead to the inference that he was associating himself with the dangerous driving.[43]

In *Martin*,[44] D was meant to be supervising a learner driver who lost control of the car and killed himself and another. The Court of Appeal sought to give more detail on the control principle. D may be liable for an offence as an accessory if, when P committed the offence, (i) D knew that P was acting with the fault element, (ii) D knew that he or she had an opportunity to stop the offence taking place, (iii) D intentionally did nothing to stop the offence taking place, and (iv) D so conducted him or herself in order to assist or encourage the commission of the offence, leading to the commission of the offence by P.

It is submitted that these authorities provide support for the following view. In cases where D has the legal power or duty to control P's criminal actions, and knowingly fails to do so with the result that P commits the crime, it is sufficient to find D complicit in P's crime that D knew of the circumstances of the offence and intentionally failed to intervene to prevent the offending (assuming there was an opportunity to do so). However, even if that proposition goes too far, as a statement of the common law of complicity, these cases nonetheless provide ample justification for the continued existence of 'connivance' alongside 'consent' as a basis for finding directors complicit in crime. The cases do not only provide such a justification for the existing rules covering cases when the wrongdoing was that of the company. The cases also provide a legal basis for extending the 'consent or connivance' rules to instances in which a director has knowingly

[42] [2006] EWCA Crim 415. See also *Story v United States*, 16 F.2d 342, 344 (DC Cir 1926).

[43] [2006] EWCA Crim 415, [29]. For further discussion of the fault element in such cases, see B Fisse, 'Complicity in Regulatory Offences' (1968) 6 *Melbourne University Law Review* 278.

[44] [2010] EWCA Crim 1450.

failed to intervene to stop offending intended to benefit the company by an individual employee, an agent, or even a subsidiary company, respecting whom that director had a legal power or duty to control and supervise its actions. As part of any reform of criminal liability arising in corporate contexts, such an extension – an amplified version of the 'responsible corporate officer' doctrine in the USA[45] – may perhaps not accord with current policy in England and Wales, which tends to be focused on the (in)action of companies themselves rather than of individual directors. For example, in its business plan for 2021–22,[46] under the heading 'Key Priorities for 2021/2', the Serious Fraud Office does not mention the need to pursue individuals within companies. Instead, it stresses:

> Encouraging good corporate compliance, and continuing to deploy Deferred Prosecution Agreements where these can help to deliver justice for victims quickly and effectively, whilst mandating improvements to avoid future fraud, bribery or corruption.

Such an approach, which places emphasis on an evolving preventative and neo-regulatory role for the SFO, in relation to corporate governance, rather than on successful prosecution of companies or individuals, has its defenders.[47] Even so, and by way of contrast, the US Department of Justice (DoJ) has placed the pursuit of high-level individual wrongdoers within companies at the top of its most recent agenda.

In her Keynote Address at American Bar Association's 36th National Institute on White Collar Crime,[48] Deputy Attorney General Lisa O Monaco indicated that DoJ policy under the Biden Administration would be shaped as follows:

> Accountability starts with the individuals responsible for criminal conduct. Attorney General Garland has made clear it is unambiguously this department's first priority in corporate criminal matters to prosecute the individuals who commit and profit from corporate malfeasance.

To that end she made it clear that, for example, any credit given to a company for co-operation with the DoJ would depend on the provision by the company to the DoJ of all non-privileged information about individuals within the company responsible for the wrongdoing in issue. As she put it, 'To be clear, a company must identify all individuals involved in the misconduct, regardless of their position, status or seniority'. Legal provisions that make it possible for directors to be found complicit, on the basis of consent *or* connivance', in the crimes of individual persons associated with the company, do something to further this objective. As the US Supreme Court put it (albeit, in justifying liability without fault) in *US v Park*:[49]

[45] See the discussion in section 4 below.

[46] See www.sfo.gov.uk/download/sfo-business-plan-2021-22/.

[47] See, eg, S Buell, 'The Responsibility Gap in Corporate Crime' (2018) 12 *Criminal Law and Philosophy* 471.

[48] See www.justice.gov/opa/speech/deputy-attorney-general-lisa-o-monaco-gives-keynote-address-abas-36th-national-institute.

[49] 421 U.S. 658 (1975).

> Courts of Appeals have recognized that those corporate agents vested with the responsibility, and power commensurate with that responsibility, to devise whatever measures are necessary to ensure compliance with the Act bear a 'responsible relationship' to, or have a 'responsible share' in, violations.[50]

In what kinds of cases might a version of the consent or connivance doctrine that has been extended to cover crime by individual company employees, agents or subsidiaries make a difference? One possible example is provided by *SFO v Serco Geografix*.[51] In this case, Serco Geografix Ltd (SG), a subsidiary of Serco Ltd (SL), had been providing electronic tagging services to the Ministry of Justice. There was an agreement with the Ministry of Justice that, in so far as the contracts proved more profitable than anticipated, the Ministry of Justice would be entitled to some 50 per cent of the difference between the anticipated and the actual profits made. By 2006, two years after the deal had been signed, it became apparent to SL that the contracts were going to be considerably more profitable than anticipated. However, individuals within SL decided that they did not wish to share increased profits with the Ministry of Justice, and conspired with directors of SG to avoid this outcome. To avoid any profit-sharing, SL charged for inflated levels of costs incurred by SG (and other parts of the business empire), including entirely fabricated costs for 'equipment, staff and overheads'. By this means, SL artificially depressed the apparent profit made from its contracts with the Ministry of Justice. The fraud was uncovered, and SG – admitting that it was guilty of fraud – entered into a deferred prosecution agreement with the SFO. More significantly, in the present context, was the fact that, whereas the knowing involvement in the fraud of management at 'directing mind and will' level within SG meant that the company itself was admitting to fraud, this was not true of SL. Although relatively senior contract managers within SL were knowingly and actively involved in the fraud, no one fitting the description of 'directing mind and will' was involved. Accordingly, SL as a company was not implicated in the fraud. Yet what if, as seems perfectly possible, senior managers with 'directing mind and will' status within SL were aware of (or suspected) what their contract managers were doing – 'cooking the books' in a conspiracy with directors at SG – and did nothing to stop it happening? Under the current law, there would be no criminal liability. That is because there was no consent or connivance on the directors' part in wrongdoing committed by SL, as a company, the company of which they were directors. The wrongdoing was committed by SL's individual contract managers and by the subsidiary company, SG. That is a glaring omission in the scope of criminal liability. If directors at SL connived at, or consented to, the fraud (intended to benefit SL) engaged in by SL contract managers or by SL's subsidiary company SG, that should be enough to establish the individual criminal liability of those directors.

[50] ibid, 672 (Berger CJ).
[51] *SFO v Serco Geografix Ltd* (2019), Case No: U20190413 (Mr Justice William Davies).

4. Wrongdoing in Corporate Contexts: Directors' Neglect

We saw in section 3 that individual liability for a crime committed by a company can in some instances be imposed on a director who knew nothing of the offending, but whose 'neglect' was a cause of the company's crime (the 'neglect doctrine'). This form of liability tends to be confined to regulatory offences, but we noted that the blurred line between regulatory and non-regulatory crimes creates a certain amount of arbitrariness in the application of the neglect doctrine. In some cases, as we saw, directors can be convicted – solely on the basis of neglect – of highly stigmatic offences committed by another person whose action nonetheless incriminates the company through the doctrine of vicarious liability. How should this issue be addressed, in terms of law reform?

The neglect doctrine bears comparison with the 'responsible corporate officer' (RCO) doctrine in the USA. In *US v Park*,[52] the President of Acme Markets, a company with a national food chain, was charged – along with the company itself – with violating section 301(k) of the Federal Food, Drug, and Cosmetic Act 1938. It was alleged that the company had caused interstate food shipments being held in Acme's Baltimore warehouse to be exposed to rodent contamination. The company pleaded guilty. However, the company President sought to avoid individual conviction, on the basis that he was not himself responsible for having exposed goods to contamination. His conviction was upheld. The Supreme Court held that it was not sufficient for the Government to show merely that D occupied a senior role in the company.[53] Instead, in the case of someone exercising authority and supervisory responsibility, it was held that the 1938 Act imposed on them not only a positive duty to seek out and remedy violations, but also, and primarily, a duty to implement measures that will ensure that violations will not occur:[54]

> the Government establishes a *prima facie* case when it introduces evidence sufficient to warrant a finding by the trier of facts that the defendant had, by reason of his position in the corporation, responsibility and authority either to prevent in the first instance, or promptly to correct, the violation complained of, and that he failed to do so.[55]

[52] 421 US 658 (1975).

[53] 421 US 658 (1975), 674–75. For a contrary holding, see *United States v Dee* 912 F.2d 741, 748–49 (4th Cir 1990), cert. denied, – US 111 S Ct 1307, 113 L Ed 2d 242 (1991), and the discussion in SM Morgan and AK Obermann, 'Perils of the Profession: Responsible Corporate Officer Doctrine May Facilitate a Dramatic Increase in Criminal Prosecutions of Environmental Offenders' (1991) 45(3) *Southern Methodist University Law Review* 1199.

[54] It is generally considered that personal liability in such cases can be established on the basis of strict liability, even if in practice prosecutions will be undertaken only where there was personal negligence: see the discussion in S Buell, '*The Responsibility Gap in Corporate Crime*' (2018) 12 Criminal Law and Philosophy 471–91.

[55] 421 US 658 (1975), 673–74.

Importantly, though, the RCO doctrine will not lead to conviction if, in the circumstances, the corporate officer was 'powerless to prevent or correct the violation'.[56]

A relatively recent illustrative case is *US v Freedom Industries; US v Southern*.[57] In this case, a major chemical leak was discovered in Charleston at the aboveground storage tank area owned and operated by Freedom Industries on the Elk River. Freedom Industries used these storage tanks to keep and process chemicals, and the leak consisted primarily of 4-methylcyclohexane methanol (MCHM), a chemical used in the coal mining industry as a cleansing agent. A significant amount of MCHM leaked into the Elk River, flowed into a water treatment plant, and contaminated the water supply of Charleston and the surrounding areas for several days. Freedom did not have a permit required by law that would have allowed the company to discharge MCHM into the Elk River. Gary Southern was the Freedom Industries President at the time of the leak. During Southern's tenure as a responsible corporate officer, Freedom never developed or implemented a storm water or groundwater plan. It was found that Southern's negligence in failing to ensure that Freedom developed and implemented a storm water and groundwater plan was a proximate and contributing cause of the chemical spill. On that basis, in 2016 Southern was sentenced to 30 days in federal prison, to be followed by a six-month term of supervised release, and a $20,000 fine.

The precise scope of the RCO doctrine is uncertain, with some cases giving it a relatively narrow scope, and others interpreting it more broadly.[58] In the *Freedom Industries; Southern case*, for example, the former President of the company was sentenced on the basis of personal negligence that causally contributed to the prohibited outcome: a basis for sentence that closely mirrors the legal ingredients of the neglect doctrine in English law. However, some cases interpreting the RCO doctrine do not require that the senior officer's involvement in what happened to be directly causal. Such a person's role is, rather, a role-responsibility relationship. If employee P adulterates food, then P is the (direct) cause of the adulteration; but if supervisor D – with authority to guide P's actions – watches on and does nothing, is asleep on the job, or even simply covers up P's wrongdoing afterwards, then D's involvement in the wrongdoing is responsibility-based as opposed to (directly) causal.[59] For example, in *US v Brittain*,[60] where D was convicted of falsely reporting a material fact to a government agency and discharging pollutants in violation of the limits of the applicable permit, the court said that D, 'would not have to wilfully or negligently cause a permit violation. Instead, the wilfulness or negligence of the actor

[56] 421 US 658 (1975), 673.

[57] (2016, unreported).

[58] See SM Morgan and AK Obermann, 'Perils of the Profession: Responsible Corporate Officer Doctrine May Facilitate a Dramatic Increase in Criminal Prosecutions of Environmental Offenders' (1991) 45 *SMU Law Review* 1199–1219.

[59] For brief, further exposition of this distinction, see S Shute, J Gardner and J Horder, *Action and Value in Criminal Law* (OUP, 1993) Introduction.

[60] 931 F 2d 1413 (10th Cir 1991).

would be imputed to him by virtue of his position of responsibility'.[61] Arguably, such a basis for conviction is more appropriate, in the case of those in authority within a company. For, such people are less likely to be involved causally in the commission of offences, when a company has employees whose job it is to the deliver 'front line' services.

Comparing the neglect doctrine and the RCO doctrine (on its broad construction):

1. Both doctrines permit personal liability in respect of corporate wrongdoing to be imposed on high-ranking corporate officers, without the need to prove knowledge or recklessness.
2. Both doctrines apply to offences (typically, regulatory offences) created by statute.
3. Whereas the neglect doctrine requires proof of a causal link between the neglect and the corporate wrongdoing, the responsible corporate officer doctrine requires proof that measures had not been put in place to prevent, or promptly to correct, wrongdoing of the prohibited type.

It is worth noting that although the RCO doctrine's focus is obviously individual corporate officers, rather than the company itself, the doctrine has some similarities with the offence and defence elements to the UK corporate crimes of failure to prevent bribery or the facilitation of tax evasion.[62] However, the doctrine is differently configured. Under the RCO doctrine, the state bears the initial burden of establishing a *prima facie* case not only that the senior officer in question failed to prevent the offending, but also that the officer failed to put in place procedures to prevent or promptly correct the violation. By contrast, under UK law, the Crown only bears the burden of showing that the company failed to prevent the relevant wrongdoing. It is for the defendant company to show that it had adequate or reasonable procedures in place to prevent such wrongdoing.

Nonetheless, in one way, the RCO doctrine provides a perhaps more satisfactory basis for convicting individual senior company officers, in cases where (in a broad sense) neglect is regarded as an adequate basis for conviction. That is because the RCO doctrine is focused on the harm-prevention or harm-mitigation procedures, which are the special (if not the unique) responsibility of management, rather than on individual instances of neglectful behaviour. Having said that, the RCO doctrine still involves conviction without subjective fault of a senior company officer for the offence itself, and that can be unfair in cases where conviction attracts significant moral stigma. So, can the RCO doctrine be modified to meet that point? Let us go back to the controversial case of corporate liability for taking indecent photographs of children, contrary to the 1978 Act.[63] Instead

[61] ibid, 1419.
[62] See Bribery Act 2010, s 7; Criminal Finances Act 2017, Pt 3.
[63] See text at n 18.

of convicting a negligent director of that self-same offence, alongside their company, it would be possible to provide that the senior officer could be guilty of a separate offence of 'failing to provide or maintain reasonable procedures to prevent or remedy the offending'. Although this would be a separate offence from that of company, it would be possible to provide that the offence is not committed unless the company has also committed the substantive offence. In that way, a purely regulatory, safeguarding failure on the part of a senior company officer would not be committed, in the absence of wrong done by the company itself.[64]

It could, of course, be argued that the same approach should be taken in cases of consent or connivance. That is to say, one might argue that, when the company has committed the substantive offence, it should be possible to charge the senior officers with a separate offence of 'consenting or conniving,' rather than these states of mind being sufficient to justify individual conviction for the company's offence.[65] However, that argument is not wholly convincing. It was argued earlier that, under the doctrine of complicity, these states of mind – when possessed by someone in authority or control over the person who commits the offence – are sufficient to justify the imposition of full liability on the person in authority for the offence itself. The law should not resile from that position.

5. Conclusion

If there is to be genuine deterrence of corporate wrongdoing, alongside strong incentives to improve anti-harm processes and procedures within companies, then it ought to be easier than it currently is to target influential senior corporate officers within companies, at whose door responsibility for such processes and procedures can be laid. We have argued that there are two main ways that this can be done, whilst honouring the value of fair labelling in criminal law. First, it ought to be possible to prosecute senior corporate officers for offences when they consented or connived at the commission of those offences by individual employees or agents under their control (not just when the offences were committed by the company itself). Second, at least in some instances, when a criminal wrong has been committed by a company, it ought to be possible to prosecute senior corporate officers for a discrete offence of 'failing to provide or maintain reasonable procedures to prevent or remedy the offending'.

There is no doubt that Parliament currently has an appetite for reform of corporate criminal liability, including the basis on which individual directors may be held liable for offences committed by their company. For example, in the

[64] For the dangers of permitting criminal prosecution purely on the basis of risk assessment, see KE Woody, 'No Smoke and No fire: The Rise of Internal Controls Absent Anti-Bribery Violations in FCP Enforcement' (2017) 38 *Cardozo Law Review* 101.

[65] The analogy being with the inchoate offences of assisting or encouraging crime, contrary to the Serious Crime Act 2007.

Economic Crime and Corporate Transparency Bill 2023, amendments were placed intended to extend the scope of individual directors' criminal liability for consent or connivance: to instances of the proposed new offence of failure to prevent economic crime:

> (1) A person ('S') commits an offence if—
>
> (a) at a time when S is a senior manager or corporate officer of a corporate body ('C'), S—
>
> (i) takes, or agrees to the taking of, a decision by or on behalf of the corporate body as to the way in which the business of the corporate body is conducted, and
>
> (ii) fails to take any steps that S could take to prevent such a decision being taken;
>
> (b) at the time of the decision, S is aware of a risk that the implementation of the decision may lead to the commission of an offence of money laundering, fraud, false accounting, bribery or tax evasion; and
>
> (c) the implementation of the decision causes C to commit such an offence.

This particular provision is inept. It would make a senior manager or company officer criminally liable when the economic crime committed by an employee or agent stemmed from nothing more than a perfectly legitimate decision by the company to invest in a country where – as the senior managers or officers knew – there were enhanced risks that investing companies would be asked to engage in economic crime. Even so, what the amendment indicates is that the current legislative climate is favourable to reform of corporate criminal liability, including the individual liability of company officers: even those below directorial 'mind and will' level. As our argument has sought to demonstrate, there is nothing especially radical or out-of-step with a regime of individual criminal liability, applicable to senior managers and company officers, that extends to consent-or-connivance based liability for the criminal actions of individual employees, agents or subsidiary companies (under the control of the managers or officers) when the crimes were intended to benefit the company. Accordingly, it should not be necessary to hold extensive consultation before bringing such provisions into effect: they can be attached to any company-related Bill going through Parliament. Such a provision might read as follows:

> (1) A person ('S') commits an offence if—
>
> (a) an employee, agent or subsidiary company of a corporate body ('C') commits bribery, fraud, false accounting or money laundering, in order to benefit C,
>
> (b) at the time of the offence, the employee, agent or subsidiary company was under the control of or directed by S, and,
>
> (c) at the time of the offence, S was a senior manager or corporate officer of C, and
>
> (d) S consented to or connived at the commission of the offence by the employee, agent or subsidiary company.

Comment on Chapter 3

Extending the Individual Liability of Senior Officers for the Crimes of Employees or Agents

ALISON CRONIN*

The discussion and insight of Professor Jeremy Horder and Gabriele Watts, provides a timely and invaluable reminder of the need to keep in view the role of individuals, and the responsibility they might bear in the overall complexity of corporate action, whilst offering the thought-provoking analysis necessary to inspire, underpin and enable future developments in the law. With that in mind, it seemed fitting that this response should, to a large extent, explore their discussion by reference to the contribution of the eminent Glanville Williams, who was, of course, particularly noted for his seminal works on the general principles of criminal liability; and the proposed reforms now contained in the Economic Crime and Corporate Transparency Bill. In addition, this chapter points to a lacuna in the law of corporate fraud evident in both the current and proposed schemes of criminal liability.

In their chapter, Horder and Watts argue that the current law of consent and connivance is too narrow, confined in application to instances where there is a corporate conviction, and that senior officers should also be liable under this doctrine when they are in a command-and-control relationship with employees or agents who commit offences. They reason that the extension is justifiable by reference to the proper understanding of the theoretical basis and laws of complicity in the light of more general common law developments in this area. Undoubtedly, Horder and Watts are correct in their assertion that the individual liability of senior officers can be justifiably extended, however, this response offers an alternative analysis that breaks free of the stringent conditions imposed under the common law's complicity doctrine.[1]

* Principal Academic in Law, Bournemouth University.

[1] Namely that the secondary party must have intentionally assisted or encouraged the offence committed, *Jogee* [2016] UKSC 8.

Furthermore, Horder and Watts suggest that the imposition of criminal liability on senior officers based on their neglect is too broad. They argue that the importation of an objective assessment of fault is undesirable since it departs from the general law of complicity which requires a subjective approach to fault. While Horder and Watts are correct to assert that the artificial distinction between *mala prohibita* and *mala in se* offences provides no principled basis upon which to determine the scope of liability for neglect, again this chapter provides an alternative analysis, that offers some justification for the objective approach.

The first section of this chapter sketches the scope of the respective forms of individual accountability: consent, connivance, and neglect, applicable only to senior company officers, and the rules of complicity that are of general application. Crucially, this includes not only the common law rules that were considered in the previous chapter, now expressed in *Jogee*,[2] but also the less restrictive encouraging and assisting provisions contained in Part 2 of the Serious Crime Act 2007,[3] which overlap with the common law. The second section in this chapter elaborates the underlying basis of liability for neglect, drawing on general principles of liability for omissions; and the final section goes on to consider the peculiar nature of dishonesty offences, such as fraud and theft, the consequent implications for the attribution of corporate fault and, by extension, the liability of senior officers for these crimes.

1. Individual Accountability: Consent; Connivance; Neglect

'Consent' requires that the senior officer knows of the facts constituting the offence and agrees (this can be inferred) to the conduct.[4] 'Connivance' is essentially a tacit agreement/ acquiescence in such knowledge, however, the courts have diluted the knowledge requirement such that a senior officer will be liable if he/she is wilfully blind to the material facts,[5] deliberately refraining from making inquiries and, according to Glanville William's seminal text, he/she negligently fails to take steps to prevent the offence.[6] 'Neglect' is defined as a lack of attention to some duty that should have been performed. Given the less stringent approach to *mens rea*, liability requires proof of a causal link between the senior officer's neglect and the company's commission of the offence.

It is important to note that a senior officer's liability under the individual accountability principles can only apply where a corporate offence has been committed. In crimes requiring proof of *mens rea*, this means that the senior

[2] ibid.
[3] Specifically, ss 45 and 46.
[4] *Chargot Ltd* [2008] UKHL 73, [8].
[5] *Westminster v Croyalgrange Ltd* [1986] UKHL 9.
[6] G Williams, *Criminal Law, The General Part*, 2nd edn (Stevens & Sons Ltd, 1961).

officer must have consented to or acquiesced in the offence committed by an individual who is of such senior status that he/she is considered the 'directing mind and will of the company'.[7] Since the provisions make little sense otherwise, this surely presupposes that to attract individual liability the senior officer must have been empowered with some control over that individual's conduct. For example, if a sales manager in a large corporation were to discover his managing director engaging in bribery, his purported withdrawal of consent to that activity would be nothing more than a powerless and inconsequential gesture, analogous with King Canute's reputed attempt to command the tide, given his inferior status in the corporate hierarchy.[8] Furthermore, the law does not impose a general duty requiring individuals to police or report the criminality of others.[9] It would be an altogether different matter if, in the same circumstances, the conduct was discovered by, for example, fellow board members. Since the individual accountability principle necessarily imports a power relationship, it is questionable whether it requires justification based on concepts of the *general* law of accessorial liability, as reasoned by Horder and Watts, or on any other premise. Indeed, case law sets out that it is the position of real authority, power and responsibility to decide and manage the affairs of the company as a whole that provides the basis for senior officer liability;[10] and, of note, in his work on the general part of the criminal law, Glanville Williams described the increase of responsibilities to corporate officers as an 'addition to common law accessorial liability' and not as an expansion of it.[11]

However, if the empowered position is not of itself a presupposed justification, and another basis is required, it is arguable whether liability for failing to prevent another's crime is well-established, as suggested in the previous chapter, where there is a power or right of control. Interestingly, Glanville Williams reviewed the decided cases in this area, some 30 years ago, in response to the Law Commission's Draft Criminal Code, Clause 27(3),[12] which proposed a version of complicity based on passive assistance or encouragement 'arising from a failure by a person to take reasonable steps to exercise any authority or discharge any duty he has to control the relevant acts of the principal in order to prevent the commission of the offence'. Describing this as creating a notion of constructive encouragement and constructive assistance based on fiction,[13]

[7] *Lennard's Carrying Co Ltd v Asiatic Petroleum Ltd* [1915] AC 705.

[8] Although Blackstone's suggests that a senior officer may be guilty of consent or connivance if he fails to report a fellow director even where he has no right of control over that director, the text provides no authority for this proposition: D Ormerod and D Perry, *Blackstone's Criminal Practice*, 33rd edn (OUP, 2023) A6.25.

[9] SF Copp and A Cronin, 'New models of corporate criminality: the developments and relative effectiveness of "failure to prevent" offences' (2018) 39(4) *The Company Lawyer* 104.

[10] *Re B Johnson & Co (Builders) Ltd* [1955] Ch 634, 661; *Boal* [1992] 1 QB 591, 598.

[11] Williams, *General Part* (1961) 867.

[12] *A Criminal Code for England and Wales* (Law Com No 177, 1989).

[13] G Williams, 'Letting Offences Happen' [1990] *Criminal Law Review* 780, 781.

Williams identified two categories of cases, both of which are relied upon by Horder and Watts, comprising: (a) the interpretation of a statute (Road Traffic Act), (b) the ownership of property; as well as (c) 'one dubious exception'.[14]

As regards the failure of the supervisor to prevent a learner driver's offence, for which *Martin* was illustrative in the previous chapter,[15] Williams describes this as a 'spurious interpretation' of the Act that does not bear general expansion in the criminal law, since the statute creates no failure to control offence, no power to instruct the learner, and no requirement on the learner's part to obey.[16] In relation to the *Webster*[17] authority, again advanced in the previous chapter, the decision that an owner of a car could, as a passenger, be found complicit in the offence committed by the driver, has its basis in the fact that a property owner can tell another person not to touch his property, or tell him to leave his (owned) premises.[18] However, in Williams' view, the court used this principle as a 'dodge'[19] in *Du Cros*[20] to make a car owner liable where the prosecution could simply not establish whether the owner was the passenger or the driver and, absent of proof of either encouragement or the intention to do so, Williams argued that it fell outside the traditional parameters of complicity liability. Although, *Webster* relies on *Du Cros*, there was no evidential problem regarding the identity of the driver in this case and *Du Cros* was itself unsound. *Martin* is equally problematic in its reliance on *Webster* since the supervisor here did not own the vehicle.

The only other case regarding this version of complicity concerns a publican being found an accessory to his customer's offence of late drinking,[21] contrary to the Licensing Act, since the pub was his and under his control, albeit there was no evidence of encouraging the offence or an intention to do so. Employing the court's reasoning, Williams argues that *Clarkson*,[22] the voyeur who watched a rape, could have been convicted of rape, if he had owned the premises in which the offence was committed and had refrained from telling the rapists to leave, and that a landowner who unreasonably failed to try to eject a would-be murderer, would be an accessory to the murder. At the time of writing, in 1990, Williams observed there was no other authority for finding encouragement based on a failure to exercise control. For example, a policeman who fails to prevent an assault does not become an accomplice to it even though he could prevent it, by arrest, and is duty bound to protect the victim and to maintain the peace. Thus, a police officer who ignored a serious violent incident was found guilty of misconduct in public office but there was no suggestion that he was complicit in the killing.[23]

[14] ibid, 783.
[15] *Martin* [2010] EWCA Crim 1450.
[16] *Rubie v Faulkner* [1940] 1 KB 571.
[17] *Webster* [2006] EWCA Crim 415.
[18] *Du Cros v Lambourne* [1907] 1 KB 40.
[19] Williams (n 13) 784.
[20] [1907] 1 KB 40.
[21] *Tuck v Robson* [1971] 1 WLR 741, 1 All ER 1171.
[22] *Clarkson* [1971] 1 WLR 1402, 3 All ER 344.
[23] *Dytham* [1979] QB 722.

Taken to the extreme, any witness to any offence, who fails to take active steps to prevent it, might find themselves an accessory to it since everybody has the statutory power to use reasonable force to prevent a crime.[24]

In the context of the employment relationship, Williams cites the case of *Cassady v Reg. Morris (Transport) Ltd*,[25] noting that it serves as both an extension and severe limitation to the 'authority to control' idea. While the employer's failure to enforce his employee's regulatory compliance might be some evidence of complicity, sufficient to defeat a submission of 'no case', it is for the court to decide, on the facts of the particular case, whether positive encouragement or assistance was given. Although the employer was acquitted, Williams cautioned that *Cassady* may be the thin end of what might become a broad wedge by which a kind of vicarious liability could be imposed on employers. His concern was not with individual liability for an offence of neglect of duty, but that the individual should not be guilty of the substantive offence he fails to prevent.[26] Indeed, Williams observed that statutes impose just such a duty through creating offences of 'permitting', and *JF Alford Transport*, discussed by Horder and Watts in the previous chapter, is a case in point. Here, in the knowledge of the managing director and other senior officers, numerous employees were involved in a systemic practice of falsifying tachographs, prohibited by section 99(5) of the Transport Act 1968. At the time of the decision, the offence was drafted to impose criminal liability on a person who 'makes or causes [the false entry] to be made', but the insertion of a consent or connivance provision had apparently been overlooked. In the circumstances of the evident knowledge of the senior management, the convictions of the company and its officers, that were arguably justified on the facts, required an exceptional straining of the general principles of accessorial liability. It is of note that the legislation was subsequently amended to include a permitting offence.

Given the shaky foundations of what amount to a limited number of hard cases, it is doubtful that they provide a sufficient basis to justify extending senior officer liability under the traditional common law principles of accessorial liability. Arguably, if a control/power duty were to exist as an established basis, there are more obvious applications that have failed to materialise. For example, although the age of criminal capacity is just 10 years, parents do not generally attract criminal liability for the failure to control their children.[27]

Perhaps the greatest cause of doubt that the proposed extension of senior corporate officers' liability must accord with the common law principles of complicity is the enactment of the general encouraging and assisting offences in Part 2 of the Serious Crime Act 2007. Sections 45 and 46 create liability when

[24] Williams (n 13); Criminal Law Act 1967, s 3.

[25] [1975] Crim LR 398.

[26] Williams (n 13).

[27] There are exceptions, eg, parents can be guilty of an offence of failing to secure their child's regular attendance at school, Education Act 1996, s 444.

an individual does an act or omission[28] capable of encouraging the commission of an offence or offences, believing that the offence(s) will be committed, and that his/her act or omission will encourage its commission. The provisions therefore offer a departure from the strict requirement of an intention to encourage or assist established at common law. Although belief (the mental element for statutory encouragement) is not synonymous with knowledge (the defining element for consent) or wilful blindness (the diluted knowledge requirement for connivance), it is defined as a state of awareness short of knowledge where the defendant believes or is reckless as to whether the other person will perform the act with the *mens rea* necessary for the offence in question.[29] Thus, if looking to justify the extension of senior officer's liability to encompass offences committed by employees and agents under their control, the encouraging and assisting offences in the Serious Crime Act provide a better basis. Although wilful blindness, sufficient to inculpate a senior officer for his or her connivance in a corporate offence, is arguably narrower than recklessness, it is certainly closer in nature to the concept of belief that underpins the statutory encouraging and assisting offences. Indeed, in *Sadique* the court uses the words belief and subjective recklessness interchangeably.[30] Imposing liability on senior officers for consent or connivance may therefore be more readily justified by reference to the statutory scheme that overlaps the traditional rules of complicity. Since this avoids the need to justify the 'resurrection' of the common law foresight rule for connivance, it also obviates the need to establish a special control relationship. Put simply, the 2007 Act does the heavy lifting, and a senior officer will be guilty if his/her conduct is capable of encouraging or assisting an offence, whether or not it is committed, if he/she believes or foresees that another person will commit the offence and that his/her conduct will encourage or assist.

Since the offences contained in the Act impose a general liability on any individual who encourages or assists in crime (not just senior corporate officers), apply to both acts and omissions, and offer the same scope in terms of *mens rea*, the real question is whether the consent and connivance doctrine is now rendered effectively obsolete. While regard might be had to the special context of the individual accountability principles, such that it may be said to have normative value, according with both the criminal law's expressive function and fair-labelling principles, insight can be gained from the approach taken in the Economic Crime and Corporate Transparency Bill in the context of its introduction of a corporate 'failure to prevent fraud' offence. Here the omission of a statutory consent and connivance provision is expressly attributed to the fact that individuals can be prosecuted under general principles of criminal law for encouraging or assisting

[28] Section 47(8)(a).

[29] Section 47(5)(a).

[30] *Sadique and Hussain* [2011] EWCA Crim 2872, but see JJ Child, 'Exploring the Mens Rea Requirements of the Serious Crime Act 2007 Assisting and Encouraging Offences' (2012) 76(3) *Journal of Criminal Law* 220.

fraud.[31] Since the scope of the statutory encouraging and assisting provisions goes further than that of the consent and connivance doctrine, being applicable to any individual complicit in the crime of any other, there is no need to extend specifically the individual accountability of senior officers, for the crimes of employees or agents, in the way that Horder and Watts have suggested and reasoned. It is also worth observing that, through the proposed 'extension' of the identification principle contained in the Bill, senior managers are much more likely to be the subject of increased scrutiny as regards the range of economic offences for which their individual liability will be in scope of attribution to the corporation.[32] If enacted, it is to be hoped that this reform, albeit through a different means, may meet the need for greater accountability of corporate senior officers that is ultimately sought by Horder and Watts.

2. Alternative Analysis of Neglect

It is of note that, in its approach to the individual liability of senior officers for neglect, where the corporation has committed an offence, the current Bill seemingly accords with the view of Horder and Watts. Government has firmly rejected the imposition of individual liability for 'failure to prevent fraud' on the basis that it would be disproportionate to impose objective fault on individuals who do not consent or know of the offence.[33] The same reasoning might equally apply to the imposition of individual liability for neglect.

However, regarding senior officers' liability for neglect, an alternative analysis under the general principles of omissions, premised on a failure to act when under a duty to do so, may lead to an alternative conclusion to that drawn in the previous chapter. Of note, omissions liability is, like neglect, subject to the usual principles of causation, and it is, as Horder and Watts observe, the causative link that does much of the justificatory work in both areas. Additionally, while the difference between the conduct of consent and connivance is broadly the distinction between act and omission, and Williams certainly viewed connivance through the lens of omissions, it is trite law that a person cannot be made responsible for an omission unless a legal rule attaches to him a personal duty to act.[34]

Reasoned as a form of omissions liability, case law seems then to support the inclusion of neglect as a head of liability for senior officers under a duty, alongside connivance, and irrespective of a subjective *mens rea* requirement. It is, perhaps, of note that the terms connivance and neglect have been used synonymously.[35] As Horder and Watts observe, the argument for imposing neglect as a basis for

[31] See *Factsheet: failure to prevent fraud offence* (Policy Paper, 2023).
[32] Economic Crime and Corporate Transparency Bill, Clause 195(2), (4) and Sch 12.
[33] Policy Paper (n 31).
[34] Williams (n 6) 867.
[35] D Ormerod and K Laird, *Smith, Hogan and Ormerod's Criminal Law*, 15th edn (OUP, 2018) 116.

individual liability is questionable in a case where corporate liability is, for example, established for taking indecent photographs of children, contrary to section 1(1) of the Protection of Children Act 1978. In *Wotherspoon* it was held that neglect would require the senior officer to have some identifiable duty arising through his position within the company that required him or her to take steps and that the issue of knowledge, or whether the accused should have been aware of the need for action, will be relevant.[36] Consistent with the general principles of omissions liability, the facts would need to be considered on a case by case basis with reference to all the evidence including that of the defendant.[37] Under neglect, the officer's duty requires clear definition, as do the steps it would be reasonable to expect him or her to take in his/her control of the principal offender, who, after all, as the company's directing mind and will, is likely to be superior to the senior officer in rank.

If a situation did arise in which the conviction of the senior officer was possible, this would of course be averted if conviction demanded that the crime was intended to benefit the company. Whether that restriction would be justifiable in every case is a matter for debate. Perhaps more pertinent in the situation postulated is the question of the duty of care owed to the children by the organiser of the party and any failure on his part to properly supervise. This person may be a more appropriate candidate for prosecution and, if so, would likewise attract the general objective approach to the matter of his negligence.

3. Corporate Fraud

Leaving aside the issue of complicit liability, this final section offers a brief comment on corporate liability for fraud, given the proposed enactment of a new corporate 'failure to prevent fraud' offence.[38] Under the current law a corporation can be convicted of the substantive offence of fraud through application of the identification principle. The new Act will not only extend the scope of attribution for corporate fraud to include senior managers,[39] it will also create a substantively different corporate offence for failure to prevent lower-level individuals aiding, abetting, counselling, procuring or committing fraud.[40] Although this form of corporate liability is essentially premised on the management's failure to establish adequate preventative measures, it is still parasitic in nature in the sense that it is dependent upon the commission of an underlying substantive offence by an individual employee or associate. In the case of fraud and tax evasion offences, for

[36] *Wotherspoon v HM Advocate* [1978] JC 74.

[37] ibid, [14].

[38] Economic Crime and Corporate Transparency Bill 2023, Clause 198.

[39] Clause 195.

[40] Similar to the failure to prevent bribery and tax evasion offences, see Bribery Act 2010, s 7, and Criminal Finances Act 2017, ss 45 and 46.

which it is the element of dishonesty that distinguishes criminal from otherwise lawful behaviour, corporate liability necessarily hinges on that individual having acted with the requisite dishonesty. In circumstances where the wrongdoing is not reducible to individuals, perhaps because the dishonest conduct was a systemic corporate practice, for example mis-selling, and the individuals involved in the conduct were not themselves dishonest, but simply doing their job, the company would evade liability.[41]

To address this lacuna, where the individuals involved lack the *mens rea* for fraud, it may be more appropriate to conceive the substantive offence as that of the company, and there is a growing call for the use of evidential presumptions, together with the inferential approach to dishonesty, as a means to attribute fault directly to it.[42] Through the addition of this distinct approach, the evidential burden would shift to the defence, and thus by practical implication to the senior corporate officers, in cases where the corporate conduct is manifestly dishonest.

4. Conclusion

The extension of senior officers' liability for consent and connivance in offences committed by employees or agents under their control or command is both desirable and justified, if not as an extension of the general principles of complicity, by reference to the encouraging and assisting offences contained in the Serious Crime Act 2007. The proposed extension of the identification principle will also serve to increase the scrutiny and accountability of senior officers. Neglect may be justified as a head of liability, albeit not on the basis of an arbitrary distinction between *mala prohibita* and *mala in se* offences, but in accordance with established principles of omissions liability in cases where a clearly defined duty to act on the part of the senior officer can be identified. Given the unique nature of fraud (and other dishonesty offences), and the lacuna in the criminal law where dishonesty cannot or should not be reduced to individuals, the addition of a new kind of corporate liability, where the company's conduct is manifestly dishonest, would complement the parasitic approach to corporate fault attribution characteristic of the identification principle, its proposed extension, and the new failure to prevent offence. The direct attribution of corporate liability can be achieved using the traditional evidential presumptions, and inference of dishonesty, and effected with a simple amendment to the Criminal Practice Directions. Since corporate convictions can be more readily established using this evidential approach, the bite of the current consent and connivance provisions would also be sharpened in their application to senior corporate officers who fail to address fraudulent corporate practice.[43]

[41] A Cronin, *Corporate Criminality and Liability for Fraud* (Routledge, 2018).
[42] ibid.
[43] Fraud Act 2006, s 12.

4

A One-sided Coin? Attributing Agency and Responsibility in Contexts of Coercive Control

VANESSA BETTINSON, VANESSA E MUNRO AND NICOLA WAKE*

In recognition of the role that domestic abuse, and particularly coercive control, can play in pathways to women's offending,[1] the Prison Reform Trust (PRT) proposed a domestic abuse defence, based on section 45 of the Modern Slavery Act (MSA) 2015, during the recent Domestic Abuse Bill debates in England and Wales.[2] Despite the advocacy of experts across the sector,[3] the Government concluded that such a provision was not required. Its reasoning was primarily based upon a perception that the existing defences were capable of ensuring just outcomes that balanced 'recognition of the abuse that has been suffered and the impact that it has had on a victim against the need to ensure that people, wherever possible, do not revert to criminal behaviour.'[4] However, it has been accepted that duress as a defence is often not fit for purpose, both in general and particularly in domestic abuse contexts.[5] Though the Law Commission has considered the ambit of duress repeatedly in the context of homicide, there is little political interest in changing the status quo. A fixation on the applicability of the defence to murder has often eclipsed a much-needed

* Professor Vanessa Bettinson, University of Northumbria, Professor Vanessa E. Munro, University of Warwick, Professor Nicola Wake, University of Northumbria. We would like to thank the reviewers for their constructive thoughts on an earlier draft of this chapter.

[1] Prison Reform Trust, '"There's a reason we're in trouble" Domestic abuse as a driver to women's offending' (2017) Prison Reform Trust; C. Barlow, *Coercion and Women Co-Offenders* (Policy Press, 2016); J Corston, 'The Corston Report: A Report by Baroness Jean Corston of a Review of Women with Particular Vulnerabilities in the Criminal Justice System.' (Home Office, 2007).

[2] Written Evidence submitted by the Prison Reform Trust (DAB05) (2019).

[3] Discussed below.

[4] Hansard, HL, Vol 809, col 2285 (3 February 2021).

[5] J Loveless, 'Domestic Violence, Coercion and Duress' (2010) *Crim LR* 93; S Yeo, 'Resolving gender bias in criminal defences' (1993) 19(11) *Monash University Law Review* 104, 107; BIZ Boland, 'Battered Women Who Act Under Duress' (1994) 28 *New England Law Review* 603.

robust reflection on the appropriateness of the defence requirements when applied to other types of offending.[6]

In this chapter, we underscore the ways in which domestic abuse can, and often does, impact victims' agency and responsibility in respect of criminal behaviour. We argue, contrary to the Government's position, that existing legal mechanisms are insufficient to allow this to be taken appropriately into account and put forward proposals for reform that build upon, and extend the remit of, those embodied in the PRT's unsuccessful legislative intervention.

We are, of course, far from alone in highlighting and seeking to challenge the failures in England and Wales, in existing doctrine and practice, to recognise offenders' experiences of domestic abuse victimisation. Previous critiques have highlighted legal mechanisms that have inappropriately leveraged claims to diminished responsibility by pathologising victims' reactions to meet diagnostic criteria for recognised 'syndromes'.[7] Others have sought (with limited success) to contain episodes of 'violent resistance' by victims within the doctrinal parameters of defences that privilege (masculinist) frames of impulsive aggression and decontextualised 'proportionality'.[8] Recent literature has also argued that the concept of coercive control must be placed within a social entrapment context, particularly in respect of defences.[9] This allows for a more complete approach to understanding the realities facing domestically abused people's 'space for action'[10] and their available options in responding to it. In other work, we have explored these difficulties within existing frameworks for self-defence, loss of control and diminished responsibility in domestic abuse contexts.[11] These concerns continue to inform our analysis, but in this chapter we focus in particular on the question of the adequacy of compulsion-based defences where a background of domestic abuse has coercively shaped, if not determined, the parameters and potential for an offenders' agency.

[6] *Murder, Manslaughter and Infanticide* (Law Com No 304, 2006); *Criminal Law Report on Defences of General Application* (Law Com No 83, 1977); *A New Homicide Act for England and Wales? An Overview* (Law Com No 177, 2005).

[7] D Nicholson and R Sanghvi, 'Battered Women and provocation: the implications of R v Ahluwalia' [1993] *Crim LR* 728; A McColgan, 'In Defence of Battered Women Who Kill' (1993) 13 *OJLS* 508.

[8] S Edwards, 'Coercion or Compulsion – Re-imagining Crimes and Defences' (2016) *Crim LR* 876; A Carline and P Easteal AM, *Shades of Grey – Domestic and Sexual Violence Against Women* (Routledge, 2014).

[9] H Douglas, S Tarrant and J Tolmie, 'Social entrapment evidence: understanding its role in self-defence cases involving intimate partner violence' (2021) 44(1) *University of New South Wales Law Journal* 326; J Tolmie, R Smith, J Short, D Wilson and J Sach, 'Social entrapment: a realistic understanding of the criminal offending of primary victims of IPV' (2018) 2 *New Zealand Law Review* 181, 209–210.

[10] N Sharp-Jeffs, L Kelly and R Klein, 'Long journeys toward freedom: the relationship between coercive control and space for action' (2018) 24(2) *Violence Against Women* 163.

[11] N Wake, 'Battered women, startled householders and psychological self-defence: Anglo-Australian perspectives' (2013) 77(5) *The Journal of Criminal Law* 433. N Wake, '"His Home Is His Castle. And Mine Is a Cage": A New Partial Defence for Primacy Victims Who Kill' (2015) 66 *Northern Ireland Legal Quarterly* 151. V Bettinson, 'Aligning partial defences to murder with the offence of coercive or controlling behaviour' (2019) 83(1) *The Journal of Criminal Law* 71. V Bettinson and N Wake, 'A new self-defence framework for domestic abuse survivors who use violent resistance in response' (2023) online first at onlinelibrary.wiley.com/doi/full/10.1111/1468-2230.12837.

Despite the vast majority of female offending involving non-violent criminality,[12] the availability of defences in these contexts has not attracted the same level of academic or public attention as cases of violent resistance. Moreover, attributions of responsibility often occur at lower levels of the criminal justice process, where there may be less scope for reflective practice, a lack of resource to facilitate that reflection, and an absence of systematic oversight.[13]

With these considerations in mind, in this chapter, we will demonstrate the inadequacy of the defence of duress in domestic abuse cases, reflect on the abolition of martial coercion and consider the limitations of the PRT's proposed defence based on section 45 of the MSA 2015. We will suggest that the solution lies with both law reform, providing a defence for victims of domestic abuse who are compelled to commit crimes as a consequence of coercive control, and a prosecutorial policy favouring non-prosecution where appropriate. Our recommendations in these respects are underpinned by a 'social entrapment' model,[14] which as others have persuasively argued allows more meaningful consideration of the mesh of relational, cultural, social and structural factors framing the offenders' reality of living within an abusive relationship. In so doing, this affords a more detailed and nuanced deliberation of an offender's agency and responsibility for committing a criminal offence.

More specifically, we will advance an entirely novel general defence of coercion by domestic abuse which when successfully raised results in an acquittal. To be found not guilty, the coercer must be personally connected to the defendant and the coercion by domestic abuse must have compelled the defendant to commit the offence charged, in that it denied the defendant fair opportunity to not commit the offence. As with existing coercion defences, this would not apply in the context of murder or attempted murder. Domestic abuse here takes the same definition as in section 1 of the Domestic Abuse Act (DAA) 2021, and inspired by the Domestic Abuse Scotland Act (DASA) 2018, the link between abusive behaviour and coercion is underscored by its having, amongst its purposes, to make victims dependent on or subordinate; to isolate them from friends, relatives or other sources of support; to control, regulate or monitor their day-to-day activities; to deprive them of, or restrict, their freedom of action; or to frighten, humiliate, degrade or punish. What amounts to denial of a fair opportunity not to commit the offence depends on the nature and type of coercion, responses by statutory and voluntary agencies when made aware of the circumstances, and any characteristics or circumstances of the defendant that affected the nature and type of coercion or the agency response to it.

[12] MoJ, 'Statistics on Women and the Criminal Justice System 2019' (2020).

[13] V Bettinson, M Burton and V Munro, 'An Offence We Could All Do With Learning More About: Identifying and Responding to Coercion in Intimate Partner Relationships' *Key Findings Report* (2023) available at wrap.warwick.ac.uk/179870/1/WRAP-identifying-responding-coercion-intimate-partner-relationships-key-findings-23.pdf.

[14] Douglas et al (n 9); J Tolmie et al, 'Social entrapment: a realistic understanding of the criminal offending of primary victims of IPV' (2018); J Ptacek, *Battered Women in the Courtroom: The Power of Judicial Responses* (Northwestern University Press, 1999).

1. Exploring the Problem – Coercive Control as a Pathway into Victim Offending

The frequent presence of domestic abuse victimisation in women's pathways to criminality has been widely documented over many decades.[15] In 2017, the PRT reported that 57 per cent of women in prison in England and Wales had been victims of domestic abuse: a figure that was 'likely to be an underestimate' given well-established barriers to disclosure.[16] Meanwhile, research has revealed that almost four in five women prisoners in Scotland had a significant history of head injury that, in most cases, occurred in the context of domestic abuse, to which they were often subjected over several years.[17]

Though there may not always be a simple or linear causal link, domestic abuse has been identified as a key driver of offending for the 'majority of women in prison'.[18] The nature, severity and circumstances of that offending will obviously vary. It has been suggested that the offending often relates to three offence types. First, 'status' offences in which victims are placed in a precarious position by an abusive partner – for example, in respect of immigration or benefits, or a failure to act to protect vulnerable others.[19] Second, 'consequential' offences in which victims are put into criminality under pressure from partners – for example, drug dealing or prostitution.[20] Third, 'liberation' offences in which victims commit crimes to improve or remove themselves from their abusive situation – such as, acquisitive crimes to mitigate a lack of access to independent finances or acts of violent resistance targeted against partners.[21] There is often overlap between these categorisations – for example, a victim may use violent resistance to protect a child, or they may commit a consequential offence, such as criminal damage, as a by-product of trying to escape from their abusive circumstances. A victim's capacity for 'choice' can be deleteriously eroded by the abuse suffered. Failure to comply with the abuser's demands may be met with a punishment potentially worse than legal consequences, and where the victim complies, the current legal framework affords little consideration of her circumstances.[22]

[15] Corston (n 1).

[16] Prison Reform Trust (n 1); SK Howes, KS Williams and H Wistrich 'Women who kill: why self-defence rarely works for women who kill their abuser' (2021) *Crim LR* 945.

[17] T McMillan et al, 'Associations Between Significant Head Injury and Persisting Disability and Violent Crime in Women in Prison in Scotland, UK: A Cross-Sectional Study' (2021) 8(6) *Lancet Psychiatry* 512.

[18] Prison Reform Trust (n 1).

[19] *Emery* (1993) 14 Cr App R (S.) 394.

[20] Barlow (n 1).

[21] See, in the related context, A Schloenhardt and R Markey-Towler, 'Non-Criminalisation of Victims of Trafficking in Person – Principles, Promises and Perspectives' (2016) 4(1) *Groningen Journal of International Law* 10.

[22] S Vickers and P Wilcox, 'Abuse, Women and the Criminal Justice System' (2011) 85(1) *Criminal Justice Matters* 24.

The UK Government's 'Female Offender Strategy' commits to a reduction in women's incarceration, particularly in respect of those serving short sentences.[23] Despite this Strategy, the All Party Parliamentary Group on Women in the Penal System recently concluded that 'imprisonment compounds the victimisation of women, the majority of whom have experienced violence or abuse prior to prison' and 'most women in prisons do not need to be there'.[24] These findings have been reinforced by the Centre for Women's Justice (CWJ), which has highlighted key failings across the justice process, particularly tied to a lack of professional understanding regarding coercive control and its impacts upon women's offending.[25] For victims of domestic abuse faced with the 'choice' of whether to comply with the abuser's demands or contact the authorities, there is often only one feasible option. In research by Howes *et al*, less than half of the victims of coercive control interviewed had reported their victimisation to police, and those who did were found to receive poor responses leading to future under-reporting. Exploring how such lack of confidence in the protection afforded by the justice system translates to victims' coerced or compelled criminality, Howes et al conclude that charges are being pursued where non-prosecution would be more appropriate, leading 'to women being convicted and serving long sentences that do not appear to be in the public interest'.[26]

Coercive Control, the Erosion of Victim's Agency and Impact Upon Responsibility

The creation of a coercive control offence – under section 76 of the Serious Crime Act (SCA) 2015 – provided an unprecedented opportunity to shift criminal justice logic and practice in England and Wales. It did this by more adequately recognising the experiences of, and harms caused by, abuse in intimate relationships; harms that might include pressure or compulsion upon victims to engage in criminal offending.

The offence recognised that the scale of infringement upon a victims' agency can only be understood by looking at the wider temporal frame in which cycles of control are established, cemented and naturalised.[27] Section 76 achieved this aim by criminalising a range of psychological and emotional injuries that experts had long known to be central to the *modus operandi* of abusive partners, but which had been excluded from a legal regime that prioritised physical and

[23] Ministry of Justice, *Female Offender Strategy* (London: Ministry of Justice, 2018).
[24] All Party Parliamentary Group on Women in the Penal System (APPG, 2022: 1).
[25] Centre for Women's Justice, *Double Standard: Ending the Unjust Criminalisation of Victims of Violence Against Women and Girls* (2022).
[26] Howes et al (n 16).
[27] V Bettinson and C Bishop, 'Is the creation of a discrete offence of coercive control necessary to combat domestic violence? (2015) 66 *Northern Ireland Legal Quarterly* 179.

psychiatric injury.[28] The offence requires a more complex and contextualised framing of the abuse in which patterns of behaviour and the cumulative effects of both micro- and macro- forms of aggression, coercion, control and abuse are made visible.[29] Taking seriously the logic underpinning this offence requires criminal justice (and other) professionals to recognise that victims of domestic abuse can be trapped in a cycle that isolates them from mechanisms of escape or safeguarding, erodes their self-esteem, controls their freedoms, and orchestrates their precarity to state intervention.[30] We do not need to position such victims as 'helpless' to see that they are often entangled in a web of control, with a restricted amount of agency to navigate the persistent background of threat and risk created and orchestrated by the perpetrator. For a consistent criminal law framework, recognition of coercive strategies should extend to the potential impact (both morally and legally) they have upon victims' responsibility for any offending prompted, encouraged, or compelled by abusers.[31]

However, this is not the current position. Recent research has highlighted the unfamiliarity of criminal justice professionals (in England and Wales, and in Scotland) in considering a background of coercive control that led to offending. Participants were largely cognisant of an empirical reality in which many female offenders have been subjected to domestic abuse. Nonetheless, when asked specifically about the potential connections between being a victim of coercive control and committing criminal offences, professionals' answers often lacked recognition of, and confidence regarding, how any such victimisation was to be taken into account.[32] Police officers observed, for example, that 'if they're committing crime because they're being forced to do so, *you'd like to think* that would be massively mitigating'[33] and that 'it's certainly something that we'd identify *if it screams out to us*'.[34] However, they were largely unable to articulate any systematic approach to the processes for identifying and responding to the existence of such abuse. It is not routine practice to proactively determine if there is a background context of abuse; and where such abuse is indicated or

[28] *Chan Fook* [1994] 1 WLR 689; *Dhaliwal* [2006] EWCA Crim 1139; V Munro and S Shah, '*R v Dhaliwal*: reconstructing manslaughter in cases of domestic violence suicide' in C McGlynn, R Hunter and E Rackley (eds), *Feminist Judgments From Theory to Practice* (Hart, 2010).

[29] C Wiener, 'From social construct to legal innovation: the offence of controlling or coercive behaviour in England and Wales' in M McMahon and P McGorrery (eds), *Criminalising Coercive Control* (Springer, 2020).

[30] Home Office, *Domestic Abuse Act Statutory Guidance* (July 2022).

[31] Edwards (n 8); V Bettinson, 'Defending the domestic abuse victim/defendant: Why the Prison Reform Trust's campaign to introduce defences for offending driven by domestic abuse is important' (2022) 102(1) *The Prison Journal* 154.

[32] For further discussion, see Bettinson et al, above (n 13). See also V Munro, V Bettinson and M Burton, 'Coercion, Control and Criminal Responsibility: Exploring Professional Responses to Offending and Suicidality in the Context of Domestically Abusive Relationships' (2023) *Social and Legal Studies*, online first at doi.org/10.1177/09646639231198342.

[33] ibid.

[34] ibid.

disclosed, there is no consistent process for assessing its impact on whether or how to proceed with charging.[35]

We suggest that the solution lies with both law reform, providing a defence for victims of domestic abuse who are compelled to commit crimes as a consequence of coercive control, alongside a prosecutorial policy favouring non-prosecution where appropriate. As noted above, both these recommendations are underpinned by the social entrapment concept.

The Social Entrapment Approach

Before assessing the inadequacy of existing compulsion defences and prosecutorial policy in this context, it is necessary to highlight the new thinking in relation to victims' experiences of coercive control that is facilitated by a social entrapment approach. Whilst the concept of coercive control has been helpful in allowing the experiences of the domestically abused victim to inform the parameters of the offence, it allows only for a partial understanding if it is not located within a broader context of social entrapment.[36] As Tolmie et al explain, this highlights the abusive behaviours by the perpetrator and the systematic patterns of harm that continue when a victim seeks to leave their abusive partner. More specifically, social entrapment, which was originally conceived by Ptacek, consists of three dimensions.[37] First, the social isolation, fear and coercion placed on the victim created by the perpetrator's use of control. The second dimension considers institutional responses to the victim's suffering; and the third, requires an exploration of how the coercive control is exacerbated by the structural inequities arising from factors such as gender, class, race, age and disability. This framework could make a difference to the legal outcomes of the victim of abuse turned offender because, as Tolmie et al argue, it 'focuses on explaining the objective realities of the circumstances in which the primary victims are located at the time of the offending, as opposed to making unwarranted assumptions about those realities or pathologizing but excusing the victim's perspective'.[38] For example, as noted above, Howes et al found that factors affecting disclosure by women experiencing coercive control who had been accused of committing a crime included fear of social service's involvement and children being removed, and concerns that they would not be believed by justice personnel.[39] Other research has demonstrated that experiences of institutional racism mean that BAME victims' experiences of state violence and neglect can compound the violence from their abusive partners.[40]

[35] ibid.
[36] Tolmie et al (n 9).
[37] Ptacek (n 14) 10.
[38] Tolmie et al (n 9) 207.
[39] Howes et al (n 16).
[40] D Wilson, K Cootes, A Mikahere-Hall, J Sherwood, K Berryman and D Jackson, 'Reflecting and learning: A grounded theory on reframing deficit views of young indigenous women and safety'

By mapping and scrutinising previous institutional responses to any attempts by victims to seek help, as well as how the failure of such efforts might have compounded perpetrators' control, a social entrapment lens increases understanding of victims' isolation and compliance.

2. The Inadequacy of Current Defences and the Case for Reform

The Government's insistence, during the passing of the Domestic Abuse Bill, that there was no need for legislative reform to address this issue, since common law already had all the potential at its disposal to secure just outcomes, is not entirely inaccurate. It is certainly true that greater judicial attention to context, and creative and progressive interpretation of existing legal principles around the defence of duress, could seek to redress many of the concerns above.

At its core, to claim duress successfully requires that the defendant genuinely and reasonably believed they had been threatened with death or serious injury;[41] and that, in the face of such threat, they exercised reasonable fortitude given some relevant characteristics.[42] An exclusionary rule has been developed for those who voluntarily place themselves at risk of coercion.[43] This may involve association through joining a criminal organisation or terrorist group, or equally through a lesser association as illustrated in *Heath*.[44] Heath was a drug user who was coerced into collecting a consignment of class B drugs after threats of physical violence were made to him by his drug dealer. The court rejected his appeal against conviction on the basis of duress, reasoning that he had formed a voluntary association with the drug dealer, and ought to have known the risks of mixing with him. This decision could be problematic for a victim of domestic abuse, who once aware that their partner is abusive but remains in the relationship, could be interpreted as forming a voluntary association with them, knowing the risk that they could be further coerced. However, in *Hasan*, (then) Baroness Hale was of the view that such an exemption would not apply where there was a pre-existing relational risk in a domestic abuse case. She observed, in obiter comments, that compulsion to carry out household chores and submit to sexual intercourse 'should not deprive [the battered wife] of the defence of duress if she is obliged by the same threats to herself or her children to commit perjury or shoplift for food'.[45] For Baroness Hale, knowing that you may be subject to

(2019) 1 *Health Care for Women International* 690; Institutional responses towards Black and Ethnic Minorities in England and Wales are outlined in Sisters for Change, *Unequal Regard, Unequal Protection – Public Authority Responses to Violence Against Black and Minority Ethnic Women in England* (2017).

[41] *Hasan* [2005] 4 All ER 685.

[42] *Bowen* [1996] 2 Cr A R 157.

[43] *Sharp* (1987) 3 All ER 103, CA; *Hasan* (n 41).

[44] *Heath* (2000) *Crim LR* 109.

[45] *Hasan* (n 41), [77].

violent threats is not enough to deny a defendant of duress. Instead, the exclusionary rule should apply to voluntary associations where the defendant ought to have foreseen the use of threats to compel them to commit crimes of the same type and gravity that are committed.[46]

More generally, offering 'green shoots' of a wider interpretation, Hale observed in her dissenting judgment in *Hasan* that there had been support for proposals made by the Law Commission to move towards a subjective duress defence.[47] This would ensure that the defendant be judged on the facts as she believed them to be, with the defence available to those who honestly believed that official protection would be ineffective, and where the particular defendant could not reasonably have been expected to resist the threat faced.[48] This approach would be important in the coercive control context, but has not been adopted with the Law Commission's proposals receiving strong criticism and progressing no further.[49]

While creative re-imaginings of judgments in leading duress cases also illustrate the latent potential for more progressive interpretations,[50] subsequent authority post-*Hasan* has evidenced that neither case law nor public policy have 'adapted to the threat posed by domestic abusers who through coercion and compulsion coerce women to commit crimes'.[51] Indeed, critics maintain that, stubbornly embedded in duress doctrine, are a range of principles and presumptions that privilege the threat of physical injury and are informed by partial – and gendered – understandings. This includes what gives rise to a 'good cause for fear', what pressures might 'impel a person to act', what levels of 'reasonable fortitude' are to be expected in the face of coercion, and what would constitute a feasible alternative via recourse to the state for protection.[52] All of this undermines its potential as a defence in the context of domestic abuse, even where the effects of victimisation are undeniable. In particular, the core tenets of duress have trivialised the harms secured through non-physical injury and failed to recognise the deleterious impact of the abuse itself – as well as prior failures by criminal justice or third sector agencies to provide protection – on victims' assessment of reasonable alternatives.

For example, the defendant in *YS*[53] argued that a defence of duress ought to have successfully applied to a number of driving offences she was convicted of.

[46] ibid, [79].

[47] ibid, [68].

[48] *Legislating the Criminal Code: Offences against the Person and General Principles* (Law Com No 218, 1993) para 29.

[49] ibid, para 63; J Horder, 'Occupying the moral high ground? The Law Commission on duress' (1994) *Crim LR* 334.

[50] See S Cowan and V Munro's Re-imagining of the Scots necessity case of *Ruxton v Lang* in 'Scottish Feminist Judgments: (Re)Imagining Law from the Outside In' (Hart, 2020).

[51] S Edwards, '"Demasculinising" the Defence of Self-Defence, the "Householder" Defence and Duress' (2022) *Crim LR* 11, 123.

[52] Loveless (n 5).

[53] *YS v DPP* [2017] EWHC 2839 (Admin).

The incidents occurred when she was dragged into the car by her abusive and intoxicated partner, where he threatened to kill her if she did not drive, and throughout the incident he screamed at her and punched her in the ribs. The harm threshold required to engage duress was met. However, the High Court rejected a first instance direction that required assessment of duress in light of what a reasonable person, not only of the defendant's age and sex but also with a history of domestic abuse, would have done in the circumstances. Instead, the court applied a standard formulation that focussed only on age, sex and any mental or physical condition as relevant characteristics.

In *A*,[54] the issue for the court was whether the defendant had been subject to duress, rather than whether she had exercised appropriate fortitude in resisting it. *A* unsuccessfully appealed against her conviction for perverting the course of justice where she had retracted a complaint of partner rape. The court emphasised that 'the circumstances in which different individuals are subjected to pressure, or perceive that they are under pressure, are virtually infinite' and that 'duress should not and cannot be confused with pressure'.[55] Thus, whilst the court accepted that threats of rape would constitute sufficiently serious injury to be relevant, they were unpersuaded that such threats had been made in this case. Notwithstanding a background of domestic abuse, it was deemed to be 'inconceivable' that the victim – had the threats made by her partner been genuine – would not have told authorities about them at the time.[56] For this reason, the court found it unnecessary to consider any other issues that may have reduced her ability to seek alternative avenues of escape. There are, of course, a myriad of rational reasons why victims of domestic abuse do not disclose abuse,[57] and adopting a social entrapment approach would have better enabled the court to delve into the perpetrator's conduct, the institutional response to the victim's help-seeking and structural inequities such as race, gender, age, socio-economic factors that might further restrict the victim's choices.

Shortly thereafter, returning to the issue of whether reasonable fortitude was exercised by the defendant, in *GAC*,[58] the Court doubled down on the requirement to differentiate pressure from duress through a focus on overbearing the offender's will. The court accepted that experiencing domestic abuse might cause a mental condition relevant to assessing the reasonableness of the accused's response to compulsion. However, it set the threshold extremely high, requiring evidence both of a recognised (battered women) syndrome and for the accused to experience 'total domination' and a will 'overborne by terror'.

Again, taking seriously the concept of social entrapment would have enabled the court in *GAC* to more clearly question the underlying assumption that, between

[54] [2012] EWCA Crim 434.
[55] ibid, [63].
[56] ibid, [66].
[57] Howes et al (n 16).
[58] [2013] EWCA Crim 1472.

incidents, victims of abuse have effective safety options that they elect not to avail themselves of.[59] Whilst the court accepted that the defendant had experienced serious domestic abuse by her ex-partner, it did not appreciate the significance of underwhelming institutional reactions to her previous help-seeking, which further exacerbated the coercive control perpetrated by the abuser. This meant the ways in which domestic abuse progressively and systematically closes down a victims' space for action, including in respect of responsibility for offending, were not fully recognised. Moreover, the extent to which this is achieved both through abusers' direct conduct and by their capitalising upon intersecting personal vulnerabilities and experiences of precarity that impact on victims' experiences of help-seeking was side-lined.[60] The decision illustrates the problematic tendency of the courts to underestimate the scale of barriers to disclosure and the regularity with which victims find engagement with services expose them to additional risk.

The implications of this are also apparent in the most recent case to emerge, notably after the Government had expressed its confidence in the potential for the common law to utilise tools already at its disposal to ensure justice is done. In *Johnson*,[61] the court concluded that an accused could not avail herself of the duress defence, having made false statements to the police decades ago during investigations into murders for which her partner was subsequently convicted. Again, the threshold for invoking a duress defence was deemed to be met as there were recorded incidents of the accused presenting with bruising to her face and neck, being assaulted by her partner whilst pregnant, and requesting alternative safe housing.

However, the Court of Appeal concluded that the defendant had not exercised reasonable fortitude and that her will was not overborne by the abuser, expressing scepticism towards her claims of being in a coercive and controlling relationship. In particular, the court considered she had the opportunity to escape from or avoid any threat posed by her partner or his family, by going to the police after the threats were made or prior to giving her incriminating testimony. This again indicates misconceptions about the real experience of the victim-offender that could have been better addressed through a social entrapment approach. Indeed here, as in *GAC*, an over-simplistic logic prevailed, which equated telling someone of the threat with being able to escape it. It is far from clear that this ever holds, but particularly in a domestic abuse context where restraining orders are broken with regularity, victims often have disappointing experiences with agencies that fail to protect them, and many endure years of grinding abuse that undermine their independence, self-esteem and erode their networks of support.[62]

[59] Douglas et al (n 9).
[60] Sharp-Jeffs et al (n 10).
[61] [2022] EWCA Crim 832.
[62] Douglas et al (n 9). For further discussion of the effects of this on victim suicidality, see S Dangar, V Munro and L Young Andrade, 'Learning Legacies: An Analysis of Domestic Homicide Reviews in Cases of Domestic Abuse Suicide' (2022), available at wrap.warwick.ac.uk/174206/1/

Moreover, the law has now statutorily recognised that ending a relationship does not necessarily end the abuse, and may in fact give rise to an escalation in its severity.[63]

Crucially, then, the legal logic that still prevails places victim-offenders in a double-bind: while prior help-seeking is seen to corroborate the existence of abuse, and potentially its duration and severity, victims' engagement with services (no matter how futile) indicates an awareness of, and willingness to, seek out alternatives, which undermines their claims to compulsion. Thus, the court were able to hold in *Johnson* that the accused's previous requests for assistance established that 'she did not consider that she had no choice – she would have welcomed and accepted police protection – yet she took no steps to secure that help'.[64]

Notwithstanding the Government's assertions to the contrary, the decision in *Johnson* continues a trajectory of case law that fails to accommodate the complex effects of coercive control on victims' agency, and in particular to recognise the uniquely difficult, and often compromised, position in which domestically abused offenders may find themselves.

Other Defence Models: Marital Coercion

The specific issue of coercion in marriage and its connection to a victim's offending was previously recognised in the marital coercion defence. Section 47 of the Criminal Justice Act 1925 allowed a defence where a wife committed a crime (except murder and treason) in her husband's presence, under his coercion.[65] This provision attracted interest in 2013 when the case of Vicky Pryce made news headlines. Pryce sought to rely on the defence in respect of a charge of perverting the course of justice after she had accepted penalty points for speeding, allegedly under pressure to do so from her husband, Chris Huhne MP, who had in fact been the driver.[66] Responding to her attempted use of the defence, commentators highlighted its discriminatory application, echoing the concern raised decades earlier by J. LL.J Edwards that 'it is certainly strange … that the presumption of coercion, never extended to any relationship within the family group other than that of husband and wife.'[67] As a result, the defence was abolished by section 177 of the Anti-Social Behaviour, Crime and Policing Act 2014.[68]

WRAP-learning-legacies-analysis-domestic-homicide-reviews-cases-domestic-abuse-suicide-2023.pdf.

[63] Domestic Abuse Act 2021, s 68 amended s 76 of the 2015 Act; see A Myhill, 'Measuring coercive control: What can we learn from national population surveys? (2015) 21 *Violence Against Women* 355; P Tjaden and N Thoennes, *Extent, nature, and consequences of intimate partner violence: Findings from the National Violence Against Women Survey* (National Institute of Justice, 2000).

[64] [2022] EWCA Crim 832, [51].

[65] J Edwards, 'Compulsion, Coercion and Criminal Responsibility' (1951) 14 *MLR* 297.

[66] BBC News (2013) 'Vicky Pryce and Chris Huhne: Recap of the court case'.

[67] Edwards (n 65).

[68] S Edwards, 'In defence of the defence of marital coercion' (2013) 43 *Family Law* 996.

A simple resurrection of this defence, albeit with the elimination of its discriminatory element and instead an application 'where A and B are personally connected,' as provided by section 2 of the DAA 2021, might on its face seem like an effective way to deal with offenders whose crimes are driven by coercive control. Certainly, a broad interpretation of 'coercion' – not limited to physical force, but instead inclusive of threats of force and moral coercion – was provided first in *Richman and Richman*[69] and later approved in *Shortland.*[70] However, ongoing forms of domestic abuse were not part of the court's discussion, and it is possible that an interpretation that corresponds with Home Office guidance on the offence of controlling and coercive behaviour[71] may cause the judiciary consternation, given their approach to duress. Moreover, the requirement that the offence must be committed within the abuser's presence, despite J. LL.J Edwards view that this was not limited to actual physical presence so long as the husband was 'near enough materially to influence her conduct'[72] would be likely to prove unduly restrictive.[73] Elkington notes that the phrase was not consistently defined, with the cases of *Hughes*[74] and *Connolly*[75] providing conflicting outcomes.[76] In addition, it is clear that the impact upon victims of coercive control occurs beyond the presence of the abuser with dynamics of threat and compliance being ongoing. Furthermore, with the evolution of technology, it is clear that an abuser no longer needs to exert demands and threats in the victim's physical presence, as they are able to track and monitor at all times.[77]

Thus, any attempt to resurrect the marital coercion defence would need to include a requirement that the defendant was acting because of the coercive or controlling behaviour at the time of the offending. Interpreting this in any meaningful way would, moreover, require careful consideration of the circumstances and social entrapment of the victim-offender. In effect, this would necessitate consideration of the extent to which a victim's agency and responsibility for offending was reduced based on an assessment of their realistic options to act, which in turn would bring analysis inevitably into the terrain of a wider duress defence.

[69] [1982] *Crim LR* 506.

[70] [1996] 1 Cr App R 116.

[71] Home Office, *Controlling or Coercive Behaviour in an Intimate or Family relationship. Statutory Guidance Framework* (London, 2015).

[72] Edwards (n 65) 310.

[73] ibid, 310.

[74] (1813) 2 Lew 229.

[75] (1929) 2 Lew 229.

[76] A Elkington, 'Allowing a Defence to Those Who Commit Crime Under Coercive Control' (2021) 86(5) *Journal of Criminal Law* 295.

[77] T Havard and M Lefevre, 'Beyond the power and control wheel: How abusive men manipulate mobile phone technologies to facilitate coercive control' (2020) 4(2) *Journal of Gender-Based Violence* 223.

Other Defence Models: The PRT Proposal/Section 45 of the Modern Slavery Act 2015

As noted above, during the drafting of the DAA 2021, the PRT advocated for reform to create a bespoke statutory defence that, it was argued, would afford more systematic protection to victims of abuse. Under this proposal, those recognised to be victims of domestic abuse would have a defence where they were compelled to commit the offence, that compulsion was attributable to their being a victim of domestic abuse, and a reasonable person in the same situation and having that person's relevant characteristics (including age, sex, and physical or mental illness or disability, and any experience of domestic abuse) might have acted in the same way. Modelled on similar provisions that exist to protect human trafficking victims, under section 45 of the MSA 2015, the proposal was not for unlimited immunity.[78] It was seen as a practical step to strengthen protection, given that concessions to a vulnerable category of defendant had already been accepted in the trafficking context, and (some) parallels in respect of power dynamics, control and coercion could be articulated.[79] It afforded a *prima facie* neat solution in many respects, but lobbying efforts for its inclusion were ultimately unsuccessful. This was a disappointment to many campaigners, and undoubtedly reflected excessive optimism (at best) from the Government regarding the adequacy of the existing common law response. Nonetheless, there were also some pitfalls to a domestic abuse defence modelled on these provisions, and its non-inclusion within the DAA 2021 thereby creates the opportunity for a more ambitious alternative to be developed.

For one thing, the domestic abuse defence proposed by the PRT provided a lower threshold compared with duress, requiring the defendant to have been compelled to commit the offence as a consequence of their situation, not limited to fear of death or serious injury. While in many respects a positive step, this raised the prospect of governmental concern that the defence's scope would be too wide, applying where there had been 'any level of abuse'.[80] In reality, that concern was likely unsubstantiated since merely demonstrating that the defendant was a victim of domestic abuse would not have been sufficient. According to the PRT proposals, it would also have to be proven that the commission of the crime was the consequence of being a victim of domestic abuse *and* a reasonable person in the same situation might have acted in the same way. In this sense, the proposals tread a closer line to existing duress logics; but as noted above, this may be significantly undermining since case law is replete with examples where awareness

[78] Schedule 4 excludes a wide range of offences from the s 45 defence including: common law offences including false imprisonment, murder, manslaughter and perverting the course of justice were excluded, as were various offences under the Offences Against the Person Act 1861, as well as a range of property, public order, criminal damage, firearm, terrorism, and sexual offences.

[79] N Wake, 'Human Trafficking and Modern Day Slavery: When Victims Kill' (2017) *Crim LR* 658.

[80] Hansard, HL, Vol 809, col 2287 (3 February 2021).

of the existence of external help has been interpreted as evidence of the availability of reasonable alternatives. Semblances of freedom or independence that victims might have (for example, access to a mobile phone or opportunities to leave home to go to work) may also be apt to be (mis)construed as undermining claims of compulsion under the proposed reform. It is true that the courts have shown a willingness to consider reasons why a victim of trafficking may not take the opportunity to escape the exploiter in respect of modern slavery provisions. In the case of *N*,[81] for example, relevant facts included having no travel documents, a history of being beaten by traffickers following an earlier escape and having no contact with anyone other than the traffickers.[82] However, the entrapment in domestic abuse cases is likely to be different, and potentially more subtle and systemic. And to the extent that the gold standard protective strategy assumes victims of abuse will seek to leave the relationship,[83] evaluations of reasonable fortitude undertaken in furtherance of the model proposed by the PRT defence may continue to be unduly restrictive.

To transpose a defence designed for human trafficking to domestic abuse cases may also be problematic for strategic and political reasons. The imperatives at stake for the government are different in trafficking and domestic abuse contexts. Indeed, the incentive for legal reform in the trafficking context came primarily from international Treaty obligations.[84] Moreover, prior to the MSA 2015, the CPS already exercised discretion when making a charging determination, which carried the strategic benefit of protecting victims from prosecution who could provide intelligence with which to target organised criminal networks.[85] By contrast, international conventions on domestic abuse are often not concerned, and certainly less categorically so in terms of their demands upon signatories, with victims' responsibility for coerced offending. There has been no consistent approach taken by the CPS in respect of the relevance and significance of compulsion in this context, meaning the implementation of a statutory defence would represent a more radical departure from current practice than was the case in respect of trafficking victims. With concerns raised about potential misuse of the modern slavery provisions,[86] there is likely to be similar anxiety in the context of domestic abuse; and, given the limited applicability of section 45 to more serious forms of offending, it is unclear that there would be appetite to expand the defence in ways that would bring meaningful protection to victims of domestic abuse. The PRT proposals include the list of exclusionary offences in Schedule 4

[81] [2019] EWCA Crim 984.
[82] ibid, [43].
[83] SL Hamby, *Battered Women's Protective Strategies* (OUP, 2014).
[84] See Council of Europe Convention on Action Against Trafficking in Human Beings 2005, Article 26, which requires states not to sanction victim whose crimes had been compelled by their trafficker. This did not create blanket immunity (*N* [2012] EWCA Crim 189).
[85] K Laird, 'Evaluating the Relationship Between Section 45 of the Modern Slavery Act 2015 and the Defence of Duress: An Opportunity Missed?' (2016) *Crim LR* 395.
[86] ibid.

of the MSA 2015 even though many are offences that victims of domestic abuse may be disproportionately prone to commit (including, failures to protect vulnerable family members over whom they have a duty of care). As Edwards notes 'it can hardly be the case that the coerced victim/defendant has any control over the particular offence s/he is compelled to commit, or can be expected to develop a more robust resistance or greater fortitude when being compelled to commit one of the crimes excluded in Schedule 4'.[87]

In addition, excluding some offences from the ambit of one defence creates practical difficulties. Where a victim offender commits more than one offence, for example, it is possible that different provisions (eg, section 45 and duress) may arise for juror consideration in the same trial, despite there being arguably little difference in their moral responsibility.[88] This is apt to cause juror confusion, and may further call into question the wisdom of the list of exceptions to the MSA defence, and by implication the PRT proposals.

Other practical problems with the interpretation and application of section 45 have also arisen. In particular, a lack of clarity regarding where the burden of proof rests has resulted in arguably unnecessary litigation.[89] In *MK; Gega*,[90] for example, each trial judge opted to follow CPS guidelines, which, at the time, articulated that the defendant held an evidential burden of establishing that they were a victim of slavery or exploitation. If the prosecution were unable to prove beyond reasonable doubt that the defendant was not a victim, the defence would be required to prove the remaining elements of the defence on the balance of probabilities. On appeal against conviction, the Court of Appeal disagreed with the CPS guidelines, and confirmed that the defendant merely had an evidential burden in respect of each element of the defence, whilst the prosecution had to disprove each element to the legal standard.[91] The Court of Appeal's judgment was influenced by the fact section 45 contains an objective element, as does duress: 'the objective test is designed to operate against the "twin dangers" that D might easily concoct a false claim and that this may operate to encourage traffickers to continue with their exploitation'.[92] The PRT proposal does not reference the issue of burden of proof, but as it seeks to mirror the section 45 provision, it would likely be approached in the same way. In turn, this may put particular pressure on a restrictive interpretation of criteria grounded in evaluation of reasonable fortitude within the operation of the defence.

[87] Edwards (n 8) 899.

[88] See *Asfaw* (HL, 2008/9) where the prosecution chose one charge to which the defence in Immigration and Asylum Act 1999, s 31, applied, and another similar offence to which the defence did not apply. There are also more general procedural issues regarding which defence applies. A variety of options are available to trafficked victims who offend, including the exercise of CPS discretion, a stay of prosecution, s 45, duress, and/or mitigation in sentencing depending upon the nature of the offence.

[89] S Mennim and N Wake, 'Court of Appeal: Burden of Proof in Trafficking and Modern Slavery Cases: *R v MK; R v Gega* [2018] Crim 667' (2018) 82(4) *Journal of Criminal Law* 282.

[90] [2018] Crim 667.

[91] ibid, [45].

[92] Above n 89.

Though there were clear strategic benefits to the PRT proposals, designed to parallel the modern slavery protections, we are in measured agreement with the government that section 45 does not provide the optimal solution.[93] A bolder vision is required – one capable of addressing the shortcomings of existing interpretations of duress and ensuring a consistent approach across the suite of offences for which victims of abuse might find themselves at risk of prosecution. In theory, the common law could be amenable to more progressive interpretations. However, this would demand a bold rediscovery of underlying principles and ambitious interpretation of the sort that tends to form the exception rather than the norm of judicial engagement, particularly when the policy issues at stake are so contentious. Thus, an alternative provision is needed, which brings fresh opportunities to reflect, in the circumstances of domestic abuse, on present assumptions about objective levels of fortitude, the availability of reasonable alternatives, and the primacy of threats of violence over other forms of circumstantial coercion asserted to be equally if not more harmful to victims.

3. Our Proposed Defence

In this section we introduce our proposed defence of 'coercion by domestic abuse'. It addresses the gap created by judicial interpretations of duress, which place offenders in a double bind whereby previous help sought from the authorities is deemed as evidence of alternative avenues available to the defendant and, as such, demonstrates a lack of reasonable fortitude in responding to the coercion. Moreover, its purpose is to provide a criminal defence aligned with the section 76 SCA offence, which captures the deep and pervasive effects of coercive control. Our recommendations invoke the social entrapment lens advocated by scholars in Australia and New Zealand, allowing – indeed requiring – the court to consider the complex reality of the defendant's circumstances at the time the offence was committed.

'Defence of coercion by domestic abuse'

s. 1 The defence of coercion by domestic abuse can be raised for an offence (excluding murder or attempted murder).

s. 2 D will not be guilty of an offence where D committed the offence under coercion by domestic abuse [as defined in s. 1 Domestic Abuse Act 2021]

(a) The coercer (A) must be personally connected to D [as defined by s. 2 Domestic Abuse Act 2021]; and
(b) The coercer (A) must have subjected D to behaviour which is abusive as defined in s. 3 below; and
(c) That abusive behaviour must have compelled D to commit the offence, in that it denied D the fair opportunity to not commit the offence.

[93] Hansard HL Deb, Domestic Abuse Bill (HL Deb) 10.03.21 1753 Lord Wolfson of Tredegar. See also N Wake, R Arthur, T Crofts and S Lambert, 'Legislative approaches to recognising the vulnerability of young people and preventing their criminalisation' (2021) (PL 2020) *Public Law* 145.

s. 3 The Abusive Behaviour must have or would reasonably be considered by others to have, amongst its purposes:

(a) to make D dependent on or subordinate to A;
(b) to isolate D from friends, relatives or other sources of support;
(c) to control, regulate or monitor D's day-to-day activities;
(d) to deprive D of, or restrict D's, freedom of action; or
(e) to frighten, humiliate, degrade or punish D.

s. 4 In assessing whether D was compelled to commit the offence, in that D was denied fair opportunity to not commit the offence, regard must be had to:

(a) the nature and coercive effects of the domestic abuse perpetrated by A;
(b) the responses by any relevant statutory or voluntary agencies when made aware of any acts of domestic abuse by A towards D; and
(c) any characteristics or circumstances of D that affected the nature and coercive effects of the domestic abuse experienced or response provided to it by any relevant statutory or voluntary agency.

s. 5 Relevant characteristics or circumstances for the purposes of s. 4 (c) include – but need not be limited to – race, age, gender, physical or mental illness or disability, socio-economic status, parental status, sexuality, religion, and immigration status.

s. 6 The defence may be raised by the accused or on his or her behalf, or by the court of its own volition or on hearing submissions from any party deciding that such a defence should be considered by the court.

Unlike the PRT proposals, this defence would extend to most offences barring murder or attempted murder, thereby bringing consistency with the common law defence of duress.[94] Behaviour that is abusive can take any of the forms set out in section 1 of the DAA 2021, but must have at least one of the effects listed in section 3 above, which are taken from the DASA 2018 and intended to provide a clearer articulation of the nexus between abusive behaviour and coercive effect at the centre of our proposal.[95]

Evidence of coercion in a domestic abuse relationship alone would not be sufficient as the coercion must have compelled the defendant to commit the offence. We suggest that compulsion, like causation, need not be singular in its operation. Just as there is no requirement for a defendant to be the sole cause of an outcome so long as they were a significant and operative one,[96] so too there ought not to be a requirement for domestic abuse to be the only reason for the offending where it can be established as a significant and influencing factor which denied the defendant a fair opportunity to exercise an agentic form of resistance. It is well-established that victims of domestic abuse are not 'only' or exclusively victims: they are often required to navigate within the parameters of their abuse, finding strategies to deflect or minimise its harms; and in that

[94] *Howe* (1987) 1 All ER 771; *Gotts* (1992) 2 AC 412.

[95] M Scott, 'The Making of the New "Gold Standard": The Domestic Abuse (Scotland) Act 2018' in M McMahon and P McGorrery (eds), *Criminalising Coercive Control* (Springer, 2020).

[96] *Smith* [1959] 2 QB 35.

process there is an agency that ought neither to be ignored nor seen to count against their claims to having experienced acute coercion and control.

Importantly, our proposed defence does not require 'reasonable fortitude' in the face of a threat. In this respect, it loosens the grip of objective evaluations that have proven impervious to critique within the common law. Unlike the PRT proposals, we do not seek to do so through inclusion of the characteristic of being a victim of domestic abuse within a modified standard, since this risks a narrowly defined understanding of that experience, which is apt to focus once more on individualised and pathologised understandings of the victim. Likewise, we do not do so by hinging reliance on the defence upon the lack of availability of 'evasive alternatives', since this is a context in which availing oneself of such alternatives is fraught with additional risk, and the prospect of achieving the evasion that these alternatives purport to offer is often uncertain. Instead, we suggest that the defence hone in on the question of whether an individual – in the circumstances in which they found themselves – had a 'fair opportunity' to act differently.[97] Section 4 makes it clear that in assessing what would count as fair opportunity not to commit the offence by acting differently, regard must be had to insights brought forward through a social entrapment approach – in particular, this requires deep engagement with the situational and structural reality of the defendant's circumstances rather than abstract insistence on the formal availability of 'rescue'.[98] It is likely that this would need to be supported at trial through the use of extended judicial directions to jurors, akin to those already developed in respect of serious sexual offences, which would be designed to ensure that evaluation of victims' reactions to abuse are not reliant upon myths or stereotypes.

Thus, our use of compulsion connects the coercion as a pathway that denies the defendant's 'fair opportunity' to choose to act differently when abusers coercively control them to participate in offending behaviour. It allows for a more expansive understanding of compulsion: one broad enough to countenance 'the possible offences a victim may have to commit to escape, endure or survive' in an abusive relationship.[99] By removing the 'reasonable fortitude' element found in both duress and section 45 of the MSA, a new way of thinking around responsibility for compelled criminality in domestic abuse contexts is possible. Here, there is not a consideration of whether a reasonable person (with some of the defendant's characteristics) would have done as the defendant did in the circumstances and whether there existed reasonably available evasive actions to avoid criminality. Instead, the driver lies in a deeper understanding of a social entrapment model that accounts for the position of the accused, and the impact of relational, social and structural coercion.[100] Our approach extends beyond an

[97] A Duff, 'Choice, Character and Criminal Liability' (1993) 12(4) *Law and Philosophy* 345.

[98] Tolmie et al, 'Understanding IPV: Why Coercive Control requires and Entrapment Framework' (forthcoming).

[99] Schloenhardt and Markey-Towler (n 21) 21.

[100] M Moore, *Placing Blame: A Theory of the Criminal Law* (OUP, 1997).

assessment simply of the capacities of individuals, to include 'a fundamentally political interpretation of the relationship between individual and state' and a consideration of the role of 'failures of education, socialization, or other external factors'.[101] This matters since, as Lacey underscores, our concern must be not only with what criminal responsibility *is* but also with what work it does in a modern, liberal justice system.[102]

Removing the reasonable fortitude test is, no doubt, likely to bring the criticism that the defence we are proposing is too far reaching.[103] In the context of duress, the Law Commission suggested a reverse burden of proof could be applied should a subjective approach be adopted[104] or the defence extended to all offences.[105] The rationale for departing from the common law approach included difficulty in disproving the defence, the potential for serious criminals to concoct false claims and the serious nature of the offences under consideration.[106] A reverse burden might, however, frustrate the aim of our defence by risking the double victimisation of the victim-offender, particularly given the resources available to the prosecution.[107] Further, the risk of false claims is not limited to compulsion-based defences, yet this has not resulted in a reverse burden in other contexts. For example, the reasonableness or otherwise of D's belief in the need for self-defence is relevant to the question of whether D genuinely held it, but D remains entitled to rely on that belief whether it was mistaken or (if it was mistaken) whether the mistake was a reasonable one to have made.[108] In this respect, a reverse burden requirement should not automatically follow a more subjectivised defence or elements thereof, providing that the parameters of the defence are appropriately drawn.

Our Proposed Changes to Prosecutorial Guidance

Of course, for many victim-offenders who have experienced the coercive effects of domestic abuse in creating their pathway to criminality what might be most appropriate is not for charges to be brought and trials contested through reliance on this statutory defence, but for discretion to be exercised against prosecution from the outset. As has been the case in respect of trafficking victims who commit crime, we recommend that there should be a policy against

[101] N Lacey, 'Socializing the Subject of Criminal Law? Criminal Responsibility and the Purpose of Criminalization' (2016) 99(3) *Marquette Law Review* 541–57, 557.
[102] ibid.
[103] Horder (n 49); W Wilson, 'The Structure of Criminal Defences' (2005) *Crim LR* 108.
[104] Law Com No 304 (n 6); Hale in *Hasan*, [71].
[105] Law Com No 304 (n 6), [6.101]. The Commission also proposed a reverse burden for duress generally in Law Commission, *Legislating the Criminal Code: Offences Against the Person and General Principles*, Law Com No 218, (1993), [3.16]. (See also *Z* [2005] 2 AC 467, [20].).
[106] Law Com No 304 (n 6), [6.101]–[6.111].
[107] See *Woolmington* v *DPP* [1935] AC 462, [481].
[108] Criminal Justice and Immigration Act 2008, s 76(4).

prosecution for victims of domestic abuse where there are good grounds to believe that the offending is caused by it. One approach here would be to apply a rebuttable presumption against prosecuting such a defendant modelled on the position that applies in Scotland to trafficking cases. There, the Lord Advocate's instructions to the Crown Office provide a 'strong presumption against prosecution' where there is 'credible and reliable information' that the accused is 'a victim of trafficking or exploitation; has been compelled to commit the offence' and 'the compulsion is directly attributable to being the victim of human trafficking or exploitation'.[109] Rebuttable presumptions at the point of making a charging decision are unusual in CPS guidance, however, and so instead we recommend an alternative approach that is likely to be more practical and is aligned with recommendations of the CWJ.

More specifically, in the context of the public interest limb, CPS guidance already currently lists, *inter alia*, coercion/compulsion as factors to consider in prosecutorial charging decisions, albeit that evidence collated by the CWJ suggests that in practice this does not occur.[110] We agree with the CWJ's recommendation that the CPS in England and Wales should introduce further guidance in respect of potential victims of domestic violence accused of offending.[111] In addition to improving the clarity of charging decisions in this context, the benefit would be to mandate consideration pre-trial of the circumstances in which the accused has found herself, using the social entrapment approach. Thus, putting to test the question of responsibility would be a deliberate decision, grounded on an evaluation of the actual rather than assumed circumstances of the defendant, instead of an arbitrary outcome of a justice process often propelled by disconnected momentums and discretionary-decision-making.

Guidance that incorporates the social entrapment concept in respect of the public interest limb would apply – as CWJ have suggested – where there is 'contextual evidence'[112] of domestic abuse. It would require the CPS to consider the principles of the social entrapment model described above, allowing an assessment of the individual's actual rather than assumed situation. Specifically, this would involve consideration of the nature of the coercive control perpetrated by the abuser and how this reduced the defendant's capacity for action,[113] as well as the responses of frontline services and what the victim (now defendant) could realistically be expected to do given that previous experience and ongoing threat. Any intersecting inequalities that might affect the nature of the coercive

[109] Crown Office and Procurator Fiscal Service, *Lord Advocate's instructions for non-prosecution of victims of human trafficking* (2022).

[110] 'A suspect is likely to have a much lower level of culpability if the suspect has been compelled, coerced or exploited, particularly if they are the victim of a crime that is linked to their offending.' Crown Prosecution Service, *The Code for Crown Prosecutors* (2018). See also, Centre for Women's Justice (n 25) 54.

[111] Centre for Women's Justice (n 25) 54.

[112] ibid, 54.

[113] See, Sharp-Jeffs (n 10).

control employed, and/or the victim's response to the abusive behaviour or frontline service involvement would also be central to enabling a more holistic evaluation.[114] Guidance would have to be supported by training which teaches prosecutors about coercive control through the social entrapment lens. Such an approach may promote the greater overall pursuit of justice by ensuring that, where the victim-offender is not meriting of prosecution, the abuser who more appropriately holds responsibility can then be identified and held accountable, for example, as an accessory to the crime.[115]

Of course, this would not preclude the need for the statutory defence outlined above to run in parallel with such prosecutorial decision-making. A requirement for 'contextual evidence' of domestic abuse which gives good grounds for believing that the offence was committed under coercion may be necessary here, but it is also clear that there will be many victims who will not be able to provide the kind of corroborative trail of disclosures that might be required. Moreover, many victims will not feel sufficiently empowered to provide disclosures of abuse at a juncture in which they are being processed as offenders, reducing the potential for prosecutors to make informed charging decisions. A substantive defence is thus required to provide protection to those coerced into criminality against whom charges are pursued. What is more, the introduction of such a defence performs an important communicative function in legally recognising the dynamics of power and responsibility in domestic abuse, which can assist in informing investigative and prosecutorial decision-making.

4. Conclusion

It is easier, no doubt, to recognise the invasive effects of coercive control upon victims' autonomy and independence when they are squarely contained by the justice process within a victim position. However, the complexity of that experience does not change when those victims are required, as part of survival in that complex and intricate web of control, to engage in offending. The Domestic Abuse Bill provided an opportunity for the Government to consider the lack of appropriate defences for victims of coercive control compelled to offend. Proposals advanced by the PRT, including those modelled on the compulsion-based section 45 defence, provided a framework for robust debate and reflection on the impact that coercive control has in terms of female offending. Disappointingly, the Government reiterated the view that extant defences, and specifically the common law of duress, could accommodate the circumstances of such domestic abuse victims. As we have demonstrated, however, the duress defence has

[114] Douglas et al (n 9).

[115] Serious Crime Act 2007, s 44; See *Bourne* (1952) 36 Cr App R 125 liability as a secondary party is established even where the principal offender has a defence to the offence charged.

stringent parameters and is severely limited in this context. While the PRT proposals offered a practical and neat solution, the Government were 'not persuaded that the model on which this amendment is based … is either apt or effective with regard to domestic abuse'.[116] Nor entirely are we. There are different political drivers underpinning section 45, the exclusion of offences limits the utility of the defence to domestic abuse, and the reasonable fortitude tests places scrutiny on the victim's apparent options of escape in a context in which leading case law has clearly evidenced that prior attempts to reach out to authorities or other service interactions, however ineffectual, are seen to undermine claims to compulsion.

In this chapter, we have argued for the creation of a bespoke statutory defence, which incorporates contemporary thinking from scholars in Australia and New Zealand about employing a social entrapment lens to defences where the defendant's crime is compelled by domestic abuse. This lens would be used to assess whether the defendant had been denied fair opportunity to conform with the requirements of the law, taking into account the abuse, institutional responses to the abuse and social inequities at play. This substantive defence should sit alongside a mandated focus in early investigative and prosecutorial decision-making around the presence, relevance, and impact of coercive control, with the public interest limb of the prosecutorial code in particular being interpreted through a social entrapment approach.

[116] Hansard, HL, Vol 811, cols 1892–9, 1891 (21 April 2021).

Comment on Chapter 4

Tackling Scourge of Domestic Abuse and Coercive Control as a Driver to Offending

PARAMJIT AHLUWALIA*

A fundamental driving factor in relation to women committing criminal offences is domestic abuse and coercive control.[1] This has been recognised for many decades – from the Corston Report of 2007,[2] to statistics published in 2018 by the Ministry of Justice Female Offender Strategy,[3] citing that at least 57 per cent of women in prison and under community supervision are victims of domestic abuse.

To cut and limit cycles of victimisation and thus the number of female offenders, Bettinson, Munro and Wake contend that legislative and policy reform is needed. In summary, their position is that the solution lies in both law reform, providing a defence for victims of domestic abuse compelled to commit crimes as a consequence of coercive control, alongside a prosecutorial policy that favours non-prosecution where appropriate. Both recommendations are underpinned by the social entrapment model.

I share many of concerns discussed in the proposal chapter. In October 2017, I provided a briefing note (on behalf of the Criminal Bar Association) for the Prison Reform Trust and spoke at a Summit on why duress was 'not working' in relation to cases where victims of domestic abuse and coercive control go on to offend. As part of the briefing, I set out a potential 'seed', utilising the framework

* Barrister at 1 Pump Court Chambers.

[1] Albeit the Domestic Abuse Act 2021, s 1 provides the statutory definition of domestic abuse as including controlling or coercive behaviour, I will use the terminology of coercive control separately as well within this paper.

[2] *A report by Baroness Jean Corston of a Review of Women with Particular Vulnerabilities in the Criminal Justice System* (Home Office, 2007). See para 5, which highlights factors that disproportionately impact female offenders, including: 'relationship problems feature strongly in women's pathways into crime, coercion by men can form a route into criminal activity for some women'.

[3] *Female Offender Strategy* (Ministry of Justice, Cm 9642, 2018). The forward notes that: 'Many experience chaotic lifestyles which are often the product of a life of abuse and trauma; almost 60% of female offenders have experienced domestic abuse.'

within section 45 of the Modern Slavery Act 2015 as a model for a statutory defence for those who have gone on to commit offences, as a result of being victims of domestic abuse. In purest terms, why should victims of domestic abuse not have similar protective mechanism in legislation as victims of trafficking and modern slavery?

Years of work later, with the collaborative (and far more extensive) expertise of individuals such as Katy Swaine Williams, Jenny Earle, Dame Vera Baird KC, Harriet Wistrich, Naima Sakande, and Clare Wade KC, such amendments bore fruit, and were debated within the House of Commons and Lords as proposals for the Domestic Abuse Bill.[4] The Joint Committee on the Draft Domestic Abuse Bill recommended, in June 2019,[5] the Government consider the proposal for a new clause to be added to the Bill to create a statutory defence for women whose offending was driven by their experience of domestic abuse. The Government agreed to consider this proposal,[6] but was of the view that a statutory defence was unnecessary in the light of the existing full and partial defences.[7]

The proposals were tabled by Jess Phillips MP for consideration in the House of Commons, but the amendments were rejected in the Commons. The amendments were then tabled in the House of Lords by Baroness Helena Kennedy, highlighting that 'legislative opportunities don't come around too often [and so] we should seize the moment and align the protections with those given to victims in other legislation'. Baroness Hamwee cited the original 2017 Briefing paper on behalf of the Criminal Bar Association:

> I came across a briefing from the Prison Reform Trust that included a paper from the Criminal Bar Association, written in 2017. It addressed the potential application of duress to domestic abuse and coercion. It quoted the noble and learned Baroness, Lady Hale, in the 2005 case of *Hasan* – as usual, she was in the vanguard – and I cannot do better than to quote her. Although it was obiter, what she said was very clear and relevant: 'I have no difficulties envisaging circumstances in which a person may be coerced to act unlawfully. The battered wife' – we have moved on from that sort of terminology, but this was in 2005 – 'knows very well that she may be compelled to cook the dinner, wash the dishes, iron the shirts and submit to sexual intercourse. That should not deprive her of the defence of duress if she is obliged by the same threats to herself or her children to commit perjury or shoplift food … It is one thing to deny the defence (of duress) to people who choose to become members of illegal organizations, join criminal gangs, or engage with others in drug related criminality. It is another thing

[4] *Domestic Abuse Bill – legal protection for survivors who offend due to domestic abuse* (Written evidence submitted by the Prison Reform Trust, 2019).

[5] Joint Committee on the Draft Domestic Abuse Bill, *Draft Domestic Abuse Bill: First Report of Session 2017–19* (HL Paper 378, HC 2071, 2019), [180].

[6] *Further Government Response to The Report From The Joint Committee on The Draft Domestic Abuse Bill* (CP 214, 2020).

[7] Instead, improved understanding and awareness of domestic abuse throughout the criminal justice system would mean that existing defences would be better able to respond flexibly and proportionately than a narrowly defined statutory defence, to the circumstances of those compelled to commit crimes as a result of domestic abuse.

> to deny it to someone who has quite a different reason for becoming associated with the duressor and then finds it difficult to escape. I do not believe that this limitation on the defence is aimed at battered wives at all, or at others in close personal or family relationships with their duressors and their associates, such as their mothers, brothers and sisters.' These are important amendments, and we support them enthusiastically.[8]

Unfortunately, despite the amendments being passed in the Lords, they were rejected when they went back to the Commons. In the debates,[9] Victoria Atkins referenced defences already potentially available to victims of domestic abuse who commit offences in circumstances where they are in an abusive relationship, namely duress, self-defence and loss of control and diminished responsibility in relation to homicide cases. Sir Robert Neill also resisted the Lords amendments.[10] His view was that the statutory reform would over-engineer a solution, given duress and self-defence already existed. He believed the Judiciary's approach had changed vastly over the years and the statutory reform was not needed, as the courts had shown themselves willing to reflect changes in social conditions and the pressures that exist.

1. Social Entrapment

The social entrapment model employed by the proposal chapter seeks to reflect upon institutional responses to a victim's suffering and how coercive control is exacerbated by the structural inequities arising from factors such as gender, class, race, age and disability. However, the proposal chapter fails to consider that the inequities from race and class (for example) are pervasive throughout the criminal justice system. Why is it appropriate that an accused who has sustained coercive control receive further protections in law, and yet the additional protections are not available to other accused who suffer similar inequities? Why would it be appropriate to limit to one strand of vulnerable victims that are now defendants, as opposed to wholescale application for all individuals within the Criminal Justice System?

Arguably, efforts to eradicate inequities should be more generally focused on all defendants and users of the Criminal Justice System. For example, the Equal Treatment Bench Book highlights:[11]

Religious, cultural and social factors may be relevant. For example:

- In some communities a woman leaving her abusive husband may be at risk of reprisals or even of being killed by her own or her husband's family for bringing 'shame' onto the family or community.

[8] Hansard, HL Vol 810, col 1748 (10 March 2021).
[9] Hansard, HC Vol 692 (15 April 2021).
[10] ibid, cols 536–538.
[11] *Equal Treatment Bench Book* (Judicial College, April 2023 Revision).

- Someone who marries from within their extended family may be particularly vulnerable, lack family support and feel pressured to stay. Speaking little or no English means an abused person may struggle to access support.
- Concern about the impact upon children of moving away from their home, school or community or the loss of a support network for the woman or her children with disabilities or special needs may mean particular hardship, isolation and the possibility that similar support may never be found in the area she moves to.[12]

2. Practical Changes – Policing and DARA Risk Assessment

Post November 2022, police forces have used the Domestic Abuse Risk Assessment (DARA) model to record domestic abuse incidents.[13] DARA replaces the DASH (domestic abuse, stalking and honour-based violence) assessment model previously used. Research by the College of Policing found the DASH model to be inconsistently implemented by police forces on the frontline, with officers prioritising physical violence and injury. The review by the College of Policing concluded that an understanding of coercive control needed to be embedded with a risk led approach, with a revised risk tool for frontline officers emphasizing patterns of abuse behaviour.[14] As a result, the DARA risk assessment tool was introduced.

To have the greatest impact, any proposed reforms need to have real and practical impact upon policing practices. Arguably, the DARA risk assessment tool already covers the first dimension within a social entrapment model in relation to considering whether there has been social isolation, fear and coercion on the victim by the perpetrator's use of control. For example, at question 7,[15] it asks 'how often do you feel isolated or like you have no one to turn to for support?' Other questions also reflect the themes of the first dimension: 'how often does X control your daily activities such as how you dress or how you perform household tasks?' and 'how often does X make you account for where you have been or monitor your phone, email or social media to check up on you?'

I recognise that the second and third dimensions of the social entrapment model – in relation to institutional responses to a victim's suffering and how coercive control is exacerbated by factors such as gender, race, age and disability – are not yet adequately reflected within the DARA risk assessment model. In my

[12] ibid, ch 6, para 66.
[13] *Domestic Abuse Risk Assessment* (College of Policing, 2022).
[14] A Robinson et al, *Risk-led Policing of Domestic Abuse and the DASH Risk Model* (College of Policing, 2016).
[15] *Domestic Abuse Risk Assessment* (College of Policing, 2022).

view, the second and third dimensions as general concepts themselves do not assist in relation to a DARA toolkit for front line police officers, but may be of assistance in terms of Statutory Guidance.

3. Statutory Guidance

The Statutory Guidance Framework for Controlling or Coercive Behaviour was issued under section 77 of the Serious Crime Act 2015 (SCA),[16] as well as Statutory Guidance in relation to Domestic Abuse,[17] post the Domestic Abuse Act 2021.

Rather than invoke legislative reform of the kind proposed, I query if real practical reform can be brought about through updating the Statutory Guidance and ensuring consistent and complete implementation on the ground. In essence, it would be better to use the social entrapment model and lens as a mechanism to enhance and update the existing Statutory Guidance. For example, the Statutory Guidance on controlling or coercive behaviour already sets out the following:

> 35. Victims may face major barriers when leaving a relationship with a perpetrator, or not want to leave at that time. There can be a lack of public and professional understanding around why victims do not "just leave", which can create further stigma around the abuse they are experiencing and be a barrier for victims accessing effective support. Some victims may also have previous experience of not being believed or not having their disclosure taken seriously, or effectively acted on. Victims also stay in the relationship as a means of managing their own risk or risk to others, if they believe that leaving the relationship may pose an increased risk to them, their children and/or their wider family.
>
> 36. When responding to a callout, it is important for police officers to use professional curiosity and look beyond what may be presented to them at the scene, in order to identify any patterns of behaviour. Police officers must always consider the wider context and that there may be other elements of the perpetrator's behaviour, or other forms of abuse being perpetrated, which could amount to controlling or coercive behaviour. To assist with this, responding officers should be informed of any previous reports.[18]

Further the Statutory Guidance sets out the following contextual matters that bear similarities with the social entrapment model:

> Individuals can be the victims of multiple and different abusive behaviours because of the way different characteristics, such as sex, race, ethnicity, disability, gender reassignment, sexual orientation, age, religion or belief can intersect and overlap, along with other factors such as socio-economic position or immigration status. These factors can create additional barriers to accessing services and support if they are not adequately designed to meet a victim's specific needs.

[16] *Controlling or Coercive Behaviour: Statutory Guidance Framework* (Home Office, Updated July 2023).
[17] *Domestic Abuse: Statutory Guidance* (Home Office, Updated April 2023).
[18] *Controlling or Coercive Behaviour: Statutory Guidance Framework* (n 16).

Other factors that can create additional barriers to a victim accessing support are listed below. Others are explored in additional detail in the rest of the Annex:

- … Language and communication – the victim may face specific challenges in communicating the abuse which may hinder them from accessing or seeking assistance.
- … Religious/community/family pressures – the victim may be under pressure from religious or community figures, or members of their extended family, not to leave, or to return if they have left.
- … Race and ethnicity – There is often under-reporting of domestic abuse within minority communities, with many victims reporting that stereotypes and assumptions were made about them coming from 'cultures where VAWG was normalised and accepted' or their experiences of domestic abuse being treated as housing and/or immigration cases by public authorities. Experiences of discrimination and racism may also make a person vulnerable to abuse.
- … Migrant victims may face barriers when attempting to escape domestic abuse relating to their immigration status or lack thereof. Some victims may have no recourse to public funds (NRPF), which can lead to greater dependence on the partner, ex-partner or family. They may also face a greater economic impact of leaving a perpetrator if they are unable to claim benefits or access housing, or if they lose their immigration status by leaving their partner, including destitution and homelessness. Perpetrators may manipulate a victim's immigration status as a tool for controlling or coercive behaviour.[19]

In my view, core principles within the social entrapment model are already encapsulated within the Statutory Guidance to the Domestic Abuse Act 2021,[20] which emphasises that police should adopt a trauma informed and trauma responsive approach including:

> An awareness of protected characteristics (as set out in section 4 of the Equality Act 2010) and any vulnerabilities that may impact on the victim and how they seek support, avoiding making assumptions based on stereotypes;
>
> Barriers that may exist for victims to disclose information or seek support, for example: fear of the perpetrator; fear that they may not be believed; pressures from family or the community – in particular for those victims in rural or closed communities; negative past experiences with the police or services; a desire to make the relationship work; economic barriers; communication difficulties; not wanting to uproot the children or fear that the children will be taken into care; fear of repercussions related to insecure immigration status;
>
> A range of offences may result from a victim's experience of abuse, including: handling stolen goods under threat of violence from a partner; possession of a controlled substance belonging to an abusive partner; use of force against an abusive partner or ex-partner; failure to ensure school attendance for fear of meeting an abusive partner or ex-partner. Agencies should always consider the possible context of domestic abuse

[19] ibid, Annex A.
[20] *Domestic Abuse: Statutory Guidance* (n 17).

> in female offending and emphasise a gender and trauma-responsive approach for supporting women at risk of entering the criminal justice system.[21]

Thus, the principles that stem from the second and third dimensions of the social entrapment model – in relation to institutional responses to a victim's suffering and how coercive control is exacerbated by factors such as gender, race, age and disability – are in fact contained and reflected within the Statutory Guidance on Domestic Abuse. The question ultimately is whether post 2021, such Statutory Guidance framework is being used in practice. And if not, why not?

Given the changes post 2021, such as the DARA risk assessment, the Domestic Abuse Act 2021, and the Statutory Guidance for Domestic Abuse and for coercive and controlling behaviour, it would be of benefit to have objective and empirical research on the outcomes and efficacy of these frameworks (inclusive of setting out failings and gaps). Further, an emphasis needs to be upon regular training to all practitioners, frontline police officers and the Judiciary to ensure awareness of the contents and impact of this Statutory Guidance.

4. Limitations of Duress

YS v DPP demonstrates the limitations of duress at present.[22] This was a case where a woman was dragged into a car and directed to drive by her abusive and violent partner who threatened to kill her if she did not drive. The High Court's judgment was that duress could not be extended. Instead the formulation was to be upon age, sex or mental or physical condition as relevant characteristics. What could not be included as a relevant characteristic was an individual with a history of 'domestic abuse.'

It is difficult to see how the concept of social entrapment itself (without specific legislative reform) would necessarily alter the outcome in *YS v DPP*, or indeed *GAC*.[23] The real issue is that duress and the definitions of 'relevant characteristics' need to be updated post *Hasan*,[24] or as an alternative, there needs to be clear and expanded prosecutorial published guidance to ensure that cases such as *GAC* and *YS v DPP* do not come before the Courts in the first instance. Further, it is of note that both the above decisions were prior to *Challen*,[25] DARA forms, and recent Statutory Guidance on Coercive Control and Domestic Abuse. I would hope that post the changes of 2021 that if a case of *YS v DPP* were arise again, that the individual would not be prosecuted. But the issue remains that the common law needs to advance and update 'relevant characteristics' as more befitting to

[21] ibid, [342].
[22] *YS v DPP* [2017] EWHC 2839 (Admin). NB. the author was the advocate for the appellant in this case.
[23] *GAC* [2013] EWCA Crim 1472.
[24] *Hasan* [2005] 4 All ER 685.
[25] *Challen* [2019] EWCA Crim 916.

2023 and the circumstances faced, perhaps to encapsulate a potential category of 'victims of domestic abuse.'

It is clear (and correctly identified by Sir Robert Neill in Commons debates) that there has been a real clear shift from the Judiciary in understanding the impact of coercive control, as can be seen in *Bowskill and Sansome*[26] where the President of the Queen's Bench Division set out that:

> Sentencing policy has clearly moved on since the comments made in *Spence*, as has the understanding of domestic abuse and controlling and coercive behaviour: see for example, the sentencing guidance given by the Sentencing Council in the 'Overarching principles on domestic abuse' and the fact that an offence (including kidnap) 'occurs in the domestic context, in particular in the context of an abusive personal relationship, will be an aggravating factor; indeed it is likely to be a seriously aggravating factor.'[27]

5. Proposed Legislative Reform – Coercion by Domestic Abuse

The proposed reform of a defence of 'coercion by domestic abuse' would apply to all offences, with the exception of murder or attempted murder. This eradicates the need for complex lists of offences to be excluded, such as within Schedule 4 of the Modern Slavery Act 2015. The essence of the proposed defence would be that the 'abusive behaviour must have compelled D to commit the offence, in that it denied D the fair opportunity to not commit the offence'.

Denial of Fair Opportunity

The proposal includes compulsion where a defendant was denied a fair opportunity to not commit the offence. In the circumstances of *YS v DPP*,[28] already discussed, it is clear that the defence may work – an individual was compelled to drive the vehicle at the behest of a violent partner and denied the fair opportunity to not commit the offence.

However, the difficult aspect of the proposed defence is the likely invocation of 'immediacy' through the back door. Take the example of a woman, X, who is subjected to threats in her house at night, when both she and her partner have consumed a certain level of alcohol. If X picks up a knife and stabs her abusive partner who sustains a serious wound, normally the issue at trial might be that of self-defence. It is unclear if a woman in the position of X would in fact be greater protected by the new proposed defence. Or whether, it would be harder for her to rely on the new proposed defence of coercion by domestic abuse.

[26] *Bowskill and Sansome* [2022] EWCA Crim 1358.
[27] ibid, [22].
[28] *YS v DPP* [2017] EWHC 2839.

The lens of social entrapment provides a more nuanced model to appreciate the true societal context and dynamics faced by a victim of domestic abuse and coercive control. However, it fails to take into account the challenges within a criminal trial of bad character applications against an accused. Enacting wording of 'denied D the fair opportunity to not commit the offence', risks placing undue weight and satellite litigation upon past events that have taken place to the accused. In addition, it is unclear how the authors see the proposed defence interacting with other current defences. For example, in the case of X, how would the defences of self-defence and the defence of 'coercion by domestic abuse' be set out in legal directions to the jury. It is unclear if a Judge would have powers to gatekeep evidence adduced at trial in relation to section 3 of the reform proposal on what would reasonably be considered:

(a) to make D dependent on or subordinate to A;
(b) to isolate D from friends, relatives or other sources of support;
(c) to control, regulate or monitor D's day-to-day activities;
(d) to deprive D of, or restrict D's, freedom of action; or
(e) to frighten, humiliate, degrade or punish D.

It is unclear if in adducing evidence under proposed section 3, an accused would have to comply with the bad character provisions legislation,[29] or if these are to be overridden.

6. Tailored Judicial Directions – Recent Advancements

The proposal authors suggest the use of similar judicial directions akin to those in serious sexual offence trials, where jurors are directed to be cautious against myths and stereotypes. In a first instance re-trial of *Magson*,[30] such judicial directions were provided by the trial judge, using adaptations from the Equal Treatment Bench Book.

The Judicial College Compendium for the last two years has set out examples of directions to be given 'in cases other than ones that involve sexual allegations, for example where a jury may need assistance as to how someone may be conditioned by the experience of long term domestic abuse.'[31] Extracts of potential judicial directions are seen at examples 15 and 16:

> W told you of a troubled relationship in which W had been both verbally and physically abused by D. W told you that whilst they separated at times D would contact W and they would get back together, D always promising that things would

[29] Criminal Justice Act 2003, s 100.
[30] 2021, Birmingham Crown Court.
[31] The Crown Court Compendium (n 8) 20-1.

be different from before. It is the experience of the courts that people who are in an abusive relationship may struggle to extricate themselves from it for a whole range of reasons including fear, lack of resources, family responsibilities, cultural or societal concerns and/or their own conflicting emotions towards their abuser. Further, their capacity to react to events may be compromised or blunted by their lived experience. Where the abuse is not physical but psychological, emotional and/or financial, those subject to it may not even recognise themselves as victims of abuse, particularly where the behaviours develop over time. Whether that is relevant here will depend upon your assessment of the evidence that you have heard. Do not fall into the trap of assessing someone's behaviour by reference to how you think you may or may not have acted or reacted in their position. Put aside any assumptions you may have had and make your judgments in this case based only on the evidence which you have heard, assessing the accounts of D and W within the evidential context and the context of their wider relationship.[32]

In assessing this area of the case you should be careful not to engage in any misguided stereotypical thinking. For example, it would be wrong to think that a partner in a relationship who is assaulted by the other will, on the first occasion that happens, leave and never come back – some may do so, others may forgive and stay and others still may come to be conditioned to endure such behaviour over time. It is common experience that victims of domestic abuse may try and hide what is going on, even from those closest to them. It is common experience that abusive relationships may last for a long time and that victims of abuse may struggle to remove themselves from such a situation. Where the abuse is not physical, but is psychological, emotional and/or financial, those subject to it may not even recognise themselves as victims of abuse, particularly where the behaviours develop over time.

There is no such thing as a typical victim of domestic abuse and no such thing as a typical abuser; domestic abuse can occur irrespective of age, gender and social circumstances.

Whether and to what extent there was domestic abuse taking place in this relationship you will need to determine with care, in accordance with the burden and standard of proof and in the light of all the evidence in the case. I am explaining these points so that you think about them in your deliberations. I am not expressing an opinion. You will of course take account of the arguments presented by the advocates in deciding the extent to which this issue assists you in reaching your conclusions.[33]

The proposal authors are right to contend that more detailed and clear published policy is required in relation to accused who have been subjected to domestic abuse and coercive control. It would be fundamental to the efficacy of any statutory defence proposed to have in tandem a published policy that implements the ethos of that new defence. Given the difficulties of disclosure, perhaps a multi-agency approach is required to be adopted at this stage, to ensure that the Crown Prosecution Service has all material before it prior to making a decision to prosecute. The authors do not go on to consider whether such tailored CPS published guidance would require the abuse of process doctrine to ensure that such guidance

[32] ibid, 20-1, Example 15.
[33] ibid, 20-1, Example 16.

is properly considered and applied. Certainly within the field of modern slavery and trafficking, the abuse of process doctrine has been utilised to ensure proper reviews of a decision to prosecute has taken place.

7. Alcohol, Drugs and Reactive Violence

The social entrapment model is an innovative lens through which to consider the issues currently before the courts in relation to accused who have been subject to coercive control and domestic abuse. However, when looking at cases concerning serious violence and domestic homicide, a large number involve juries having to grapple with other contextual dynamics. These often include:

(i) Alcohol usage and level of intoxication at time of index offence
(ii) Drug usage at time of index offence.
(iii) Reactive violence – bad character and propensity issues in relation to accused.

A difficulty to tackle at trial relates to the interplay between how in law culpability can truly be extinguished where there has been usage of alcohol, drugs or reactive violence. Often the issue for a jury is not the lack of empathy with a survivor of domestic abuse or coercive control, but rather what weighting to afford to this context of coercive control and domestic abuse, in light of other factors such as reactive violence/bad character, and alcohol or drug usage immediately prior to the index offence. These are not easy issues to tackle for juries, prosecutors or courts alike. And it is unclear how the social entrapment model will engage with such difficulties, and the ramifications for those whose lives are affected by alcohol and drug abuse that in turn may well have played a part in the offending behaviour alleged.

8. Conclusion

In conclusion, I broadly support the objectives of the proposal. However, I would urge that given the recent changes with the DARA assessment tools, and post the Statutory Guidance for Domestic Abuse and for Coercive and Controlling Behaviour, that there is a need for empirical research (both qualitative and quantitative) before advancing any legislative reform. The landscape we face as practitioners and academics in the field is changing at a rapid pace – one example being the Judicial Compendiums of 2022 and 2023 highlighting the use of tailored guidance directions to guard against myths and stereotypes in relation to victims of domestic abuse. The emphasis at this juncture in my view should be on consistent and effective implementation and awareness of the Statutory Guidance Frameworks, through training and awareness of all agencies within the Criminal Justice System.

5

Post Appeal Decision-Making: Reforming the Powers of the Criminal Cases Review Commission

LUCY WELSH*

The CCRC was established following recommendations of the Royal Commission on Criminal Justice.[1] That Royal Commission had been established on the same day that the convictions of the Birmingham Six were quashed,[2] and in light of public concerns surrounding a series of miscarriages of justice.[3] The contemporary system of Home Office case review lacked independence, so one recommendation was the creation of an independent body to review suspected miscarriages of justice. The Royal Commission also recommended that the new body should operate independently of the Court of Appeal (CoA) given its investigatory function, with the role of considering 'allegations put to it that a miscarriage of justice may have occurred'.[4]

The CCRC reviews convictions and sentences from magistrates' and Crown courts, and refers them to the CoA when appropriate. The organisation derives all of its powers from the Criminal Appeal Act 1995 (CAA). While the CCRC is generally viewed as a significant improvement on its predecessor,[5] it attracts criticism about the way it uses its powers to decide which cases are referred to the CoA.[6]

* Dr Lucy Welsh, Reader in Criminal Justice, University of Sussex. The empirical research in this article was generously funded by UKRI ESRC, under grant ES/R008515/1. We are grateful to the CCRC for allowing us access to the organisation, and to all project participants. I also thank Jo Wilding and Richard Vogler for their comments on earlier drafts of this chapter.

[1] Royal Commission on Criminal Justice *Report* (CM 2263, 1993).

[2] *McIlkenny and Others* [1992] 2 All ER 417.

[3] See *Hill and others* (1989) *The Times* (20 October); *Maguire* (1992) 94 Cr App R 133.

[4] Royal Commission (n 1) 182.

[5] See, eg, P May. '"Partly excellent, partly abysmal": 20 years of the CCRC' (*The Justice Gap*, 31 March 2017).

[6] M Naughton (ed), *The Criminal Cases Review Commission: Hope for the innocent?* (Palgrave Macmillan, 2012); C Hoyle 'The Challenges for England's Post-Conviction Review Body (2020) 4 *Erasmus Law Review* 33–43.

In 2021, the All-Party Parliamentary Group on Miscarriages of Justice published the report of its inquiry into the CCRC (the Westminster Commission).[7] It recommended reform of the CCRC, and of the tests the organisation applies when considering cases. The Westminster Commission recommendations included that:

(i) the CCRC should relax its approach to finding 'exceptional circumstances' when considering applications;

(ii) the test that the CCRC uses to determine whether a case should be referred to the CoA should be reformed; and

(iii) post-conviction disclosure provisions for prospective appellants should be expanded.

Following the Westminster Commission but also in 2021, several colleagues and I reported our findings about the impact of funding cuts on lawyers who advise clients about making applications to the CCRC.[8] Lawyers' assessments about client eligibility for publicly funded legal assistance are grounded in a 'sufficient benefit' test set out by the Legal Aid Agency, and interpreted by lawyers with reference to the way in which the CCRC conducts its work. Lawyers must consider whether, based on their client's instructions, the case is one that the CCRC could investigate, and whether the case might meet the CCRC's referral criteria.[9] Thus, a prospective client's eligibility for publicly funded advice – acknowledging that many CCRC applicants are in prison and indigent – is dependent on lawyers' perceptions about how the CCRC applies statutory tests for referral, and how it uses its investigatory powers. Our own (and previous) research found that applications involving lawyers had a significantly greater chance of being fully reviewed than those which did not involve lawyers.[10] Uncertainty about tests used by the CCRC has, therefore, an impact on access to justice, because lawyers are required to predict how the CCRC will respond to applications. During the course of our project, we asked lawyers about their perceptions of the CCRC's powers and the statutory provisions. We found that difficulties created for lawyers and their clients by funding cuts were exacerbated by problems surrounding interpretation of the CCRC's tests for 'exceptional circumstances' and for referral, and the limited nature of post-conviction disclosure available to would-be CCRC applicants. Our findings thus provided further reasons to reconsider the statutory powers of the CCRC.

[7] Westminster Commission on Miscarriages of Justice, 'In the Interests of Justice. An inquiry into the Criminal Cases Review Commission' (APPG on Miscarriages of Justice, 2021).

[8] The team consisted of Prof Richard Vogler (Sussex), Dr Amy Clarke (Sussex), Dr Liz McDonnell (Sussex), Dr Susann Wiedlitzka (Auckland) and myself. See R Vogler et al, *The Criminal Cases Review Commission: Legal Aid and Legal Representatives. Final Report* (University of Sussex, 2021).

[9] Legal Aid Agency, *Standard Crime Contract Specification* (Ministry of Justice, 2022), paras 11.19 and 11.20.

[10] J Hodgson and J Horne, *The extent and impact of legal representation on applications to the Criminal Cases Review Commission (CCRC)* (University of Warwick, 2009).

This chapter proceeds by outlining the CCRC's present powers. It then discusses whether change is required and offers recommendations for reform to the test for referring cases, the exceptional circumstances test, and powers to assist with post-conviction disclosure. The recommendations are made by drawing on case law, our data, and by, at times, making comparison with the Scottish CCRC (SCCRC) and New Zealand's CCRC, Te Kāhui Tātari Ture (Te Kāhui).

1. A Brief Explanation of the CCRC's Powers

The CCRC impartially reviews suspected miscarriages of justice, thereby promoting public confidence in the criminal justice system.[11] Reviews are usually instigated on request from the convicted party (or their representative). Applicants seeking review can raise their concerns about their case with the CCRC either by letter setting out the reasons why the applicant believes review is necessary, or by using the CCRC's Easy Read application form. Occasionally, the CoA will ask the CCRC to investigate a case under section 15 of the CAA. Even more occasionally, the CCRC can review a case brought to its attention by another criminal justice agency. There is no time limit on being able to make an application to the CCRC but, before approaching the organisation, applicants are usually expected to have exhausted traditional appeal avenues.[12] If an applicant has not done so, the CCRC is likely to deem an application ineligible for more than a preliminary review and to invite the applicant to consider making an (often out of time) application directly to the CoA. Furthermore, the CCRC cannot refer a case that it considers to be based on grounds that have already been raised at trial or on appeal.[13] Sections 17–21 of the CAA grant the CCRC extensive powers to investigate an applicant's concerns. The CCRC notifies applicants (and their representatives) about the progress of reviews, but – as an inquisitorial body – does not represent any party to the proceedings.

The CCRC refers cases to the CoA when new information (either evidence or points of law) indicates that there is a 'real possibility' the CoA will not uphold the original decision.[14] The CoA is obliged to consider cases referred to it by the CCRC, though under section 14(4A) the subsequent appeal cannot be based on a ground that is unrelated to the CCRC's reason for referral. It is well known that the CCRC's referral rate is low.[15] The CCRC receives approximately 1,500 applications for review each year.[16] To March 2022, the CCRC had received 28,561

[11] Criminal Cases Review Commission (2020) Corporate Plan 2020 to 2023 [online].
[12] CAA, s 13(1)(c).
[13] CAA, s 13(1)(b).
[14] CAA, s 13 (1)(a).
[15] G Maddocks, KC, 'An argument for reforming the Court of Appeal' *Law Society Gazette* (4 November 2019); K Kerrigan, 'Real Possibility or Fat Chance?' in Naughton (n 6).
[16] Vogler et al (n 8); CCRC, 'Annual Report and Accounts 2018/19' (CCRC, 2019).

applications, and referred 788 cases to the CoA (of which 539 appeals were allowed).[17] Hoyle pointed out that in the five years to 2020, around seven per cent of applications received were referred to the CoA.[18] The CCRC, however, asserts that success should not be judged only on the basis of the number of referrals made[19] (especially as a low referral rate may indicate that the criminal process is functioning well). Roberts found that if a case is referred to the CoA, there is an almost 70 per cent chance that a conviction will not be upheld.[20] It should be noted that the appropriate success rate (where success is that a conviction or sentence is not upheld) is not a subject about which there can be an exact science. A 100 per cent success rate would suggest that the CCRC is overly cautious in its decisions to refer only cases they are certain of being overturned, and some commentators argue that a 70 per cent success rate is also too high.[21] The CCRC's own Key Performance Indicators suggested that a success rate of between 60 per cent and 80 per cent is appropriate.[22]

2. Examining Real Possibilities: The Case for Reform

The CCRC will refer a case to the CoA if, after review, it takes the view that there is a 'real possibility' that appellate judges will not uphold the conviction/sentence. In order to judge whether a case crosses this threshold, the CCRC must appraise the ways in which the CoA manages potential miscarriages of justice. As the High Court stated, in the exercise of this function, '[t]he judgment required of the CCRC is unusual, carrying with it the predictive exercise as to the view the CACD might take', yet the test operates as 'an important filter' to ensure that unmeritorious cases do not reach the appellate court, and to uphold the principle of finality.[23] The CoA will overturn a conviction that is 'unsafe'.[24] The meaning of 'unsafe' is not defined in the Criminal Appeal Act 1968, and the courts have shown a desire to retain some flexibility in its interpretation. In *Pearson*, Lord Bingham stated:

> The expression 'unsafe' in section 2(1)(a) of the 1968 Act does not lend itself to precise definition. In some cases unsafety will be obvious, as (for example) where it appears

[17] CCRC 'Facts and Figures' (CCRC, 2022) [online].
[18] Hoyle (n 6).
[19] Criminal Cases Review Commission, *Annual Report and Accounts 2019/20* (HC521, 2020).
[20] S Roberts, 'Post-Conviction Review in England and Wales: Perpetuating and Rectifying Miscarriages of Justice.' in G Lennon et al (eds), *Counter-terrorism, Constitutionalism and Miscarriages of Justice: A Festschrift for Professor Clive Walker* (Hart, 2019) 249–67. The CCRC recently broke their success rate into distinct categories, and indicated that doing so brought their success rate to 55% (L Lee and J Curtis, 'CCRC Update' (Criminal Appeal Lawyers' Association Conference, 19 November 2022)).
[21] M George KC, 'Why blame the CCRC? It's the Court of Appeal that needs to change' (*The Justice Gap*, 19 April 2015); Justice Committee, *Criminal Cases Review Commission Twelfth Report of Session 2014–15* (HC 850, 2015).
[22] Justice Committee (n 21).
[23] *R (Charles) v CCRC* [2017] EWHC 1219 (Admin), [47].
[24] Criminal Appeal Act 1968, s 2.

> that someone other than the appellant committed the crime [...] or where a conviction is shown to be vitiated by serious unfairness [...] Cases however arise in which unsafety is much less obvious: cases in which the court [...] is subject to some lurking doubt or uneasiness whether an injustice has been done (R v Cooper [1969]1 QB 267 at 271). If, on consideration of all the facts and circumstances of the case before it, the court entertains real doubts whether the appellant was guilty [...] the court will consider the conviction unsafe. In these less obvious cases the ultimate decision of the Court of Appeal will very much depend on its assessment of all the facts and circumstances.[25]

While the court was at pains to avoid a comprehensive definition of the meaning of safety, it seems that convictions may be considered unsafe:

- on the basis of new evidence or an error leading to concerns about the defendant's guilt; or
- where there has been procedural irregularity or abuse of process; or
- where there has been serious unfairness in the conduct of the trial (including a breach of the right to a fair trial under Art. 6 European Convention on Human Rights); or
- where there is lurking doubt about the safety of the conviction.[26]

However, even where concerns exist about fairness, a conviction is not automatically rendered unsafe.[27] As Bennathan et al said, '[t]he Court has repeatedly emphasised that there is a single statutory test of unsafety and has shown considerable flexibility in its application.'[28] Thus, asking the CCRC to judge whether there is a 'real possibility' that the CoA would not uphold a conviction requires the CCRC to predict the outcome of whether or not an appellate court will consider the conviction 'unsafe'. The CCRC must also necessarily address guidance that has been issued by the CoA, and issues its own guidance notes on particularly difficult or unclear issues.[29]

The high success rate of referred cases suggests that the CCRC is adept at predicting how the CoA will judge 'safety'. However, the Westminster Commission heard evidence which suggested that the CCRC could and should be bolder in its approach to referring cases to the CoA, and that doing so would increase public confidence in the organisation.[30] While the CCRC should not refer plainly unmeritorious cases, as that would also undermine public confidence and the organisation's credibility, stakeholders clearly feel that the organisation could

[25] *Criminal Cases Review Commission (ex parte Pearson)* [1999] EWHC Admin 452, [10].

[26] J Bennathan KC, R Trowler KC and G Stewart, *Criminal Appeals Handbook* (Bloomsbury Publishing, 2019).

[27] *Togher* [2001] 1 Cr App R 33; *Abdurahman* [2019] EWCA Crim 2239.

[28] Bennathan et al (n 26) 22.

[29] Hoyle (n 6); C Hoyle and M Sato *Reasons to Doubt* (OUP, 2019).

[30] Westminster Commission (n 7).

strike a better balance. The Justice Committee also suggested that the CCRC could be less cautious in referring cases to the CoA.[31] As is discussed below, the SCCRC refers a greater proportion of cases with a lower 'success' rate, yet seems to have maintained credibility with the appellate court.[32]

While the CAA sets the 'real possibility' threshold, it does not define it. Recognising that the test is imprecise, Lord Bingham offered judicial interpretation in *Pearson*, indicating that a real possibility 'is more than an outside chance or a bare possibility, but … may be less than a probability or a likelihood or a racing certainty.'[33] Lawyers who participated in our study suggested that a lack of clarity around the meaning of what amounts to a 'real possibility' inhibited applicant understanding of the CCRC's review process. Furthermore, despite its relevance and importance, there were varying levels of understanding among participants about the 'real possibility' test. When surveyed, nine of the 16 participants expressed concern about the test's clarity. One interview participant (of 45) described it as a fresh evidence test and two interviewees needed prompting about the tests used by the CCRC. A couple of interviewed lawyers thought there was a lack of clarity over the CCRC's interpretation and application of the test, and one interviewee felt that the subjective nature of the test worked to protect the CCRC from criticism:

> It's so vague … it allows them to do what they like. If they don't want to refer, they don't have to refer, because they can say, 'Well, we know … we've applied the predictive test and we've applied it properly' – R27

Newby, in his analysis of historical abuse cases, highlighted that inconsistent applications of the 'real possibility' test have posed a particular challenge for the CCRC.[34] It is, by nature, a predictive test that requires the CCRC to consider how the CoA will view cases in light of the decision in *Pendleton*, which asserted that, in difficult scenarios, appellate judges may consider what the jury might reasonably have done rather than substituting its own view for that of the jury.[35] As Hoyle and Sato said, *Pendleton* seemed to raise the threshold of the test for the CCRC. Consequently '[c]ommissioners may have become more "timid" in

[31] J Robins, 'A watchdog that has lost its teeth' (*Law Society Gazette*, 15 March 2021). This has been a long-standing criticism of the CCRC: C McCartney, and C Walker, 'Criminal Justice and Miscarriages of Justice in England and Wales' in CR Huff and M Killias (eds), *Wrongful Conviction International Perspectives on Miscarriages of Justice* (Temple University Press, 2008) 183–212.

[32] I Callander and F Leverick, 'The Scottish Criminal Cases Review Commission and the Appeal Court at 20 years: relationship status – it's complicated?' (2019) 4 *Juridical Review* 287–307.

[33] *Pearson* (n 25).

[34] M Newby, 'Historical Abuse Cases: Why They Expose the Inadequacy of the Real Possibility Test' in Naughton (n 6).

[35] *Pendleton* [2001] UKHL 66. This decision was discussed at length in *Park* [2020] EWCA Crim 589, their Lordships concluding that the potential impact of fresh evidence on the jury is not of itself determinative of safety. The ultimate question is whether the new information casts doubt on the safety of the conviction.

deciding which cases meet the test for referral'.[36] McCartney and Walker described the CCRC as working to a 'real possibility of a real possibility test', representing a narrow interpretation of powers granted under section 13 of the CAA.[37] Importantly, the test grants the CCRC a power to refer cases, not a duty to do so.[38] This adds another layer of discretion to an imprecise test (the 'real possibility' test), which requires the CCRC to try and predict the outcome of another imprecise test (the safety test).

Participants in our study did not express united views about the propriety of the 'real possibility' test. As one solicitor put it: 'You've got, in my view, the wrong test, and then even if it was the right test, they don't apply it correctly. But when they're applying the wrong test incorrectly, it's just hopeless' (R19). Other participants felt that the test should be changed, pointing to the CCRC's low referral rate. The data generally implied a consensus that the CCRC should (be empowered to) refer more cases to the CoA. Interviewees commonly expressed the view that the test was being applied too conservatively by the CCRC following criticism from the CoA, which they felt had made the organisation 'supine' or 'obsequious'. Participants said, for example:

> The CCRC should be a bit more willing to take a chance on cases, and a bit more willing to incur the displeasure of the CoA – R3
>
> I'm not asking them to lose all sense of perspective, but where there are two choices, to err on the side of generosity – R33

These perceptions had consequences for whether lawyers believed the legal aid threshold of sufficient benefit could be satisfied; the lower the likelihood of referral, the less likely sufficient benefit could be found.[39]

These findings echo those of the Westminster Commission, whose respondents referred to the vague nature of the real possibility test, alongside the way in which it required the CCRC to defer to the CoA.[40] CCRC staff indicated to us that they do not feel inhibited by the real possibility test, and staff seemed to experience a genuine sense of job satisfaction if they found a case with a real possibility of the decision not being upheld. However, the organisation also welcomed reconsideration of the 'real possibility' test.[41] While overly rigid approaches would not increase access to justice, layers of imprecision appear to complicate access for applicants and to undermine the credibility of the justice system.

[36] Hoyle and Sato (n 29) 31.

[37] McCartney and Walker (n 31) 198.

[38] Hoyle and Sato (n 29).

[39] We also recommended that the sufficient benefit test in CCRC casework should be reviewed: Vogler et al (n 8).

[40] Westminster Commission (n 7).

[41] The CCRC welcomed the Westminster Commission's suggestion that the real possibility test be reviewed, but asserted that the test itself is deferential, not CCRC staff. See CCRC, *Response to Report of Westminster Commission on Miscarriages of Justice* (CCRC, 2021) [online].

3. Recommendation: Referring When a Miscarriage of Justice Might (Reasonably) have Occurred

The Royal Commission's proposal that the post-appeal review body should be able to refer a case if, after investigation, 'there were reasons for supposing that a miscarriage of justice might have occurred' should be reconsidered.[42] If the test for referral was that the CCRC felt there was reason to believe a miscarriage of justice might have occurred, this would set a lower threshold than a 'real possibility', making the test less deferential to the CoA. The Royal Commission recommended that the role of the organisation should be to review *potential* miscarriages of justice. This arguably justifies a lower threshold than reviewing whether there is 'real possibility' that the CoA will not uphold the conviction. The Royal Commission did not envisage that the review body would predict outcomes.

As the body established to review potential miscarriages of justice, the threshold for referring a test should arguably be much lower than the point at which a conviction will likely be quashed. This is not the same as suggesting that threadbare cases should be referred to the CoA. As Callander and Leverick suggested, review commissions depend, for their effective operation, on 'the respect of the appeal court'.[43] A new test in the manner originally envisaged by the Royal Commission – that the CCRC refers if it believes a miscarriage of justice might have occurred – does not remove the power or duty of the commission to make a measured judgment about the applications that it receives. It would require the CCRC to examine safety directly and in its own (inquisitorial) view to determine whether a miscarriage of justice might have occurred. By realigning the test with the statutory ground for appeal, the CCRC would need to focus on whether it believes a miscarriage of justice might have occurred in its own view, rather than predicting whether the CoA will find that a miscarriage of justice has occurred. In doing so, the CCRC should become more independent of the CoA, while having a duty only to refer cases which cross the threshold for being a potential miscarriage of justice.

A test which supposes that a miscarriage of justice might have occurred could allow the CCRC to retain a flexible yet less predictive approach. Use of the word 'might' is not necessarily problematic. Indeed, the CoA relies on the concept of 'might' when examining safety. In *Pendleton*, Lord Bingham suggested that the possibility that a conviction might be unsafe was sufficient to overturn a conviction:

> [...] it will usually be wise for the CoA, in a case of any difficulty, to test their own provisional view by asking whether the evidence, if given at the trial, might reasonably

[42] Royal Commission on Criminal Justice (n 1) 183.
[43] Callander and Leverick (n 32) 287.

> have affected the decision of the trial jury to convict. If it might, the conviction must be thought to be unsafe.[44]

Furthermore, in *Lundy*, Lord Kerr stated – in relation to cases where new evidence is presented:

> … the proper test to be applied by an appellate court in deciding whether a verdict is unsafe […] is whether that evidence might reasonably have led to an acquittal.[45]

Since the CoA uses the word 'might' in assessing whether or not a conviction is unsafe, it would not be inappropriate for the CCRC to use the same term. If the term 'might reasonably' is preferred, the test would still be closer to the test envisaged by the Royal Commission than the present test. In fact, the appellate court's inconsistency around using the words 'real possibility' together with 'might' blurs judicial assessment further: 'if there is a real possibility that […] a jury might reasonably have come to a different verdict'.[46] This blur seems to add complexity to the CCRC's work, as finding a balance between 'real possibility' and 'might' is no simple task. That complexity has the potential to hinder comprehension of the test, exacerbating concerns about legitimacy.

Requiring the CCRC to turn its focus away from predicting CoA decision-making and towards investigating possible miscarriages of justice through a direct consideration of safety, could emphasise its inquisitorial purpose to examine the potential basis on which a miscarriage of justice might have occurred. Only if, having conducted that investigation, the CCRC believes that a miscarriage of justice might (reasonably) have occurred, should it refer the case to the CoA for the court to adjudicate whether, as a matter of law, a conviction is unsafe. This would return the CCRC to its core function as an inquisitorial body investigating potential miscarriages of justice and referring cases to the CoA where it believes miscarriages of justice might (reasonably) have occurred. This is congruent with the aims of the CCRC proposed by the Royal Commission. It is also in line with the decision in *Park*,[47] in which the court held that appellate courts must only consider whether or not, in light of the information, the safety of the conviction is in doubt. Allowing the CCRC to focus on safety, as opposed to predicting the CoA view of safety could increase the independence of decision-making at the organisation.

Implementing a change of this nature would require a clear definition of the meaning of 'miscarriage of justice'. A miscarriage of justice could arise from either substantive or procedural injustice, or a combination of the two. Given the practical difficulty in finding innocence,[48] and the due process requirement of the

[44] *Pendleton* (n 35), [19].
[45] *Lundy v The Queen* [2013] UKPC 28, 150.
[46] *McInnes v HM Advocate* [2010] UKSC 7, 30.
[47] [2020] EWCA Crim 589.
[48] H Quirk, 'Identifying Miscarriages of Justice: Why Innocence in the UK is Not the Answer.' (2007) *MLR* 70, 759–77.

criminal process to be able to hold state agencies accountable,[49] it seems right that substantive and procedural injustice could each alone give rise to a potential miscarriage of justice. Wrongful guilty pleas and wrongful acquittals also fall within the definition of a miscarriage of justice, though the latter would be beyond the scope of the CCRC's powers. A miscarriage of justice might reasonably have occurred whenever there is reason to doubt the safety of a conviction.[50] Reasons to doubt the safety of a conviction could arise from a procedural error which casts doubt on the safety of the conviction or sentence; new information or argument that casts doubt on the safety of the jury's conviction; or serious unfairness or procedural irregularity which calls into question the validity of the conviction/sentence.[51]

This approach would follow the Criminal Appeal Act 1968, but make the tests used by the CCRC less deferential to the CoA. A change of this nature could allow the CCRC to '[t]alk the same language as the appeal court and present cases in the same terms'.[52] The test of the SCCRC references the ground of appeal against conviction in its jurisdiction, and is not regarded – by Callander and Leverick at least – to be deferential to the appeal court.[53] A test of this proposed nature means not predicting what the appellate court might do, but considering whether it appears that a miscarriage of justice might (reasonably) have occurred. This is not dissimilar to the test employed by Te Kāhui, which allows a referral to be made on the basis of the interests of justice, considering a number of factors (including an assessment of likely success).[54] New Zealand's Ministry of Justice indicates that Te Kāhui may refer cases when it considers a miscarriage of justice might have occurred.[55]

While there will always be some reliance on how the court has interpreted the meaning of safety to determine whether a miscarriage of justice might have occurred, the focus of recommending a referral where there is reason to suppose a miscarriage of justice might have occurred both sets a lower threshold for the CCRC to apply, and shifts focus more onto the grounds for allowing an appeal and further from predicting the culture of the CoA. The fact that applications must be based on something not previously raised at first instance or on appeal protects the sovereignty of the trial and – where relevant – first appeal court, limiting the possibilities for conflict to occur between the institutions and Article 6. Where

[49] H Packer, 'Two Models of the Criminal Process' (1964) 113(1) *University of Pennsylvania Law Review* 1.

[50] In the case of sentencing, a miscarriage might reasonably have occurred where there are grounds to believe that the sentence imposed is manifestly excessive.

[51] Unfairness in the Article 6 sense, as discussed by Bennathan et al (n 26) and abuse of process.

[52] Callander and Leverick (n 32) 6.

[53] ibid. Although they argue that the CCRC's test also follows the same, but reframed, test as the CoA, I disagree. The CCRC must consider there to be a real possibility that the court will not uphold the conviction, which seems to require another layer: safety may be an issue, but is there a real possibility of the decision not being upheld?

[54] Criminal Cases Review Commission Act 2019, s 17.

[55] Ministry of Justice, *Te Tāhū o te Ture Key Initiatives, Criminal Cases Review Commission* [online].

the CCRC would effectively be working in an inquisitorial way, employing a test with a lower threshold, the CoA will continue to work to the criminal standard in the adversarial process. While referring cases using a lower threshold test than at present might occasionally fruitlessly raise defendant expectations,[56] there are two criminal due process values which ought to counter this issue.

First, it is for the court to determine whether a miscarriage of justice has in fact occurred in law. As the High Court reiterated, 'ultimate responsibility for deciding whether a conviction is safe rests with the CACD'.[57] Amending the threshold test might encourage the CCRC to request that the CoA consider more cases where a problem may exist, such as where there is lurking doubt about the safety of a conviction. Currently so few convictions are quashed on the basis of lurking doubt that it is of little practical use to would-be appellants,[58] meaning that it is an area where challenging the CoA could prove fruitful. As Callander and Leverick argued, referrals based on slightly broader points 'might encourage the court to define particular grounds of appeal more broadly'.[59] Consequently, the CCRC could be more 'mindful of how it could, in turn, try to shape the Court's evolving jurisprudence', especially as the CCRC might currently be inclined to endure flawed jurisprudence and the reluctance of the CoA to overturn jury decision-making.[60] Interestingly, when asked to reflect on power relationships in the post-conviction criminal justice system, CCRC staff did not appear to see themselves as having any influence over the CoA. This seemed to support Hoyle and Sato's argument that the CCRC sets the frames within which decisions are made, yet rarely recognises its power in this regard,[61] and overlooks the contributions that the CCRC has made within the criminal justice system. For example, research into asylum-related cases commissioned by the CCRC identified a systemic problem with the way in which offences relating to passports were being prosecuted,[62] leading to amended prosecutorial and defence practice and providing an example of the way in which the CCRC can influence procedural change. A lacking sense of empowerment to affect change was evidenced in the comments of a focus group participant:

> We have more [power] than applicants, but we are powerless in that we can only interpret the cases in relation to the law, so we have no power to change things. I don't know how better to express that, but I see the power as the people who can actually change the outcomes, and that is entirely with the CoA – R10

[56] *Cleobury* [2012] EWCA Crim 17, 22; Callander and Leverick (n 32).
[57] *R (on the application of Cleeland) v Criminal Cases Review Commission* [2022] EWCA Civ 5, [10]; *R v Noye* [2011] EWCA Crim 650.
[58] L Welsh et al, *Sanders and Young's Criminal Justice*, 5th edn (OUP, 2021).
[59] Callander and Leverick (n 32) 8.
[60] Hoyle (n 6) 37.
[61] Hoyle and Sato (n 29).
[62] M Sato et al, 'Wrongful Convictions of Refugees and Asylum Seekers: Responses by the Criminal Cases Review Commission' (2017) *Crim LR* 106.

Lowering the threshold for referral might remind the CCRC that although it may be required to defer to the CoA to an extent, 'it is not powerless to act in the difficult cases that cause disquiet', and may make it more inclined to act in cases where there is 'lurking doubt' about the safety of the conviction.[63]

Second, amending the threshold test could go some way to improving the integrity of the process and public confidence in the criminal justice system, which was a core reason for the CCRC's establishment. The aim of the recommendation is to shift from a test that is layered higher than unsafe – a real possibility that the conviction will not be upheld because it is unsafe – to a threshold which is lower than the Court will address; there might (reasonably) have been a miscarriage of justice meaning that the conviction might be unsafe. This would be congruent with the threshold test used in other parts of the justice system, such as the permission stage in an application for Judicial Review, which leaves final determination of substantive issues to the High Court. The original recommendation for the CCRC's establishment – to consider allegations put to it that a miscarriage of justice may have occurred – implies that it is not for CCRC to try to predict whether a conviction is likely to be quashed, but to investigate whether there might have been a miscarriage of justice.

4. Reviewing Exceptional Circumstances: The Case for Reform

The conditions for review and referral are subject to the provision in section 13(2); in the absence of an appeal or new evidence/argument, the CCRC can only make a referral to the CoA where it considers there are exceptional circumstances that justify doing so. Exceptional circumstances are likely to be argued when an applicant has not exhausted their formal appeal opportunities before making an application to the CCRC; so-called 'no appeal' cases.[64] Exceptional circumstances are not defined in the CAA, although the CCRC has developed a casework policy that allows 'considerable discretion' to CCRC staff making decisions about the existence of exceptional circumstances.[65] The existence of a 'real possibility' does not, of itself, amount to an 'exceptional circumstance'. CCRC casework staff can make recommendations about exceptional circumstances, and decisions are ultimately made by Commissioners. This seemed to result in 'some variability among screening commissioners' in how they processed no appeal cases.[66]

[63] Hoyle (n 6) 43.
[64] J Hodgson et al, *The Criminal Cases Review Commission. Last resort or first appeal?* (University of Warwick, 2018); Hoyle and Sato (n 29).
[65] Hoyle and Sato (n 29) 52.
[66] ibid.

Following Horne's finding that the CCRC tended to take an inconsistent approach to the meaning of exceptional circumstances,[67] Hodgson et al conducted a review of the way that the CCRC interprets the exceptional circumstances provisions.[68] Their research, and that conducted by Hoyle and Sato, found that although the CCRC has improved the consistency with which it approaches no appeal cases since 2016, it has also taken a more restrictive view of what amounts to exceptional circumstances.[69] There still remained, however, some inconsistency in casework screening decisions.[70] The CCRC believes that it should not usurp usual appeal processes,[71] but it has also indicated in its evidence to the Westminster Commission that more checks and balances were introduced into its system of dealing with no appeal cases.[72]

Very few people who have their applications rejected for lack of exceptional circumstances proceed to lodge an application with the CoA,[73] a situation made more difficult by the short time limit placed on lodging an application for leave to appeal.[74] As Hodgson et al said, those applicants 'are in danger of falling through the criminal justice system's safety net',[75] especially given the difficulties of finding a lawyer willing to examine the case in light of cuts to legal aid.[76]

In line with the Westminster Commission, our study revealed that participants generally agreed that it was appropriate to have an exceptionality test to prevent appellate bodies being overwhelmed with applications.[77] However, some criticised the test in practice, stating that the meaning of 'exceptional circumstances' was unclear and that the bar for exceptionality was too high, agreeing with Hodgson et al's finding that the CCRC tends to interpret the exceptional circumstances test narrowly. Participants who had managed to persuade the CCRC to review on an exceptional circumstance basis had usually done so on the grounds of obtaining documents. One participant, however, felt that even in those cases the bar was set too high, explaining that 'even then, they will often say your reason is based on speculation' (R35). Several participants at both survey and interview stages were unclear about the meaning of exceptional circumstances.[78] These findings

[67] J Horne, *A plea of convenience: an examination of the guilty plea in England & Wales* (PhD thesis, University of Warwick, 2016).

[68] Hodgson et al (n 64).

[69] ibid; Hoyle and Sato (n 29).

[70] Hoyle (n 6).

[71] CCRC, *Casework Policy on Exceptional Circumstances in 'No Appeal' cases* (2020) [online].

[72] Westminster Commission (n 7).

[73] Hodgson et al (n 64).

[74] Section 18 of the Criminal Appeal Act 1968 places a 28-day time limit (from the original finding) for seeking leave to appeal to the CoA.

[75] Hodgson et al (n 64) 28.

[76] ibid; Vogler et al (n 8).

[77] Westminster Commission (n 7) 37–38.

[78] Hodgson et al (n 64) also suggested that lawyers were uncertain about the application of exceptional circumstances when advising clients about their eligibility for case review at the CCRC.

demonstrated the consequences of ambiguity in narrow tests, with further negative consequences for peoples' ability to access legal advice.

One of our key findings was that lawyers can make a significant contribution to the CCRC by filtering unmeritorious – especially unmeritorious no appeal – cases. In these circumstances, it is concerning that in the small number of cases where lawyers considered that exceptional circumstances existed, they felt that the CCRC was unlikely to conduct a full case review. Some participants suggested that no appeal cases were too quickly rebuffed, such as the participant quoted below:

> I had one, in particular, […] where it did stick in the craw a bit that, having done a huge amount of work preparing it […], they just went, 'Yeah, you've had no appeal move along.' And I feel that client was short changed […] It feels like they don't want to investigate no appeal cases […] and it's very easy for them to say, 'Well go to the Court of Appeal' – R30

As with the 'real possibility' test, respondents suggested that opaqueness around 'exceptional circumstances' meant the test was difficult for applicants to understand. Hodgson et al found that nearly 80 per cent of applicants either failed to answer the question about exceptional circumstances, or offered circumstances that were specifically excluded from CCRC guidance, including lack of legal representation.[79] The same research further found that the CCRC seemed to place undue weight on the possibility of an applicant lodging an appeal in person to remedy this issue.[80] When we conducted file reviews, we found that many unrepresented applicants seemingly failed to understand that they must either have had an appeal rejected, or an exceptional circumstance justifying the absence of an appeal, in order for the CCRC to review the case. A handful of applicants' submissions that we reviewed tried to persuade the CCRC that inability to access legal advice was an exceptional circumstance. In focus groups with CCRC staff, some participants indicated that increasing numbers of applicants had attempted to argue exceptional circumstances existed because they were unable to get legal assistance. Focus group participant two explained:

> We normally won't say what is exceptional circumstances, but an inability to get Legal Aid is one of the few things we have specifically listed because on our budget and with our resources we can't deal with hundreds of millions of pounds worth of cuts ourselves. We cannot say that lack of Legal Aid is exceptional circumstances because we would be overwhelmed.

While it was clear to lawyers and CCRC staff that lack of legal advice *would not* amount to exceptional circumstances, there remained a lack of clarity about what *would* be regarded exceptional circumstances. We found (during quantitative data analysis) that applications with the outcome 'Recommend no

[79] ibid.
[80] ibid.

exceptional circumstances' increased slightly after 2012. This might suggest that more speculative applications began being made around 2012, when the CCRC introduced its Easy Read form. Some interview participants implied that the problems faced by CCRC applicants who have not previously applied to the CoA and/or considering renewing their application to appeal to the full court[81] were exacerbated by the complexity of CoA processes and tests, especially for unrepresented appellants. These included restrictions imposed by the loss of time rule,[82] funding for first-time appeals and renewals, and problems understanding the CoA's requirements (among applicants and some lawyers). For example, lawyer R34 said:

> What's even worse is the people who write us who haven't exhausted their first appeal, but they couldn't even get there. I find the proceedings of the CoA quite complex. It's going to be really difficult for someone to pursue that, and then obviously, if they're then writing to the CCRC having not appealed, they're even more likely to get their case rejected.

Evidence from our interviews with lawyers indicated that firms were increasingly unlikely to take on work pro bono for potential applicants to ascertain whether exceptional circumstances (or grounds for review) existed, in the vague hope of future remuneration if successful. This suggested that (prospective) applicants are less likely to be able to access advice about exceptional circumstances, increasing the likelihood /frequency with which the CCRC receives unmeritorious applications. The Westminster Commission also recommended that the CCRC take a broader approach to exceptional circumstances. While the CCRC agreed to review this, it is not yet clear whether there has been a review and/or a change of procedure. Problems with understanding 'exceptional circumstances' appear linked to inability to seek legal advice to sift meritorious cases. Greater clarity around the exceptional circumstances test might alleviate some of these issues.

5. Recommendation: Introducing an Interests of Justice Provision for Exceptional Circumstances

'Exceptional circumstances' should include an interests of justice provision. Flexibility needs to be retained while ensuring that the CCRC is not inundated with unmeritorious applications. Combining an interest of justice test with a less

[81] Two participants suggested that easier and better funding to renew an application for leave to appeal at Court, would reduce the CCRC's caseload because appropriate cases could be better redirected there instead of to the CCRC.

[82] Criminal Appeal Act 1968, s 29.

predictive test for referral could assist in this area. The SCCRC also operates with an interests of justice test (though when considering referral), so the existence of a similar test is not in principle objectionable.[83]

A test similar to that used by Te Kāhui could be adopted. Te Kāhui refers cases based on a multifactorial analysis of the interests of justice. A similar multifactorial test could be used to consider exceptional circumstances. This could allow the CCRC to find exceptional circumstances taking into account:

- Whether appeal rights have been exercised and the difficulty involved in doing so (especially in relation to out of time appeals).
- The extent to which issues raised have previously been argued or considered.
- The prospects of the issues raised indicating that a miscarriage of justice might reasonably have occurred.
- Any other matter the CCRC considers relevant.

Amending the statutory wording to allow the CCRC to find exceptional circumstances wherever it appears to be in the interests of justice to do so might soften the CCRC's approach to such cases by broadening the circumstances that can be taken into consideration. It would enable applicants to frame requests for review around factors highlighted by statute, rather than being wholly reliant on CCRC casework policies. This could increase clarity and transparency of processes surrounding no appeal cases, limiting unmeritorious applications while allowing stronger applications to be framed around statutory provisions.

6. Post Appeal Disclosure: The Case for Reform

The CCRC's determination about whether a 'real possibility' for referral exists is influenced by the nature of applicants' representations, and material discovered as a result of the issues raised in the application. As Hoyle pointed out, '[m]ost applicants, even those with legal representation, do not have access to all the records from the trial, and so the first stage of any review is to collate and analyse relevant material for the investigation'.[84] The CCRC may also uncover, of its own volition during the course of investigation, new information upon which referrals could be based. Key, then, to referral decision-making is access to information about the case, especially given the requirement for something not previously raised upon which a referral might be based. Non-disclosure of scientific or other forensic evidence can be especially problematic, as the infamous cases of Judith Ward,[85]

[83] Callander and Leverick (n 32).
[84] Hoyle (n 6) 39.
[85] *Ward* [1993] 2 All ER 577.

Stefan Kiszko, the Birmingham Six, Maguire Seven, Guildford Four, and – recently – the near miss for Liam Allan illustrate.[86] As McCartney and Shorter stated, 'problems with police/prosecution disclosure of evidence, (and lack thereof), are an enduring feature of criminal justice crises, with many famous miscarriages of justice having non-disclosure of evidence at their heart'.[87]

Disclosure problems are no historical artefact, and expert witnesses are themselves concerned about the sustainability and quality of work that they can conduct for the defence under legal aid payment schemes.[88] As McCartney and Shorter said '[i]t is widely acknowledged that effective pre-trial disclosure is presently far from assured, making an effective appellate system vital'.[89] Furthermore, scientific opinions evolve over time, meaning that the something new which the CCRC requires could be found in a re-examination of evidence. Moreover, simple disclosure failings (not necessarily involving scientific evidence) continue to result in the wrongful imprisonment of people.[90] Despite these problems, practices of post-conviction disclosure remain under-scrutinised, and McCartney and Shorter highlighted a concerning level of inconsistent practices regarding what should be retained by police forces, what can be disclosed, and when. These failings occurred despite guidance on retention of materials contained within the Criminal Procedure and Investigations Act 1996, and guidance issued by the National Police Chiefs Council.[91] Statutory and professional guidance each specifically refer to retaining materials to assist an investigation being conducted by the CCRC.

Another of our significant findings was that lawyers faced problems obtaining evidence, or examining gaps in existing evidence, especially since the decision in *Nunn*, in which the court ruled that the duty of disclosure post-conviction is more limited than the duty during proceedings.[92] The CCRC recently observed that case files are being destroyed by state agencies increasingly early, creating potential problems with their investigations.[93] These problems exist despite prosecutorial guidance which acknowledges that there is a duty to consider disclosure where material surfaces which may case doubt on the safety of a conviction.[94]

[86] T Smith, 'The "near miss" of Liam Allan: Critical problems in police disclosure, investigation culture, and the resourcing of criminal justice' (2018) *Crim LR* 711–31.

[87] C McCartney and L Shorter, 'Exacerbating Injustice: Post-conviction disclosure in England and Wales' (2019) 59 *International Journal of Law, Crime and Justice* 1.

[88] L Welsh and A Clarke, 'United by cuts: Exploring the symmetry between how lawyers and expert witnesses experience funding cuts' (2022) *Amicus Curiae* 3.

[89] McCartney and Shorter (n 87) 2.

[90] ibid.

[91] ibid.

[92] [2014] UKSC 37. For discussion see C McCartney and N Speechless, 'The Supreme Court, post-conviction disclosure and "fishing expeditions": *R (Nunn) v Chief Constable of Suffolk Constabulary & Anor* [2014] UKSC 37' (2015) 19(2) *International Journal of Evidence & Proof* 120–26; H Greenwood and D Eady, 'Re-evaluating post-conviction disclosure: A case for "better late than never"' (2019) 59 *International Journal of Law, Crime and Justice* 100328.

[93] Lee and Curtis (n 20).

[94] McCartney and Shorter (n 87).

However, to obtain post-conviction disclosure, applicants must demonstrate that evidence has come to light that casts doubt on the safety of conviction (subject to a good reason not to disclose proviso), and that there is a real prospect that further enquiry will uncover information which might affect the safety of the conviction.[95] Where *Nunn* was mentioned during the course of our study, lawyers suggested that the law was being incorrectly interpreted to justify withholding evidence. Participants were concerned that the police and CPS were overly obstructive when considering the propriety of post-conviction disclosure. Similarly, McCartney and Shorter described lawyers expressing concerns about decreased co-operation with disclosure requests *since Nunn*, depicting access to post-conviction disclosure as 'a lottery'.[96] Given the powers of the CCRC to compel disclosure by public bodies under section 17 of the CAA, there is scope for the CCRC to remedy this problem (to an extent).

The CCRC's ability to disclose information is governed by the provisions in section 23 of the CAA. Subject to some exceptions, the CCRC is prohibited from disclosing information obtained during the exercise of its functions. Non-compliance with section 23 amounts to a criminal offence. Public bodies may, under section 25 CAA, notify the CCRC that disclosure cannot be made without their consent. Section 24 of the CAA allows, however, the CCRC discretion to disclose information. The comments in *ex parte Hickey* also guide the CCRC in its decision-making around disclosure:

> The guiding principle should always be that sufficient disclosure should be given to enable the petitioner properly to present his best case. That can only be done if he adequately appreciates the nature and extent of the evidence elicited from the [...] enquiries.[97]

According to its casework policy, the CCRC considers that disclosure of material to applicants (or their representatives) is generally justifiable under subsections 24(e) or (f). These subsections refer to reports made by the CCRC and work done in the CCRC's exercise of its functions. The CCRC's casework policy on disclosure states that:

> [a]s a general rule, all material which supports the decision for referral or non-referral together with any further information that may assist the applicant in making his best case will be disclosed.[98]

The CCRC thus retains broad discretion about what to disclose to applicants and their representatives, and their powers under sections 17–19 of the CAA increase the likelihood of the CCRC being able to access information that applicants and

[95] *Nunn* (n 92), [33].
[96] McCartney and Shorter (n 87) 7.
[97] *Secretary of State for the home department, ex parte Hickey (No 2)* [1995] 1 All ER 490, 501.
[98] CCRC, *Casework Policy. Disclosure by the CCRC* (2021) [online] 11.

their representatives cannot access. The casework policy takes – in principle – a generous approach to disclosure according to the facts of each case. It seems, therefore, that the CCRC is potentially in a position to assist applicants and their representatives with post-conviction disclosure issues. McCartney and Shorter nonetheless argued that 'the (resource stretched) CCRC has demonstrated reluctance to seek further testing of materials [...] Indeed, the CCRC has come under sustained criticism, with a growing lack of confidence in the CCRC to carry out diligent investigations ....'[99] Greenwood and Eady argued that the decision in *Nunn* can only be accepted if – among other things – the CCRC operates as 'an effective safety net for disputed disclosure requests',[100] yet it appears that both restrictive statutory provisions and resourcing issues exacerbate problems with post-conviction disclosure. Pragmatic restrictions, such as resource issues, operate alongside restrictive statutory provisions to limit access to (post-)appeal systems and appear together to damage the appearance of legitimacy in the criminal process.

Applicants (and their lawyers) are in a difficult situation. They struggle to obtain information that could uncover a real possibility for referral, and this might weaken the strength of submissions that can be made. While the CCRC does not require supporting material to be present at the point of application, and their role is not to obtain information so that others can conduct their own investigations, unsupported assertions are more difficult to evaluate than evidentially supported ones. This could hamper the assessment of case strength in relation to referral criteria. Unless either applicants make a very strong case about information that they cannot access in support of that application, or the CCRC is persuaded to obtain information of its own volition, the chances of a case being referred as a result of new evidence appear – according to lawyers we interviewed, and to McCartney and Shorter[101] – to be diminished following *Nunn*. As McCartney and Shorter said, '[c]onvicted persons who are deemed to have insufficient grounds for appeal may thus be denied access to the material that could provide those grounds'.[102]

During focus groups, CCRC staff demonstrated an appreciation of the disclosure difficulties faced by lawyers preparing cases for CCRC submission. If lawyers and the CCRC could better negotiate around disclosure, this could also mitigate lawyers' funding difficulties and allow earlier, and perhaps more thorough, decisions to be made about the potential sufficient benefit attached to publicly funded cases. It would, however, require review of the CCRC's disclosure obligations under sections 23–25 CAA. While the CCRC is an inquisitorial body that has to also consider the interests of various stakeholders, amending and clarifying the

[99] McCartney and Shorter (n 87) 7.
[100] Greenwood and Eady (n 92).
[101] McCartney and Shorter (n 87).
[102] ibid, 8.

law in this area could be beneficial for all parties, and may help mitigate the deleterious effects of changes to legal aid funding. In light of increased concerns around disclosure, there is a case for reforming the ability of the CCRC and lawyers to work more collaboratively in relation to post-appeal disclosure. It is incongruous that police forces may retain and re-examine materials when they consider a wrongful acquittal has occurred,[103] yet the defence are not afforded the same opportunities in the event of suspected wrongful convictions. While it would be impractical to expect the police to retain files in all cases for an indefinite period of time, research indicates that retention practices are inconsistent,[104] suggesting that a revised formalised mechanism for disclosure would be beneficial to those seeking to have their case reviewed, and therefore to the perceived legitimacy of the criminal process.

7. Recommendation: A Four Tier Disclosure Process

While some restrictions on disclosure might be necessary in the context of the sensitive nature of information examined by the CCRC,[105] disclosure provisions could also be amended. The CCRC indicated it was not opposed to the Law Commission reviewing 'the CoA's test and issues around post-conviction disclosure', though it is concerned about being able to conduct potentially sensitive investigations in an unfettered manner.[106] Scotland provides for post-conviction disclosure using a statutory regime found in section 133 of the Criminal Justice and Licensing (Scotland) Act 2010. This provision requires disclosure at the conclusion of proceedings where appeal proceedings have been instigated, and section 135 allows an appellant to apply for further disclosure from the prosecutor.[107] Drawing on those provisions, I suggest a four-stage statutory process for post-conviction disclosure.

1. A provision that enables the appellant to request disclosure directly from the police or CPS. In doing so, the applicant should explain why the material is requested, putting the police and CPS on notice of a potential appeal and/or CCRC review. If disclosure is refused, the applicant could move to stage 2.
2. If the CCRC considers the application to be potentially meritorious, provisions could enable the CCRC to specifically request the materials considered potentially capable of undermining the safety of the conviction. The CCRC could be required to disclose the material where it is of assistance to the

[103] See, eg, H Siddique, 'Brighton "babes in the wood" killer Russell Bishop jailed for life' *The Guardian* (11 December 2018).
[104] McCartney and Shorter (n 87).
[105] See also Westminster Commission (n 7).
[106] CCRC (n 41).
[107] McCartney and Shorter (n 87).

applicant's case, subject to certain exceptions. This provision would not undermine the CCRC's inquisitorial nature by assisting the defence, but would speak to its role as an investigatory body while also retaining their ability to withhold sensitive material, or that which is subject to Public Interest Immunity, for example.

3. Where there continues to be non-disclosure (by the police/CPS/other first instance investigatory body) or where the information requested has been destroyed, non-disclosure or destruction of material could provide an automatic ground of appeal because it provides reason to suppose a miscarriage of justice might (reasonably) have occurred.
4. An overall interests of justice test which allows for (non-)disclosure where appropriate, but the CCRC should be expected to detail reasons for non-disclosure where it is considered necessary.

Additionally, provisions should enable applicants to trigger stages two, three, and four as an issue for exceptional circumstances. This would involve introducing a new aspect to the CCRC application process; a procedure whereby applicants have not previously tried to appeal but the failure is related to disclosure issues. This might go some way to remedy the problem identified by McCartney and Shorter, in which 'reliance on the "safety net" disregards the fact that individuals who have not had a first appeal are ineligible for case review by the CCRC (their first appeal may require post-conviction disclosure) …'.[108]

There exist examples of cases in which non-disclosure of materials remains a cause for concern, yet the cases have been rejected by the CCRC and/or on appeal. Robins's analysis of the case of Eddie Gilfoyle,[109] based on accounts of police officers that lines of enquiry were not pursued, and where police initially withheld interview notes, highlights that problems with disclosure may hinder case reviews. Eventually an investigative editor from *The Times* was able to obtain interview notes via a Freedom of Information request, but the CCRC refused to refer the case (for a second time) in 2016. The notes may have been easier to obtain using the proposed disclosure scheme, and, in light of their disclosure, a lower threshold for referral might have assisted Gilfoyle.

Robins also pointed to the case of Omar Benguit, whose ability to pursue an appeal has been 'significantly hindered by the absence of court transcripts and other paperwork'.[110] In the case against Danny Major – a former police officer accused of a serious assault – the police failed to disclose CCTV evidence which was only uncovered following an inquiry, and the withholding of forensic evidence from the jury has been a long running problem in the Jeremy Bamber case.[111]

[108] ibid, 9.
[109] J Robins, *Guilty Until Proven Innocent* (Biteback Publishing, 2018).
[110] ibid, 104.
[111] ibid.

Bamber's case goes further and provides us with an example that not only relates to disclosure but also connects to the present operation of the 'real possibility' test. Bamber has made multiple applications to the CCRC, most recently seeking his third appeal in 2021 (with the assistance of experienced appellate lawyers). In 2012, Bamber judicially reviewed the CCRC's decision not to refer his case. Although the application was unsuccessful, Sir John Thomas noted that the claimant's arguments were attractive.[112] The then President of the King's Bench Division concluded that the views reached by the CCRC were ones that it was open to them to make, ie, they were not irrational or unlawful. That conclusion was based on the CCRC's two stage interpretation of the admission of further evidence:

> first, is there a real possibility that the evidence would be received by the Court of Appeal, and secondly, if so is there a real possibility that the court would conclude that it might have affected the decision to convict?[113]

In this case, the CCRC acknowledged that the first stage could be satisfied, but came to the view that the second stage could not be passed. It should be noted that in the more recent case of *Cleeland*, a different two stage test was said to be appropriately applied. Although the first stage was whether there was a real possibility that the court would accept the fresh evidence, the second stage was whether the court 'in the light of it would consider the conviction unsafe'.[114] If the test that the CCRC applied to Bamber's case was less predictive, it might have come to a different conclusion. If we accept that the CCRC were correct to believe that the CoA would accept the new evidence, applying a lower threshold test of whether, as a result, there might (reasonably) have been a miscarriage of justice, might have led to a different conclusion at initial case review, which would have avoided (impliedly meritorious, given the then President's comments) reconsideration of the case by the High Court. Furthermore, the application of a different test in *Cleeland* could be said to betray inconsistent application of the real possibility test. We know, however, that the High Court will be slow to intervene in CCRC decision-making where the organisation has come to a defensible and not irrational view.[115] Therefore, while the bar is set high at Judicial Review because its function is not to consider the correctness of the CCRC's decision, it seems that the predictive layers that the CCRC is presently required to address may hinder potentially

[112] *R (on the application of Bamber v Criminal Cases Review Commission* [2012] EWHC 3768 (Admin).
[113] ibid, [16].
[114] Curiously, in the more recent case of *Cleeland* (n 57), [12], a different two stage test was said to be appropriately applied. Although the first stage was whether there was a real possibility that the court would accept the fresh evidence, the second stage was whether the court 'in the light of it would consider the conviction unsafe'. Here the court seemed to omit repetition of the real possibility element from the second limb of the test. Unfortunately, the rest of the judgment is silent on whether that omission was deliberate or meaningless. If it was not a meaningless omission, the application of a different test in Cleeland might be said to betray inconsistent application of the real possibility test.
[115] *Charles* (n 23).

meritorious cases, resulting in time consuming and costly (sometimes multiple) applications for Judicial Review (as has occurred in both *Bamber* and *Cleeland*).

Each of the cases discussed above have undergone several stages of review by the appellate courts and CCRC, yet the process by which information has been obtained has been slow, piecemeal, and halting.[116] Each time new information is discovered, applicants and their representatives have to produce more information and ever stronger arguments to have the cases considered for review, and to the reach the high standard for referral of presenting a 'real possibility' of the decisions not being upheld. A process which sets out much clearer obligations for disclosing documents and information of concern, with clear consequences for failure to disclose (the automatic grounds of appeal) might avoid delay, avoid duplication of work, and allow miscarriages of justice to be properly identified and analysed in a much more efficient manner.

8. Contextual Considerations

During our study, we uncovered numerous instances where applicants' problems obtaining funding for legal advice were exacerbated by tests the CCRC is obliged to use. As Hoyle said, 'the challenge for any post-conviction review process must be to balance the principle of finality and deference to the jury's decision with opportunities for rigorous post-conviction review'.[117] The above recommendations aim to improve opportunities for rigorous review yet leave the CCRC with considerable discretion. Given increased concern about the ability of people to access legal assistance in relation to suspected miscarriages of justice, the CCRC should adopt the same approach as the SCCRC, which 'believes, as a rule, that the interests of justice are better served by correcting substantial injustice than through an overly rigid application of the principle of finality'.[118] Even if the core issues lie with the CoA, resources, declining availability of representation, etc, the perception of the test used by the CCRC is important if the organisation is to retain legitimacy. Presently, layers of questionable clarity create layers of predictive guesswork, causing problems with accessibility, and with public perceptions of the justice system. Given that the CCRC was established following crises of confidence in the justice system resulting from high profile miscarriages of justice, upholding perceptions of trust and legitimacy are of crucial importance for the viability of this organisation.

Commentators might suggest that lowering the threshold at which a referral should be made could cause a backlash from the CoA, if it believes that 'too many' unmeritorious cases are being referred. This fear has not materialised for

[116] Robins (n 109).
[117] Hoyle (n 6) 34.
[118] Callander and Leverick (n 32).

the SCCRC, whose test arguably tracks more concretely onto that jurisdictional ground of appeal so it may not materialise in England and Wales. The SCCRC has a lower 'success rate' than the CCRC, but still has a mutually respectful relationship with appellate court.[119] Callander and Leverick describe the relationship between the SCCRC and the appellate court as one of 'healthy independence'.[120] While, given the nature of the work it does, the CCRC will always be required to have regard to the decisions of the CoA, the key is to make its tests less deferential to that court, hence the recommendation to implement broader tests for exceptional circumstances, and for referral. As the CCRC is described as 'somewhat risk averse',[121] implementing broader tests would be helpful to those cases that are perhaps more complex, of wider concern, or sit at the borderline of safety. While there is a need to avoid delaying the passage of meritorious cases, and a risk that lowering the threshold for referral will create more work for CCRC and possibly more applications for Judicial Review from disappointed applicants, these are resourcing issues that should be considered separately from primary concerns about whether the statutory tests and legal guidance are working effectively. The cases discussed above provide examples where ineffective practices challenge the very legitimacy of the CCRC and the effectiveness of the criminal process more broadly is called into question. As Crawford and Hucklesby said, compliance is directly impacted by perceptions and experiences of legitimacy.[122] As things stand, Eddie Guilfoyle's family believe the 'CCRC simply won't stand up to the Court of Appeal'.[123] If, therefore, provisions can be enacted to improve people's perceptions of legitimacy, better resourcing should follow for the integrity of the criminal process.

The final point to consider is whether changing the tests in the ways described would actually effect change. Many of the issues discussed in this chapter might be addressed by shifting cultural and organisational paradigms, or frames.[124] Organisational cultures in legal professions are arguably entrenched.[125] While the CCRC has shown itself willing to consider research findings and adapt practices accordingly, insufficient change has been achieved in terms of practical outcomes for referral rates and perceptions of the CCRC among practitioners. As such, I suggest that a more forceful approach to change – amendment to legal provisions themselves – is required to affect the type of changes needed to address evident concerns about legitimacy and effectiveness. Changes of this nature may also make the CCRC feel less powerless and more willing to send cases that cause disquiet or raise broader concern to the CoA, and provide an opportunity for the CCRC to

[119] ibid.
[120] ibid, 20.
[121] Hoyle (n 6) 41.
[122] A Crawford and A Hucklesby (eds), *Legitimacy and Compliance in Criminal Justice* (Routledge, 2012).
[123] Robins (n 109) 137.
[124] ibid; Hoyle and Sato (n 29).
[125] E Cooke, 'The Working Culture of Legal Aid Lawyers: Developing a "Shared Orientation Model"' (2022) 31(5) *Social & Legal Studies* 704–24.

redouble its efforts to address inconsistency (though some inconsistency is likely to be inevitable). As Hoyle said, the CCRC's 'decision-making demonstrates that the surround is not static. It shifts according to wider social and political changes beyond the institution', suggesting that change is possible. Thus, amending the legislation might encourage a shift in decision-making at the CCRC by altering the context in which decisions are made.[126]

9. Conclusion

Currently, lawyers are required to predict outcomes for funding as the CCRC is required to assess exceptional circumstances and to predict a real possibility of the conviction not being upheld. These issues had consequences for how lawyers interpreted their delegated powers to assess eligibility for funding, creating uncertainty about client suitability for legal assistance. This potentially increases the number of (unmeritorious) applications received by the CCRC, having an impact on its overall caseload and an impact on resources for meritorious applications. Hoyle correctly stated that the CCRC is 'required to consider how the Court will respond to a referral, [so] its decision-making is inextricably linked to the test subsequently applied by the Court',[127] and this will always be the case. However, granting the CCRC powers to act in the broader interests of justice and to disclose more material, combined with a less predictive test for referral could go some way to improving access to justice in an area of practice that has suffered greatly at the mercy of austerity.

The recommendations for reform set out in this chapter – especially in relation to the real possibility test – serve several purposes. Reducing the predictive nature of the test for referral might move the CoA to adjust its own practices, while sitting better with the CCRC's inquisitorial role. Aligning the test for referral more with the original recommendation of the Runciman Commission could also align it further with the test for safety set out in the Criminal Appeal Act 1968 and mean that the English and Welsh CCRC adopts similar approaches to the SCCRC and Te Kāhui. Additionally, these proposed reforms could make it easier for applicants to obtain legal advice (itself a filter for merit) while also promoting greater public confidence in appellate processes. The proposed reforms may or may not lower the CCRC's 'success' rates, and might increase the number of referrals in which convictions are upheld, with possible costs implications. However, public perception of the criminal process is important from due process perspectives, and the possible (yet unpredictable) costs implications may be neutralised by a reduction in multiple and/or unmeritorious applications to the CCRC and for Judicial Review.

[126] Hoyle (n 6) 41.
[127] ibid, 35.

Comment on Chapter 5

Reforming the Powers of the Criminal Cases Review Commission

JOHN CURTIS AND MILES TRENT*

As representatives of the CCRC, we were delighted to be invited to attend the conference on which this collection is based and to contribute to the plenary sessions. Similarly, we are pleased to provide this response chapter. This builds on a longstanding collaboration between the CCRC and academics: one that the CCRC is proud of, and which is overseen by the CCRC's dedicated Research Committee.[1]

The work of the team from the University of Sussex, led by Dr Welsh, highlighted the impact of drastic cuts to legal aid both in terms of reducing access to justice and causing a corresponding increase in the CCRC's workload. In addition to facilitating the Sussex research, the CCRC met with Lord Bellamy KC (Chair of the Independent Review of Criminal Legal Aid, 2020–2021) to explain its concerns and provided written submissions to the government urging an immediate uplift in fees and a reduction in bureaucracy surrounding payments to legal representatives. The CCRC recognises that legal representatives do incredibly valuable work and the ability to secure professional representation is fundamental to a properly functioning justice system.

To acknowledge a few more valuable academic contributions, detailed research by Professor Carolyn Hoyle and Dr Mai Sato assisted in making improvements to the CCRC's casework process, with their work reporting on the effect of policy changes that were already underway, making informed observations and publishing an incisive account of the CCRC's working practices.[2] Malcolm

* John Curtis is In-House Counsel at the CCRC and Miles Trent is a Senior Case Review Manager.

[1] The CCRC's Research Committee was established in 2015 and seeks to stimulate independent academic research into subjects of benefit to the CCRC and the wider criminal justice system. See further: ccrc.gov.uk/ccrc-research. We also endorse the observations of the new Lord Chief Justice, Lady Justice Carr, on the importance of legal academics: '"Delicate Plants", "Loose Cannons" or "A Marriage of True Minds"? The Role of Academic Literature in Judicial Decision-Making' (Harris Society Annual Lecture, 17 May 2023).

[2] C Hoyle and M Sato, *Reasons to Doubt* (OUP, 2019).

Birdling's doctoral thesis supported the creation of a CCRC in New Zealand,[3] and Jaqueline Hodgson's research[4] together with the CCRC's own expertise has prompted work on accessibility and the development of 'easy-read' application forms in appeals to the Crown Court – and now to the Court of Appeal Criminal Division.

In recent years, the CCRC has invested more in outreach work and in discussions with stakeholders. It also welcomed the 2021 report of the All-Party Parliamentary Group (APPG) on Miscarriages of Justice.[5] Members of the CCRC and its staff attended the APPG's evidence sessions, gave extensive evidence and answered questions on a wide range of issues. The CCRC provided a full response to the Westminster Commission's recommendations, embracing many and explaining why it disagreed with others.[6]

At the time of writing this response, the Law Commission has published its 'Criminal Appeals: Issues Paper'.[7] The Paper runs to some 160 pages: it highlights matters that are perceived as problematic and will serve to facilitate discussion, submissions and a formal consultation process on reform. It includes what we regard as a detailed and balanced chapter on the role of the CCRC and the application of the statutory test for a reference. The CCRC has engaged in preliminary discussions with the Law Commission and will actively participate in the next stages of that process. To some extent then, this chapter foreshadows the CCRC's response to the Law Commission, but it also engages with Welsh's observations on the statutory test for CCRC references, explains the CCRC's application of 'exceptional circumstances' (in both of its statutory contexts[8]) and the concerns regarding post-conviction disclosure.

As Welsh notes, since inception the CCRC has had its critics and, as a particularly useful 2012 collection of essays demonstrates,[9] many of the current criticisms and concerns are not new. Just as we observed in 2012, there is much more that can be said in the CCRC's favour, in terms both of its contribution to correcting miscarriages of justices and the improvements it has made to its own working

[3] M Birdling, *Correction of Miscarriages of Justice in New Zealand and England* (University of Oxford Doctoral Thesis, 2012).

[4] See ccrc.gov.uk/ccrc-research.

[5] Westminster Commission on Miscarriages of Justice, *In the Interest of Justice: An Inquiry into the Criminal Cases Review Commission* (APPG on Miscarriages of Justice, 2021).

[6] See ccrc.gov.uk/news/ccrc-releases-official-response-to-the-westminster-commission-report/.

[7] Law Commission, *Criminal Appeals: Issues Paper* (2023).

[8] Criminal Appeal Act 1995, s 13(2), modifying s 13(1)(c) to permit references in exceptional circumstances where there has been no appeal. Section 13(2) also permits references where, contrary to the usual requirement in s 13(1)(b)(i), there is nothing new by way of evidence or legal argument. In each case there must still be a 'real possibility' that the conviction will be quashed. We discuss this in more detail later.

[9] In preparing this chapter, we were struck by the ongoing relevance of a collection of essays published in a dedicated edition of the Solicitors Journal: *Wrongly Accused: Who is Responsible for Investigating Miscarriages of Justice?* (Solicitors Journal, 2012). The edition was compiled in conjunction with the Justice Gap, contained a foreword by Mr Justice Sweeney, and included contributions by Michael Mansfield KC, Campbell Malone, and a former CCRC commissioner, David Jessel.

practices. The CCRC's reflective and ongoing commitment to improvement is integral to its operation; we have seen waiting times reduce and communications with applicants and stakeholders improve. In 2012, in his contribution to the volume of essays, Alastair MacGregor QC, then Deputy Chair of the CCRC, described the combination of reflective practice and our passion for our work in the following terms:

> Throughout its existence the Commission has been engaged in an almost constant process of self-analysis, self-improvement and reform. None of its critics is more committed to remedying miscarriages of justice or to optimising the process for doing so.

Another statement that MacGregor made in 2012 contains a characteristic combination of modesty and spirited flourish. In the interests of having both properly informed discussions and readerships, MacGregor invited critics to respond to a challenge, saying:

> The Commission makes no claim to perfection. It does, however, suggest that those who express concerns about its role and performance should first acknowledge its considerable achievements.

Those words still chime today. At the time of writing,[10] 819[11] cases have been referred to the appellate courts; and of the 792 of those which have been decided by the courts to date, 557 appeals have been allowed. Each one of those successful appeals will have had a profound impact on the individuals concerned and their families. The miscarriages of justice include Mahmood Mattan,[12] Derek Bentley,[13] Barry George,[14] Sean Hodgson,[15] Sam Hallam,[16] Alexander Blackman (Marine A),[17] Sally Clark,[18] Angela Cannings,[19] Andrew Malkinson,[20] and over 60 Post Office convictions arising from the Horizon computer scandal;[21] as well as many less well known but equally deserving cases. As noted by Welsh, the CCRC has also assisted many victims of trafficking and modern slavery. Other cases include those affected by the activities of undercover police officers,[22] the Shrewsbury pickets,[23] Winston Trew,[24] and other victims of racist and corrupt

[10] August 2023.
[11] See ccrc.gov.uk/facts-figures/.
[12] *R v Mattan*, unreported *The Times* (5 March 1998).
[13] *R v Derek William Bentely (deceased)* [1998] EWCA Crim 2516.
[14] *R v Barry George* [2007] EWCA Crim 2722.
[15] *R v Robert Graham Hodgson (also known as Sean Hodgson)* [2009] EWCA Crim 490.
[16] *R v Sam Hallam* [2012] EWCA Crim 1158.
[17] *R v Alexander Wayne Blackman* [2017] EWCA Crim 190.
[18] *R v Clark* [2000] EWCA Crim 54.
[19] *R v Angela Cannings* [2004] EWCA Crim 1.
[20] *R v Andrew Malkinson* [2023] EWCA Crim 954.
[21] See ccrc.gov.uk/postofficecases/. See also *R v Josephine Hamilton & Others* [2021] EWCA Crim 577.
[22] *R v Warren & Others* [2021] EWCA Crim 413.
[23] *R v Christie & Others* [2019] Crim 2474.
[24] *R v Martin McCauley* [2014] NICA 60.

police misconduct from the 1970s. In Northern Ireland, convictions from the Troubles have been overturned including those of Martin McCauley ('the hayshed shooting'), Danny Morrison and others,[25] and Michael Devine.[26]

Through CCRC references we have also been able to shape law reform or bring about clarification in areas including the standards expected from expert witnesses in cases involving scientific analysis and medical opinion; the application of modern standards of fairness; safeguards around disclosure; the effects of police misconduct; defendants with mental health conditions; those who have been wrongly advised on the state of the law; and miscalculations in sentencing (recently including time to be served following periods on remand or on tagged bail).

We say this because it seems essential when debating reform to bear in mind the good which the CCRC has been able to do under the present system. But we turn now to some of the recurrent points of challenge.

1. The 'Real Possibility' Test

The CCRC notes the critical comments made by some practitioners and set out in Welsh's chapter. These are couched in general terms and surround the nature of the 'real possibility' test and its application. Unfortunately, the quotations do not permit us to know which cases the practitioners have in mind, and that inhibits discussion. As Professor Hoyle and Dr Sato noted, few critics have ever stepped into the CCRC's workspace and there is a consequent lack of empirical evidence to support such assertions. Although perception is important, some of the comments may have been made by those who were not fully aware of the extent of the reviews on which they are commenting or who have not had sight of the detailed decision document (the Statement of Reasons) for the cases in question – although as we later comment, it may well be that the Commission should be allowed to make some such Statements publicly available, precisely in order to facilitate informed debate. One researcher who did undertake detailed analysis of our files, Dr Steve Heaton, commented to the Justice Select Committee as follows:

> The question of whether the test has been applied appropriately was a fundamental part of my doctoral thesis. I was interested to narrow down my sample of cases to examine those where the application of the real possibility test presented a finely balanced decision. I was able to do that because of the statutory provision which requires a decision of three commissioners before a referral can be made. By examining a sample [of] 172 Committee refusals to refer I was able to analyse the application of this decision.

[25] *R v Daniel Morrison & others* [2009] NICA 1. See also, 'Danny Morrison's Conviction Quashed' *Belfast Telegraph* (24 October 2008).
[26] *R v Michael Devine* [2021] NICA 7.

> My conclusion, based on that research, is that CCRC does apply the test appropriately. Of the 172 Committee refusals I examined there were a group of 26 in which, from my own perusal of the case papers, I harboured genuine doubts about the conviction. However, in each of those cases I could understand the careful analysis and reasoning of the Commission in reaching a decision not to refer. Commissioners and staff monitored the decisions of the Court of Appeal carefully. This is essential since the Commission is undertaking a predictive role about the likely decision of the Court. The knowledge of the Court of Appeal's approach was evident in CCRC's decision making and it underpinned the refusal to refer.[27]

It seems to us that it is the absence of evidence of demonstrable errors in individual cases which prompts critics to rely on international comparisons and statistics. But there are dangers in these (indirect) methods of criticism.

International comparisons are interesting to a point, but the numbers of cases considered by our counterparts in Scotland and New Zealand are much smaller, and different jurisdictions have different issues. It is interesting that notwithstanding its multifactorial test, the New Zealand Commission has so far referred just one case back to its appellate court and has made around 300 negative decisions – although other references are no doubt in the pipeline.

The Scottish test is sometimes cited as preferable because it uses the phrase 'miscarriage of justice' and combines that with a public interest element. In Scots law, the phrase 'miscarriage of justice' is linked to the test that the Scottish appellate court applies.[28] Both the Criminal Appeal Act 1995 and the Criminal Procedure (Scotland) Act 1995 therefore use the test for references to ensure that the respective commissions are mindful of the practice of the courts. As Welsh observes, incorporating the term 'miscarriage of justice' may need a statutory definition – or alternatively, case law would lead to the Court to defining it – possibly in language that equates to a conviction which might reasonably be expected to be overturned on appeal. Certainly, the definition of a 'miscarriage of justice' set out in section 133 of the Criminal Justice Act 1988 (as amended) would be overly restrictive, since it requires a 'new or newly discovered fact' to 'show beyond reasonable doubt that the person did not commit the offence'. We also note that the Court of Appeal in *R v Park*[29] (a CCRC reference), following its own previous decision in *R v Garland*,[30] concluded that there was no material difference between the legal principles applied on appeal in Scotland and in England and Wales.

We might also ask to what extent it is useful to look at the referral rate and the success rate in percentage terms. The CCRC's intake includes a large proportion

[27] Written evidence to the Justice Committee, December 2014 at p 10, available at committees.parliament.uk/committee/102/justice-committee/publications/written-evidence/.

[28] For a further discussion of this concept see G Sinclair, 'The relationship between the Scottish Criminal Cases Review Commission and the appeal court, and their respective views on what constitutes a miscarriage' (*Law Society of Scotland*, 15 Aug 2005).

[29] *R v Park* [2020] EWCA Crim 589, [167].

[30] *R v Garland* [2016] EWCA Crim 1743.

of people who have not yet appealed (typically around 40 per cent). The CCRC can review these cases if there are exceptional circumstances, but in a significant majority there are no such circumstances and the cases are thus ineligible. The CCRC includes these cases in its reporting because they require work and assessment of exceptionality (rather than real possibility). Thus, in an annual intake of 1500 cases with 30 references for appeal, the pool of eligible cases would be significantly smaller and closer to 900. Changing the denominator has a corresponding shift on the percentage – so 30/900 gives a rate of 3.3 per cent rather than the 2 per cent figure that 30/1500 yields. Although neither percentage may be perceived as high, it illustrates that the lower figure is derived from including a large amount of cases that Parliament intended to be classed as ineligible. Numbers can depend on themes – so currently, the high success rate is influenced by a high quashing rate in the Post Office cases. Likewise, summary convictions that are referred to the Crown Court for appeal are rarely opposed, and cases in Northern Ireland connected to the Troubles have seen a higher rate of quashing. It does not follow that more references would produce more quashings because, importantly, the Court of Appeal approaches references on the criterion of safety and not on a statistical or normative basis.

Those who see a low referral rate and high success rate as evidence that the CCRC is not adequately discharging its function are silent on what they believe the numbers ought to be. Put simply: how many miscarriages of justice could the system be expected to produce? Again, we understand the pull of statistics and the idea of numerical analysis, but we consider that better information lies in qualitative analysis of the cases of those individuals who have or have not had their cases referred – and convictions that have or have not been quashed.

The 'real possibility' test has also been criticised in principle. Indeed, David Jessel, a former CCRC Commissioner, once colourfully described it as a 'wicked fairy at the christening of the CCRC', a 'baptismal curse' introduced as a 'political compromise with a judiciary jealous of their own rights and suspicious of a bunch of amateurs in Birmingham set up to mark their homework'.[31] However, two important points have been reiterated consistently in reply.

First, the Runciman Commission was adamant that a separation of powers should be maintained and that the power to quash convictions should rest with the Courts – and not with the new statutory body whose creation it recommended. So, the test which was debated by Parliament and included in primary legislation could be said to have embodied the recommendation of the Royal Commission. Further, for as long as it remains the Court's decision whether to quash a conviction, there will remain a predictive aspect to the CCRC's case decisions; and it will be the Court's criterion – at present, the test of 'safety' – which will continue to be integral to those decisions.

[31] D Jessel, 'Time to reconnect' in *Wrongly Accused: Who is Responsible for Investigating Miscarriages of Justice?* (Solicitors Journal, 2012) 17.

We do wonder whether there is a compelling answer to the question what purpose is to be served by the CCRC asking the Court of Appeal to consider a case when there is *not* thought to be a real possibility of the conviction being quashed or the sentence changed. Further, in response to some of the practitioners quoted by Welsh, from our perspective, in any case where a decision on the merits appears to be borderline, we have always erred on the side of referring the case for appeal and giving the benefit of any doubt to the applicant. With regards to the existing test, the CCRC pushed back on the Westminster Commission's suggestion that it could shift towards a 'bolder' approach. The threshold is imprecise and permits flexibility. A real possibility is equivalent to a reasonable prospect – and there are plenty of similar formulations in criminal and civil law.

We note also that there appears to be an assumption within some of the commentary on this subject that there are a significant number of 'lurking doubt' cases which the CCRC would refer for appeal if 'real possibility' were no longer the test. Would a change of statutory wording materially alter the assessment of the merits of individual cases which the CCRC's Commissioners carry out? Would additional cases, in fact, be referred for appeal if the wording were changed? If so, would that mean that all cases which have been referred would have also come within the new formulation – and would past cases which the CCRC has turned down need to be revisited in the light of the new statutory wording? The CCRC notes that to inform its work, the Law Commission has asked respondents to focus on any evidence where known miscarriages of justice have at some point failed the 'real possibility' test. This could, usefully in our view, move the discussion towards real life examples and away from more abstract concepts such as perceived (and disputed) deference to the Court of Appeal and the percentage threshold of a 'real possibility'. The CCRC will await the responses to the Law Commission consultation with interest.

The second important point is that, as the 'real possibility' test is predictive of how an appeal would be determined, calls for reform would surely be better aimed at the courts themselves, however difficult this might be. Some practitioners and academics have, to our mind, rightly queried whether a change in wording to the tests (real possibility and safety) would make any difference in practice, both in respect of volume of convictions that might be overturned and/or the types of case that would come within or fall outside the new formulations. Professor Michael Zander, a member of the Runciman Commission, whose views on criminal justice matters are highly regarded, recently wrote:

> My concern is that a great deal of time will be wasted by everyone involved in the review – both the Law Commission and those who take part in the consultation – by going over well-trodden, though hotly contested, ground, when the issues above [i.e. the wording of the tests] are not actually the problem.[32]

[32] M Zander KC, *Wrongly Accused: Who is Responsible for Investigating Miscarriages of Justice?* (Solicitors Journal, 2012) 7.

Others endorse Zander's comments and would rather see criticism of the 'real possibility' test directed at the approach of the courts in deciding appeals. They may take comfort from the fact that the Law Commission is also considering the Court's approach to matters including fresh evidence, safety and substantial injustice.

We should be clear that the CCRC has always been open to considering possible reforms. In 2012, we suggested that there might be a case for our being able to make 'contrarian referrals'[33] and canvassed the possibility of a power to refer based purely on the perceived public interest, notwithstanding that there was not thought to be a real possibility of the conviction being declared unsafe.[34] However, in a climate where the rights of victims are (properly) being given more weight than has been the case in the past, and where finite legal resources are in high demand, it must be asked whether the public interest could justify an appeal with no reasonable prospect of success? The CCRC is acutely aware that a criminal appeal is not an abstract exercise and that real people are profoundly affected by the appeal process and its outcome. It can be immensely painful for victims and defendants to revisit the circumstances of a criminal case, sometimes many years after the trial in question. As Welsh notes, 'referring cases using a lower threshold test than at present might occasionally fruitlessly raise defendant expectations'. The CCRC considers that causing such unnecessary distress to defendants and victims would need to be counterbalanced by significant public interest benefits to justify such a change in approach.

2. Exceptional Circumstances

'Exceptional circumstances' are often misunderstood and, as Welsh suggests, are criticised both for vagueness and because of the perceived inconsistency in the way the CCRC applies them. By section 13(2) of the Criminal Appeal Act 1995, the legislation applies the phrase to two distinct contexts: section 13(1)(b)(i) and section 13(1)(c). Commentators often either conflate or confuse the two, or do not specify which they are referring to. We deal with them separately below.

'No Appeal' Cases

Procedurally, following receipt of an application, the first context for considering 'exceptional circumstances' arises in relation to so called 'No Appeal' cases.

[33] A MacGregor QC, 'Unrealistic expectations' in *Wrongly Accused: Who is Responsible for Investigating Miscarriages of Justice?* (Solicitors Journal, 2012) 13.

[34] A reference without any prospect of success would be permissible in New Zealand. There, the Commission must have regard to the prospects of a successful appeal but need not regard this as the determinative factor.

The CCRC should in principle only review a case where the individual's appeal rights have been exhausted. Parliament created the exception to assist individuals who could not appeal without the CCRC's assistance, although an annual figure of around 600 'No Appeal' applications is perhaps much higher than anyone expected when the CCRC was founded. Those applications can only proceed to review where there is something exceptional which justifies the CCRC's involvement.

Although the statutory requirement for something 'exceptional' by definition prevents an expansive approach to 'No Appeal' cases, we do not accept that the CCRC is unduly restrictive on this issue. Indeed, the available evidence suggests otherwise. Each year, a significant number of 'No Appeal' applications are accepted for a full review and such cases are well represented among those which the CCRC has referred. Indeed, approximately a third of all CCRC references are cases where there had been no previous appeal.

The CCRC keeps under review whether we are being fair and accessible to all, including in how we treat 'No Appeal' applications. At the same time, it is vital that we do not usurp the conventional appeal process or unnecessarily delay an applicant in appealing directly to the Court of Appeal where there are no potential exceptional circumstances. The CCRC must also continue to conduct timely and high-quality case reviews for those applicants who come to us having exhausted the appeal process. These are the important considerations which the CCRC seeks to balance.

There is no closed list of scenarios which constitute 'exceptional circumstances'. Examples in the past have included: cases where the defendant pleaded guilty in a magistrates' court (and so had no conventional right of appeal); where the CCRC's special access to public body material might be required; and where the applicant was extremely vulnerable. However, the term could cover a variety of different scenarios, and so the fact that there is no prescribed list has provided the CCRC with considerable flexibility. In fact, it is arguable that the current regime is already wide enough to – in Welsh's words – 'allow the CCRC to find exceptional circumstances wherever it appears to be in the interests of justice to do so'.

We have striven to understand why so many people apply to the CCRC instead of applying directly to the Court of Appeal for leave to appeal. One reason has been that the CCRC's 'easy-read' application form is perhaps more accessible than the Court of Appeal's 'Form NG'. For this reason, we have worked with the Court of Appeal to develop an 'easy-read' Form NG to assist unrepresented applicants. This form is now widely used and we send it to each applicant whose 'No Appeal' application is not accepted for a full review. Another reason why applicants might prefer to approach the CCRC relates to misconceptions about 'loss of time orders' which are sometimes made by the Court of Appeal. Those in prison consistently report to us their (mistaken) belief that the Court of Appeal could require them to restart their sentences if their appeal is heard but thought to be groundless. Our outreach team has worked hard to correct this myth, but there is no doubt that it persists in the prison estate and is dissuading some applicants from attempting to appeal.

No New Evidence or Argument

The second context where the phrase 'exceptional circumstances' arises is where we are asked to refer a case where there is no new evidence or argument but there nevertheless exists a real possibility that the conviction[35] will be overturned. In practice, the CCRC has made only one reference of this kind (although others are under consideration). In the referred case, we considered that the Court had misunderstood an argument on a previous appeal, and that there was a real possibility that the Court might accept the argument if it were put correctly. Ultimately, however, the conviction was upheld again.[36]

We have found it difficult to find other examples of cases where there is nothing new but there is nevertheless a real possibility that the Court would overturn the conviction. The Court will always be mindful that it did not hear or see the witnesses at trial and that it will have an imperfect view of proceedings. Some have argued that 'lurking doubt' cases could be referred for appeal on this basis. The courts have acknowledged that lurking doubt exists as a concept – in cases such as *Pope*[37] in England and Wales, and *Pollock*[38] in Northern Ireland (where it was framed as a 'sense of unease') – albeit this is undoubtedly a rare occurrence. We ask rhetorically, how many cases can be categorised as ones of 'lurking doubt'? Lurking doubt is sometimes used as shorthand for an as yet unarticulated ratiocination. We think that once the reason for the doubt is examined, it is often found to be based on new argument or fresh evidence that may, in turn, be based on information from similar cases – and it is this new material which supplies grounds on which the courts will be more comfortable to quash.

3. Post-Appeal Disclosure

We welcome the attention which Welsh has given to the important subject of the disclosure of evidence to the defence within the criminal justice system. She rightly recognises that problems with disclosure have been a feature of many miscarriages of justice. That is reflected in our own experience: at least one fifth of all CCRC references to the appeal courts over the past 26 years have featured non-disclosure in some form. The problem has reared its head in many different types of

[35] This does not apply to sentence cases, where the statute requires that there must be new legal argument or information (s 13(1)(b)(ii)).

[36] *R v Stock* [2008] EWCA 1862, [43]–[45].

[37] *R v Pope* [2012] EWCA Crim 2241, [14].

[38] *R v Pollock* [2004] NICA 34, [32], [36] and [45].

cases, from Northern Ireland 'Troubles' era convictions, to the recent CCRC referrals connected with the Post Office Horizon scandal. Wherever we have referred cases for appeal on the basis of non-disclosure, we have also done whatever we can to draw public attention – and the attention of key stakeholders – to those issues. When it comes to disclosure by the CCRC, Welsh rightly notes that we are governed by the provisions in sections 23–25 of the Criminal Appeal Act 1995. When the CCRC was created it was granted the significant and unique power to require any other public body to provide it with material (including material of the highest sensitivity). However, alongside that formidable ability, Parliament put in place protections which were designed to ensure that the CCRC acts carefully and responsibly with the 'public body' material it obtains; hence the specific criminal offence within section 23 of the Act.

Nevertheless, case law[39] enables and requires the CCRC to disclose information which is relevant to the case decisions that it takes. More specifically, in every case and irrespective of whether it refers or not, the CCRC must supply the applicant with the information on which it relies as well as anything new that is necessary to enable them to present their best case for appeal. That is an assessment for the CCRC to make on a case-by-case basis, and we do so with care. Importantly, the law does not require disclosure of material that is neutral or irrelevant to an applicant's case.

We do not accept that the CCRC takes an overly restrictive approach in deciding whether evidence meets our test for disclosure; we make such disclosures routinely in the course of our casework. We also do not recognise the suggestion that disclosure decisions are in any way constrained by resources. The decision is taken in each case in accordance with the law, not by reference to cost. We understand that legal representatives and campaigners will have a natural curiosity about what other case material we hold and would prefer to 'double-check' our assessment of whether that material is capable of assisting their cases – but when Parliament created the CCRC, it entrusted us both with the power to obtain material and the responsibility to evaluate its potential relevance to the safety of the convictions in question.

We note with interest Welsh's proposed four-stage process for post-conviction disclosure. To the extent that it is suggested that the CCRC should be used as a vehicle to permit wider defence access to police and prosecution files, this would of course require a significant extension to the CCRC's statutory remit – one which the relevant agencies would not necessarily support. There would also be a need for greater funding, and practical challenges for the workability of such a system. However, it is worth noting that some elements of the process proposed by Welsh are already reflected in current CCRC processes. For instance, where

[39] *R v Secretary of State for the Home Department, ex parte Hickey and others (No 2) and other appeals* [1995] 1 All ER 490.

an appeal is being prepared, but public body material of potential relevance to that appeal cannot be accessed by the convicted person or his representatives, then that may in itself qualify as an 'exceptional circumstance' which justifies the CCRC's involvement in the absence of a previous appeal. Likewise, if the CCRC's review then confirms that there is 'material [which] is of assistance to the applicant's case',[40] then it would already fall to be disclosed in accordance with the current law. This is not a 'new aspect' to the CCRC's work, but, as alluded to above, is already a key reason why 'exceptional circumstances' may be found to exist in 'No Appeal' cases.

One consequence of the current rules governing CCRC disclosure is that they generally prevent the publication of CCRC case decisions, or 'Statements of Reasons'. As part of the Law Commission's review, we will consider whether to call for legislation which would enable us to publish some Statements of Reasons – or at least particular sections from them – where we consider this in the public interest. Very few applicants and campaigners have made Statements of Reasons available for public consideration, as is their right.[41] This can lead to some mistrust of the CCRC and its casework – although we often suggest that inferences can be drawn where a campaign group publicly criticises a CCRC decision while failing to make available the document which contains the detailed reasoning which underpins that decision. In practice, the CCRC would often like to be able to comment publicly on the various materials which it has considered and lines of enquiry which it has followed, and explain why these have not resulted in a referral for appeal. If we were able to be more transparent about the reasons for our decisions, then this might increase public confidence in our decision-making. We note that the New Zealand Commission is required to publish decisions (albeit not necessarily as full documents). We believe this is an issue which warrants further consideration, and we would be interested in others' views.

4. Conclusion

We would like to express our thanks, once again, for the invitation to attend the conference and to comment on Welsh's chapter for this collection. She has addressed some important issues and the focus on the 'real possibility' test is timely in view of the Law Commission's current review. The CCRC looks forward to reading submissions to the Law Commission, participating in its consultation and considering any proposals for legislation. We will be particularly interested in any proposed changes to the statutory test for referral, and the potential impact of such changes in theory, in public perception, and in practice.

[40] The second stage of Welsh's suggested four stage process.

[41] A notable exception is the decision in the first Oliver Campbell review. Access to the decision document is via: www.thejusticegap.com/oliver-campbell/.

The need to identify and remedy miscarriages of justice is as important today as it was when the CCRC was formed in 1997. After 26 years in operation – with over 800 cases referred to the appeal courts to date – there can be little doubt that the CCRC continues to fulfil a vital public function. We welcome detailed public scrutiny of our work, with the aim of continuous improvement to how we discharge that function.

6

Consent to Bodily Harm and the 'Public Interest'

DANIEL BANSAL AND TRACEY ELLIOTT*

If A deliberately knocks B to the ground, it would be uncontroversial to state that A's conduct is harmful, wrongful, and criminal.[1] However, suppose A and B are playing rugby when such interaction occurs. In that case, because both players have (impliedly) consented to such contact, B is not wronged by a legitimate tackle, and no criminal offence is committed. The criminal law recognises B's voluntary 'factual' consent[2] as legally transformative and provides a defence.[3] Indeed, the classic Millian view provides that B's voluntary factual consent to A's conduct, which would otherwise amount to a set-back to B's interests, negates *any* wrongdoing on the part of A.[4] This is because, on this liberal view, the criminal law should only be used to prevent harm to others, and state intervention is unjustified if the 'harm' in question is self-regarding and freely consented to.[5]

English criminal law, however, does not always take this Millian stance and frequently disregards B's sovereignty of choice. In fact, regarding serious non-fatal, non-sexual offences against the person, with which this chapter is concerned, the current doctrinal position offers little space for autonomous decision-making. The category-based approach to consent favoured by appellate courts (in cases where bodily injury has been caused) has resulted in inconsistent and unprincipled

* Dr Daniel Bansal, Associate Professor of Law, University of Leicester; Dr Tracey Elliott, Lecturer in Health Care Law, University of Leicester. We are grateful to Mandy Burton, Sally Kyd, Stephen Riley, and the editors of this volume, for their helpful comments on earlier drafts of this chapter. All errors remain our own.

[1] This assumes A does not have a valid defence.

[2] Westen distinguishes between 'factual' and 'legal' consent, and we adopt this terminology within this chapter. P Westen, *The Logic of Consent* (Ashgate, 2005).

[3] We argue that, at the level of assault and battery, consent forms part of the *actus reus*, but for more serious non-fatal, non-sexual offences, it operates as a defence. G Williams, 'Consent and Public Policy' [1962] *Crim LR* 74, 75.

[4] JS Mill, *On Liberty* (Penguin Classics, 2006). Similarly, Feinberg suggests that fully voluntary consented to harms do not count as 'harms' for the purposes of the Harm Principle: J Feinberg, *Harmless Wrongdoing* (OUP, 1990) 211–12.

[5] P Roberts, 'The Philosophical Foundations of Consent in the Criminal Law' (1997) 17 *OJLS* 389.

development of legal doctrine. For example, bodily injury caused during cosmetic genital surgery, piercing for decorative purposes, and contact sports have been recognised as lawful. However, female genital mutilation (FGM), non-surgical body modification, and sadomasochistic sexual activities are not.

The Law Commission, in recognition of these issues, recommended reform of the common law defence of consent in 1994 and 1995.[6] However, since the publication of those papers, no such reform has occurred. In this chapter, we argue that the current legal framework on consent to bodily injury is incoherent, lacks moral justification, and fails to adequately recognise individual autonomy. We propose replacing the current law with a statutory 'public interest' defence to resolve some of these issues. Our proposal argues that the causation of injury to another person, falling short of serious disabling injury (SDI), should not be criminal if the other person provided valid consent to injury of the type caused. Once this threshold of harm is exceeded, it is argued that 'consent' is not really what it is at issue, but whether it is in the *public interest* to permit the causing of such injury to another. We argue that a statutory public interest defence specifying the circumstances in which consent, or public utility, will be regarded as justifying the causing of harm would better reflect the reality of the defence and bring much-needed clarity to the law.

To achieve this, our chapter assumes the following structure. First, we examine the role that the concept of consent plays in legal jurisprudence and explore the problems in relation to the current legal framework. Then, we outline our reform proposals, offering a statutory 'public interest' defence to the causation of bodily injury. The remainder of the chapter outlines the key features of our defence, defining the threshold of harm that can generally be consented to (injury falling short of SDI), and reviewing the two circumstances in which our defence privileges the causation of harm at and above the SDI threshold (medical and surgical procedures and regulated sports). Finally, we review the implications that our defence has on the lawfulness of sexual conduct that causes bodily injury.

1. The Role of 'Consent' in Criminal Law

'Consent' is a core concept in legal and moral philosophy. Indeed, the ability to consent is a central manifestation of personhood and individual autonomy.[7] This importance is embodied by the maxim *volenti non fit injuria*, which provides that a person is not *wronged* by that to which they consent.[8] However, this maxim is not an accurate statement of criminal jurisprudence. In English criminal law, although consent can transform unlawful conduct into entirely lawful conduct, B's consent

[6] Law Commission, *Consent and Offences Against the Person* (Consultation No 134, 1994); Law Commission, *Consent in the Criminal Law* (Consultation No 139, 1995).

[7] H Hurd, 'The Moral Magic of Consent' (1996) 2 *Legal Theory* 121, 121.

[8] T Ingman, 'A History of the Defence of *Volenti Non Fit Injuria*' (1981) 26 *Juridical Review* 1.

to A's conduct does not *always* change the legal quality of their conduct. B has no unlimited right to authorise A's harming of them.

At a fundamental level, the nature of consent depends on the type of harm and wrongdoing it seeks to legitimise. For instance, consent to death or serious bodily injury differs significantly from consent to sexual conduct. Engaging in sexual conduct is not *itself* unlawful. Here, non-consent is *inculpatory*. Or, in familiar legal terms, the 'absence of consent' forms a fundamental part of the *actus rei* of these offences; for example, rape requires non-consensual penile penetration.[9] The presence of consent precludes wrongdoing.

Conversely, the causation of death or serious bodily injury is morally different. These are harms that should usually be avoided. For this reason, the criminal law constructs offences prohibiting the *acts* of causing death or serious injury.[10] Therefore, if the state legitimises the causation of harm in such circumstances, consent is *exculpatory* and provides A with a supervening defence. Thus, if A breaks B's nose during a boxing match, B's consent does nothing to alter the offence elements for a serious non-fatal offence. Instead, A is provided with a defence to exculpate A *in those circumstances*, recognising that breaking noses should usually be avoided.

Although consent is fundamental to autonomy, we do not believe it offers B *carte blanche* to authorise A causing harm to them at all levels. This restriction can be justified by distinguishing between public and private spheres of concern, recognising that some issues are not the law's business.[11] The implication is that some harms are so egregious that they fall within the domain of the law. However, this leaves the dilemma of determining how serious harm must be before it sufficiently violates B's protected interests and dignity such that prohibition is justified. It is our view that consent becomes legally ineffective when A *significantly* sets back B's protected interests and disregards their dignity.[12] This, we argue, occurs when A causes B harm that is serious and disabling. At this point, there are two dignitarian concerns. First, the seriousness of the harm has moved into the sphere of objectification and is simply inconsistent with treating B as sentient. Second, B is no longer being treated as an end in themselves; B is no longer meaningfully included in A's actions and deliberations as a setter of ends or possessor of value.[13]

[9] Sexual Offences Act 2003, s 1.

[10] Subject to the necessary exceptions, eg, self-defence.

[11] The 'public-private' distinction can be drawn in many ways. Here, we use the distinction in a primarily normative sense; conduct is 'private' if it does not prejudicially affect the interests of others. To establish whether conduct (and results) is public or private, it is necessary to question the nature of the activity, the nature of the choices by A and B, and the consequences of the conduct. If 'descriptively' private conduct concerns the legitimate interests of society, state intervention may be justified on the grounds that it is normatively public. See E Wicks, *The State and the Body* (Hart, 2016) 17–34.

[12] M Dan-Cohen, 'Basic Values and the Victim's State of Mind' (2000) 88 *California Law Review* 759, 777; RA Duff, 'Harms and Wrongs' (2001) *Buffalo Crim LR* 13, 39–44; and V Bergelson, 'Autonomy, Dignity, and Consent to Harm' (2008) *Rutgers Law Review* 724, 730.

[13] I Kant, *The Metaphysics of Morals* (CUP, 1999); S Riley, 'Why is law necessary for human dignity?' (2020) 11(2) *Jurisprudence* 248, 249.

2. Problems with the Current Legal Framework

When does B's factual consent to A's conduct, which causes B bodily harm, provide A with a defence to non-fatal, non-sexual criminal wrongdoing? It is clear that B's consent is an answer to a charge of common assault or battery. Within the *actus rei* of these offences, the 'absence of consent' is an essential criterion the prosecution must prove.[14] This is true irrespective of the circumstances in which the harm is caused (eg, violent sex). It is important to recognise 'non-consent' as an offence element to ensure that behaviour not intended to be criminalised (eg, *any* consensual contact between A and B, such as a handshake) does not require a defence to be lawful.[15]

However, when A causes B actual bodily harm or worse, the relevance of B's consent to the assault or battery is more problematic. For a section 47 offence,[16] an offence of constructive liability, if there is no base offence (assault or battery), there can be no liability. However, the courts have been reluctant to permit A to escape liability for causing actual harm simply because B provided factual consent to the underlying assault or battery. A can only escape liability if they were not intentional or reckless as to causing further harm.[17] If A were intentional or reckless as to causing actual harm or worse, A can only escape liability if the restrictive 'defence of consent' is satisfied. Sections 20 and 18 do not require such analysis since they criminalise wounding and the causation of grievous bodily harm, with no need for an underlying assault or battery.[18]

Thus, for sections 47, 20, and 18,[19] consent is only relevant as a supervening defence, with its presence doing nothing to alter the offence elements. However, B's factual consent will only be relevant if the circumstances in which the harm was caused fall within one of the recognised 'exceptional categories'. The leading authority on this matter remains *Brown*.[20] In *Brown*, the appellants engaged in consensual BDSM (bondage, domination, submission, masochism) practices. Those involved 'willingly and enthusiastically participated in the commission of acts of violence against each other for the sexual pleasure which it engendered in the giving and receiving of pain'.[21] By a bare majority, the court held that factual consent by B to the causation of actual or serious harm for sexual gratification is irrelevant to A's liability for serious non-fatal offences. Furthermore, the court reaffirmed the restrictive category-based approach to consent to bodily injury. This, it

[14] *Barnes* [2005] EWCA Crim 3246, [16].

[15] The Law Commission's latest recommendations favoured this position: Law Commission, *Reform of the Offences against the Person* (n 6) paras 5.29–5.3.

[16] Offences Against the Person Act 1861.

[17] *Meachen* [2006] EWCA Crim 2414.

[18] Although section 20 criminalises the 'infliction' of grievous bodily harm, this is now taken to mean 'cause' per *Dica* [2004] EWCA Crim 1103 and *Konzani* [2005] EWCA Crim 706.

[19] Offences Against the Person Act 1861.

[20] [1993] UKHL 19; [1994] 1 AC 212.

[21] *Brown* [1992] QB 491, 496 (Lord Lane).

has been argued, is to (*inter alia*) protect social order, advance the public interest, and 'protect people from themselves'.[22]

The six exceptional categories that have been recognised are: (a) proper medical treatment and reasonable surgical interference, (b) regulated sports, (c) tattooing, piercing, and body modification, (d) harms related to religious or cultural practices, (e) bravado and horseplay, and (f) sexual pleasure and transmission of diseases.[23] These categories are *ad hoc*; they have not been developed per legal principles but have evolved as a matter of public policy. Each category was recognised at a time when there was a perceived social utility of the conduct and the circumstances in which it occurred. Unfortunately, these categories have been widely criticised as arbitrary, moralistic, and unclear.[24] Consequently, the general rule can be stated: if A causes B actual bodily harm or worse, B's factual consent is irrelevant if A intentionally or recklessly causes B further harm, unless the harm is caused in circumstances that closely align with one of the six categories above.

There are numerous problems with the current legal framework, many of which are well documented in the academic literature.[25] Here, we outline some key issues supporting the case for law reform.

First, despite widespread criticism and calls for reform, the current legal framework has been codified by section 71 of the Domestic Abuse Act 2021, primarily in response to political pressure and radical feminist ideology to protect against a narrative of 'rough sex gone wrong' claims to evade homicide convictions.[26] The vociferous campaign by the group 'We Can't Consent To This' celebrated this enshrinement as a means of combating the so-called 'rough sex defence' and as a victory for women. Unfortunately, the practical and theoretical limitations of section 71 mean that celebrations by campaigners will be short-lived as the victory is symbolic only. While codification by statute carries some intrinsic weight, the section does no more than state the clear position at common law. As such, the law continues to fail to articulate what distinguishes BDSM from abuse, forecloses productive legal reform, and represents a departure from liberal legal method.[27]

[22] *Brown* (n 20) 235 (Lord Templeman) and 246 (Lord Jauncey); Cf W Wilson, 'Is Hurting People Wrong?' (1992) 14 *Journal of Social Welfare and Family Law* 388, 393–95.

[23] This is limited to incidental injury caused during sexual conduct and conduct that risks the transmission of a disease or infection, where B is fully informed as to A's sexual health status, per *Slingsby* [1995] *Crim LR* 570 and *Dica* (n 18). It does not permit the causing of bodily injury *for* sexual pleasure, per DAA 2021, s 71.

[24] J Tolmie, 'Consent to harmful assaults: the case for moving away from category-based decision making' [2012] *Crim LR* 656.

[25] See, eg, D Kell, 'Social disutility and consent' (1994) 14 *OJLS* 121; M Giles, 'Consensual harm and the public interest' (1994) 57 *MLR* 101.

[26] S Edwards, 'Assault, Strangulation and Murder – Challenging the Sexual Libido Consent Defence Narrative' in A Reed et al (eds), *Consent: Domestic and Comparative Perspectives* (Routledge, Abingdon 2016) 88–103.

[27] E Bradley, 'Reacting to Rough Sex: The Unexpected Toll of Section 71 Domestic Abuse Act 2021' in H Bows and J Herring, *Rough Sex and the Criminal Law: Global Perspectives* (Emerald Insight, 2022) 167–83.

It would have been beneficial for Parliament to have consulted other stakeholders, particularly those groups seeking to practise safe BDSM, so that there could have been meaningful debate and the inconsequentiality of this provision avoided.

Second, the 'actual bodily harm' threshold within the general rule causes unnecessary uncertainty. One unfortunate implication of this is that, definitionally, the threshold for harm that can be legally consented to is set remarkably low. All injuries more than 'transient or trifling' constitute actual harm and cannot be lawfully consented to/caused unless they fall within a recognised exceptional category. Injuries need not be significant, with minor injuries such as cuts and bruises falling within this definition.[28] In addition to physical injuries, the scope of the offence is further broadened through the inclusion of psychiatric injuries[29] and an elastic interpretation of 'occasioning', now taken to mean 'causing'.[30] This captures a wide scope of conduct that should *not* be criminalised. For example, when A (a hairdresser) cuts a substantial amount of B's hair at their request, A has completed the offence elements for a section 47.[31] Consequently, enormous scope is afforded to prosecutorial discretion.

Third, a significant problem with the current position is that it is unclear whether the list of exceptional categories can be extended to admit new categories of lawful activity. That new categories might be permitted was implicit within *Brown*,[32] and in *Dica*, the court held that the stated categories are 'neither closed nor immutable'.[33] Moreover, if new categories were admitted, it would be on 'social utility' grounds. However, it appears this is no longer an option. In *BM*, the Court of Appeal held that bar Parliamentary intervention, new forms of activity may only be considered lawful if there is a 'close analogy' to an existing category.[34]

Consequently, the outer limits of the boundaries of existing categories of lawful conduct further blur the lines of criminality. Take, for example, tattooing, piercing, and body modification. Local authorities regulate and monitor businesses offering cosmetic body piercing, permanent tattooing, semi-permanent colouring, electrolysis, and acupuncture, and it is a criminal offence to trade without a licence and to be in breach of relevant byelaws.[35] However, the scope of this category needs clarification.

While 'extreme' body modifications, involving the 'removal of parts of the body' and 'mutilation', are unlawful, it is unclear whether less extreme modifications

[28] *Donovan* [1934] 2 KB 498; *T v DPP* [2003] EWHC 266.

[29] *Miller* [1954] 2 QB 282.

[30] Cf Gardner claimed that 'occasion' is broader than 'cause' and can be used to attribute responsibility where there is no causal basis. J Gardner, 'Rationality and the rule of law in offences against the person' [1994] *CLJ* 502, 509.

[31] *DPP v Smith* [2006] EWHC 94.

[32] *Brown* (n 20) 267 (Lord Mustill).

[33] *Dica* (n 18), [41].

[34] *BM* (2018) EWCA Crim 560, [41].

[35] Local Government (Miscellaneous Provisions) Act 1982, s 15 (as amended by the Local Government Act 2003, s 120). Local authorities in London are subject to the London Local Authority Act 1991.

performed by tattoo and piercing artists, such as branding and scarification, fall within the scope of this category.[36] These procedures fall outside local authorities' regulatory jurisdiction and framework, meaning that if performed by a registered tattoo or piercing artist in studio, they may potentially be liable to criminal proceedings. Yet, in *Wilson*,[37] the Court of Appeal found branding to be analogous to tattooing when performed between a married couple in their own home. Therefore, it is uncertain whether such procedures would be deemed analogous to tattooing and lawful, or analogous to extreme body modifications and unlawful, with much appearing to depend on *who* performs the procedure and *where* it is performed.[38] The other categories of exception are similarly vulnerable to criticism.

Fourth, although the activities of medical practitioners and tattooing and piercing businesses are regulated, following *Richardson*[39] and *Melin*,[40] it is unclear when a deception as to qualifications or regulatory status will vitiate consent. Although the Court of Appeal in *BM* stressed the unregulated nature of the appellant's activities,[41] the significance of regulation and whether standards of regulation should be required for more serious harms remains unclear.

For these reasons, we offer a proposal for reform that acknowledges the morally and legally transformative nature of consent within a framework that protects and advances the public interest.

3. The 'Public Interest' Defence

Our reform proposal provides that a statutory 'public interest' defence should replace the current legal framework on consent to bodily injury. This defence, grounded in Millian liberalism, provides that it is *not* in the public interest for the state to interfere with citizens' private lives. This liberal view provides that one of the law's core functions is to respect and uphold individual liberties in conformity with the principle that each should be accorded the greatest possible liberty compatible with respecting that of others; individuals must be free from interference in self-regarding matters.

Nevertheless, B's consent does not render A's conduct permissible *tout court*. It is necessary to strike an effective balance between the values of autonomy and authoritarian communitarianism, allowing greater weight to the former

[36] Scarification is the process of scratching or cutting the skin to create a pattern, and branding is the burning of the skin to create a pattern, both producing a permanent scar in the form of a design.

[37] [1997] QB 47.

[38] R Clement, 'Consent to body modification in criminal law' (2018) 77(3) *CLJ* 451; D Bansal, 'Body Modifications and the Criminal Law' (2018) 28 *Journal of Criminal Law* 496.

[39] [1999] QB 444.

[40] [2019] EWCA Crim 557.

[41] *BM* (n 34), [7]–[8].

but denying the validity of choices made by B that are not in B's best interests. Moreover, the criminal law has a role in curtailing the legally transformative force of consent to protect against *public* harm.[42]

For these reasons, we argue that A should be able to raise a statutory 'public interest' defence to the causation of bodily injury falling short of SDI, provided that B provides effective consent to the level of harm intended or risked.[43] Once at the level of SDI, the gravity of the harm means that, unless there is a regulatory framework encapsulating the circumstances in which the harm occurs, B can no longer be said to be acting in their best interests.[44] Therefore, if A intentionally or recklessly causes B SDI, A will be subject to criminal liability and B's consent ineffective. This approach concedes that although B can factually consent to harms of all levels, morally transforming A's conduct, it fails to *legally* transform the moral quality of A's conduct in criminal law.[45] Here, the 'moral magic' of consent runs out, and A's conduct takes B as its victim.[46]

However, we recognise that in limited circumstances, it may be permissible for A to cause B SDI, either where it is in B's best interests and/or whether there is sufficient regulation to secure the interests of all parties involved. For this reason, we suggest two regulatory-based exceptions to our general rule. B *can* legally consent to SDI in the context of: (a) medical and surgical procedures, and (b) regulated sports. Our proposal does leave open the *possibility* for SDI to be permitted in other contexts should adequate state- or self-regulation develop in the future. This would require regulatory bodies to oversee and enforce standards for businesses and individuals that offer (say) BDSM, extreme body modification, and dangerous exhibition services.

On this basis, the public interest defence is both a 'sword' and a 'shield'. It is a sword used by the state in performing its *ex-ante* and *ex-post* functions to criminalise unregulated behaviour that causes or risks SDI. However, it is also used as a shield by citizens who cause or risk harm falling short of SDI, or at the level of SDI

[42] Bergelson lists several considerations that are employed to legitimise the overriding of consent. These include social order, social utility, and immorality. V Bergelson, 'The right to be hurt: Testing the boundaries of consent' (2007) 75 *George Washington Law Review* 165, 190–200.

[43] We acknowledge that there are difficult questions surrounding complicity and secondary liability. For reasons of space, we are unable to deal with these matters in full. However, we indicate our preference for preservation of a *Tyrrell* [1984] 1 QB 710 exemption, which provides that a 'victim' of SDI cannot be convicted of committing the offence as an accessory where either: (a) consent was not voluntarily obtained or (b) the relevant act was committed under the evidential presumption circumstances because they exist for a victim's protection. See G Williams, 'Victims and other exempt parties in crime' (1990) 10 *Legal Studies* 245.

[44] Our proposal is not wholly dissimilar to the position in New Zealand. See *Lee* (2006) 22 CRNZ 568; Tolmie (n 24).

[45] This may strip B of standing to complain against A, but this is of no consequence in criminal law. B has no standing to complain against A in any event; all that matters is whether the State has standing to complain against A. A Harel, 'Why only the state may inflict criminal sanctions' (2008) 14 *Legal Theory* 113 and MM Dempsey, *Prosecuting domestic violence: A philosophical analysis* (OUP, 2009) 185–210.

[46] MM Dempsey, 'Victimless conduct and the *volenti* maxim: how consent works' (2013) *Crim Law & Philosophy* 11, 15.

where sufficient regulatory framework permits, providing consent as an effective exculpatory defence.

In cases where it *is* in the public interest to permit bodily injury, B's consent will legally transform A's harmful conduct into conduct that does not *wrong* B.[47] Thus, making the distinction between harms that adversely affect B's interests, and those harms that adversely affect B's interests *and* in doing so wrongs B. If A's conduct is different to what B consented to, goes beyond the proposed limit of consensual harm, or it is proven that A did the relevant act in an abusive capacity, A will be subject to the normal rules of non-fatal offences against the person and homicide. For this reason, our defence is subject to three important caveats:

1. B must provide effective consent to the causation of bodily harm. B consents if they expressly or impliedly consent to A's conduct, which B knows or believes to be intended to cause injury of the type caused, and B understands the possible consequences of such harm;
2. A must hold an honest and reasonable belief that B consents to the relevant act; and
3. If there is evidence that A did the relevant act in an abusive capacity, it is to be evidentially presumed that B did not consent, and A did not hold a reasonable belief in consent.

If such a framework were to be adopted, we recognise a lacuna exists where A *risks* the causation of SDI, and does cause SDI, but the conduct and harm ought not to be criminalised and do not fall within an exception. Here, we envisage conduct that risks the transmission of diseases and infections as being of particular concern. However, not all instances of disease or infection transmission should be criminalised.[48] Otherwise those who enter a supermarket or their workplace with a common cold, not intending to infect anyone, but nevertheless spreading their infection to others, might fall within the purview of the criminal law.

We therefore propose distinguishing between the transmission of communicable diseases and that of sexually transmitted diseases. For the non-intentional transmission of communicable diseases, we are of the view that although this should remain predominantly a public health matter,[49] transmissions could give rise to criminal liability where the harm is sufficiently serious, causation can be proven, and it was unjustified in the circumstances to risk transmission to another.[50] Convictions are likely to be rare because of the difficulty in proving

[47] This analysis is based Feinberg's interpretation of the *volenti non fit injuria* maxim, which explains the morally transformative nature of consent. See Feinberg (n 4) xxix, 115.

[48] M Weait, 'Limit Cases: How and Why We Can and Should Decriminalise HIV Transmission, Exposure, And Non-Disclosure' (2019) 27(4) *Med LR* 576.

[49] Public Health (Control of Disease) Act 1984 and Public Health (Infectious Diseases) Regulations 1988, SI 1988/1546.

[50] See K Laird, 'Criminalising Contagion – Questioning the Paradigm' in C Stanton and H Quirk (eds), *Criminalising Contagion* (CUP, 2016) 201.

causation and the presence of tacit consent; entering a supermarket with an everyday illness conforms with the social expectation of what types of risks people tacitly consent to take. However, the sexual transmission of diseases and infections is a discrete form of transmission, related to a particular set of behaviours, and thus warrants separate treatment. If A fails to disclose their sexual health status, there can be no tacit consent by B to the transmission of a disease or infection through unprotected sex on the basis of A's deception and breach of trust.[51] Consequently, there is no informed consent. However, where B *is* informed as to A's status, any non-intentional transmission should fall outside the purview of the criminal law, even if the harm is at or above the level of SDI.[52] This result could be obtained in two ways. Either, through formal decriminalisation by the state on public health grounds, effectively retaining section 71(4) of the DAA. Or, should section 71 of the DAA be repealed, one could achieve the same result through the courts finding that unprotected sex between A and B, where B is fully informed as to A's status, is *justified* risk-taking, thus failing to satisfy the criteria for recklessness.[53]

SDI Threshold

What do we mean by 'serious disabling injury'? Our proposal adopts a modified version of Glanville Williams' definition.[54] SDI includes loss of a bodily member or organ, permanent bodily injury, permanent functional impairment, serious or permanent disfigurement, severe or prolonged pain, serious impairment of mental health, and prolonged unconsciousness. We have omitted the prerequisite that injury must cause 'serious distress', since this would render the definition very complicated to apply, especially where B offers testimony or evidence to the contrary.

The rationale for setting the threshold of harm at SDI is two-fold. First, we consider this to be the point at which injury is, without state regulation, most likely to adversely affect B's interests and dignity. Second, we reject the view that to protect the ostensibly consenting 'victim', it is only safe to allow very modest interference in *any* case. It is possible to ensure that B's consent is valid, that their will is not overborne or subject to abuse, and that they know what they are consenting to, through the inclusion of an evidential presumption of non-consent in cases of abuse. Therefore, in addition to the normal rules of consent, this presumption, effective above and below the SDI threshold, protects abused victims and promotes the autonomy of others who wish to engage in the causation of harm with others consensually. We discuss the evidential presumption in further detail below.

[51] J Herring, 'Mistaken sex' (2005) *Crim LR* 511; J Slater, 'HIV, trust and the criminal law' (2011) 75(4) *Journal of Criminal Law* 309.

[52] We adopt Judge LJ's rationale for legitimising such conduct per *Dica* (n 18), [51].

[53] JR Spencer, 'Liability for reckless infection – part 1' (2004) 154 *NLJ* 384.

[54] The Law Commission adopted Williams' full definition in their proposal: Law Commission, *Consent in the Criminal Law* (n 6) paras 4.29–4.40.

The line we have drawn is, we concede, somewhat arbitrary. That is, it is not grounded in unanimous public opinion. However, relying on public opinion would be futile. There would be a marked lack of consensus over what freely chosen activities disrespect the moral worth of the participants such that we can find that they are not acting in their best interests. This is owing to the diverse cultural, social, and religious groups within England and Wales.

Ormerod and Gunn criticised the Law Commission's use of SDI, and its definition, within their reform proposals for two principal reasons.[55] First, they argued that the 'serious and permanent disfigurement' criterion contradicted the Commission's stance regarding the permissibility of tattoos and piercings. Second, if adopted, there would be a resulting offence-defence mismatch; there is no offence of causing SDI. Thus, if A were charged with causing grievous bodily harm contrary to sections 20 or 18, and relied on B's consent as a defence, defence counsel would have to prove that the injuries fell short of SDI, which would add confusion and complexity to proceedings.

We offer three rebuttals to address their criticism of the incoherence regarding the permissibility of bodily modifications. First, we argue that male circumcision should fall within the confines of medical treatment. Second, we do not regard tattooing and piercings as *dis*figurements; rather, they are enhancements. Finally, we are of the view that 'extreme' bodily modifications, which a registered medical professional does not perform, should at present remain unlawful. Modifications such as branding, scarification, ear-pointing, and tongue-splitting are all irreversible and carry an inherent risk of unwanted injury. As indicated above, our proposal does leave open the possibility for bodily modifications at or above the SDI level to be permitted *if* enhanced and responsible self-regulation, approved by the state, were adopted by modifiers.[56] However, a regulatory body would have to be created to oversee the training and practice of body modifiers and enforce these standards.[57]

Regarding the offence-defence mismatch, we concede this point and the implications stated by Ormerod and Gunn. However, reforming the defence of consent to bodily injury *should* occur as part of a root and branch reform of non-fatal, non-sexual offences against the person. Ideally, a newly reformed non-offences ladder would see the offences of: (a) intentionally causing SDI, and (b) recklessly causing SDI at the top of the ladder, to which the public interest defence would not apply unless within the context of medical procedures and regulated sport.[58]

Furthermore, by raising the threshold to SDI, much of the dissatisfaction within the current legal framework will be remedied, and the vast majority of injuries

[55] D Ormerod and M Gunn, 'Second Law Commission consultation paper on consent: (2) consent – a second bash' (1996) *Crim LR* 694, 700–701.

[56] For an analysis of self-regulation in the context of body modification, see S Pegg, 'Not so clear cut: the lawfulness of body modifications' (2019) *Crim LR* 579, 591–93.

[57] This option was not considered by the Court of Appeal in *BM* (n 34).

[58] This ensures full compliance with the principle of correspondence. See J Horder, *Ashworth's Principles of Criminal Law*, 10th edn (OUP, 2022) 102.

caused during consensual interactions will become *de jure* lawful. To explore some of the implications and benefits of our proposal, the remainder of this chapter focuses on the conduct that our public interest defence privileges at and above the SDI level, namely medical procedures and regulated sports. However, we also examine the impact our defence has on the lawfulness of sexual conduct that causes bodily injury.

Medical Exemption

It has been recognised at least since the nineteenth century that surgical and medical treatment enjoy a special position so far as this part of the criminal law is concerned,[59] and judicial authority has expressly regarded 'proper medical treatment'[60] and 'reasonable surgical interference'[61] as being lawful, in the public interest, and an exception to the general rule that consent is not a defence to the causation of bodily injury. However, the limits of this so-called medical exception remain uncertain because the courts have not defined what amounts to 'proper medical treatment' or 'reasonable surgery',[62] apart from indicating that treatment 'in accordance with good medical practice'[63] is lawful. Since 'Good Medical Practice' is the term used by the General Medical Council (GMC) to denote acceptable standards for medical practice,[64] this suggests that professional standards concerning qualification and practice are key to determining what is in the public interest and support for this approach may be found in *BM*.[65]

We have considered whether the consent of adult patients with capacity should be a sufficient condition to render medical treatment lawful, removing the need for any regulation concerning the medical exception. A broader approach to consent would accord greater respect to individual autonomy and accord with Millian and Feinbergian liberal principles. However, there are cogent reasons for not adopting such an approach. First, some non-therapeutic surgery is so harmful that its prohibition may be justified based on its violation of the would-be patient's dignity. An example of this is the case of 'Stalking Cat', an American man who underwent multiple body modification procedures to resemble a female tiger, including having his upper lip surgically split, septum relocated, ears reshaped,

[59] JF Stephen, *A Digest of the Criminal Law*, 4th edn (Macmillan, 1997) Art 204, n 1.

[60] *A-G's Reference (No 6 of 1980)* (1981) 73 Cr App R 63, 66 (Lord Lane); *Airedale NHS Trust v Bland* [1993] AC 789, 891 (Lord Mustill); *Brown* (n 20) 266 (Lord Mustill).

[61] *Brown* (n 20) 231 (Lord Templeman); 243 (Lord Jauncey); 266 (Lord Mustill).

[62] M Brazier and S Fovargue, 'Transforming wrong into right: What is 'proper medical treatment'?' in S Fovargue and A Mullock (eds), *The Legitimacy of Medical Treatment: What Role for the Medical Exception?* (Routledge, 2016) 14.

[63] *Brown* (n 20) 258–59.

[64] GMC, *Good Medical Practice* (2019). The GMC is the public body responsible for the registration and regulation of medical practitioners.

[65] *BM* (n 34), [13], [17], [19] and [44]; cf *Paterson* [2022] EWCA Crim 456, [8].

and subdermal silicone implants inserted.[66] Second, the reality of the doctor/patient relationship needs to be recognised: medical practitioners play a key role in shaping the patient's knowledge and understanding of their condition and available treatments; patients who are (or believe themselves to be) unwell are likely to be pre-disposed to accept available therapeutic interventions offered by a doctor.[67] As Mullock has observed, the patient's ability 'to consent in a truly autonomous fashion, is restricted'.[68] Unfortunately, experience has shown us that 'bad-apple' surgeons are willing to manipulate the consent process, betray patients' trust, transgress professional, ethical and regulatory requirements, and cause harm to their patients. In these circumstances, we argue that there is a proper role for the criminal law to intervene in protecting patients from such harm.

Whilst the medical profession may properly be criticised for being insufficiently proactive in protecting patients from harmful procedures and practitioners,[69] there is a danger that reform of the medical exception to incorporate a more patient-focused conception of 'reasonableness' would blur the line between the criminal law and the tort of negligence, and lead to less certainty as to which treatments are acceptable and lawful.[70] In practice, whether a patient is offered a treatment, which they can then decide to consent to, depends on medical opinion as to whether a treatment is appropriate, based on medical evidence and professional guidance. Therefore, we propose that the test for determining whether the treatment falls within the medical exception should be whether the treatment is regarded as appropriate by a responsible body of medical practitioners.[71] Medically unnecessary treatment, such as the surgeries performed in *Paterson*, and treatment regarded as inappropriate,[72] would not fall within the exception. In relation to innovative procedures, case law suggests this test would not lead to criminal liability provided the clinician regards the treatment as being appropriate, the treatment is not futile or improper, and the patient either consents to the treatment or, in the case of an incapacitated patient, the treatment is in their best interests.[73]

In 1995 the Law Commission recommended that the law be reformed to create a statutory exception recognising the lawfulness of 'proper medical treatment'.[74] However, this recommendation has not been followed by successive Governments,

[66] F Minerva, 'Cosmetic surgery and conscientious objection' (2017) 43 *Journal of Medical Ethics* 230, 231.

[67] See *Paterson* (n 65).

[68] A Mullock, 'Surgical harm, consent, and English criminal law: When should "bad-apple" surgeons be prosecuted?' (2021) 21 *Medical Law International* 343, 361.

[69] P Lewis, 'The Medical Exception' (2012) 65 *Current Legal Problems* 355, 373; Mullock (n 68) 366–67.

[70] Cf *Paterson* (n 65), [33].

[71] This test is known as the *Bolam* test: *Bolam v Friern Hospital Management Committee* [1957] 1 WLR 582, although in the context of our proposed defence the test focuses upon the appropriateness of the treatment, not the quality of the treatment provided.

[72] Brazier and Fovargue (n 62) 24–25.

[73] *Simms v Simms; A v A and another* [2002] EWHC 2734, [49]–[51], [58]; *NHS Trust v J* [2006] EWHC 3152; Brazier and Fovargue (n 62) 28–29.

[74] *Consent in the Criminal Law* (n 6) paras 8.49–8.52.

and subsequent reports relating to the reform of non-fatal offences have not considered this 'exception'.[75] We recognise one might argue governmental inactivity reflects that, despite legal uncertainty, the legality of most medical and surgical procedures is uncontroversial because the treatment is either accepted as being therapeutic or statute provides a lawful basis for treatment; and the patient either provides valid consent or, if incapacitated, it is in their best interests. However, there are cogent reasons why reform is necessary:

1. There has been extensive regulation of healthcare professions since the Law Commission last considered this matter,[76] with the requirement of registration being introduced to protect patients from so-called quacks and practitioners who did not meet professional standards. We take the view that, where medical practitioners are legally required to register with their professional body and the Care Quality Commission and/or to obtain a licence to practise, they should not be able to avail themselves of the' medical exception' if they fail to do so. The introduction of a such a requirement would also clarify the law relating to deception vitiating consent in cases where patients are treated by unqualified/unregulated practitioners. In *Melin*,[77] a deception that the appellant was medically qualified was held to amount to a deception as to professional status which was inextricably linked to identity and capable of vitiating consent. Yet, in *Richardson*,[78] a failure by a qualified and registered dentist to inform patients that she was suspended from practice did not amount to a deception as to identity. Our proposal would mean that arguments that a failure to be registered or licensed did not vitiate the patient's consent to treatment would not result in the defendant's acquittal because the medical exemption would not apply.
2. The increasing social acceptance and popularity of cosmetic surgery procedures (including procedures which carry significant risks of mortality),[79] conducted for aesthetic reasons and offer no physical and limited psychological benefit to the patient. In particular, labiaplasty, a form of aesthetic genital surgery (AGS), has increased dramatically, with a twenty-three per cent worldwide increase in procedures between 2017 and 2021.[80] However,

[75] CLRC Cmnd 78344 (1980); L Com No 143 (1985); L Com No 177 (1989); L Com CP No 122 (1992); HO CP, *Violence: Reforming the Offences Against the Person Act 1861*(1998); L Com CP No 217 (2014) and L Com No 361 (2015).

[76] See, eg, Health and Social Care Act 2008 (Regulated Activities) Regulations 2014, SI 2014/2936, Sch 1; Health and Social Care Act 2008 (Regulated Activities) Amendment Regulations 2015, SI 2015/64; Health and Care Act 2022, Sch 19.

[77] *Melin* (n 40) [30]–[40].

[78] *Richardson* (n 39).

[79] See, eg, the 'Brazilian Butt-Lift' procedure. This carries a significant risk of death from fat embolus (as high as 1:2351): MM Mofid et al, 'Report on Mortality from Gluteal Fat Grafting: Recommendations from the ASERF Task Force' (2017) 37 *Journal of Aesthetic Surgery* 796.

[80] International Society of Aesthetic Plastic Surgery (ISAPS), *ISAPS Survey on Aesthetic/Cosmetic Procedures performed in 2021* (2023).

there is undesirable uncertainty regarding the borderline between lawful AGS and unlawful FGM, which is prohibited save in very limited specified therapeutic circumstances.[81] Clarity on this issue has not been provided by Crown Prosecution Service guidance, which suggests that the medical exception provided in section 1(2)(a) of the 2003 Act 'is unlikely to apply where the surgery is purely to alter the appearance of the genitals'.[82]

3. Doubts and inconsistency exist regarding the legality of surgery to treat psychiatric/psychological conditions. For example, gender reassignment surgery to treat Gender Identity Disorder is lawful. However, it has been suggested that limb amputation to treat Body Integrity Identity Disorder is not,[83] although the only surgeon to conduct such procedures in the UK was neither investigated nor prosecuted for his conduct.[84]
4. There is some dispute as to whether the common law offence of mayhem or maim, to which consent is not a defence, may apply to certain forms of surgical practice (eg, healthy limb amputation).[85] Although it may be argued that this offence is obsolete,[86] and ought no longer to be charged,[87] we believe that statutory reform should clarify that this offence is abolished.

Sports

Despite the often-high risk of bodily injury, regulated sports offer clear personal and social benefits.[88] However, there are obvious difficulties in determining which sports should fall within the scope of the defence, and how the rules of those sports inform the availability and limits of the defence. To that end, we defer to the National Governing Bodies and Parliament[89] to determine which sports offer sufficient regulation to fall within the scope of the exception and how those regulations are constructed and interpreted, which are both likely to develop and change over time.[90]

[81] Female Genital Mutilation Act 2003.

[82] CPS, *Female Genital Mutilation Prosecution Guidance* (2019). Cf C Dyer, 'FGM: Surgeons who do cosmetic surgery may risk prosecution' (2019) 367 *British Medical Journal* 16094.

[83] See J Johnston and C Elliott, 'Healthy Limb Amputation: Ethical and Legal Aspects' (2002) 2 *Clinical Medicine* 431.

[84] T Elliott, 'Body Dysmorphic Disorder and the Limits of Consent' (2009) 17 *Med LR* 149.

[85] ibid, 171–72. PDG Skegg, *Law, Ethics and Medicine* (Clarendon Press, 1984) 43–6.

[86] *Brown* (n 20) 262 (Lord Mustill); cf 247–48 (Lord Lowry).

[87] *Rimmington; Goldstein* [2006] 1 AC 459, [30].

[88] The public benefits for those engaging in regulated sports are numerous, including the societal and health benefits, instilling of discipline, and opportunity for self-advancement.

[89] It is important to note that Parliament is not obliged to accede to any rule changes instituted by NGBs and should oversee the regulation of sports.

[90] Our view is that the time has come for the state to determine those sports that can lawfully rely on a special exemption from the criminal law. While we believe that while boxing and (some) martial art sports should be afforded exemption, others fly too close to prizefighting by another name. The legal

The legal jurisprudence on sports and bodily injury distinguishes between sports that do/do not involve fighting as the defining activity. In sports that do not involve fighting as the defining activity, if the injury is intentionally caused, criminal liability may arise even if the incident falls within the rules of the game.[91] Where the injury is non-intentional and a foreseeable consequence of participating in the sport, the rules of the game are likely to be attested as potent evidence of what risks are consented to by the players.[92] However, the rules of the game are not the sole determinant of liability. In competitive sports, conduct outside the rules can occur in the heat of the moment and still not reach the threshold level required to be criminal. To determine whether a player impliedly consented to the *risk* of injury occurring outside the rules of the game, we recommend codification of *Barnes* and the Canadian position espoused in *Cicarelli*.[93] This requires an objective assessment, independent of the individual players, that considers the type of sport, the safety rules and level and conditions under which the game is played, the nature of the injuring act, the extent of the force employed, the degree of risk of injury, and the state of mind of the offending player. Therefore, for non-fighting sports, the public interest defence only provides players with a defence to the reckless causation of SDI, having regard to the stated objective criteria.

In the case of sports that involve rule-governed fighting, all injuries, up to and including death,[94] seem to be within the purview of effective consent, provided the injury is caused within the rules of the sport. This is likely only to be true for well-established fighting sports, like boxing,[95] and the position is much less clear for newer fighting sports, like Thai boxing and cage-fighting. However, whether boxing and newer fighting sports, which may cause SDI and worse, fall within the scope of the exception should depend on Parliamentary approval. For those rule-governed fighting sports that receive approval, the defence provides players with a defence to the intentional and reckless causation of SDI, per the objective criteria above.

For all sports, including fighting sports, all instances of intentionally caused injuries falling outside the rules of any game, including the zone of tolerance, should lead to criminal liability.

status of these sports is controversial and should be subject to scrutiny and special consideration by Parliament.

[91] *Bradshaw* (1878) Cox CC 83.

[92] *Barnes* (n 14).

[93] (1989) 54 CCC (3d) 121. The Law Commission similarly advocated for this position at one time. See Law Commission, *Consent and Offences Against the Person* (n 6) paras 10.7–10.23.

[94] In the circumstances where serious bodily injury is intended, and death is caused.

[95] The legality of boxing does not rest on any statute or significant appellate decision, but the generally held assumption of legality based on social facts. M Gunn and D Ormerod, 'The Legality of Boxing' (1995) 15 *LS* 181.

Sexual Conduct

To review the implications of our public interest defence on the lawfulness of harm caused during sexual conduct, it is helpful first to review the current position.

Consent serves a dual function in determining the lawfulness of sexual conduct. For sexual offences, non-consent serves an inculpatory function; it is for the tribunal of fact to determine whether there was an absence of consent to satisfy the *actus rei* of those offences. However, for non-fatal offences involving sexual conduct, consent serves an exculpatory function, providing A with a defence to *prima facie* wrongdoing. This occurs when B factually consents to the causation of injury at the hands of A *during* or *for* mutual sexual gratification. In such circumstances, if the state recognises B's consent to injury as legally transformative, A's conduct moves from a crime of violence to private sexual conduct.

Sexual conduct involves the causation and risk of harm at all levels. At its very core, it involves contact between two or more persons. However, no battery is committed if A and B consensually engage in such conduct. The justification for this is uncontroversial and has been stated above; the 'absence of consent' forms a fundamental part of the *actus reus* of battery. This is true even if it is a BDSM encounter. Unfortunately, once this low harm threshold is exceeded, and A causes B actual harm or worse, there is a distinct lack of doctrinal certainty as to when B's consent provides A with a defence. To determine the lawfulness of such conduct, the current framework requires us to distinguish injuries caused *incidentally* to the pursuit of mutual sexual gratification from injuries caused *for* sexual gratification.[96]

Suppose A causes B actual harm or worse but did not intend or foresee the risk of injury. In that case, B's consent to the 'battery' prevents A's criminal liability for a more serious offence, including homicide. B's injury is incidental to the primary objective of mutual sexual gratification.[97] Conversely, if A intentionally or recklessly causes B actual harm or worse *for* sexual gratification, B's consent is immaterial to A's criminal liability.[98] *Brown* illustrates this. For this reason, all instances of BDSM that involve the causation of actual or serious harm are presently unlawful.[99]

Unfortunately, the current position implies that many common sex injuries are *de jure* unlawful. For instance, 'injuries' such as 'love bites', scratches, and teeth marks from affectionate biting may give rise to section 47 liability. These are deliberately inflicted injuries, meaning they fall within the scope of the general rule espoused in *Brown* and section 71, and render any consent by B ineffective. It is hard to describe such injuries as incidental to sexual conduct and lawful, given how they are caused; they are *part of* the sexual interaction.

[96] This view is also supported in the academic literature: Duff (n 12) 39.
[97] *Meachen* (n 17) citing *Slingsby* (n 23).
[98] *Emmett* [1999] EWCA Crim 1710.
[99] DAA 2021, s 71.

Whether injuries sustained during sexual conduct are incidental or for sexual gratification is not binary. Many sexual acts traverse the boundary between pain and pleasure. Indeed, a wide array of sexual acts are commonly performed between consenting adults where the risks of injury are well known, with anogenital injury from penile, digital, or object penetration commonly reported.[100] If A and B take precautions (eg, lubrication) before engaging in sexual activity, that is potent evidence they are aware of the risks of such conduct, even if the risk is slight. If A is aware of such risk, A's only 'defence' is that the conduct was justified to preclude a finding of recklessness. However, the courts have not analysed these cases in this way, and a court would likely think it inconsistent with *Brown* and section 71 to recognise the satisfaction of BDSM desires as a justified reason for risk-taking.

The current position also seeks to establish A's *desire* to cause B's injury. In *Dica*, Judge LJ, in a discussion of *Brown*, distinguished between cases where A wants to cause pain as a vehicle for pleasure from cases where there was a risk that harm might occur, but not desired.[101] On this account, to determine the lawfulness of injuries inflicted during sex we must assess whether A wanted B to feel pain. However, we argue that this is a tenuous distinction that fails to account for sexual practices where pleasure and pain are intertwined.

Returning to our proposal, recall that the 'public interest' defence provides A with a defence to the causation of bodily harm, up to the level of SDI, provided that B consented to (the risk of) such harm. Raising the harm threshold to this level encapsulates the majority of BDSM practices, rendering them *de jure* lawful without the need for special exception.[102] However, the intentional or reckless causation of SDI and above remains unlawful. The principal reason we do not extend our defence to BDSM at or above SDI is because of the lack of state regulation and oversight of such practices. In this way, regulated sports and medical procedures are distinctly different.

For those who engage in BDSM practices, our proposal offers three benefits over the current position. First, by raising the threshold of harm where consent is effective to harms falling short of SDI, the issue of the causation of minor injuries during sex is resolved. Second, it removes A's *motivation* from the legal analysis of whether consent is lawful. As such, it no longer matters *why* A causes B bodily injury; if A and B derive pleasure from (the risk of) pain, that is to be treated in law as the same as the incidental causation of injury during sexual activity. Finally, our defence includes an evidential presumption that protects against the inauthentic use of the defence within the context of abuse.

[100] JS Jones et al, 'Anogenital injuries in adolescents after consensual sexual intercourse' (2003) 10 *Academic Emergency Medicine* 1378; Martin Dahlberg et al, 'Retained sex toys: an increasing and possibly preventable medical condition' (2019) 34 *International Journal of Colorectal Disease* 181.

[101] *Dica* (n 18), [51].

[102] This is an important implication of our proposal given the empirical research illustrates BDSM practices are more prevalent than ever. A Brown et al, 'A Systematic Scoping Review of the Prevalence, Etiological, Psychological, and Interpersonal Factors Associated with BDSM' (2020) 57 *The Journal of Sex Research* 781.

There are, however, two concerns that need addressing. The first relates to the theoretical and moral problem of sadists who engage in BDSM practices. The second relates to the efficacy of our abuse safeguards. We address both of these in turn.

Regarding the moral problem of sadists, Dempsey argues that caution must be exercised if we adopt a Feinbergian justification for permitting consent to the causation of harm in cases of BDSM.[103] We have argued the importance of consent from a liberal standpoint, where B's consent allows A to exclude some of the reasons against acting in that way based on the *prima facie* assumption that the act is contrary to B's well-being. However, this causes issues for sadists. One implication of adopting our liberal philosophical approach is that it only provides A with a defence insofar as A acts *for* those reasons. Or, as Herring writes, A can only rely on B's consent if A seeks to *promote* B's well-being.[104] However, for a sadist, Dempsey argues that A takes B as his victim, for, in virtue of A's sadistic explanatory reasons, B's consent fails to bear transformative normative force on the moral quality of A's conduct.[105] However, our response is that, during BDSM practices, A (a sadist) *may* act with mixed motives, and pain is not necessarily against B's well-being.[106] It seems integral to *legitimate* instances of BDSM, and not abuse, that A is acting to give B an experience that is *both* painful and pleasurable and that this is desired by A. Furthermore, by raising the threshold of harm that can be lawfully consented to, we acknowledge that serious harm is not *always* against B's interests. However, we agree that if A is motivated solely by desire for sexual gratification, the defence should be unavailable since B's factual consent fails to transform A's wrongdoing into permissible conduct.

Regarding the potential abuse of the defence, our proposal seeks to protect abuse victims while respecting the freedom for *any* self-regarding choice made by competent adults to engage in sexual activity that may cause injury falling short of SDI. However, caution must be exercised so as not to surreptitiously permit violence under the guise of lawful sexual conduct and protect those most vulnerable who are manipulated into participating in BDSM without valid consent.[107] We recognise the political objections to permitting the causing of *any* harms during sexual encounters. In our view, these objections stem, *inter alia*, from two primary sources: (1) a desire to prevent violent sex in abusive relationships,[108] and (2) the feminist and gendered connotations that women have been historically subjected

[103] Dempsey (n 46).
[104] J Herring, '*R v Brown* (1993)' in Philip Handler et al (eds), *Landmark Cases in Criminal Law* (Hart, 2017) 346.
[105] Dempsey (n 46) 24.
[106] Herring (n 104) 346.
[107] See *Keeble* [2001] EWCA Crim 1764.
[108] J Horn, 'Fifty Shades of Oppression: Sadomasochism, Feminism, and the Law' (2015) 4 *Journal of Women, Gender, and the Law* 1; J Herring and S Choudhry, 'Righting Domestic Violence' (2006) 20 *International Journal of Law Policy and the Family* 95.

to violence at the hands of men.[109] Notwithstanding these concerns, our view is that the criminal law *should* permit such conduct where abuse is absent.

To protect against the inauthentic use of the defence and A advancing the narrative of 'rough sex gone wrong', our proposal offers two layers of protection. The first resides within the threshold of harm that can be consented to; if A intentionally or recklessly causes SDI, A is afforded no defence of consent *tout court*. The second layer is secured through an evidential presumption. This provides that if A did the relevant act in an abusive capacity, it is evidentially presumed that: (a) B did not consent to the relevant act, and (b) A did not hold an honest and reasonable belief that V consented to the relevant act. We adopt the non-gendered definition of 'abuse' in section 1(3) of the DAA and do not propose limiting it to domestic abuse cases only.[110] If the presumption is successfully raised, the burden of proof shifts to A to prove that they were not acting in an abusive capacity and B's consent valid. It is for the tribunal of fact to determine whether there is sufficient evidence of abuse to vitiate B's consent.

Furthermore, since section 71 of the DAA ostensibly covers all sexual relationships, not just abusive relationships, we propose that the intention behind enacting section 71 of the DAA is better served through an evidential presumption, which does not encroach on the personal autonomy of others who wish to engage in legitimate and consensual BDSM practices.[111]

We acknowledge that the efficacy in dealing with abuse cases lies as much in implementing the law as in the letter of the law, perhaps more so. This is demonstrated by the difficulties in successfully prosecuting individuals for section 76 of the SCA 2015, the offence of controlling and coercive behaviour in an intimate or family relationship.[112] While the standard response for addressing the deficiencies in implementing abuse provisions is to recommend judicial training, the impact of this is likely to be short-term.[113] Burton argues that critical elements to successfully implementing and prosecuting abuse offences are better policing and stronger consequences for their poor practices.[114] We share this view and argue that better policing, improved CPS decision-making processes, and judicial training are needed to address the structural gender inequality evident in abuse cases to prevent the inauthentic use of our defence.

[109] In England and Wales, every known instance of death caused during sex games were by the acts of another man. WCCTT found that 59 women and seven men were killed in sex games gone wrong, where the defendant claimed the deceased had been an enthusiastic participant. Also see E Stark, *Coercive Control: The Entrapment of Women in Personal Life* (OUP, 2007) 363.

[110] This includes a wide definition of abuse, mapping onto a broader understanding of the nature of abuse and includes 'coercive control'.

[111] Cf the evidence submitted by WCCTT for the Public Bill Committee: Domestic Abuse Bill 2019–21.

[112] M Burton, *Domestic Abuse, Victims and the Law* (Routledge, 2022) ch 5.

[113] I Brennan et al, 'Policing a new domestic abuse crime: Effects of force-wide training on arrests for coercive control' (2021) 31(10) *Policing and Society* 1153.

[114] Burton (n 112) ch 2.

4. Conclusion

The defence of consent to serious non-sexual, non-fatal offences is a complex and controversial area of law. As such, we have been unable to explore all aspects of, and difficulties with, consent to bodily injury within this chapter. What we have sought to do is to set out a framework for a statutory public interest defence, which would provide greater clarity for the criminal law, both at the *ex-ante* and *ex-post* stages, in drawing a much-needed boundary between legality and criminality.

To summarise, we propose a statutory 'public interest' defence to reform the law on consent to bodily injury. Our proposal offers three principal benefits over the current framework. First, by providing A with a statutory defence to the causation of injury falling short of SDI, and permitting the causation of SDI and above in the context of medical procedures and regulated sports, we give greater deference to autonomy. Second, including an evidential presumption, which vitiates consent where there is evidence of abuse, provides a considered means for protecting victims of abuse while respecting the freedom for *any* self-regarding choice made by competent adults. Third, we move from an arbitrary category-based rationale for justifying injury caused above the permitted threshold to a regulatory-based rationale.

Comment on Chapter 6

Consent to Bodily Harm and the Public Interest

MICHELLE MADDEN DEMPSEY*

Daniel Bansal and Tracey Elliott's proposal to reform the law regarding consent to bodily harm is persuasive and appealing.[1] This brief response outlines the need for law reform in this area, examines key features of Bansal and Elliott's proposal, and raises three considerations that may require further clarification in order to appropriately implement their reforms.

1. The Need for Reform

Under existing English law, the 'threshold for harm that can be legally consented to is set remarkably low': anything more than 'transient or trifling' harm cannot be consented to, unless the circumstances fall within a narrow category of cases.[2] Each time a hairstylist cuts a client's hair – no matter how specifically requested the style, how expertly the stylist performs the task, or how delighted the client is with the results – the cutting of hair could very well amount to a crime, unless the defendant can successfully plead a defence. So, too, with ear piercing and tattooing. In each case, the client's consent to the hair cutting, ear piercing, or tattooing would provide a defence – and so there would be no crime. Yet surely something has gone wrong when the criminal law defines offences so expansively that one must rely upon a criminal defence to avoid conviction in such cases.[3]

* Harold Reuschlein Scholar Chair and Professor of Law, Villanova University Charles Widger School of Law. My thanks to John Child, Jonathan Rogers, and Melissa Bone for organising this volume and inviting me to contribute. Many thanks to Daniel Bansal and Tracey Elliott for their informative and insightful chapter.

[1] D Bansal and T Elliott, 'Consent to Bodily Harm and the "Public Interest"' (this volume).

[2] Bansal and Elliott (n 1) fn 31, citing *DPP v Smith* [2006] EWHC 94 to support the view that the offence has been committed. Other commentators view the matter as uncertain. JJ Child, et al, *Simester and Sullivan's Criminal Law: Theory and Doctrine*, 8th edn (Hart, 2022) 880.

[3] As Antony Duff argues, criminal offences should generally be defined in terms of *pro tanto* wrongs, not mere *prima facie* wrongs. RA Duff, 'De Minimis and the Structure of the Criminal Trial' (2023) 42 *Law and Philosophy* 57, 79–84.

The problem doesn't end there. For while a consent defence is available in cases involving haircuts, ear piercing, and tattoo artistry, things are considerably less clear in cases involving 'love bites' (known as 'hickeys' in the US). No matter how welcome, desired, or explicitly requested – it remains an open question in English law as to whether giving someone a 'love bite' constitutes a complete crime.[4] If a 'love bite' does amount to more than a 'transient or trifling' harm, then actual bodily harm arises and there is no defence clearly available under existing English law.[5]

The potential overbreadth and lack of clarity regarding the legal status of 'love bites' arise from the fact that existing English law allows for a consent defence to causing bodily harm only in a limited range of cases. Specifically, the consent of the 'victim' will not provide a defence in cases involving the intentional or reckless infliction of anything more than 'transient or trifling' harm to another person, unless the activity clearly falls within (or can be considered a 'close analogy' to) a limited range of categories, such as medical treatment, regulated sports, tattooing, and horseplay.[6] Notably absent from this 'exceptional categories' framework is a defence in cases where consensual bodily harm is caused for the purpose of sexual gratification: thus, the precarious legal status of 'love bites'.[7]

Even where the legal framework is more clearly defined, it remains problematic for at least three reasons.[8] First, the framework is grounded in the notoriously poorly reasoned *R v Brown*, a case that 'fits the stereotype of judges being out-of-touch dinosaurs, whose judgments are motivated more by personal prejudice than respect for legal principle'.[9] The facts of *Brown* involved a group of homosexual men engaging in sadomasochist sex. Homophobic anxieties were on full display in expressions of concern regarding the 'corruption' of one of the younger participants, with Lord Lane (later quoted by Lord Templeman) remarking, 'It is some comfort … that [he] has now settled into a normal heterosexual relationship'.[10] While the majority's reasoning has been widely criticised as heterosexist,

[4] The term 'crime' is used herein to reflect a criminal offence for which there is no valid defence. For similar usage, see J Edwards, 'Criminalization Without Punishment' (2017) 23 *Legal Theory* 69, 72.

[5] As Bansal and Elliott observe, harm that exceeds this level 'need not be significant, with minor injuries such as cuts and bruises falling within this definition' (n 1), citing *Donovan* [1934] 2 KB 498; *T v DPP* [2003] EWHC 266.

[6] Bansal and Elliott organise the activities into five categories (n 1) fn 23. Compare the eight categories set out in J Herring, *Criminal Law* (Hart, 2023) 110–12. On the extension to cases that constitute a 'close analogy', see *BM* (2018) EWCA Crim 560, [41].

[7] If the bodily harm consists of, or is a result of, being infected with a sexually transmitted infection, there is a defence available where 'V consented to the sexual activity in the knowledge or belief that D had the sexually transmitted infection'. Domestic Abuse Act 2021, s 71(4). Aside from this exception, the Domestic Abuse Act 2021 tracks the general rule of *Brown*, according to which there is no defence in cases where consensual bodily harm is caused for the purpose sexual gratification. Domestic Abuse Act 2021, s 71(2).

[8] Bansal and Elliott outline further reasons for concern (n 1) 192–195. For the sake of brevity here, I will focus on just these three concerns.

[9] J Herring, '*R v Brown* (1993)' in P Handler, H Mares and I Williams (eds), *Landmark Cases* (Hart, 2017) 333.

[10] *R v Brown* [1994] 1 AC 212, 236 (Lord Templeman), citing [1994] 94 Cr App R 302, 310 (Lord Lane).

prudish, and illiberal, the substance of the legal ruling – that consent is no defence to causing bodily harm to another during BDSM[11] – remains the leading authority on the issue.[12]

Second, insofar as the current legal framework relies on the 'exceptional categories' approach, it may deny a consent defence in cases involving even low levels of bodily harm (such as 'love bites'). No matter how much people may desire and actively seek out an activity that causes or risks causing them a low-level of harm, the criminal law denies normative force to their consent unless the activity falls within (or is closely analogous to) one of the 'exceptional categories'. As a result, 'the threshold for harm that can be legally consented to is set remarkably low'.[13]

Third, the existing legal framework obscures the significance of vulnerability and abuse in cases involving the infliction of bodily harm. By framing the inquiry in terms of whether the conduct was consensual, the law fails to address cases in which the harmful conduct is nonetheless abusively inflicted. As Bansal and Elliott note, this failure is problematic insofar as it leaves the law without adequate resources to 'protect those most vulnerable who are manipulated into participating in' harmful activities.[14]

In their proposal to reform the law regarding consent to bodily harm, Bansal and Elliott abandon the framework grounded in *Brown* and its progeny. In its place, they recommend a legal framework that respects the value of individual autonomy in cases involving low levels of harm, acknowledges the relevance of abuse to the proper scope of criminalisation, and enlists the power of the regulatory state to demarcate the boundaries of legality in cases involving the most serious forms of harm.

2. Summary of Reforms

Bansal and Elliott's key move is to draw a sharp distinction between cases involving 'serious disabling injury' (SDI) and cases involving the infliction of bodily harm falling short of SDI.[15] This move is similar to the one endorsed by the Law Commission in 1995, albeit with a slightly amended definition of SDI.[16] For Bansal and Elliott, harm exceeds the SDI threshold if it includes the 'loss of a bodily member or organ, permanent bodily injury, permanent functional impairment,

[11] BDSM is an acronym for bondage, dominance, sadism, and masochism: the acronym will be used here interchangeably with the term sadomasochistic sex.

[12] Indeed, as noted above n 7, the substance of the judgment in *Brown* has largely been consolidated in Domestic Abuse Act 2021.

[13] Bansal and Elliott (n 1) 205.

[14] Bansal and Elliott (n 1) 207.

[15] Bansal and Elliott (n 1) 198–200.

[16] Law Commission, *Consent in the Criminal Law* (Consultation No 139, 1995) paras 4.29–4.40.

serious or permanent disfigurement, severe or prolonged pain, serious impairment of mental health, and prolonged unconsciousness'.[17]

With the SDI threshold in place, Bansal and Elliott articulate a general rule to govern each kind of case. In cases where the harm falls below the SDI threshold, Bansal and Elliott propose that a consent defence *should* generally be available.[18] Whereas, in cases involving SDI or death, a consent defence generally *should not* be available.[19] Of course, as we will see, these general rules come with some exceptions.

One exception to Bansal and Elliott's proposal carves out concerns cases involving abuse.[20] Specifically, in cases where there is evidence that bodily harm was abusively inflicted, this exception creates an evidential presumption that the victim did not consent to the harm, and that the defendant did not hold an honest and reasonable belief that the victim consented.[21] Once the presumption is triggered, the defendant bears a burden to establish that they were not acting abusively, and that the victim validly consented to the bodily harm.[22] If defendants fail to satisfy these burdens, they can properly be convicted.[23]

Bansal and Elliott's phrasing regarding the abuse exception strikes me as somewhat unclear when it comes to identifying the issue(s) that are subject to the evidential presumption. 'If the presumption is successfully raised', they explain, 'the burden of proof shifts to [the defendant] to prove that they were not acting in an abusive capacity *and* [that the 'victim's'] consent [was] valid.'[24] This sentence suggests that their abuse exception triggers burdens as to two distinct issues: (1) abuse, and (2) consent. However, the authors follow up this point by noting, that 'it is for the tribunal of fact to determine whether there is sufficient evidence of abuse to vitiate [the 'victim's] consent.'[25] This latter phrasing suggests that consent is the only issue, and evidence of abuse is simply relevant to determining whether consent is valid or vitiated. Since it is my view that abuse and consent are properly regarded as distinct issues and that treating them as such will better serve the goals that Bansal and Elliott envision, my discussion in the next section below will proceed on the assumption that their proposal triggers burdens as to abuse *and* consent, as separate issues.

[17] Bansal and Elliott (n 1) 198. This definition omits any requirement of 'serious distress'.

[18] '[C]ausation of injury to another person, falling short of serious disabling injury (SDI), should not be criminal if the other person provided valid consent to the injury of the type caused.' Bansal and Elliott (n 1) 190.

[19] Bansal and Elliott (n 1) 191.

[20] As Bansal and Elliott explain, 'this presumption [is] effective above and below the SDI threshold'. Ordinarily, however, it will only be relevant in cases involving harm below the SDI threshold, since consent is generally not available as a defence in cases involving more than SDI. Bansal and Elliott (n 1) 198.

[21] Bansal and Elliott (n 1) 197.

[22] Bansal and Elliott (n 1) 197.

[23] On the nature of the burdens created by evidential presumptions, see Child, et al (n 2) 1005–1006.

[24] Bansal and Elliott (n 1) 208 (emphasis added).

[25] Bansal and Elliott (n 1) 208.

A second exception to the general rules set out in Bansal and Elliott's proposal concerns cases involving the infliction of harm above the SDI threshold. I will refer to this as the regulatory exception. This exception will have immediate application in two kinds of cases: regulated medical treatment and sports. In cases where SDI is caused in the course of medical treatment, the general rule ('no consent defence to harm above SDI') will not apply, provided the medical treatment is regarded as appropriate by a responsible body of medical practitioners.[26] So, too, they propose that SDI caused in sporting activities should be legally permitted, so long as the relevant sport is regulated by National Governing Bodies and Parliament.[27]

Notably, the kind of cases that can, in principle, fall under the regulatory exception is not a closed list. As Bansal and Elliott explain, '[t]he principal reason we do not extend our defence to [other conduct that causes harm] at or above SDI is because of the lack of state regulation and oversight of such practices'.[28] Indeed, they explicitly 'leave open the possibility for SDI to be permitted … [if] regulatory bodies [were established] to oversee and enforce standards for businesses and individuals that offer (say) BDSM, extreme body modification, and dangerous exhibition services'.[29]

3. Three Considerations

There is much to commend Bansal and Elliott's proposed reforms. While the general framework they propose is appealing and well supported by their arguments, I offer the following considerations in hopes of adding further clarity in implementing their proposals.

The Need for 'Root and Branch' Reform

As the authors acknowledge, the key distinction in their proposal, between harms that fall above or below the SDI threshold, is not currently recognised in English criminal law. Rather, the key distinction in existing law is between 'actual bodily harm' (ABH), 'grievous bodily harm' (GBH), and 'wounding'.[30] Since the offence classifications (ABH, GBH, and wounding) do not track Bansal and Elliott's proposed defence classifications (below SDI and above SDI), implementing their

[26] Bansal and Elliott (n 1) 201, fn 71, citing *Bolam v Friern Hospital Management Committee* [1957] 1 WLR 582.

[27] The regulation of recognised sports will fall under existing National Governing Bodies, while any future regulation of newer sports, such as cage-fighting, will fall under the regulatory exception if and when Parliament decides to regulate them.

[28] Bansal and Elliott (n 1) 206.

[29] Bansal and Elliott (n 1) 196.

[30] J Herring, *Criminal Law*, 13th edn (Hart, 2023) 102–105.

reforms would create an 'offence-defence mismatch'.[31] Bansal and Elliott recognise this point and thus correctly call for their proposal to be implemented as part of 'a root and branch reform of non-fatal, non-sexual offences against the person'.[32]

Root and branch statutory reform regarding offences against the person would be welcome not only to eliminate the offence-defence mismatch, but to achieve two further goals. First, it would provide a welcome opportunity to explicitly replace *Brown* as the organising framework for this area of law, thus relegating the infamous case to 'the history books of judicial freaks and aberrations'.[33] Second, in defining crimes involving lower-level harms, comprehensive statutory reform would provide an opportunity to unequivocally confirm that lack of consent is an element of the actus reus, not an affirmative defence. By clarifying this matter, the law would avoid the risk of overbreadth illustrated above in cases of hair cutting, ear piercing, and tattooing, and would thereby promote important rule of law values regarding certainty and fair warning.[34]

Is this a 'Public Interest' Defence?

Bansal and Elliott call their defence a 'public interest' defence, but the label is potentially misleading. For, despite their own suggestion to the contrary, they are *not* proposing that each case be individually assessed to determine whether the particular facts establish that the conduct is in the public interest. That is, they are *not* proposing an approach like the one adopted in New Zealand.[35] Rather, the key question under Bansal and Elliott's proposed reform is whether conduct causing SDI falls into a *category* of conduct that is *regulated* by a public authority, not simply whether the conduct in a particular case is in the public interest all-things-considered.

Moreover, Bansal and Elliott have surprisingly little to say about what constitutes 'the public interest' when it comes to causing bodily harm. For example, rather than taking on that question directly when it comes to controversial conduct such as cage fighting and extreme (SDI-inflicting) BDSM, Bansal and Elliott simply defer to Parliament to determine when, whether, and how such conduct should

[31] D Ormerod and M Gunn, 'Second Law Commission Consultation Paper on Consent: (2) Consent – a second bash' (1996) *Crim LR* 694, 700–701, criticising the Law Commission's use of SDI on these grounds. See discussion in Bansal and Elliott (n 1) 199–200.

[32] Bansal and Elliott (n 1) 199.

[33] The quote comes from Herring (n 9) 333–34; but Herring argues in favour of salvaging *Brown* in substance, while remaining critical as to the Lord's poor reasoning in the case.

[34] J Horder, *Ashworth's Principles of Criminal Law*, 10th edn (OUP, 2022) 88–91.

[35] *Lee* (2006) 22 CRNZ 568 CA, [316] (emphasis added). J Tolmie, 'Consent to Harmful Assaults: The case for moving away from category-based decision making' [2012] *Crim LR* 656. Bansal and Elliott claim that their proposal is 'not wholly dissimilar' to the New Zealand approach, (n 1) 196 fn 44. However, insofar as they continue to ground their defence to SDI in terms of regulated categories of conduct, their approach seems quite dissimilar to New Zealand's particularistic, fact-specific approach.

be regulated. Once such regulation is in place, they would permit the infliction of SDI in such contexts, without any further inquiry regarding whether the conduct serves the public interest. As such, the proposed reforms (at least in cases involving SDI) seem better labelled as a 'regulatory defence' rather than a genuine 'public interest' defence.

The Abuse Exception

The most promising and important aspect of Bansal and Elliott's proposed reforms concerns the abuse exception. Recall that according to this exception, where evidence of abuse is present, the defendant bears the burden of proving that they were not acting abusively and that the victim validly consented to the bodily harm.[36] If the defendant fails to satisfy these burdens, they can properly be convicted.

As a conceptual matter, the framing of this exception is attractive because it acknowledges the possibility that competent, consenting adults can also be subject to abuse. As noted above, some phrasing by Bansal and Elliott occasionally seems in tension with this view. For example, they characterise their abuse exception as a means of 'protecting victims of abuse while respecting the freedom for any self-regarding choice made by competent adults'.[37] This phrasing risks embracing a false dichotomy between 'competent adults' on the one hand, and 'victims of abuse' on the other. However, a more generous interpretation of Bansal and Elliott's point – and one that is in keeping with the legal framework they have proposed – embraces the view that bodily harm, abusively inflicted, should be criminalised, even if consensual. Bansal and Elliott's framework allows for this possibility if we interpret the evidential presumption created by the abuse exception to require the defendant to carry the burden of proof on *two distinct issues*: (1) that they were not acting abusively, *and* (2) that the victim validly consented to the bodily harm. If the defendant merely succeeds in proving that the victim consented, but fails to prove that they themselves were not acting abusively, they can be convicted.

However, to avoid unfair burden shifting in cases where the defendant has established that they were *not* acting abusively, the prosecution should ultimately bear the burden of proof on the issue of consent.[38] So, in cases, where evidence of abuse is raised, the first question (on which the defendant should bear the burden of proof), is whether there was abuse in fact. If the defendant fails to carry this burden, they should be convicted. If the defendant proves there was no abuse,

[36] Bansal and Elliott (n 1) 207–208.

[37] Bansal and Elliott (n 1) 207, 209.

[38] This solution may require somewhat complicated jury instructions, with the jury being charged, first, to resolve the issue of abuse with the defendant carrying the burden on that issue; and (if the defendant meets their burden on the abuse issue) then, second, to resolve the issue of consent with the prosecution carrying the burden on that issue.

then we reach the second question: whether the harm was consensual. Here as elsewhere the burden of proving non-consent should fall on the prosecution. One further advantage of this formulation is that, where factual consent by itself is in issue, the prosecution must still always prove its case; to propose might otherwise might easily run into various obstacles which need not be encountered.[39]

As a policy matter, the abuse exception addresses valid and important concerns raised by feminist advocates who are rightly concerned about any expansion of a consent defence in cases involving the infliction of bodily harm.[40] Given the increasing use of 'rough sex' defences and the prevalence of dangerous conduct such as strangulation during sex, there is good reason to suppose that allowing a general consent defence in cases involving less than SDI will further hamper the ability of the criminal law to protect victims and hold abusers accountable.[41] The abuse exception, properly interpreted, will address some of these concerns by creating presumptions in cases where there is evidence of abuse.

As a practical matter, the abuse exception generates normatively appealing results in a range of cases. Taking just three examples, explored below: (1) *Brown*, which reached the right outcome, but for the wrong reasons;[42] (2) *Wilson*, which reached the wrong outcome for the wrong reasons;[43] and (3) *Emmett*, which reached the right outcome for the wrong reasons.[44] In all three cases, Bansal and Elliott's abuse exception would allow the courts to reach the right outcomes, for the right reasons.

As noted above, *Brown* involved a group of men engaging in BDSM. Since the infliction of harm during sadomasochistic sex did not fall within an 'exceptional category' and the Lords were unwilling to expand the categories to embrace such facts, the defendants' convictions were upheld. As already explained, the reasoning in *Brown* was notoriously problematic. However, the disposition (affirming conviction) seems justifiable as to at least some of the charges, if we apply Bansal and Elliott's abuse exception. As Herring observes, 'there must be concerns over whether the relationship between [at least some of] the defendants and the victims was abusive' given the significant age disparity and evidence that 'drink or drugs were employed to obtain consent'.[45] Given such evidence of abuse, the case could have proceeded to trial with defendants carrying a burden as set out above: first, they must prove that they were not acting abusively, and only then can they avail themselves of a defence that the victim(s) validly consented to bodily harm. Ultimately, it would be for the tribunal to determine these facts, but with the abuse

[39] My thanks to Jonathan Rogers for helping to refine and clarify these points.

[40] See research briefing submitted by We Can't Consent to This, 'Consent Defences and the Criminal Justice System further submission' (DAB73, June 2020).

[41] J Herring, 'Coercive Control and Rough Sex' in H Bows and J Herring (eds), *Rough Sex and the Criminal Law: Global Perspectives* (Emerald Publishing, 2023).

[42] *Brown* (n 10).

[43] *Wilson* [1996] 2 Cr App R 241.

[44] *Emmett* [1999] EWCA Crim 1710.

[45] Herring (n 9) 349, citing *Brown* (n 10) 236.

exception in place, some of the defendants could still have been convicted – albeit for different, and more justifiable, reasons.

In *Wilson*, a husband was convicted of an offence for branding his initials into his wife's buttocks with a hot knife at their shared home. The Court of Appeals reversed the conviction, distinguishing *Brown* despite echoing similar hetero-patriarchal social norms. 'Consensual activity between husband and wife, in the privacy of the matrimonial home is not, in our judgment, normally a proper matter for criminal investigation, let alone criminal prosecution.'[46] Consider, however, the following facts: the defendant claimed that his wife asked to be branded, but Mrs Wilson never gave evidence and thus never testified as to whether the branding was consensual; Mrs Wilson's injuries were only discovered a few days later when she visited her doctor, who then notified the police. As Jonathan Herring notes, '[o]ne of the few reasons why a doctor would breach confidentiality in this way is in cases of domestic abuse.'[47] While it is of course possible that the doctor's referral was merely made out of an abundance of caution and not due to other evidence indicating abuse, it seems at least possible that there could have been sufficient evidence to trigger the abuse exception in *Wilson*. Indeed, as Herring notes, '[t]he branding of a man's name on his female partner's buttocks seems like the nadir for an abuser seeking the ultimate control over his spouse.'[48] If the abuse exception were to be applied in *Wilson*, the defendant could have been convicted due to his failure to offer any evidence and resulting failure to carry his burden as to both abuse and consent.[49]

The final case, *Emmett*, is noteworthy for extending the ruling in *Brown* to a case of heterosexual sadomasochism.[50] Yet, while the disposition is laudable, the reasoning of the court is plagued by the deficiencies of the 'exceptional categories' framework. In *Emmett*, the male defendant was convicted of assault occasioning actual bodily harm against his female partner, based on the following facts: in one incident, he tightened a plastic bag over his female partner's head, such that she was unable to communicate with him and lost consciousness; in another, he set her breasts on fire with lighter fluid, resulting in third-degree burns.[51] As was the case in *Wilson*, the defendant claimed the infliction of bodily harm was consensual – but Emmett's partner never gave evidence. The victim's doctor, concerned by the injuries and her explanation of how they were caused, notified the police. At trial, the doctor was permitted to explain the nature of the injuries, but not the explanation of how the injuries occurred. Instead, the only explanation came from the

[46] *Wilson* (n 43) 244.
[47] Herring (n 41) 54.
[48] Herring (n 41) 54.
[49] Of course, if the abuse exception burden-shifting framework had been applicable in *Wilson*, the defendant may have chosen to offer evidence. Indeed, perhaps Mrs Wilson would have even testified. In that case, it would be for the factfinder to determine whether the branding was both consensual and non-abusive.
[50] *Emmett* (n 44).
[51] *Emmett* (n 44).

defendant's statements to the investigating police officers. Neither the defendant nor victim testified at trial. In light of reasonable inferences that might have been drawn if the matter had been addressed head-on (say, by allowing the doctor to testify more fully, or through testimony of family, friends, or neighbours who may have witnessed past abuse), Bansal and Elliott's abuse exception would likely have applied in *Emmett*, and thus the defendant would have carried a burden on the issue of abuse. Given the defendant's lack of evidence at trial and resulting failure to meet this burden, the disposition (conviction) could have remained in place, with improved reasoning that takes abuse into account.[52]

4. Conclusion

Bansal and Elliott are to be congratulated for presenting a convincing case for reforming the law on consent to bodily harm. While the key move in their proposal – separating cases that fall above and below the SDI threshold – echoes previous attempts at reform, it is no less appealing for that reason. Moreover, in creating their abuse exception, Bansal and Elliott add an important new tool for law reform: one that promises to address modern feminist concerns and hold abusers accountable for the harms they inflict.

[52] The caveats in n 49 apply.

7

Is it Time for the Next Seminal Economic Crime Statute? Modernising and Simplifying Tax Evasion Offences in the UK

SAM BOURTON*

Historically, little use was made of the criminal justice system in addressing tax evasion in the UK, with tax authorities preferring to conduct civil investigations, resulting in the imposition of civil penalties. From 1998–2002, the Inland Revenue brought only 263 prosecutions for tax offences,[1] with, at its lowest point in 2001/2, a mere 30 individuals prosecuted.[2] By 2007, His Majesty's Revenue and Customs (HMRC) only prosecuted two in a thousand cases of suspected tax evasion,[3] with the prosecution rate subsequently declining by a further 41 per cent by 2010.[4] Following the financial crisis and public dissatisfaction with responses to high-profile tax evasion scandals, the next decade saw a transformation in the enforcement of tax offences. In particular, a Parliamentary inquiry followed the HSBC (Suisse) scandal, where over 1000 UK account holders were investigated for tax evasion, yet only one individual was prosecuted.[5] Accordingly, HMRC were tasked with increasing the number of prosecutions for tax

* Senior Lecturer in Law, University of the West of England.

[1] *Tackling Fraud against the Inland Revenue: Report by the Comptroller and Auditor General* HC 429 (2002–03) 39.

[2] Inland Revenue, *Report of the Commissioners of Her Majesty's Inland Revenue for the Year Ending 31st March 2002, One-Hundred and Forty-Fourth Report* (Cm 5706, 2002). Customs and Excise typically made greater use of the criminal justice system in addressing tax offences, bringing 127 prosecutions in 1998–9, Lord Grabiner QC, *The Informal Economy* (HM Treasury, March 2000) 34.

[3] *Committee of Public Accounts, HMRC: Tackling the Hidden Economy* HC 712 (2007–08) 6.

[4] *Treasury Committee, Closing the Tax Gap: HMRC's Record at Ensuring Compliance* HC 1371 (2010–12) 11.

[5] *Public Accounts Committee, Oral Evidence: Tax Avoidance and Evasion: HSBC* HC 1095 (2014–15); *Public Accounts Committee, Oral Evidence: Increasing the Effectiveness of Tax Collection: A Stocktake of Progress Since 2010* HC 974 (2014–15).

evasion from 165 in 2010 to 1,165 prosecutions annually by 2014/15, by making sufficient referrals to the Crown Prosecution Service.[6] In response, the number of tax evasion prosecutions dramatically and steadily increased, from 420 in 2010/11 to 1288 in 2014/15.[7] Following this, 880 individuals were prosecuted from 2015–16,[8] followed by 886 prosecutions from 2016–17,[9] 917 prosecutions from 2017–18,[10] and 691 prosecutions from 2019–20.[11] Primarily owing to the impact of the COVID-19 Pandemic, from 2020, the number of prosecutions for tax evasion declined, with a mere 163 prosecutions from 2020–21 and 215 prosecutions from 2021–22.[12]

Despite this volte-face in tax law enforcement, insufficient attention has been paid by both academics and policy makers to the increasing use of the criminal justice system in combatting tax evasion.[13] Tax evasion offences have been enacted on an ad hoc basis and are comprehensive, separately criminalising the evasion of most types of taxation, as well as many of the underlying behaviours involved. However, to date, there has been little attempt to systematise and rationalise this patchwork of offences, causing duplicity and redundancy. To attempt to remedy the gap in existing literature, this chapter begins by providing a doctrinal analysis of tax evasion offences in the UK, highlighting the expansive scope of statutory offences, as well as the overuse of broad common law offences. The second part of this chapter provides an original comparison of the UK legal framework with its more rational US counterpart. This section also contrasts recent efforts to consolidate and modernise the law pertaining to other financial crimes, such as terrorism financing, money laundering, fraud and bribery. Ultimately, this chapter argues that the criminal offences pertaining to tax evasion should be simplified and modernised through the enactment of a contemporary statute, returning doctrinal coherence to this increasingly utilised area of criminal law. In particular, the UK should consider enacting a US-style system of tax evasion offences, which apply to a range of taxes and clearly distinguish culpable actions from omissions.

[6] *HM Treasury, Summer Budget 2015* HC 264 (2015–16) 43.

[7] *National Audit Office, Tackling Tax Fraud: How HMRC Responds to Tax Evasion, The Hidden Economy and Criminal Attacks* HC 610 (2015–16) 33; *HM Revenue and Customs, Annual Report and Accounts 2014–15 (For the year ended 31 March 2015)* HC 18 (2014–15) 16.

[8] *HM Revenue and Customs, Annual Report and Accounts 2015–16 (For the year ended 31 March 2016)* HC 338 (2015–16) 22.

[9] *HM Revenue and Customs, Annual Report and Accounts 2016–17 (For the year ended 31 March 2017)* HC 18 (2016–17) 24.

[10] *HM Revenue and Customs, Annual Report and Accounts 2017–18 (For the year ended 31 March 2018)* HC 1222 (2017–18) 25.

[11] HM Revenue & Customs, *HMRC Quarterly Performance Report: October to December 2020* (HMRC Corporate Report, 4 February 2021) Data Table.

[12] HM Revenue & Customs, *HMRC Quarterly Performance Report: January to March 2022* (HMRC Corporate Report, 18 July 2022) Data Table.

[13] At present, the only comprehensive study is P Alldridge, *Criminal Justice and Taxation* (OUP, 2017).

1. United Kingdom – Tax Evasion Offences

A plethora of offences are used to prosecute conduct associated with the evasion of taxation, from specific offences criminalising the evasion of each type of taxation, to general offences that criminalise the underlying fraudulent conduct. In fact, over 20 offences are used to prosecute tax evasion in the UK.

There are several statutory offences concerning income tax evasion, including an offence of being 'knowingly concerned in the fraudulent evasion of income tax by that or any other person'.[14] As a conduct offence, no loss or gain actually needs to be incurred by HMRC.[15] The offence can be committed by an act or omission,[16] and by single events as well as courses of conduct.[17] The offence captures not only those liable to pay income tax, but also, any person 'knowingly concerned' in the evasion, including professional facilitators and those who otherwise incite or collude in the offence.[18] Additional strict liability offences were enacted to criminalise the failure to give notice of chargeability to tax,[19] failure to deliver a return,[20] or the making of an inaccurate return,[21] in relation to offshore income, assets or activities in excess of £25,000 of potential lost tax revenue per year.[22]

The Value Added Tax Act 1994 contains five offences related to the evasion of VAT,[23] including the offence of being knowingly concerned in, or taking steps with a view to, the fraudulent evasion of VAT.[24] The phrases 'knowingly concerned' and 'taking steps with a view to' enable its application to not only those who evade VAT, but also (again) to those who facilitate this offence.[25] Additionally, there is a catch-all offence, which covers conduct that 'must have involved the commission by him of one or more offences under the preceding provisions.'[26] This offence is wide-ranging and is used when the specific offence is not identifiable, but the

[14] Enacted as a summary offence in the Finance Act 2000, s 144. The offence is now contained in s 106A of the Taxes Management Act 1970 and is triable either way.
[15] D Salter, 'Some Thoughts on the Fraudulent Evasion of Income Tax' (2002) 6 *British Tax Review* 489, 503.
[16] *Tuck* [2018] EWCA Crim 2529, [11].
[17] *Martin and another* [1998] 2 Cr App R 385 (CA); Although reflected in sentencing, *Khan* [2017] EWCA Crim 703.
[18] DC Ormerod, 'Summary Evasion of Income Tax' [2002] *Crim LR* 3, 14.
[19] Taxes Management Act 1970, s 106B.
[20] ibid, s 106C.
[21] ibid, s 106D.
[22] ibid, s 106B(1)(b), s 106C(1)(c), s 106D(1)(b), s 106F(2); The Sections 106B, 106C and 106D of the Taxes Management Act 1970 (Specified Threshold Amount) Regulations 2017, SI 2017/988, Reg 3. The offence applies to income tax and capital gains tax, and encompasses all offshore income and gains that are not reportable under the Common Reporting Standard, ibid, Reg 2C.
[23] Value Added Tax Act 1994, s 72(1), s 72(3)(a) & (b), s 72(8), s 72(10), s 72(11).
[24] ibid, s 72(1).
[25] *Binfield* [2019] EWCA Crim 1812; [2020] Lloyd's Rep FC 18.
[26] Value Added Tax Act 1994, s 72(8).

facts suggest an offence has been committed.[27] Despite laudable aims, the offence seemingly fails to cohere with fundamental principles of criminal law, specifically, the necessity for the specification of the particulars of an offence to enable the defendant to ascertain the nature and extent of the allegations.[28] Nevertheless, the offence has withstood challenges based on Article 7 of the European Convention on Human Rights (ECHR).[29]

Several offences pertaining to the evasion of duty, or smuggling offences, are contained in the Customs and Excise Management Act 1979.[30] The primary offence pertaining to the evasion of duty is contained in section 170 and can be committed in two ways. First, it is an offence for an individual to knowingly acquire possession of goods on which duty has been evaded,[31] or goods that are entirely prohibited or restricted,[32] such as drugs,[33] or protected wildlife,[34] as well as being knowingly concerned in activities relating to such goods.[35] Second, it is an offence for an individual to be 'knowingly concerned in any fraudulent evasion or attempt at evasion' of any duty, prohibition or restriction on the goods, or any applicable provision in the Act.[36] The second offence is much wider than the first and has been referred to as a 'sweeping up or catch all provision', owing to its ability to criminalise conduct by those outside of the initial smuggling operation.[37]

Other statutory offences criminalise being knowingly concerned in the fraudulent evasion of other taxes, such as stamp duty land tax.[38] Owing to the persistent issues surrounding the attribution of criminal liability to legal entities,[39] corporate offences of failing to prevent the facilitation of UK and foreign tax evasion have also been introduced.[40] The strict liability offences are designed to circumvent the common law's demand for identification of fault with the senior managers of a corporation,[41] by merely requiring proof that a person associated with the corporation facilitated a tax evasion offence.[42] It is a defence for

[27] J O'Donnell, 'Vat Investigation' (2007) 57 *VAT Dig* 1, 16.

[28] Alldridge (n 13) 59.

[29] Article 7 of the Convention for the Protection of Human Rights and Fundamental Freedoms (Rome, 4 November 1950); *Pattni* [2001] Crim LR 570 (CC).

[30] Customs and Excise Management Act 1979, s 167(1), s 167(3), s 168(1), s 170(1)&(2), s 170B.

[31] ibid, s 170(1)(ii).

[32] ibid, s 170(1)(i), s 170(1)(iii).

[33] See for instance, *Bhegani* [2016] EWCA Crim 2109; *Birks* [2017] EWCA Crim 810; *Jhurry* [2018] EWCA Crim 2799; [2019] 1 Cr App R (S) 40.

[34] See for instance, *Lendrum* [2011] EWCA Crim 228; [2011] 2 Cr App R (S) 69.

[35] Customs and Excise Management Act 1979, s 170(1)(b). Specifically, 'carrying, removing, depositing, harbouring, keeping or concealing or in any manner dealing with any such goods'.

[36] ibid, s 170(2).

[37] *Neal* [1984] 3 All ER 156 (CA); (1983) 77 Cr App R 283, 287.

[38] Finance Act 2003, s 95.

[39] Law Commission, *Corporate Criminal Liability: An Options Paper* (2022).

[40] Criminal Finances Act 2017, ss 45–46.

[41] *Serious Fraud Office v Barclays Plc* [2018] EWHC 3055 (QB); [2020] 1 Cr App R 28.

[42] Criminal Finances Act 2017, s 45(1), s 46(1).

the company to prove that it implemented reasonable prevention procedures.[43] However, the offence has not been prosecuted since its enactment.[44]

Additionally, general offences including fraud and false accounting can apply to fraudulent activities taken in furtherance of tax evasion, including the use of falsified documents or the provision of false information to HMRC.[45] Like tax evasion offences, fraud offences are notoriously expansive in scope.[46] Moreover, tax evasion is a predicate offence for the purposes of the anti-money laundering (AML) framework,[47] meaning that money laundering offences can be used against those who have evaded taxation.[48] When used as an additional, rather than a substitute charge, this is a form of 'uncritical over-criminalisation', whereby tax evaders face additional punishment despite failing to undertake any extra criminal conduct.[49]

Irrespective of these statutory offences, some of the most commonly utilised tax evasion offences are the common law offences of cheating the public revenue and conspiracy to defraud.[50] The offence of cheating the public revenue is long established,[51] and, unlike other common law cheats,[52] survived abolition upon the enactment of the Theft Act 1968.[53] It is widely used owing to the broad scope of the offence, encompassing the evasion of most taxes, through a wide range of acts and omissions,[54] both by the individual concerned and any facilitators.[55] As cheating can be a 'conduct offence', there is no need to prove any resultant loss.[56] In essence, 'cheating can include any form of fraudulent conduct which results in

[43] ibid, s 45(2), s 46(3).

[44] HM Revenue & Customs, *Number of Live Corporate Criminal Offences Investigations* (HMRC FOI Release, updated 30 June 2022).

[45] Fraud Act 2006, ss 2–3; Theft Act 1968, s 17. See for instance, *Backhouse v HM Revenue & Customs Prosecution Office* [2012] EWCA Civ 1000; [2013] Lloyd's Rep FC 1.

[46] See, eg, D Ormerod, 'The Fraud Act 2006 – Criminalising Lying?' [2007] *Crim LR* 193, 196.

[47] Proceeds of Crime Act 2002, ss 327–329, s 340.

[48] See for instance, *K* [2007] EWCA Crim 491; [2007] 1 WLR 2262; *William and William and William* [2013] EWCA Crim 1262; [2015] Lloyd's Rep FC 704.

[49] V Mitsilegas and N Vavoula, 'The Evolving EU Anti-Money Laundering Regime: Challenges for Fundamental Rights and the Rule of Law' (2016) 23 *Maastricht Journal of European and Comparative Law* 261, 267. This was recognised by the Supreme Court in *GH* [2015] UKSC 24; [2015] 1 WLR 2126, [48].

[50] TaxWatch, *Equality before the Law? HMRC's Use of Criminal Prosecutions for Tax Fraud and other Revenue Crimes. A Comparison with Benefits Fraud* (TaxWatch, 2021).

[51] G McBain, 'Modernising the Common Law Offence of Cheating the Public Revenue' (2015) 8(1) *Journal of Politics and Law* 40, 76.

[52] ibid, 40; see also D Ormerod, 'Cheating the Public Revenue' [1998] *Crim LR* 627, 628.

[53] The offence was expressly preserved in the Theft Act 1968, s 32(1)(a), despite the recommendation of the Criminal Law Revision Committee in its *Eighth Report: Theft and Related Offences* (Cmnd 2977, 1966).

[54] *Mavji* [1987] 1 WLR 1388, 1392 (CA).

[55] See for instance, *Whitson-Dew and Richards* [2019] EWCA Crim 2131; [2020] 1 Cr App R (S) 56; *Charlton* [1996] STC 1418 (CA).

[56] *Hunt* [1994] Crim LR 747, 748 (CA). If the offence is charged as a 'result offence', the prosecution may need to demonstrate loss, see *Lunn* [2017] EWCA Crim 34, [24].

diverting money from the revenue'.[57] As a common law offence, the maximum penalty is an unlimited fine or life imprisonment.[58] The breadth of the offence and its lack of certainty has led to allegations that the cheating offence is incompatible with the ECHR.[59] Many commentators have called for the abolition of the offence,[60] or for placing it on a statutory basis.[61]

Conspiracy to defraud also survived the abolition of other common law conspiracies, which were replaced by statutory offences.[62] There are said to be two forms or variants of the common law offence, specifically, 'agreeing dishonestly to prejudice another's economic interests' or 'agreeing to mislead a person with intent to cause him to act contrary to his duty'.[63] The offence is useful in tax evasion cases involving misrepresentation, falsification and/or concealment by several defendants,[64] or for prosecuting the facilitators of tax fraud schemes.[65] The offence is extraordinarily broad in nature, lacking any requirement to prove an intent to deceive,[66] or an intent to cause loss to the victim, or even any ill-motive; merely requiring a demonstration that the victim's, in this case HMRC's, interests have been set back in some way.[67] Indeed, the offence has been labelled 'one of the most controversial offences',[68] and has been subject to repeated calls for abolition from academics,[69] and from the Law Commission.[70]

Breadth, Overlap and Redundancy

The preceding section showed considerable overlap between the statutory and common law offences. Indeed, upon the enactment of the income tax evasion

[57] *Less*, *The Times* (30 March 1993).

[58] JH Howard, 'Cheating the Public Revenue' [2010] *Tax Journal* 16, 16.

[59] Specifically, Article 7. See, eg, G Virgo, 'Cheating the Public Revenue: Fictions and Human Rights' (2002) 61 *CLJ* 47. Yet challenges brought on this basis have been unsuccessful, *R. v Pattni* [2001] Crim LR 570.

[60] Ormerod (n 52) 645.

[61] McBain (n 51) 76; G Virgo, 'Cheating the Public Revenue' (2000) 59(1) *CLJ* 42, 45.

[62] Criminal Law Act 1977, s 1, s 5(2).

[63] *Evans* [2014] 1 WLR 2817, [36], quoting D Ormerod and DH Williams, *Smith's Law of Theft*, 9th edn (OUP, 2007), [5.12].

[64] See, eg *Bache* [2014] EWCA Crim 2464; *Bobrovas* [2014] EWCA Crim 752; *Hodges, Lineker and Stacey* [2006] EWCA Crim 2706.

[65] See for instance, *Hughes* (16 August 2018, unreported), Southwark Crown Court.

[66] *Scott v Metropolitan Police Commissioner* [1974] 3 WLR 741 (HL).

[67] *Wai Yu-Tsang v The Queen* [1992] 1 AC 269, 276–7 (PC); *Allsop* (1977) 64 Cr App R 29 (CA).

[68] D Ormerod and K Laird, 'Ivey v Genting Casinos – Much Ado about Nothing?' (2018) 9 *UK Supreme Court Yearbook* 380, 393.

[69] See, eg, ATH Smith, 'Conspiracy to Defraud' [1988] *Crim LR* 508; JC Smith, 'Conspiracy to Defraud: Some Comments on the Law Commission's Report' [1995] *Crim LR* 209.

[70] Law Commission, *Fraud* (LC No 276, 2002) 57. Earlier reports recommended the retention of the offence, 'until ways can be found of preserving its practical advantages' *Criminal Law: Conspiracy to Defraud* (LC No 228, 1994) 63; *Criminal Law: Report on Conspiracy and Criminal Law Reform* (LC No 76, 1976) 43.

offence, it was explicitly recognised that the offence would do little more than place cheating on a statutory basis for the purposes of income tax.[71] Additionally, for a significant period, the cheating offence was used to address all VAT frauds, notwithstanding the existence of statutory offences. This was due to HMRC's position that VAT frauds did not encompass economic activity (which would be subject to VAT) for the purposes of withholding repayments from fraudsters. The denial of economic activity, and thus liability to pay VAT, was also thought to prevent the use of the section 72 offence in such circumstances.[72] While case law later restored the ability of prosecutors to charge the VAT evasion offence in cases concerning carousel and missing trader frauds,[73] it also illustrates the duplicity and redundancy of the statutory offence while the cheating offence is retained. While codification of the criminal law is a worthwhile endeavour,[74] this implies that the common law offence will be abolished or, at least, that its use will be restricted. However, many years after the enactment of these offences, cheating the public revenue is still the preferred charge.[75]

This is problematic considering the especially expansive scope of common law tax evasion offences, which have a detrimental impact on legal certainty, fair labelling, and the wider Rule of Law. The ambiguous contours of the common law offences are further obscured by the mens rea element of such offences, dishonesty, or, more accurately, the test for its determination.

Dishonesty

The actus reus of common law tax evasion offences is so extraordinarily broad – being satisfied by any form of fraudulent conduct or agreement[76] – that the fault element of dishonesty is often the 'only live issue at trial'.[77] Moreover, even though some of the statutory offences may be narrower in scope, often the actus reus of the offence is usually predetermined or admitted, leaving the trial to focus on dishonesty.[78] As such, 'the notion of dishonesty is central to considerations

[71] Inland Revenue, *Tax Bulletin – Issue 49* (Inland Revenue, 2000).

[72] *Hashash* [2006] EWCA Crim 2518; [2008] STC 1158, [3]–[5].

[73] ibid, [29]–[33].

[74] Law Commission, *Codification of the Criminal Law: A Report to the Law Commission* (LC No 143, 1985); See more recently, E Steiner, 'Challenging (Again) the Undemocratic Form of the Common Law: Codification as a Method of Making the Law Accessible to Citizens' (2020) 31(1) *King's Law Journal* 27.

[75] In *Rimmington*, Lord Bingham stated that 'good practice and respect for the primacy of statute (…) require that conduct falling within the terms of a specific statutory provision should be prosecuted under that provision unless there is good reason for doing otherwise.' [2005] UKHL 63; [2006] 1 AC 459, [30]. However, courts will 'be slow to interfere' *DS* [2017] EWCA Crim 1410; [2018] 1 WLR 5609, [48].

[76] *Less, The Times* (30 March 1993), *Scott v Metropolitan Police Commissioner* [1974] 3 WLR 741 (HL).

[77] Ormerod (n 52) 630; Law Com 276 (n 70) 86.

[78] P Kiernan and G Scanlon, 'Fraud and the Law Commission: The Future of Dishonesty' (2003) 24 *Company Lawyer* 4, 6.

of criminality in tax non-compliance'.[79] Nonetheless, the failure to clearly define dishonesty in English Law has itself long been regarded as problematic.

In *Feely*,[80] it was determined that dishonesty is an ordinary word, which should not be defined judicially, but rather, should be regarded as a question of fact to be determined by the jury. Accordingly, in contrast to the traditional approach taken to the interpretation and application of criminal offences in English Law, the dishonesty test does not provide a legal definition of the term for the jury to apply to the defendant's conduct; rather, it asks them to characterise his conduct, in effect, making a moral judgement as to whether it is sufficiently reprehensible to warrant criminalisation.[81] The *Ghosh* test was the accepted test for dishonesty for 35 years.[82] In *Ghosh*, Lord Lane CJ stated that the test to be applied is as follows:

1. Was the defendant's conduct dishonest according to the ordinary standards of reasonable and honest people?
2. If it was so dishonest, did the defendant himself realise that what he was doing was by those standards dishonest?[83]

The *Ghosh* test was subject to intense and widespread criticism from academics,[84] and senior judges.[85] Many feared that diverse perceptions of dishonesty would lead to inconsistent outcomes,[86] as well as longer and more difficult trials, with the ambiguity meaning that it was logical for a defendant to 'take his chance with the jury'.[87] The second limb of the *Ghosh* test was also perceived to be problematic because it allowed the defendant to advance something akin to mistake of law as a defence.[88] Accordingly, in *Ivey*, the Supreme Court held that the second limb 'does not correctly represent the law and that directions based upon it ought no longer to be given'.[89] Instead, the Court held that the test for dishonesty should involve a subjective assessment of the individual's knowledge or beliefs as to the facts, followed by an application of the objective standards of ordinary decent people in light of this assessment. The defendant's own perceptions of the honesty of his conduct are irrelevant. *Ivey* was itself a civil case but, in *Barton*,[90] the Court of

[79] S Bourton, 'Revisiting Dishonesty – The New Strict Liability Offence for Offshore Tax Evaders' in C Monaghan and N Monaghan (eds), *Financial Crime and Corporate Misconduct: A Critical Evaluation of Fraud Legislation* (The Law of Financial Crime Series, Routledge, 2018).

[80] *Feely* [1973] QB 530 (CA).

[81] Law Commission, *Legislating the Criminal Code: Fraud and Deception: A Consultation Paper* (LC No 155, 1999), [5.11].

[82] *Ghosh* [1982] QB 1053 (CA).

[83] ibid, 1064 per Lord Lane CJ.

[84] See, eg, E Griew, 'Dishonesty: Objections to Feely and Ghosh' [1985] *Crim LR* 341; JR Spencer, 'Dishonesty: What the Jury Thinks the Defendant Thought the Jury Would Have Thought' [1982] *CLJ* 222.

[85] Ormerod and Laird (n 68) 386, citing *Starglade Properties Ltd v Nash* [2010] EWCA Civ 1314; [2011] Lloyd's Rep FC 102 and *Cornelius* [2012] EWCA Crim 500.

[86] Law Com 155 (n 81) 60–65.

[87] Griew (n 84) 343.

[88] Spencer (n 84) 224.

[89] *Ivey v Genting Casinos UK Ltd (t/a Crockfords Club)* [2017] UKSC 67; [2018] AC 391, [74].

[90] *Barton* [2020] EWCA Crim 575; [2020] 2 Cr App R 7.

Criminal Appeal held that the correct test of dishonesty in English criminal law was now that established in *Ivey*.[91]

While the decision has been welcomed by many who support the eradication of the subjective limb,[92] the decision to replace *Ghosh* with *Ivey* does not resolve the issues inherent in the test of dishonesty. As Ormerod and Laird note, the sustained objections to *Ghosh* were primarily focused on the objective, rather than subjective, limb.[93] However, this has since become its 'most prominent feature',[94] exacerbating the issues identified above. *Ivey* has compounded concerns surrounding legal certainty, particularly considering the sheer breadth of many dishonesty offences.[95] This is because, divergent interpretations of dishonesty will not only prevent the defendant from being able to determine whether any one jury would characterise his conduct as dishonest in advance, but also, *Ivey* ensures that he no longer even has to appreciate his conduct would be so characterised.[96] In this respect, the subjective limb served an important function in the criminal law, providing increased legal certainty,[97] and narrowing the scope of application of some of the widest offences.[98] The *Ghosh* test was defended on this basis by the Law Commission.[99]

The issues surrounding dishonesty are exacerbated in the tax evasion context where dishonesty is used as a positive element of the offence, forming the key determinant of both its nature and definition.[100] Ormerod persuasively argues the failure to define dishonesty is exacerbated in 'specialised cases', where juries, in the absence of relevant experience, fail to understand or appreciate the context in which the conduct is undertaken, preventing them from accurately determining the defendant's honesty.[101] Tax evasion is an example of such a specialised case, as it often involves complex and contrived tax arrangements, which are unfamiliar to many jurors.[102] Many will be unable to determine whether a defendant is to be regarded as dishonest using their own standards, let alone the abstract standards of 'ordinary decent people'. Moreover, the jury is prohibited from hearing

[91] ibid, [84].
[92] See, eg, M Galli, 'Oh my Ghosh: Supreme Court Redefines Test for Dishonesty in Ivey v Genting Casinos' (2018) 29(2) *Entertainment Law Review* 55.
[93] D Ormerod and K Laird, 'The Future of Dishonesty – Some Practical Considerations' (2020) 6 *Archbold Review* 8, 9.
[94] ibid.
[95] GR Sullivan, AP Simester, 'Judging Dishonesty' (2020) 136 *LQR* 523, 526.
[96] ibid.
[97] The *Ghosh* test was considered to meet the requirements of Article 7 of the ECHR, *Pattni* [2001] Crim LR 570.
[98] 'The Court may have inadvertently broadened a number of criminal offences that were already stretching the limits of what can legitimately be criminalised', Ormerod and Laird (n 68) 394.
[99] Law Com 276 (n 70) 43.
[100] Contrary to the recommendations of the Law Commission, which believed that dishonesty should act as a negative element of an offence, negating, rather than establishing, liability, ibid, 41.
[101] Ormerod (n 52) 635.
[102] J Freedman, 'Tax and Corporate Responsibility' (2003) 695(2) *Tax Journal* 1, 3.

any evidence pertaining to the meaning of dishonesty in particular contexts,[103] including evidence of common market practice,[104] and regulatory attitudes to the conduct in question.[105] These concerns are further exacerbated when tax has been evaded through the concealment of income, assets or activities offshore; as well as being complicated and unfamiliar to most jurors, the activities involved will be hidden, inhibiting the collection of evidence.[106]

Accordingly, the role of dishonesty within these offences creates a lack of certainty for individuals, who should be able to foresee in advance the legal consequence of a certain course of action, as well as for prosecutors, who must decide whether to charge a defendant according to the prosecution's prospects of success.[107] Additionally, the test is likely to hinder prosecutions for tax evasion, as a tax authority with discretion to select appropriate response to criminality is likely to be cautious, imposing cost-effective civil penalties, rather than a costly and uncertain prosecution, in all save for the most straightforward cases.[108] This was demonstrated following the introduction of prosecutorial targets in 2010, which led HMRC to 'focus on less complex cases', particularly 'lower-value cases', with prosecutions being undertaken for tax losses as small as £250.[109] The difficulties inherent in the dishonesty test are also at least implicitly recognised by the introduction of a strict liability offshore tax evasion offence.[110]

The failure to clearly define dishonesty and to propound a suitable test for its determination has thus had a detrimental impact on prosecutions for tax evasion offences. Nevertheless, dishonesty fulfils an important role in the delineation of tax offences, by excluding conduct from the scope of the offence, which is either not morally blameworthy, or insufficiently blameworthy for the purposes of criminalisation, as well as activities the defendant genuinely believes he has a right to lawfully undertake.[111] In this respect, the test arguably implements justice over consistency.[112] This is particularly important in a tax evasion context where the

[103] K Campbell, 'The Test of Dishonesty in R v Ghosh' (1984) 43 *CLJ* 349, 358.

[104] This was formerly only relevant to the second question of *Ghosh*, see *Hayes* [2015] EWCA Crim 1944; [2016] 1 Cr App R (S) 63; Common market practice might be considered when ascertaining the defendant's subjective beliefs as part of the *Ivey* test, see *Hussein v FCA* [2018] UKUT 186 (TCC); [2018] Lloyd's Rep FC 574; Z Leggett, 'The New Test for Dishonesty in Criminal Law – Lessons from the Courts of Equity?' (2020) 84(1) *Journal of Criminal Law* 37, 47.

[105] *Hayes* [2015] EWCA Crim 1944; [2016] 1 Cr App R (S) 63, [19].

[106] Fisher discusses these issues in relation to the HSBC scandal in J Fisher, 'HSBC, Tax Evasion and Criminal Prosecution' (2015) 1253 *Tax Journal* 6.

[107] M Wasik, 'Mens Rea, Motive and the Problem of Dishonesty in the Law of Theft' [1979] *Crim LR* 543, 552.

[108] HM Revenue & Customs, *HMRC's Criminal Investigation Policy* (HMRC Guidance, 2021).

[109] *National Audit Office* (n 7) 33.

[110] Taxes Management Act 1970, s 106B, s 106C, s 106D. S Bourton, 'Revisiting Dishonesty – The New Strict Liability Offence for Offshore Tax Evaders' in C Monaghan and N Monaghan (eds), *Financial Crime and Corporate Misconduct: A Critical Evaluation of Fraud Legislation* (The Law of Financial Crime Series, Routledge, 2018).

[111] Law Com 155 (n 81) 7.40.

[112] R Tur, 'Dishonesty and the Jury' in AP Griffiths (ed), *Philosophy and Practice* (CUP, 1985) 83.

sheer breadth of the offences means that dishonesty is the only element that distinguishes a failed tax avoidance scheme, or even a simple mistake, from a serious criminal offence.[113] It is of vital importance to the Rule of Law that such distinctions are made, for those who attempt to act within the boundaries of the law should be treated differently from those who do not.[114] In this respect, the dishonesty criterion more accurately captures the meaning attributed to tax evasion, as it permits an examination of the accused's motive, or, his knowledge, intentions and beliefs.[115] This is essential, as it is these aspects of the accused's state of mind which are pivotal in transforming a simple failure to notify, or a failure to correctly declare a tax liability, into an act or omission warranting a criminal response. Accordingly, dishonesty may be the most appropriate form of mens rea for UK tax evasion offences and its application should not be avoided through the enactment of strict liability offences. However, the preceding analysis demonstrates that if dishonesty is to be retained, it should be defined subjectively for the purposes of tax offences, as formerly required by the *Ghosh* test. This argument is also supported by analysing the scope and operation of US tax evasion offences, including the positive impact of clearly defining the mens rea element of wilfulness.

2. United States – Tax Evasion Offences

The US is a country the UK often looks to for inspiration regarding optimal law and enforcement practice, especially for the purposes of combatting financial crime.[116] This section argues that the UK could gain significant insights from the logical US framework of tax evasion offences. This is because, in contrast to the UK, US tax evasion offences centre on the underlying conduct giving rise to the offence, as opposed to the type of tax involved. In this respect, the US has been able to enact a 'complete criminal code' of tax offences, obviating the need to rely on other general white-collar offences, and enabling different labels and

[113] Honest mistakes are highly likely considering the complexity and length of the UK's tax code. 'At more than ten million words it is the world's longest.' D Frisby and A Oury, 'Budget Revolution' (2020) 185(4736) *Taxation* 8, 8.

[114] P Alldridge, 'Tax Avoidance, Tax Evasion, Money Laundering and the Problem of "Offshore"' in S Rose-Ackerman and P Lagunes (eds), *Greed, Corruption and the Modern State* (Essays in Political Economy, Edward Elgar, 2015) 332.

[115] Wasik notes that accepting motive as relevant to the consideration of criminal liability underscores much of the criticism of *Ghosh* (n 107) 550. However, Jiang states 'motive is irrelevant qua motive; the relevance of motive is always traceable to intention and belief (…) It is the intention, not its motivating force, that matters in the sight of the law'. Z Jiang, 'Unifying and Defining 'Dishonesty' in the Law of Trusts' (2020) 26(5) *T&T* 429, 437. Nevertheless, these concepts are inextricably connected, with someone's motive, or their reason for doing something, informing their knowledge and intention. The dishonesty test enables juries to consider all these aspects of a defendant's state of mind.

[116] For instance, the UK introduced Deferred Prosecution Agreements (DPAs) owing to the US use of this enforcement tool, Ministry of Justice, *Consultation on a New Enforcement Tool to Deal with Economic Crime Committed by Commercial Organisations: Deferred Prosecution Agreements* (Cm 8348, 2012) 19.

sanctions to be attached to different categories of offending.[117] Importantly, the US clearly differentiates between culpable actions and omissions in respect of tax crimes.

The 'capstone' of the US criminal sanctions regime[118] is the felony offence under §7201 of the Internal Revenue Code (IRC) of wilfully attempting in any manner to evade or defeat any tax imposed by the IRC, or the payment thereof.[119] The offence has been used to combat the evasion of income tax, including tax on illicit income,[120] but is also applicable to the evasion of other taxes, such as excise, estate and gift taxes.[121] The offence can be committed in two ways, namely, an attempt to evade or defeat the assessment of tax, or an attempt to evade or defeat the payment of tax.[122] The first form of the offence requires proof of a tax deficiency, an affirmative act constituting evasion or attempted evasion of assessment, and wilfulness.[123] The second has similar elements, but does not require proof of a tax deficiency, instead requiring proof that a tax has been assessed, is due and owed by the taxpayer.[124] Both iterations of the offence apply to 'any person', expanding the application of the offence to those who are not personally responsible for the payment,[125] including officers and shareholders of corporations that have evaded taxation,[126] as well as professional facilitators, such as attorneys and accountants.[127] However, in such cases, the offence of aiding and assisting tax fraud is more likely to be used,[128] as it does not require proof of a tax deficiency.[129]

For evasion of assessment cases, although the prosecution must demonstrate a tax deficiency, it is not compelled to demonstrate the exact amount of any deficiency.[130] Such an endeavour is viewed as unnecessary in the course of imposing criminal penalties, as opposed to recovering evaded taxation.[131] Accordingly, both

[117] G Szott Moohr, 'Tax Evasion as White Collar Fraud' (2009) 9 *Houston Business and Tax Law Journal* 208, 209; The offences were 'calculated to induce prompt and forthright fulfillment of every duty under the income tax law and to provide a penalty suitable to every degree of delinquency.' *Spies v United States* 317 US 492, 497 (1943).

[118] L Brown, A Jamali, 'Tax Violations' (2014) 51 *American Criminal Law Review* 1751, 1759.

[119] 26 USC § 7201.

[120] *James v United States*, 366 US 213 (1961).

[121] I Comisky, L Feld and S Harris, *Tax Fraud & Evasion: Offenses, Trials, Civil Penalties* [Vol 1] (Thomson Reuters, 2020) § 2.03[7].

[122] MA Turner, 'Build an Awareness of Unlawful Tax Evasion to Ensure Avoidance' (2008) 81 *Practical Tax Strategies* 230, 233.

[123] *Sansone v United States*, 380 US 343, 351 (1965).

[124] Comisky et al (n 121) § 2.03[4].

[125] ibid, § 2.03[5].

[126] See, eg, *United States v Irwin*, 593 F2d 138 (1st Cir. 1979).

[127] See, eg, *United States v Helmsley*, 941 F2d 71 (2d Cir. 1991).

[128] 26 USC § 7206(2).

[129] *Hull v United States*, 324 F.2d 817, 823 (5th Cir 1963); *United States v Chon*, 713 F3d 812, 820-21 (5th Cir 2013).

[130] SD Shimick, 'Heisenberg's Uncertainty: An Analysis of Criminal Tax Pretextual Prosecutions in the Context of Breaking Bad's Notorious Anti-Hero' (2014) 50 *Tulsa Law Review* 43, 54.

[131] *United States v Johnson*, 319 US 503, 517 (1943).

direct and indirect methods of proof can be used to demonstrate a tax deficiency.[132] The direct method of proof refers to the use of specific items to demonstrate the deficiency, whereas indirect methods involve the use of circumstantial evidence to demonstrate inaccurate reporting of, or a failure to report, income.[133] Although the amount need not be precisely determined, the majority of circuit courts have held that the amount of the deficiency must be 'substantial'.[134] This is a 'relative term' that must be interpreted with regard to the context and circumstances of the case.[135] The statutory requirement of 'an attempt in any manner' requires an affirmative act to evade or defeat a tax, as opposed to an omission or 'passive neglect'.[136] Indeed, it is this element of the offence that differentiates it from the misdemeanor offences contained in §7203.[137] As such, the simple failure to file a tax return does not fall within the scope of the section, that is, unless it is accompanied by an affirmative act, including the concealment of income or the making of a false statement to the IRS.[138]

In contrast, §7203 provides for four misdemeanor offences of wilfully failing to 'pay any estimated tax or tax', to 'make a return', 'keep any records', 'or supply any information'.[139] The offences should not be used when an affirmative attempt to evade can be demonstrated.[140] Failing to file a return is the most heavily utilised offence under section §7203.[141] The offence requires proof that the defendant '(1) was required to file a return, (2) failed to file a return, and (3) acted wilfully in failing to file.'[142] The first element is usually satisfied by demonstrating that the defendant's taxable income exceeded the minimum amount required to file.[143] There is no need to prove a tax deficiency, although this may be helpful in determining wilfulness.[144] The second element of the offence is satisfied either by a complete failure to file, or the filing of a document that contains so little information that it is incapable of being labelled a tax return.[145] The final element, wilfulness, has the same meaning as for other tax evasion offences, specifically, a 'voluntary intentional violation of a known legal duty'.[146] However, it is important

[132] Shimick (n 130) 59.
[133] L Brown, A Jamali, 'Tax Violations' (2014) 51 *Am Crim L Rev* 1751, 1761.
[134] Shimick notes that the Supreme Court has declined to address the issue, despite the circuit court split (n 130) 54.
[135] IRS, *Internal Revenue Manual: 9.1.3.3.2.2.1 26 USC §7201 – Additional Tax Due and Owing* (24 February 2010).
[136] *Spies v United States* 317 US 492, 499 (1943).
[137] ibid, 499.
[138] The traditional list of affirmative acts is outlined in *Spies v United States* 317 US 492, 495 (1943). This type of evasion is known as a 'Spies evasion', Comisky et al, above n 121, at § 2.03[2]. See also, *United States v Copeland*, 786 F2d 768, 770 (7th Cir. 1985).
[139] 26 USC § 7203.
[140] Department of Justice, *Criminal Tax Manual* (29 June 2022), § 10.02.
[141] ibid, § 10.03; Comisky et al (n 121) §2.09[1].
[142] *United States v Hassebrock*, 663 F3d 906, 919 (7th Cir 2011).
[143] See, 26 USC § 6012. This is unnecessary for corporations, 26 USC § 6012(2).
[144] Comisky et al (n 121) § 2.09[1].
[145] *United States v Marston*, 517 F3d 996, 1001 (8th Cir 2008).
[146] *United States v Bishop*, 412 US 346, 361 (1973).

to note that, under this form of the offence, the duty is to file a return.[147] As such, wilfulness does not require an intent to evade taxation, but rather a 'voluntary, purposeful, deliberate, and intentional, as distinguished from accidental, inadvertent, or negligent' failure to act.[148]

Other US offences criminalise tax perjury,[149] aiding and assisting tax fraud,[150] attempting to interfere with the administration of Internal Revenue Laws,[151] delivering or disclosing fraudulent returns, statements, or other documents,[152] and unlawfully recovering property following its lawful seizure by the IRS.[153] Additionally, general offences, such as conspiracy,[154] mail and wire fraud,[155] may be used to address tax evasion. However, use of these offences is restricted by enforcement policies. Such charges will only be brought when there is a 'large fraud loss or a substantial pattern of conduct and there is a significant benefit to bringing the charges instead of or in addition to Title 26 violations.'[156] This is in contrast to the UK, which has not provided official guidance, leaving the courts to prevent over-criminalisation; In *R v GH*, the Supreme Court held that 'it would be bad practice for the prosecution to add additional counts of [money laundering] unless there is a proper public purpose in doing so'.[157] However, this is entirely at the court's discretion.[158]

The US has not enacted a specific statutory offence pertaining to the corporate facilitators of tax crimes. This is because the US is able to attribute criminal liability to corporations through the 'Respondeat Superior' doctrine, which attributes criminal liability to a corporation based on the acts of its employees.[159] As such, the Respondeat Superior doctrine provides for a much wider basis of corporate criminal liability than the Identification doctrine in the UK and has proved far more successful in addressing the corporate facilitators of tax crimes.[160] For instance, the US has reached a plethora of Deferred Prosecution

[147] 26 USC § 7203; *United States v Smukler*, 986 F3d 229, 241 (3rd Cir 2021).

[148] IRS, *Internal Revenue Manual: 9.1.3.3.4.1.3 26 USC §7203 – Willfulness* (15 May 2008).

[149] 26 USC § 7206(1).

[150] 26 USC § 7206(2).

[151] 26 USC § 7212(a).

[152] 26 USC § 7207.

[153] 26 USC § 7212(b).

[154] 18 USC § 371. *United States v Klein*, 247 F2d 908, 921 (2nd Cir 1957).

[155] 18 USC §§ 1341 and 1343. *Pasquantino v United States*, 544 US 349, 125 S.Ct. 1766 (2005); *Fountain v United States*, 357 F3d 250, 256 (2nd Cir 2004).

[156] Department of Justice, *Justice Manual* (June 2020), § 6-4.210.

[157] Including, where the conduct involved 'some added criminality' or it was impossible to prosecute the defendant for the predicate offence, *GH* [2015] UKSC 24; [2015] 1 WLR 2126, [48].

[158] ibid; see also AM Maugeri, 'Self-laundering the Proceeds of Tax Evasion in Comparative Law: Between Effectiveness and Safeguards' (2018) 9(1) *NJECL* 83, 102.

[159] N Ryder, '"Too Scared to Prosecute and Too Scared to Jail?" A Critical and Comparative Analysis of Enforcement of Financial Crime Legislation against Corporations in the USA and the UK' (2018) 82(3) *Journal of Criminal Law* 245, 249.

[160] ibid, 262; R Luskin, 'Caring about Corporate "Due Care": Why Criminal *Respondeat Superior* Liability Outreaches its Justification' (2020) 57(2) *American Criminal Law Review* 303, 313.

Agreements and Non-Prosecution Agreements (DPAs/NPAs) with numerous corporations for their facilitation of the use of fraudulent tax shelters.[161] The US has also concluded a significant number of DPAs/NPAs with foreign banks for their facilitation of tax evasion by US citizens through offshore accounts.[162] For instance, the US reached NPAs with 80 Swiss banks through the Swiss Bank Program, imposing over $1.36 billion in penalties for their facilitation of tax evasion by US citizens.[163]

Wilfulness

Most US tax evasion offences require proof of wilfulness.[164] Indeed, wilfulness has acted as the mens rea element of US tax evasion offences since 1919.[165] The inclusion of this form of mens rea is intended to effect the Congressional intention of constructing 'penalties that separate the purposeful tax violator from the well-meaning, but easily confused, mass of taxpayers'.[166] In *United States v Murdock*, the Supreme Court held that wilfulness not only requires an act 'which is intentional, or knowing, or voluntary, as distinguished from accidental', but also, 'an act done with a bad purpose' or an 'evil motive'.[167] In *United States v Bishop*, the Supreme Court explained that the term wilfully should be afforded an identical interpretation for both the misdemeanour and felony offences, clarifying that the term wilfully refers to a 'voluntary, intentional violation of a known legal duty'.[168] In *United States v Pomponio*, the Court reiterated this definition, but declined to recognise improper motive as a necessary component of wilfulness.[169] After *Pomponio*, circuit courts differed on their interpretation of the knowledge component of wilfulness, with most applying a subjective standard of evaluation, but with others requiring that a defendant's claims to lack knowledge had to be objectively reasonable.[170]

[161] See, eg, the DPAs and NPAs reached with KPMG, Ernst and Young LLP and Deutsche Bank. See, Comisky et al (n 121) § 1.08.

[162] See, eg, Department of Justice, *Mizrahi-Tefahot Bank Ltd Admits its Employees Helped US Taxpayers Conceal Income and Assets* (Department of Justice Press Release 19-215, 12 March 2019).

[163] Department of Justice, *Justice Department Announces Final Swiss Bank Program Category 2 Resolution with HSZH Verwaltungs AG* (Department of Justice Press Release 16-093, 27 January 2016).

[164] *Cheek v United States*, 498 U.S. 192, 201 (1991); *United States v Trevino*, 419 F.3d 896, 901 (9th Cir. 2005); *United States v Bishop*, 412 US 346, 360-361 (1973).

[165] J Stein, 'Criminal Liability for Willful Evasion of an Uncertain Tax' (1981) 81(6) *Columbia Law Review* 1348, 1355.

[166] *United States v Bishop*, 412 US 346, 361 (1973); ibid.

[167] *United States v Murdock*, 290 US 389, 394-5 (1933).

[168] *United States v Bishop*, 412 US 346, 360-361 (1973).

[169] *United States v Pomponio*, 429 US 10, 12 (1976).

[170] NA Mirkay III , 'The Supreme Court's Decision in Cheek: Does It Encourage Willful Tax Evasion?' (1991) 56(4) *Missouri Law Review* 1119, 1131.

This conflict was resolved in *Cheek v United States*, which confirmed the application of the higher subjective standard,[171] while also holding that constitutional objections to taxation will not negate wilfulness.[172] As a result, individuals are not considered to have acted wilfully if they misunderstand the meaning or application of tax laws in good faith.[173] This includes misunderstandings based on advice given by a professional, providing that the advice was sought and relied on in good faith, and that all material facts were disclosed.[174]

Additionally, the uncertainty of the law in question may prevent a finding of wilfulness,[175] for uncertainty prevents a defendant from possessing the requisite intent to violate the tax laws.[176] Circuit courts are split as to whether uncertainty negates wilfulness absolutely, or whether the defendant must rely on the uncertainty.[177] Some US courts have held that uncertainty is a legal inquiry to be resolved by the court by looking at the relevant authorities,[178] while others have held that uncertainty is also factual inquiry to be resolved by the jury through the ascertainment of its impact on the defendant's mental state.[179] Several circuits have held that the law must be unknowable, rather than simply unknown.[180] Alternatively, this could be perceived as part of a 'vagueness defence', grounded on a violation of the due process clause of the Fifth Amendment, which requires fair warning of criminalisation and bears similarities to Article 7 of the ECHR.[181] Effectively, constitutional challenges in the US centre on the application of wilfulness to unclear tax laws, as opposed to the definition of wilfulness itself.

Although ignorance of the law is not typically recognised as a defence to a criminal charge in the US, the Court explicitly held that criminal tax offences should be afforded special treatment 'due to the complexity of the tax laws'.[182] The holding in *Cheek* bears similarities to the *Ghosh* interpretation of dishonesty in the UK and has garnered similar criticisms; specifically, that employing a subjective test will allow tax evaders with 'outrageously unreasonable' beliefs

[171] *Cheek v United States*, 498 US 192, 200 (1991).

[172] ibid, 206.

[173] Comisky et al (n 121) § 2.03[3][a].

[174] *United States v Renner* 648 F3d 680, 687 (8th Cir 2011); *United States v Wright* 798 Fed. Appx. 849, 852 (6th Cir 2019).

[175] *James v United States*, 366 U.S. 213 (1961).

[176] *United States v Critzer*, 498 F2d 1160, 1162 (4th Cir 1974).

[177] MM Kwon, 'The Criminality of Tax Planning' (2015) 18(4) *Florida Tax Review* 153, 180.

[178] *United States v Mallas*, 762 F2d 361, 364 (4th Cir 1985).

[179] *United States v Garber*, 607 F2d 92 (5th Cir. 1979). In Harris, the Court held that 'the doubtfulness of a tax law can influence a criminal trial in two ways. The law can be objectively ambiguous, (…) Alternatively, the defendant or the defendant's tax advisors may have subjectively, but wrongly, seen an ambiguity' *United States v Harris*, 942 F2d 1125, 1132 (7th Cir. 1991).

[180] *United States v George* 420 F3d 991 (9th Cir 2005); *United States v Kahre*, 737 F3d 554, 570 (9th Cir 2014).

[181] Stein (n 165) 1357. See also *United States v Dahlstrom*, 713 F2d 1423 (9th Cir 1983).

[182] *Cheek v United States*, 498 US 192, 200 (1991) citing *United States v Murdock*, 290 US 389, 396 (1933).

to escape liability and will prompt tax evaders to 'cling to frivolous views of the law in the hope of convincing a jury of their sincerity', inhibiting law enforcement.[183] Nonetheless, as in the UK, the reasonableness of a belief will no doubt be influential in determining its sincerity.[184] Additionally, subjective wilfulness can be inferred from circumstantial evidence of the defendant's conduct, including affirmative attempts to evade taxation.[185] The court will take into account the defendant's previous conduct and compliance history,[186] as well as their knowledge and abilities.[187] Further, wilfulness extends to wilful blindness, encapsulating defendants who claim ignorance owing to their deliberate attempts to ignore the facts,[188] thus mitigating the impact of a subjective standard on the ability to bring prosecutions for this offence.[189] Many US commentators also lamented defendants' ability to rebut wilfulness through obtaining professional advice, arguing that it will encourage tax evaders to avoid liability by seeking professional services, as well as increase the number of unscrupulous legal professionals.[190] However, seeking legal advice should be encouraged and demonstrating good faith reliance on the advice is an onerous task.[191] Moreover, even if the doctrine 'errs on the side of under inclusion',[192] arguably, it should be dishonest facilitators, rather than clients acting in good faith, who should face criminal sanction. In this respect, when a defence of legal uncertainty is raised by a facilitator in relation to a tax avoidance shelter, it is often rejected when their role extended to fraudulent implementation.[193]

In fact, rather than unjustifiably inhibiting law enforcement, by placing such emphasis on the subjective intention of the perpetrator or facilitator to comply with their obligations, US case law pays greater deference to the inherent nature of criminal tax evasion than its UK counterpart, following the decision in *Ivey*.

[183] *Cheek v United States*, 498 US 192, 210 (1991); Mirkay (n 170) 1139; MD Yochum, 'Cheek is Chic. Ignorance of the Law is an Excuse for Tax Crimes – A Fashion that Does Not Wear Well' (1993) 31 *Duq Law Review* 249, 253.

[184] *Cheek v United States*, 498 US 192, 203-4 (1991); *United States v Pensyl*, 387 F.3d 456, 459-60 (6th Cir. 2004); DE Field, 'Sincerity & Credibility: The True Concerns in Assessing Willfulness – An Analysis and Criticism of United States v. Pensyl' (2005) 59(1) *Tax Law* 283, 294.

[185] *United States v Guidry*, 199 F.3d 1150, 1157 (10th Cir. 1999); *Spies v United States* 317 US 492, 499 (1943).

[186] *United States v Lavoie*, 433 F3d 95, 98 (1st Cir 2005); *United States v Daraio*, 445 F3d 253, 264-65 (3rd Cir 2006).

[187] *United States v Guidry*, 199 F3d 1150, 1157–58 (10th Cir 1999); *United States v Bok*, 156 F3d 157, 166 (2nd Cir 1983) M Angelo, A Welles Hasen, U Hindberg, R Kesselring and H Perlman, 'Tax Violations' (2020) 57 *Am Crim L Rev* 1349, 1367.

[188] *United States v Jinwright*, 683 F.3d 471, 478 (4th Cir, 2012).

[189] R Zuraw, 'Sniping Down Ignorance Claims: The Third Circuit in United States v Stadtmauer Upholds Willful Blindness Instructions in Criminal Tax Cases' (2012) 56(4) *Villanova Law Review* 779, 801.

[190] See, eg, L Hall and SJ Seligman, 'Mistake of Law and Mens Rea' (1940) 8 *University of Chicago Law Review* 641, 652.

[191] SW Buell, 'Good Faith and Law Evasion' (2011) 58(3) *UCLA Law Review* 611, 642–43.

[192] ibid, 643.

[193] See, eg, *United States v Solomon*, 825 F2d 1292, 1297-98 (9th Cir 1987); *United States v Smith*, 424 F3d 992 (9th Cir 2005). Department of Justice, *Criminal Tax Manual* (16 November 2020), §13.07.

This is supported by the fact that wilfulness is afforded a narrower interpretation in tax offences than for other offences,[194] including BSA violations, such as, structuring offences,[195] and FBAR violations.[196] Additionally, the courts have persistently emphasised that tax offences are a rare exception to the fundamental principle of criminal law that ignorance of the law is not an excuse, owing to the complexity of the tax law and the numerous errors that result from its application, even by honest taxpayers.[197] The fact that Congress has not interfered with these decisions in the tax context, despite having done so for structuring offences,[198] and despite approving this interpretation in other statutory contexts,[199] demonstrates its approval of the judicial interpretation of wilfulness, as well as its intention to clearly distinguish tax evasion from other criminal offences, paying greater respect to the labelling function of the criminal law. More importantly, although wilfulness is determined by a jury, the term is not left for the jury to define.[200] Rather, as the case law suggests, the meaning of the term has been refined over 100 years through binding judicial decisions, providing greater clarity to this area of criminal law than the decisions that abdicate responsibility for defining dishonesty to juries in the UK.

3. Comparison and Reform

Both jurisdictions have comprehensive legal frameworks providing for the criminalisation of tax evasion, as well as the facilitation of these crimes by both individuals and corporations. Indeed, there appear to be few omissions in the scope of liability imposed in each jurisdiction. However, while the UK has enacted several offences pertaining to the evasion of different types of taxes, US tax evasion offences centre on the underlying conduct giving rise to the offence. The US has been able to enact a 'complete criminal code' for tax offences, obviating the need to rely on other general white-collar offences, and enabling different labels and sanctions to be attached to different categories of offending.[201] The US clearly

[194] *United States v Kay*, 513 F.3d 432, 447 (5th Cir. 2007); *United States v Skilling*, 554 F.3d 529, 548-49 (5th Cir 2009); Szott Moohr (n 117) 212.

[195] In *Ratzlaf v United States*, 510 US 135, 144–149 (1994) the Supreme Court held 'we are unpersuaded by the argument that structuring is so obviously "evil" or "inherently bad" that the "willfulness" requirement is satisfied irrespective of the defendant's knowledge of the illegality', Congress later amended 31 USC § 5324 to reverse this decision. I Comisky, L Feld and S Harris, *Tax Fraud & Evasion: Offenses, Trials, Civil Penalties* [Vol 2] (Thomson Reuters, 2020) at § 11.06[2][b].

[196] See, eg, *United States v Horowitz*, 978 F.3d 80, 88 (4th Cir 2020).

[197] *Spies v United States*, 317 US 492, 496 (1943); *United States v Bishop*, 412 US 346, 360 (1973); *Ratzlaf v United States*, 510 US 135, 149 (1994).

[198] See n 195.

[199] Congress intended the term 'wilfully' in the Child Support Recovery Act, 18 USC § 228 (1994) to be afforded the same interpretation as for tax offences. SL Davies, 'The Jurisprudence of Willfulness: An Evolving Theory of Excusable Ignorance' (1998) 48(3) *Duke Law Journal* 341, 405.

[200] As it is in the UK, owing to *Feely* [1973] QB 530 (CA).

[201] Szott Moohr (n 117) 209.

differentiates between culpable actions and omissions in respect of tax crimes. In contrast, the UK rarely uses its statutory offences and prefers charging the common law offence of cheating the public revenue, a catch-all crime with a severe sentence of imprisonment. Both jurisdictions use one form of mens rea consistently for almost all tax evasion offences. However, whereas the judicial failure to clearly define dishonesty in the UK has left the application of this term fraught with uncertainty, US case law provides a higher level of clarity in the interpretation of the term wilfulness. Accordingly, the US framework illustrates the benefits that would stem from a reconsideration of the UK's approach to criminalising tax evasion, enacting offences based on the underlying conduct, rather than retaining a patchwork of duplicitous offences for each type of tax evaded. This would help to limit the sheer number, as well as circumscribe the overly broad scope, of UK tax evasion offences. The US also demonstrates that, while the UK does not necessarily have to alter the chosen form of mens rea, significant benefits could be gained in providing a statutory or judicial definition of this term, including a higher level of certainty for prosecutors and defendants. On the other hand, while the US approach to attributing criminal liability to corporations for the facilitation of tax crimes appears to be more effective than its UK counterpart, reform must take place within wider ongoing efforts to reform corporate criminal liability more generally.[202]

Aside from a US-style system of offences, thought should be given to other reform options.[203] For instance, the common law offences could be abolished, or their use severely restricted, in preference to the statutory offences. Otherwise, the offence of cheating the public revenue could be placed on a statutory basis, with a clear definition of dishonesty, and many of the tax-specific offences could be removed from the statute book. This would help to define the nature of criminal tax evasion in the UK; a task that has been neglected so far by both national and international stakeholders.[204] However, this would be a less preferable solution than a US-style system of offences, with clearly defined mens rea elements. A system of offences based on the underlying conduct characterising tax evasion, as opposed to the particular type of tax evaded, would more effectively address the Rule of Law's demands for clarity and certainty. This reform should be accompanied by the adoption of enforcement policies. In particular, prosecutors should be restricted in their ability to use general white-collar offences, such as fraud and money laundering, in addition or in preference to statutory tax evasion offences. While money laundering or fraud charges may be appropriate in some cases, these offences should not be used simply because they have less demanding forms of mens rea.

[202] See Law Commission (n 39).

[203] Alldridge identifies several options for reform (n 13) 69.

[204] See generally, U Turksen, 'The Importance of a Common Definition of Tax Crime and its Impact on Criminal Countermeasures in the EU: An Explorative Study' (2020) 20 *European Law Enforcement Research Bulletin* 91.

4. Conclusion

The historic relative disinterest in tax evasion from both politicians and academics may be explained by the lack of prosecutions.[205] However, given the increasing use of the criminal justice system, this position is no longer tenable. This chapter demonstrated that the criminal offences pertaining to tax evasion need simplification and modernisation through the enactment of a contemporary statute, returning doctrinal coherence to this increasingly utilised area of criminal law. There are several options for a logical tax evasion framework, including a statutory cheating offence. However, this chapter calls for a US-style system of offences based on the underlying conduct, with different sanctions for different degrees of culpability. In contrast to the current patchwork of tax evasion offences, significant efforts have been taken to consolidate and modernise other financial crimes in the UK, such as terrorism financing, money laundering, fraud and bribery, through the enactment of the Terrorism Act 2000, the Proceeds of Crime Act 2002, the Fraud Act 2006 and the Bribery Act 2010 respectively. As such, this chapter calls for the next seminal economic crime statute, enacting a logical scheme of tax evasion offences.

[205] J Roording, 'The Punishment of Tax Fraud' [1996] *Crim LR* 240, 248.

Comment on Chapter 7

Is it Time for the Next Seminal Economic Crime Statute?

JONATHAN FISHER*

Dr Bourton presents in her chapter a solution in search of a problem. Contending that 'the criminal offences pertaining to tax evasion should be simplified and modernised through the enactment of a contemporary statute',[1] Bourton contends that the UK 'should consider enacting a US-style system of tax evasion offences, which apply to a range of taxes and clearly distinguish culpable actions from omissions'.[2] Bourton submits that her proposed solution would 'return doctrinal coherence to this increasingly utilised area of law'.[3]

Bourton demonstrates that there is a miscellany of statutory offences which can be used to prosecute tax evasion. This ranges from generic offences applicable to fraudulent conduct contrary to section 2 of the Fraud Act 2006 and false accounting in contravention of section 17 of the Theft Act 1968, to five specific offences relating to the evasion of VAT contrary to section 72 of the Value Added Tax Act 1994. There is also a myriad of statutory offences capable of commission where a taxpayer fails to make a disclosure, for example by failing to give notice of chargeability to tax contrary to section 106B of the Taxes Management Act 1970 or failing to deliver a tax return contrary to section 106C.

In addition, there are two common law offences of cheating the public revenue and conspiracy to defraud commonly deployed to prosecute serious instances of tax evasion. Bourton expresses concern about the breadth of these offences and questions whether they should be abolished. Both offences require the prosecutor to establish that a taxpayer, individual or corporate, was acting dishonestly. Typically, in tax evasion cases, it is the common law offence of cheating the public revenue which is deployed.

* Jonathan Fisher KC, Red Lion Chambers London; Visiting Professor in Practice at The LSE. Between 1991 and 2003, he was Standing Counsel (Criminal) to the Commissioners of Inland Revenue at the Central Criminal Court and London Crown Courts.

[1] Burton 222.

[2] ibid.

[3] ibid.

At this point, Bourton develops the central plank of her attack, focusing on the problems associated with determining the element of dishonesty in the wake of the decision by the Supreme Court in *Ivey v Genting Casinos*.[4] As with many other offences relating to property, the element of dishonesty is central in the offence of cheating the public revenue, involving 'any form of fraudulent conduct which results in diverting money from the revenue'.[5] Bourton explains that 'use of the offence of cheating the public revenue is problematic considering the especially expansive scope of common law tax evasion offences, which have a detrimental impact on legal certainty, fair labelling, and the wider Rule of Law'.[6]

Bourton's solution is to replace the existing landscape of revenue offences with the offence of wilfully evading tax, adopting the model in the United States of the felony offence under section 7201 of the Internal Revenue Code:

> The first form of the offence requires proof of a tax deficiency, an affirmative act constituting evasion or attempted evasion of assessment, and wilfulness. The second has similar elements, but does not require proof of a tax deficiency, instead requiring proof that a tax has been assessed, is due and owed by the taxpayer.[7]

Bourton perceives that decided cases in the US provide a higher level of clarity in the interpretation of wilfulness, as compared with the cases in the UK on the meaning of dishonesty. Also, the reform 'would help to limit the sheer number, as well as circumscribe the overly broad scope, of UK tax evasion offences'.[8] The US approach '[enacts] offences based on the underlying conduct, rather than retaining a patchwork of duplicitous offences for each type of tax evaded'.[9]

This response articulates a different narrative. It argues that, when properly particularised, the offence of cheating the public revenue does not cause unfairness to a defendant and serves as an adequate vehicle for prosecuting complex tax offences. It also argues that focused statutory offences can play a valuable role in appropriate cases.

1. In Defence of Cheating the Public Revenue

Bourton shares good company in her criticism of the common law offence of cheating the public revenue, and in particular, the key role played by the notion of dishonesty in defining the offence. The weight of academic opinion is unhappy with the decision in *Ivey v Genting Casinos*, and there is concern about unfairness

[4] [2017] UKSC 67.

[5] *Less and Depala*, 2 March 1993 (transcript) cited with approval by Stuart-Smith LJ in *Hunt* [1994] STC 819, 827.

[6] Burton (n 1) 227.

[7] ibid 232.

[8] ibid 239.

[9] ibid 239.

to a defendant since the subjective content of the test of dishonesty has been degraded.

Jeremy Horder, writing in *Ashworth's Principles of Criminal Law*, worries that 'the judgment of dishonesty comes as an *ex post facto* assessment of [a defendant's] conduct'.[10] Although as Horder notes, around one-half of all indictable charges tried by the courts include proof of dishonesty, '[i]t's uncertainty also brings it into conflict with the principle of maximum certainty in the criminal law'.[11]

In relation to the determination of dishonesty in commercial settings such as the planning and implementation of carefully planned tax schemes, David Ormerod and Karl Laird's criticism is equally forthright:

> [T]e problems appear obvious: it seems ludicrous to ask jurors to apply the test of whether a reasonable and honest person would see it as dishonest when they (probably) have little or no understanding of the very complex civil law tax position or commercial background.[12]

The criticism resonates strongly in cases where a taxpayer is alleged to have established sham transactions to evade tax. A sham transaction takes place where the acts done were intended to give the appearance of creating legal rights different from those which were actually created.[13]

In fact, these concerns are exaggerated. Whilst Bourton is correct to record the diffuse array of criminal offences available to prosecute tax evasion, the present combination of common law and statutory offences are fit for purpose and prosecutions for tax offences have not been characterised by legal impediments which have prevented their pursuit in the criminal courts.

Moreover, the combination of common law and statutory offences is not as incoherent as may appear at first blush. Broadly speaking, analysis of offences for tax evasion falls into three categories. The first category of offences, which embrace the common law offences of cheating and conspiracy to defraud, as well as general offences such as fraud contrary to section 2 of the Fraud Act 2006 and false accounting contrary to section 17 of the Theft Act 1968, are deployed in the most serious cases. The second category consists of statutory offences relating to the evasion of a specifically identified tax. These are supported by a third category of offence which criminally penalise a taxpayer's failure to declare their liability to pay tax or misinform the revenue as to the existence or extent of their tax liability. The level of intention or awareness of the commission of these offences varies from offence to offence, affording a prosecutor considerable latitude in matching the severity of the taxpayer's misconduct to the appropriateness of the criminal offence which is deployed.

[10] J Horder, *Ashworth's Principles of Criminal Law*, 10th edn (OUP, 2022) 439.
[11] ibid, 438.
[12] D Ormerod and K Laird, *Smith, Hogan & Ormerod's Criminal Law*, 16th edn (OUP, 2021) 1033–1034.
[13] See *Hitch's Executors v Stone* [2001] STC 214.

The fact that there are comparatively few criminal prosecutions for tax evasion in the UK does not testify to any perceived deficiency in the weaponry available to the prosecutor in a criminal prosecution. Rather, it is unexceptional in the light of HM Revenue & Customs' deep-rooted and declared policy which focuses on tax collection, with criminal process initiated rarely and for deterrent purposes only. As Stuart-Smith LJ explained in *Inland Revenue Commissioners ex pate Mead and Cook*:

> The crucial factor … is that the Revenue operate a selective policy of prosecution. They do this for three main reasons: first their primary objective is the collection of revenue and not the punishment of offenders; second they have inadequate resources to prosecute everyone who dishonestly evades payment of taxes; and third and perhaps most importantly they consider it necessary to prosecute in some cases because of the deterrent effect that this has on the general body of taxpayers, since they know that if they behave dishonestly they may be prosecuted.[14]

Legal Uncertainty

Turning to the concerns articulated about legal uncertainty in the offence of cheating the public revenue, the first and most obvious point to make is that, as with other common law and statutory offences in the criminal lexicon, particulars of the conduct alleged to constitute tax evasion will always be set out in the indictment. The statement of offence will reference generically the offence of cheating the public revenue contrary to common law in much the same way as an indictment for serious assault will specify the offence of causing grievous bodily harm contrary to section 18 of the Offences Against the Person Act 1861. However, the statement of offence is always accompanied by the particulars of the offence, which sets out a carefully crafted narrative in short form identifying the precise nature of offending conduct which the defendant is alleged to have committed. The jury will have an opportunity to consider these particulars, and the defendant will know the detailed allegations which must be met.[15] Section 3(1) of the Indictments Act 1915 stipulates that '[E]very indictment shall contain, and shall be sufficient if it contains, a statement of the specific offence or offences with which the accused person is charged, together with such particulars as may be necessary for giving reasonable information as to the nature of the charge'.

[14] [1992] STC 482, 492 a–b.

[15] In *Pattni* [2001] CrimLR 570 (Crown Ct (Southwark)), the Crown Court rejected a submission by defendants in an alleged tax fraud that the indictment should be quashed on grounds of legal uncertainty where the common law offence had been charged. The Court held that the offence of cheating if properly particularised was readily understood by a jury, and if a defendant had sought competent legal advice, he would have been advised that his conduct would be likely to be regarded as dishonest by a jury. There was no infringement of Article 7 of the European Convention on Human Rights which requires certainty in the understanding of law.

It is not simply a question of the defendant appreciating the nature of the case which must be answered. In the event of conviction, whether by guilty plea or jury verdict, the Judge requires clarity regarding the offending conduct for the purpose of imposing sentence. If the particulars in an indictment are insufficient, application may be made to the court for an order requiring the prosecution to give further particulars,[16] and where the judge considers it necessary the court may direct the giving of further particulars even though no application is made.[17]

Applied in a case involving tax evasion where cheating the public revenue is involved, it follows that the conduct constituting the acts of cheating must be identified by the prosecutor in the indictment before the case comes to trial. This is not problematic but simply good practice.

In *Lunn*,[18] the indictment charged an offence of cheating the public revenue, with the particulars of offence identifying the manner of cheating as submitting misleading tax returns and accounts for two named companies by falsely overstating losses, sales, and costs. The precise amounts involved were specified in the particulars, and the Court of Appeal concluded that the count was 'sufficiently clear in its terms'.[19]

Similarly, in *Hunt*,[20] the Court of Appeal approved an indictment which included extensive details of the conduct which constituted the offence.[21] The particulars of the indictment alleged that the appellant had cheated the public revenue of corporation tax by producing invoices, agreements and correspondence which were misleading, false or deceptive in that they purported to show that certain specified commercial transactions between the parties had been made genuinely in good faith, when in fact they had not.

Determining Dishonesty

The second concern that jurors will struggle to apply the test of dishonesty as reformulated in *Ivey v Genting Casinos* is similarly misconceived, since it fails to consider the nature of the key factual elements which are placed before the jury to decide.

As recognised by the Court of Appeal in *Dosanjh*,[22] cheating the public revenue is the appropriate charge for the small number of most serious revenue frauds, where the statutory offences will not adequately reflect the criminality involved

[16] *Savage; DPP v Parmenter* [1992] 1 AC 699, 737 (per Lord Ackner).
[17] *Warburton-Pitt* [1991] 92 Cr App R 136.
[18] [2017] EWCA Crim 34.
[19] ibid, [74].
[20] [1994] STC 819.
[21] ibid, 827.
[22] [2014] 2 Cr App R (S) 25, [33] (per Hallett LJ).

and where a sentence at large is more appropriate than one subject to statutory restrictions. Typically, these cases will involve a straight-forward allegation that a taxpayer has lied to the revenue authorities in answer to questions the revenue has raised, or in reliance on a document such as an invoice or account which represents that a payment has been made in circumstances where the payment does not accurately and genuinely reflect the true position.

It was recognised more than 40 years ago by Lord Keith in his seminal report that criminal prosecution in the most serious cases will be initiated only when the case fell within the 'heinous' category where the nature of the dishonest conduct was blatant and obvious:[23]

> The presence of one of the 'badges' of heinousness as viewed by the Department makes a case more likely to be selected for prosecution. Bearing in mind that the presence of intention to deceive is crucial we find it difficult to find anything to object to in the Department's selection as criteria of –
>
> …
>
> (b) evidence of collusion between the taxpayers and others;
> (c) evidence that documents have been forged with intent to deceive the Revenue; or
> (d) evidence of other irregularities which are denied on challenge.[24]

The short point is that a jury will not experience any difficulty in determining the issue of dishonesty in a complex tax evasion case which falls into one of these categories, set in the context of complicated commercial transactions.

The former Director of Public Prosecutions, Sir Keir Starmer KC, made the point clearly in 2013, in a speech entitled 'Prosecuting Tax Evasion'.[25] Addressing the prosecution of dishonest tax avoidance schemes:

> These cases typically involve highly intelligent individuals, not infrequently skilled professionals with close knowledge of the tax laws, who go to great lengths to dress up a dishonest a fraudulent tax evasion scheme as a legitimate investment scheme attracting tax relief or other tax advantages. Those setting up the schemes often use extremely complex financial instruments and corporate entities to create a subterfuge. Long and complicated audit trails are then used to disguise the scheme. But an experienced investigator and a skilled prosecutor can spot the tell-tell signs of dishonesty, whether that be false or misleading documents, false turnover figures, hidden trading transactions or payments that do not reflect commercial reality. And we demonstrated this last year when we successfully prosecuted the first ever large-scale dishonest tax avoidance scheme case: a case known as Operation Reciprocal.

[23] *Committee on Enforcement Powers of the Revenue Departments* (HMSO, Cmnd 8822, March 1983) Vol 2, para 22.1.7.

[24] ibid. The categories of case are set out and identified from (a) to (g) at Chapter 9.11.1: where such cases are identified early enough they are worked as potential criminal prosecution cases from the outset.

[25] *Prosecuting Tax Evasion* (Speech by Keir Starmer KC, 23 January 2013, Crown Prosecution Service).

> Operation Reciprocal involved a scheme devised and operated by so-called expert tax consultants to claim tax relief for high earners. It was the first of its kind and the successful prosecution sends an important message not only about the determination of HMRC and the CPS to bring those involved in such schemes to justice but also about the reach of the criminal law.
>
> … As part of the scheme, more than 600 taxpayers were encouraged to buy shares for a few pence in each of four companies set up for the purposes of the scheme. These companies were then listed on a Stock Exchange [Channel Islands]. There followed two or three days of what we were able to demonstrate was contrived trading, as a result of which the share price increased dramatically – a share ramping exercise.
>
> The taxpayers were then advised that the shares were now worth £1 each and that if they donated them to charity they could claim tax relief on the value of 1 pound each and not the few pence they had originally paid. The taxpayers donated well over 300 million shares to various registered charities, including a hospital trust. Had the scheme been completed as intended more than £70 million of tax relief would have been claimed back from HMRC from income and company profits. As it was, the fraud was detected and stopped when £5 million had been paid out. The share trading consisted entirely of purchases instigated and funded by the defendant and associates. At the heart of the scheme was a simple dishonesty: the donated shares were not worth anything like the claimed £1 each.[26]

Explaining the test of dishonesty in *Ivey v Genting Casinos*, paraphrasing Lord Hughes' words, when dishonesty is in question the jury must first ascertain, subjectively, the actual state of the defendant's knowledge or belief as to the facts. The reasonableness or otherwise of his belief is a matter of evidence going to whether the defendant held the belief, but it is not an additional requirement that his belief must be reasonable; the question is whether it is genuinely held. When the defendant's state of mind has been established, the question whether his conduct was honest or dishonest is to be determined by the jury by applying the objective standards of ordinary decent people. There is no requirement that the defendant must appreciate that the conduct was dishonest by those standards.[27]

The fact that the prosecution does not need to establish that the defendant appreciated the conduct was dishonest by the standards of ordinary decent people should not lead to unfairness in a case involving the commission of a serious tax fraud where complex commercial transactions are involved. To quote from *Smith, Hogan & Ormerod*:[28]

> Under the first limb, the jury is required to assess the defendant's conduct *and* state of mind broadly including [the defendant's] beliefs about all the circumstances. We suggest that defendants are entitled to adduce evidence of their perceptions of the honesty of their conduct. When the jury is using that information in applying the

[26] ibid.

[27] *Ivey* (n 4), [74], paraphrased in Ormerod and Laird (n 12) 915. See also *Floreat Investment Management Limited v Benjamin Churchill* [2023] EWCA Civ 440, [66] (per Males LJ).

[28] ibid, Ormerod and Laird, 917–18.

> second (objective) limb, the jury must surely have regard to that evidence but, crucially, they should not treat what the defendant believed about others' perception of dishonesty as determinative.
>
> ...
>
> Where necessary, juries should be directed to approach the issue of dishonesty as follows.
>
> (1) What were the facts or circumstances at the time [the defendant] did what he was alleged to have done by the prosecution?
> (2) What was the [the defendant's] knowledge or belief to the facts or circumstances? You are entitled to consider [the defendant's] explanation for his conduct, his experience and his intelligence.
> (3) Having regard to the facts *and* [the defendant's] state of mind about them, was his conduct dishonest according to the standards of ordinary decent people?
> (4) [The defendant's] belief about the dishonesty of his conduct, or what others think about his conduct, is not conclusive. The standard of honesty in law is that of ordinary decent people, which is a matter for you and not the defendant.

2. The Case for Statutory Offences

As for the suggestion that the 'patchwork of duplicitous offences' should be replaced by an overarching codified offence of wilfully evading tax along the lines of the US system, the proposal overlooks the case for the establishment and subsequent retention of the statutory offences.

The principal advantage for retaining focused statutory offences is that it affords the prosecution options in less serious cases where specific taxes have been evaded but the weight of the common law offence or more general fraud offences is not required. It is to be remembered that the common law offence of cheating the public revenue, as well as conspiracy to defraud, is indictable only and punishable by a maximum of life imprisonment. By way of contrast, statutory offences are triable either way, in the Magistrates Court or Crown Court, and subject to maximum sentences of imprisonment as stipulated in the statute creating the offence or limited by the jurisdiction of the Magistrates Court. Typical statutory offences involve the evasion of specific taxes such as insurance premium tax,[29] landfill tax,[30] gaming duty,[31] climate change levy,[32] aggregates levy,[33] machine games duty,[34] and stamp duty land tax.[35]

[29] Finance Act 1994, Sch 7, Pt IV.
[30] Finance Act 1996, Sch 5, Pt IV.
[31] Finance Act 1997, Sch 1.
[32] Finance Act 2000, Sch 6, Pt VIII.
[33] Finance Act 2001, Sch 6, Pt 1.
[34] Finance Act 2012, Sch 24.
[35] Finance Act 2003, s 95.

3. Conclusion

Therefore, in conclusion, whilst Bourton makes an interesting and valuable contribution to the discussion about the retention of the existing framework within which prosecutions for tax evasion are presently brought, the case for exchanging the present arrangements for a US style offence is not made out.

The 'wilfulness' of a taxpayer is the key mental ingredient of the US tax evasion offence, and as Bourton explains, instead of focusing on the feature of dishonesty, the test of wilfulness seeks to distinguish 'voluntary, purposeful, deliberate, and intentional [conduct]' from 'an accidental, inadvertent, or negligent' failure to act. Yet as Bourton acknowledges, the application of wilfulness in the US has not been free from doubt, with the issue occupying the attention of the appellate courts on several occasions, especially in complex cases where criminal tax evasion has been masquerading as lawful but failed tax avoidance. There is a danger that if the UK adopted wilfulness in place of dishonesty, it would exchange one set of problems for another.

As recorded in Aesop's' Fables (The Old Man and Death), proponents of a US codified system for the prosecution of tax offences should be careful about for what they wish.

8

Anonymity, Criminal Suspicion, and Mud That Sticks

JOE PURSHOUSE*

Should criminal suspects enjoy a right to anonymity before charge? This question has generated considerable debate among policymakers, practitioners, and academics. It has resulted in piecemeal legal reform through a series of appellate decisions and revisions to policy documents over the last decade. Owing to the complex constellation of countervailing interests it brings into conflict, the debate has exposed fault lines within the major political parties and has been the subject of a succession of abortive Private Members' Bills.[1] Through this debate a general, although by no means universal,[2] consensus has emerged that there should not be an open season on the public identification of criminal suspects.[3] This consensus reached an apex in the recent decision of *Bloomberg LP v ZXC*,[4] where the UK Supreme Court unanimously held that those falling under criminal suspicion by an agent of the state generally hold a reasonable expectation of privacy over any information linking them to the investigation until the point of charge. The argument in this chapter is that the Supreme Court in *ZXC* was correct, as a matter of principle, to recognise a general right to anonymity for criminal suspects. However, there are sound reasons to reform the law by placing the protection of suspects' anonymity on a statutory footing through the creation of an automatic reporting restriction, supplemented by a criminal sanction for breach. It is submit-

* Senior Lecturer in Criminal Law and Justice, University of Sheffield. I am grateful to Áine Clancy and the editors of this volume for comments on an earlier draft. A version of this chapter was presented at the Criminal Law Reform Now Conference 2021. I thank all participants at this event for their valuable feedback, and particularly Matthew Dyson and Monica Stevenson for their thoughtful engagement with the chapter. Any errors are mine.

[1] See Anonymity (Arrested Persons) Bill [HC] Session 2010–12. The second reading of the Bill can be found at HC Deb 4 February 2011, vol 522, col 1160. See also Anonymity (Arrested Persons) Bill [HL] Session 2017–19.

[2] F Gerry QC, 'Does the UK Really Need a Right to Anonymity?' *Huffington Post* (13 January 2015).

[3] See the discussion of Mann J in *Sir Cliff Richard v The British Broadcasting Corporation; The Chief Constable of South Yorkshire Police* [2018] EWHC 1837 (Ch), [234]–[238].

[4] *Bloomberg LP v ZXC* [2022] UKSC 5.

ted that this reform is necessary, as the current legal framework is fractured and fails to provide a consistent, simplified, and principled approach to balancing the competing rights and interests at play. It is only with the creation of a criminal offence that the harmful practices of publishers can be effectively deterred in the digital age.

Following this introduction, the analysis comprises four sections. Sections 1 and 2 analyse how harmful publication practices and the consequent destruction of suspects' reputations in several high-profile cases led to general principles of police information management at common law being hardened into narrow legal rules and formal guidance governing the dissemination of suspects' personal information in various separate contexts. Through discussion of the courts' development of the misuse of privacy information tort to enhance protection of suspects, and resultant academic debates, this chapter defends the approach taken by the senior courts in extending the misuse of private information action. However, the legal framework still suffers from several deficiencies which leave suspects vulnerable to having their private lives disrupted and their reputations permanently tarnished from the very earliest stages at which they become the subject of a criminal investigation. Section 3 surveys these gaps in protection. It contemplates the future of anonymity protection, and particularly how the recent expansion in the misuse of private information tort to create a general presumption in favour of anonymity may soon be subject to more restrictive interpretation in the face of broader reforms in domestic human rights law. Section 4 proposes a draft legislative provision to ensure statutory anonymity protection for criminal suspects until the point of charge, which could remedy some of the deficiencies of the current legal framework whilst ensuring that core democratic values of press freedom and open justice are not unduly abrogated.

1. Early Attempts to Protect Anonymity

For over 60 years, the police have recognised that the public dissemination of personal information on their records can have detrimental consequences for suspects, and such disclosures should only be made where the interests of the individual are outweighed by the public interest. In 1954, a working party of chief officers of police outlined some of the principles which have underpinned the dissemination of personal information held on police records:

> It has been a fundamental rule that police information should not be used except for the purposes for which it was acquired, and therefore that it should not be disclosed to persons in authority however responsible, other than those concerned with police functions, unless the consideration of public interest is sufficiently weighty to justify departure from this general rule.[5]

[5] See Home Office, *Disclosure of Criminal Records for Employment Vetting Purposes*, Cm 2319 (HMSO, 1993) 4.

The question of whether suspects should enjoy anonymity has also been the subject of long-standing debate amongst legislators. At several junctures, Parliament has legislated to provide anonymity for suspects in the following particularised contexts:

1. The Sexual Offences (Amendment) Act 1976 extended anonymity protections to defendants at the same time as introducing these for complainants in rape cases. However, the provision was controversial and was ultimately removed by the enactment of the Criminal Justice Act 1988, s 158. When considering repeal of the defendant anonymity protections, legislators focused on the importance of ensuring that criminal trials were open to scrutiny. However, dissenting voices in the Commons highlighted how failing to protect the anonymity of defendants may lead to their accusers being identified through their known association to the defendant.[6] In 2011, the Coalition Government introduced a very specific anonymity provision restricting the reporting of alleged offences by a teacher in a school up to the point at which that teacher is charged. It created a criminal offence for breach of those reporting restrictions.[7] The provision was designed to protect teachers from spurious allegations by pupils in their school. It has drawn criticism not only from the Society of Editors and national newspapers, who were critical of this measure for undermining press freedom,[8] but also from those who favour increased anonymity for suspects, for focusing too narrowly on teachers subject to allegations in a school, to the exclusion of other professionals who might face similar complaints.[9]
2. The Contempt of Court Act 1981 also affords suspects some protection from harmful publication practices. Under section 1 of the Act – the 'strict liability rule' – it is a contempt of court to publish any matter which creates a substantial risk of serious prejudice or impediment to the course of justice in legal proceedings, irrespective of the intention behind the publication. Section 4(2) of the Act empowers a court to order that the publication of any report of its proceedings, or any part of the proceedings, be postponed for such period as the court thinks necessary for avoiding a substantial risk of prejudice to the administration of justice in those proceedings, or in any other proceedings pending or imminent. The Contempt of Court Act 1981, s 11 also gives a court the power to make a direction prohibiting the publication of a name or other specific matter in limited circumstances. These provisions provide some enduring protection for suspects' anonymity, but do not offer anything like the general protection of a suspect's privacy rights which is advanced in this chapter. The Contempt of Court Act 1981 is generally aimed at ensuring

[6] HC Deb 28 June 1988, vol 136, colls 205–214.

[7] Education Act 2011, s 13.

[8] O Bowcott, 'Teachers accused of crimes against pupils to be granted anonymity' *The Guardian* (28 September 2012).

[9] See, eg, the comments of Baroness Hughes of Stretford in HL Deb 6 July 2011, vol 729, col 157.

the proper administration of justice, and not specifically protecting the individual rights of those subject to its administration or regulating the reporting practices of the press generally.[10] Thus, the Act affords peripheral and limited protection for the broader harms that can come from the dissemination of information linking an individual to a criminal investigation.

3. Children or young persons under the age of 18 enjoy far stronger and entrenched anonymity protections than adults, which go beyond the investigation stage to protect the anonymity of defendants. Section 49 of the Children and Young Persons Act 1933 automatically imposes restrictions on the reporting of the identity of persons subject to proceedings in youth courts and to proceedings under the Sentencing Act 2020, Sch 7. The Children and Young Persons Act 1933, s 49(4–8) empowers a court to dispense with the restriction order (i) in the public interest; (ii) to avoid injustice; or (iii) where this is necessary for the purpose of apprehending a young person unlawfully at large for certain serious offences. Under s 45 of the Youth Justice and Criminal Evidence Act 1999, where a person under the age of 18 is subject to criminal proceedings, other than a youth court subject to the s 49 restriction, the court enjoys a discretionary power to direct that no matter be included in any publication if it is likely to lead members of the public to identify him as a person concerned in the proceedings.

At common law, any personal information, that is not generally available to the public and comes into the possession of a public body during the course of performing its public duties, ought not to be disclosed except where disclosure is judged necessary for the protection of the public.[11] On its face, this necessity requirement sets a high bar for the police to clear before releasing the identifying particulars of suspects to the media or circulating such information more widely. In practice, however, this has not served as a strong protection against the public identification of suspects. First, the rule only regulates what public authorities can disseminate. Moreover, prior to the enactment of the Human Rights Act 1998, there was no obvious domestic cause of action to remedy the 'unnecessary' dissemination of such information. Even in the years following the development of the tort of misuse of private information,[12] the disclosure practices of the police were subject to light touch regulation through Association of Chief Police Officers (ACPO) guidance. This guidance contained more caveats and equivocations highlighting the lack of legal constraint on police dissemination practices than

[10] The criteria for the strict liability rule are narrow, with the rule biting only where a publication creates a substantial and serious risk that court proceedings are impeded or prejudiced, applying the criminal burden and standard of proof. See *Attorney General v MGN* [1997] Entertainment and Media Law Reports 284, 289–91, per Schiemann LJ. The s 4(2) provision is also limited as it is aimed at postponement of publication rather than an indefinite restriction. See *R (Press Association) v Cambridge Crown Court* [2012] EWCA Crim 2434.

[11] See *Devon County Council, Ex parte L* [1991] 2 FLR 541.

[12] *Campbell v Mirror Group Newspapers Limited* [2004] UKHL 22.

rules regulating police conduct, as the emphasised text in the following passage indicates:

> 4.3. **Although there is no specific law** to prevent forces identifying those they have arrested, in practice they give general details of arrests which are designed to be informative but not to identify – for example 'a 27-year-old Brighton man'. In high profile cases which may cause major public concern – such as terrorism or murders – forces **sometimes provide** substantial detail about their investigations without identifying individuals.
>
> 4.4. The media frequently discover the name of people under investigation and seek confirmation. **Again, there is no law to prevent** forces giving confirmation. **Some forces do choose** to confirm the name; others choose not to do so but **may indicate** that a name is incorrect.
>
> 4.5. If a suspect is released without charge or bailed to reappear at a police station, the fact of the police action occurring is **generally released**, though the person remains unidentified. Again, **this is practice, rather than an approach dictated by any law.**[13]

The Guidance left vast discretion in the hands of individual police forces, which would result in inconsistent approaches to naming suspects between police forces. The approach described in paragraph 4.4 above, led some forces to indulge the media in a 'guessing-game' over who was being held in their custody and created a space for corrupt relationships between police officers and the media to develop, whereby the former would supply to the latter information about arrests and other records held on police computers.[14]

In the early 2000s, there was growing evidence of the existence of an 'illicit organised trade' in confidential personal information between journalists, corrupt public authority representatives such as police or prison officers, and private investigators acting as intermediaries.[15] Early investigations into this relationship, such as the Information Commissioner's Office's *Operation Motorman*, indicated that this illicit trade predominantly targeted celebrities and other public figures such as senior politicians.[16] However, further reports in *The Guardian* of phone hacking and police bribery by journalists working for the now defunct *News of the World* newspaper, revealed evidence suggesting that the voicemails of high-profile child murder victims and relatives of British soldiers killed in action in Iraq and Afghanistan had also been wire-tapped.[17] These developments had significant

[13] Association of Chief Police Officers, *Communication Advisory Group 2010 Guidance* (2010) 6. My emphasis.

[14] H Tomlinson QC, 'Leveson, "'secret arrests" and the rights of suspects: a question of balance' (10 April 2013) at: www.simkins.com/news/leveson-secret-arrests-and-the-rights-of-suspects-a-question-of-balance-hugh-tomlinson-qc.

[15] Information Commissioners' Office, *What Price Privacy? The Unlawful Trade in Confidential Personal Information* (TSO, 2006).

[16] ibid.

[17] N Davies and A Hill, 'Missing Milly Dowler's voicemail was hacked by News of the World' *The Guardian* (4 July 2011).

repercussions, leading not only to the dissolution of *News of the World*, but also to the Leveson Inquiry into the culture, ethics and practices of the media, and Operation Elveden – a police investigation into police bribery that led to the conviction of nine police officers and two journalists.[18]

The Emerging Anonymity Consensus

In the second volume of his report of his Inquiry into the Culture, Practices and Ethics of the Press, Brian Leveson LJ addressed the case of Christopher Jefferies. Jefferies was arrested on suspicion of the murder of Joanna Yeates in 2010. Jefferies was Yeates' landlord and was wholly innocent. Vincent Tabak, who lived in the same building as Yeates, was later convicted of her murder. However, Jefferies was subject to a vitriolic campaign of innuendo and vilification, such that he felt forced to leave his home and change his appearance. Jefferies later succeeded in a defamation claim against a national newspaper.[19] The case clearly demonstrated the ease with which arrest may generally be associated with guilt in the media. Leveson observed that 'save in exceptional and clearly identified circumstances (for example, where there may be an immediate risk to the public), the names or identifying details of those who are arrested or suspected of a crime should not be released to the press nor the public.'[20]

In a formal response of the judiciary to the Law Commission's 2013 consultation on Contempt of Court, Treacy LJ and Tugendhat J endorsed Leveson's view, drawing attention to the imbalance of publicity surrounding the initiation of proceedings versus subsequent decisions to discontinue them or take no further action. They also emphasised the role of the internet in creating searchable records of information surrounding an individual's arrest, that are freely accessible to the public.[21] Later in the same year, Theresa May, then Home Secretary, wrote to the College of Policing to express concern about inconsistent approaches taken by police forces regarding public identification and to urge that there should be a presumptive right to anonymity at arrest.[22] This prompted the College of Policing to issue new guidance on police relations with the media and suspect anonymity, which stated that 'save in clearly identified circumstances, or where legal restrictions apply, the names or identifying details of those who are arrested or suspected of a crime should not be released by police forces to the press or the public.'[23]

[18] 'Operation Elveden corruption probe ends' (BBC News, 26 February 2016).

[19] Above (n 4) para 82. See Lord Justice Leveson, *An Inquiry into the Culture, Practices and Ethics of the Press: Report* HC 780-II (2012) vol 2; E Freer, 'Human rights: Bloomberg LP v ZXC' [2022] *Crim LR* 500, 504.

[20] HC 780-II (2012) vol 2 at 791.

[21] Treacy LJ and Tugendhat J, *Contempt of Court: A Judicial Response to Law Commission Consultation Paper No 209* (2013) 5.

[22] M Easton, 'Suspects should have right to anonymity at arrest – Theresa May' (*BBC*, 15 May 2013).

[23] College of Policing, 'Guidance on Relationships with the Media' (2013) para 3.5.2.

Further recognition of the potentially ruinous impact of the publication of criminal allegations followed in Sir Richard Henriques' independent review of the Metropolitan Police Service's handling of non-recent sexual offence investigations.[24] This review was commissioned following the collapse of Operation Midland, an ill-fated criminal investigation that the Metropolitan Police conducted into (what we now know to be false) accusations of past child abuse made by Carl Beech against a series of high profile public figures. Henriques expressed concern at what he described as a 'culture of belief' in policing, consisting of the failure of the police to 'appreciate the danger of false complaints'.[25]

Henriques highlighted one weakness of the police guidance and practice of not naming arrestees, but instead disclosing offence, age, and location – namely, that even the disclosure of this information would be 'all but certain' to result in loss of anonymity in cases involving a high profile arrestee, such as a celebrity or senior politician.[26] The routine release of such information as part of Operation Midland enabled journalists and the broader public to quickly identify arrestees, as anyone could 'piece together the jigsaw' of publicly available information using internet search engines and social media. Henriques made a formal recommendation that a suspect should have the right to anonymity prior to charge enforced by statute and criminal sanctions, and that any pre-charge identification should be exceptional and subject to strict control.[27]

Whilst statutory protection of anonymity has not yet taken hold, there have been further developments to strengthen such protections. The 2013 College of Policing guidance was supplemented by an Authorised Professional Practice in 2017, which has periodically been updated.[28] The guidance is *sans* the equivocation which characterised the ACPO approach pre-Leveson, and reflects an operational response to criticisms about the unfairness of previous police approaches to naming suspects.[29] It indicated that any pre-charge naming of criminal suspects should be authorised by a chief officer after consultation with the Crown Prosecution Service. The guidance sets out a general approach to be taken by all forces:

Police will not name those arrested, or suspected of a crime, save in exceptional circumstances where there is a legitimate policing purpose to do so …

> A legitimate policing purpose may include circumstances such as a threat to life, the prevention or detection of crime, or where police have made a public warning about a wanted individual …
>
> When someone is arrested, police can proactively release the person's gender, age, the place – for example, the town or city – where they live … This should not apply in cases

[24] Sir Richard Henriques, *An Independent Review of the Metropolitan Police Service's handling of non-recent sexual offence investigations alleged against persons of public prominence* (2016).

[25] ibid, para 1.41.

[26] ibid, para 1.52.

[27] ibid, para 1.67.

[28] College of Policing, 'APP: Engagement and Communications: Media Relations' (24 May 2017).

[29] See *ZXC v Bloomberg LP* [2020] EWCA Civ 611, [80], per Simon J.

where, although not directly naming an arrested person, this information would nevertheless have the effect of confirming their identity.[30]

This guidance echoes the obligations on police under the Data Protection Act 2018, and human rights law more broadly, to only process personal information in a law enforcement context lawfully and fairly, in accordance with a specified legitimate aim.[31] It should be welcomed for clarifying the police position at national level. But the guidance also has its limits. It is not legally binding and only regulates what the police disclose to the media. Problems have persisted where the media identify individuals as the subject of a criminal investigation without relying on the police disclosing this information to them. For example, in 2018 dozens of flights were cancelled at Gatwick Airport following successive reports of drone sightings close to the runway over a period of three days. As part of the investigation into who was operating drones a couple were arrested on suspicion of a series of offences under the Aviation and Maritime Security Act 1990, but were later released without further action. Although wholly innocent, they were named by a series of media outlets and described feeling 'violated' by the treatment they received in certain sections of the media with one outlet famously running the headline 'Are these the morons who ruined Christmas?' underneath a picture of the couple.[32]

The guidance warns of the risks of disparate information about a suspect being pieced together to enable 'jigsaw identification'. However, as jigsaw identification is a continuing problem, it may be questioned whether this guidance alone will be sufficient to protect suspects from jigsaw identification, even where it is followed to the letter.[33] Added to this, there have been occasions where the police disclose such information contrary to their own guidance;[34] and where Members of Parliament use their parliamentary privilege to name a criminal suspect.[35]

2. Can Anonymity be Protected Through the Courts?

By virtue of section 6 of the Human Rights Act 1998, courts must act in a way which gives effect to individual's 'right to respect for a private life' under Article 8

[30] See n 28.

[31] See Data Protection Act 2018, Pt 3, Ch 2; Article 8 of the Convention for the Protection of Human Rights and Fundamental Freedoms (Rome, 4 November 1950) (ECHR).

[32] See S Murphy, 'Pair held and released over Gatwick drone say they feel "violated"' *The Guardian* (24 December 2018).

[33] See, eg, the facts in *Sicri v Associated Newspapers Ltd* [2020] EWHC 3541 (QB).

[34] See n 3.

[35] In 2014, Jimmy Hood MP stated in a Parliamentary debate that there had been 'accusations of improper conduct with children' made against former Home Secretary, Sir Leon Brittan. Sir Leon Brittan was posthumously cleared of any wrongdoing once after it was established that these allegations were among the prolific lies of Carl Beech. See 'Suspect anonymity: The hypocrisy of parliamentary privilege' (*Brett Wilson Media and Communication Law Blog*, 2020) at www.brettwilson.co.uk/blog/suspect-anonymity-the-hypocrisy-of-parliamentary-privilege/.

of the European Convention on Human Rights. The common law tort of 'misuse of private information' emerged out of this obligation, and the senior courts have recognised this action as the primary mechanism of redress for the unjustified dissemination of information that someone is the subject of a police investigation before they have been charged. In *Sir Cliff Richard v The British Broadcasting Corporation*, the claimant successfully brought an action against the BBC for a broadcast showing police officers searching his home as part of an investigation into child sex abuse allegations made against him. The BBC were notified of the search by the South Yorkshire Police in advance, after an employee of the BBC gave the impression to police that the BBC had details of the investigation and were prepared to publish them. Senior officers provided the information on the proviso that the BBC would not publish a story based on the details they already had.

In finding that the claimant had a reasonable expectation of privacy with respect to this information, Mann J focused on the stigmatising effect and reputational damage that would likely result from the dissemination of information that an individual has been investigated, particularly in relation to offences related to child sexual abuse.[36] Whilst Mann J held that the balance of case law and extra-judicial material heard in argument (several of which are discussed above)[37] support the proposition that 'as a matter of general principle, a suspect has a reasonable expectation of privacy in relation to a police investigation',[38] he held that such an expectation should not be equated with an 'invariable right to privacy' and that '[t]here may be all sorts of reasons why, in a given case, there is no reasonable expectation of privacy, or why an original reasonable expectation is displaced'.[39] Mann J held that the public interest in the disclosure did not outweigh the claimant's interest in privacy in the immediate case, primarily as the information was disclosed with a 'significant degree of breathless sensationalism'.[40]

This approach was confirmed by the Court of Appeal in *ZXC v Bloomberg LP*, where it was held that, in general, a person has a reasonable expectation of privacy over details of their being subject to a police investigation, up to the point of charge. The defendant media company, Bloomberg, published details of an unnamed United Kingdom law enforcement body's investigation into a businessman's alleged involvement in corruption and bribery offences. The defendant's article was based on a Letter of Request for Mutual Legal Assistance sent by the UK law enforcement body to another authority abroad. It is not clear how Bloomberg obtained this letter, but it was marked as confidential.

[36] See n 3, [224].
[37] ibid, [234], citing *Hannon v News Group Newspapers Ltd* [2015] EMLR 1; *PNM v Times Newspapers Ltd* [2014] EMLR 30; *ERY v Associated Newspapers Ltd* [2017] EMLR 9; and *ZXC v Bloomberg LP* [2017] EMLR 21 inter alia.
[38] See n 3, [248].
[39] ibid, [251].
[40] ibid, [300].

Simon J, with whom Underhill LJ and Bean LJ concurred, focused on the damaging impact of being linked to a criminal investigation, given 'the human characteristic to assume the worst (that there is no smoke without fire); and to overlook the fundamental legal principle that those who are accused of an offence are deemed to be innocent until they are proven guilty.'[41] In rejecting the defendant's arguments regarding their justification for publishing the information, Simon J held that there was a significant distinction between 'a report about the alleged criminal conduct of an individual; and a report about a police investigation into that individual and preliminary conclusions drawn from those investigations', with only the latter falling within the sphere of protection.[42] Thus, whereas one could rarely be said to hold a reasonable expectation of privacy over his involvement in criminal activity, one could reasonably expect a prima facie expectation of privacy surrounding police investigations and suspicions, particularly at the early stages of an investigation.

The Court of Appeal's decision in *ZXC* was subsequently applied by a Divisional Court in *Sicri v Associated Newspapers Ltd*. The facts in *Sicri* exemplify the devastating impact of reports naming criminal suspects in high profile cases.[43] On 29 May 2017, in the aftermath of the Manchester Arena suicide bombing, the claimant was arrested on suspicion of offences contrary to the Terrorism Act 2000. The police issued a press release that a 23-year-old man had been arrested in connection with the attack but did not name the claimant. However, an article published by the *Mail Online* provided details of the claimant's name, nationality, the location of his home and his photograph. The claimant was subsequently released without charge. The *Mail Online* neither published this fact nor took down the online article. The article was published internationally, leading the claimant to fear for his safety, receive abusive messages on social media, and lose his employment. The *Mail Online* eventually took down the article in February 2018 when the claimant's solicitor sent a letter of claim.

Warby J held that English law now recognises 'a general rule in favour of pre-charge anonymity for suspects'[44] and that the rationale for this rule was based on the fact that 'disclosure of such information is likely to have a seriously harmful impact on the person's reputation, and thus their private life.'[45] Warby J went onto to summarise the exceptions to the 'general rule' or 'legitimate starting point' that had emerged in previous authorities, including the public nature of the activity under consideration,[46] and a decision by the police to release the suspect's name. Warby J also observed that the misuse of private information tort had developed in

[41] See n 29, [82].
[42] ibid, [96].
[43] See n 33. This point is also made in R Craig and G Phillipson, 'Privacy, reputation and anonymity until charge: *ZXC* goes to the Supreme Court' (2021) 13 *Journal of Media Law* 152.
[44] See n 33, [85].
[45] ibid, [75].
[46] ibid, [86].

a manner consistent with data protection laws in recognising 'personal data relating to "the … alleged commission by [the data subject] of any offence" as "sensitive personal data", the processing of which requires additional justification'.[47]

Finally, in 2022, the UKSC unanimously dismissed an appeal from Bloomberg in the *ZXC* case. Bloomberg argued that the Court of Appeal had been wrong to hold that, as a general rule, a person under criminal investigation had a reasonable expectation of privacy in respect of this information before the point of charge. Lord Hamblen and Lord Stephens (with whom Lord Reed, Lord Lloyd-Jones and Lord Sales agreed) clarified that the general rule or legitimate starting point described by the Court of Appeal was not a legal presumption: whether there was a reasonable expectation of privacy in the relevant information remained a fact-specific enquiry.[48] If the expectation did not arise, the information could be published and if the facts were such that an objective expectation of privacy was significantly reduced, that would bear on the weight to be attached to the Article 8 rights in the stage two balancing analysis. They explained that the rationale for the starting point was that publication of such information ordinarily caused damage to the person's reputation and to multiple aspects of the person's physical and social identity protected by Article 8 ECHR, as had been set out in the lower courts.[49]

Bloomberg further argued, among other things, that the application by the courts below of the starting point was unsound because it significantly overstated the capacity of publication of the information to cause damage to the claimant's reputation given the public's ability to observe the presumption of innocence. The Court rejected this argument, finding that when the fact that an individual is subject to criminal suspicion is publicised 'the person's reputation will ordinarily be adversely affected causing prejudice to personal enjoyment of the right to respect for private life such as the right to establish and develop relationships with other human beings.'[50]

The judicial development of protection for suspect anonymity under the misuse of private information tort has sparked academic debate. Moreham has criticised the extension because it unsettles the established principle of defamation law that a defendant should not be compensated for loss of a reputation which he or she might not deserve, and for creating an avenue for potential claimants to circumvent the defamation action's strong public interest expression protections.[51]

Commenting on the Court of Appeal decision in *ZXC*, Moreham argues that the *Marcel* principle under the tort of breach of confidence – that 'no person who obtains information pursuant to a legal power or in furtherance of a public duty

[47] ibid, [85]; Data Protection Act 2018, s 11(2)(a).
[48] See n 4, [68].
[49] ibid, [72].
[50] ibid, [108].
[51] See NA Moreham, 'Privacy and police investigations: *ZXC v Bloomberg*' (2021) 80 *Cambridge Law Journal* 5, 7 citing *Flood v Times Newspapers Ltd* [2012] UKSC 11 and *Bonnard v Perryman* [1891] 2 Ch 269.

is free to disclose it to others unless that disclosure is consistent with the original purpose for which the information was obtained'[52] – provides a better basis for liability in cases like *ZXC* and *Richard* than misuse of private information. Moreham advances several arguments in favour of this approach. First, breach of confidence 'homes in better than privacy on the central concern in these situations – namely, the fact that the police are sharing information about their investigations into named individuals without a good operational reason for doing so'.[53] Second, targeted liability in breach of confidence for the wrongful disclosure of police information would have less of a 'chilling effect' on media outlets and victims of crime than liability in misuse of private information.[54] Third, information pertaining to an individual falling under criminal suspicion is not related to private life in the traditional sense. Rather, the real complaint of individuals such as the claimant in *ZXC* is that publication is deleterious to reputation. For Moreham, in allowing claimants to protect their reputations through the misuse of private information tort, English courts risk compensating claimants for damage to reputations they may not deserve in the circumstances.[55]

In a recent article defending the emergent consensus that suspects should be anonymous until charge and that the misuse of private information tort is the appropriate action to protect this right, Craig and Phillipson provide a persuasive rebuttal of Moreham's main conclusions. On Moreham's argument that the expansion of the misuse of private information tort unsettles the established principle of defamation law that a claimant should not be compensated for loss of a reputation which he or she might not deserve, Craig and Phillipson argue that this concern is not well founded in practice as damages purely to vindicate reputational loss might not ordinarily be awarded in misuse of private information cases; and, in many cases, it will be clear by the time the civil case comes to trial that the claimant faces no prospect of being charged or convicted (as in *Sicri* and *Richard*). Moreover, in the rare cases that awarding damages in respect of an undeserved reputation may seem real, Craig and Phillipson contend that the civil case hearing could simply be deferred until after the criminal proceedings had concluded.[56]

Craig and Phillipson argue that the presumption of innocence (taken as a broad principle of political morality that the state should organise the criminal process in such a way as to treat all suspects as though they are innocent[57]) should

[52] See *Marcel v Commissioner of Police of the Metropolis* [1992] Ch 225.

[53] NA Moreham, 'Police investigations, privacy and the Marcel Principle in breach of confidence' (2020) 12 *Journal of Media Law* 1; NA Moreham, 'Police Investigations, Privacy and Breach of Confidence, Part 2' (30 July 2020) at inforrm.org/2020/07/30/police-investigations-privacy-and-breach-of-confidence-part-2-n-a-moreham/.

[54] ibid (2020) 12 *Journal of Media Law* 1.

[55] NA Moreham, 'Privacy, reputation and alleged wrongdoing: why police investigations should not be regarded as private' (2019) 11 *Journal of Media Law* 142, 152.

[56] See n 43 (2021) 13 *Journal of Media Law* 153, 169.

[57] ibid, 179. The authors noted that this broad conception of the presumption of innocence has found favour with ECtHR jurisprudence, which courts are specifically bound to act compatibly with by virtue of the Human Rights Act 1998. See, eg, *Worm v Austria* (1998) 25 EHRR 44; *Jishkariani v Georgia* App no 18925/09 ECtHR 20 September 2018.

serve as a 'guiding light' for judges in misuse of private information cases.[58] Craig and Philipson argue that, whilst it may be acceptable for the state to arrest, search, or detain criminal suspects on the basis of a reasonable suspicion, these necessary investigatory steps contrast sharply from the public identification of suspects in most cases. Such identification generally occasions unnecessary intrusions into the individual's private life and is potentially deleterious to the administration of justice.[59] Thus, to expose the fact of an individual's subjection to criminal process before the point of charge is to have inadequate respect for the individual's status of innocence.

By invoking the presumption of innocence as the grounding normative principle or 'guiding light' to navigate such cases, the authors introduce an unnecessary layer of conceptual complexity to their argument, which distracts from their central conclusion. Granted, the ECtHR has considered that an individual is 'not being treated as innocent' when assessing the impact of measures taken by the state against a suspect that may inflict stigma or reputational damage under the Article 8 heading.[60] However, this line of jurisprudence has prompted concern that the presumption of innocence is being extended too far beyond its traditional procedural parameters, and that this risks diluting its potency and eclipsing the normative value of the narrower procedural protection.[61] The authors do not engage with these broader debates on the scope and normative value of the presumption of innocence. However, it is submitted that such debates might be avoided altogether, as the harms occasioned by publication flow from the unjustified intrusion into the individual's private life occasioned by stigmatising publicity, and not from the state abrogating the individual's status of legal or factual innocence.

As the authors highlight, Moreham's point that information pertaining to an individual falling under criminal suspicion is not related to private life runs against a strong legal consensus cutting across European Court of Human Rights (ECtHR) jurisprudence, EU data protection law and domestic transposition and interpretation of these provisions through statutes and the common law.[62] It has been firmly established that an individual's reputation is an aspect of private life under Article 8 ECHR, and the authors are correct to conclude that public identification generally occasions unnecessary intrusions into the individual's enjoyment of this right. It is true that the ECtHR has held that Article 8 ECHR could not be relied on in order to complain of a loss of reputation which was the foreseeable consequence of one's own actions such as, for example, the commission of a criminal offence.[63] This modest limitation on article 8 prevents the use of this right to

[58] ibid (2021) 13 *Journal of Media Law* 153, 178.
[59] ibid, 178.
[60] See *S and Marper v United Kingdom* (2009) 48 EHRR 50, [119].
[61] See, eg, L Campbell, 'Criminal Labels, the European Convention on Human Rights and the Presumption of Innocence' (2013) 76 *MLR* 681, 691.
[62] See n 43 (2021) 13 *Journal of Media Law* 153, 169.
[63] *Sidabras v Lithuania* (2006) 42 EHRR 6.

suppress information pertaining to the individual's reputationally harmful actions, rather than the mere fact of being the object of suspicion by a public authority.

In *Mikolajová v Slovakia*, where police disclosed information pertaining to the applicant's arrest to the health insurer of his spouse, the ECtHR held that the dissemination of this information fell firmly within the sphere of Article 8 protection, finding that the text of the police decision to arrest the applicant 'cannot be considered to be the foreseeable consequence of the applicant's own doing, precisely because she has never been charged with, let alone proved to have committed, any crime.'[64] Here, the ECtHR seems to recognise that privacy protection is often warranted because, at the earliest stages of a criminal process, there is a high level of uncertainty as to whether any reputational damage concomitant to being the subject of police attention is or is not deserved.

There is good reason for human rights law to protect individuals from arbitrary reputational damage. This is because an individual's reputation functions to help them to form and maintain social relationships. Reputational damage can negatively impact health and well-being and reduce opportunities to gain access to resources in a community.[65] There is evidence to suggest that reputation loss increases the risk of suicide even in people for whom there existed no previous signs of mental disorder.[66]

A growing body of empirical research supports the accounts of reputational damage, loss of resources, and diminished well-being reported by the claimants in cases such as *Sicri* and *ZXC*, notwithstanding the accuracy of the reporting in these cases. A classic study by Schwartz and Skolnick – in which the researchers prepared four sets of resumes with varying criminal record disclosures to prospective employers – demonstrated that employers were significantly less likely to consider applicants who had prior contact with the criminal justice system, even if the applicant was not subsequently convicted.[67] The study even showed that, where a job applicant with an acquittal on their record supported their application with a letter from the judge certifying the applicant's acquittal and emphasising the presumption of innocence, this applicant was still less likely to be shortlisted for the position than the control applicant with no criminal record.[68] More recent studies have demonstrated similar findings,[69] and other empirical research indicates that

[64] *Mikolajová v Slovakia* 4479/03 ECtHR 18 April 2011, [57].

[65] For a very impressive summary of empirical research on the negative effects of social ostracism and reputation loss see D Howarth, 'Libel: Its Purpose and Reform' (2011) 74 *MLR* 845, 849–52.

[66] S Pridmore and M McArthur, 'Suicide and reputation damage' (2008) 16 *Australasian Psychiatry* 312, also discussed in Howarth, ibid, 849–52.

[67] R Schwartz and J Skolnick, 'Two Studies of Legal Stigma' (1962) 10 *Social Problems* 133.

[68] D Kirk and RJ Sampson, 'Juvenile Arrest and Collateral Educational Damage in the Transition to Adulthood' (2013) 86 *Sociology of Education* 36.

[69] See D Pager, 'The Mark of a Criminal Record' (2003) 108 *American Journal of Sociology* 937; C Uggen, M Vuolo, and S Lageson, 'The Edge of Stigma: An experimental audit of the effects of low-level criminal records on employment' (2014) 52 *Criminology* 627, 649.

the dissemination of arrest records can have detrimental impacts on educational attainment and school dropout rates.[70]

Although it may seem counterintuitive, anonymity may also serve the public's interest in crime prevention and public safety. This is because publishing information linking an individual to a criminal investigation could constitute a form of disintegrative stigmatisation:[71] it outcasts the individual, blocking his or her access to an avenue of legitimate participation in society (namely, through the pursuit of a chosen career). In doing so, such disclosure may – as is well documented in criminological literature – diminish the individual's social bonds to the community, increasing the likelihood that the individual will engage in offending behaviour.[72]

Given the analysis above, Moreham's point on breach of confidence providing more appropriate protection for suspects seems inadequate because the 'Marcel principle' is only equipped to remedy deliberate leaks of details of an investigation by the authorities to the press.[73] Moreham's position seems to be based on a mistaken premise that '*whenever* police are investigating a suspect there will be some reason to think that he or she might be guilty of an offence'.[74] This overlooks that mere investigation can be undertaken on any level of suspicion, and there will inevitably be situations where an individual will be wrongly suspected. Craig and Phillipson highlight that 'it is known that the police sometimes investigate multiple persons, where only one can have committed the offence, simply to eliminate them from their inquiries'.[75] Moreham's approach, which would restrict the protection of suspects' reputational interests only to cases where they are either outright defamed by the media or where there is a breach of confidence by the authorities, would leave the media free to identify criminal suspects at the earliest stages of police inquiries and the consequences of such publicity for suspects can be devastating.

3. Human Rights Reform and the Uncertain Future of Anonymity for Criminal Suspects

The preceding sections of this analysis have demonstrated that there is a broad and defensible consensus that those subject to criminal investigation should gener-

[70] For example, empirical research from the United States shows that the dissemination of an arrest on a job applicant's criminal record certificate will have a deleterious impact on his or her chances of gaining employment. See ibid (2014) 52 *Criminology* 627.

[71] J Braithwaite, *Crime, Shame and Reintegration* (CUP, 1989) 101.

[72] D Downes, P Rock, and E McLaughlin, *Understanding Deviance*, 7th edn (OUP, 2016) 160–84. For further discussion in the context of non-conviction criminal record disclosure, see J Purshouse, 'Non-conviction disclosure as part of an enhanced criminal record certificate: Assessing the legal framework from a fundamental human rights perspective' [2018] *Public Law* 668.

[73] See n 43 (2021) 13 *Journal of Media Law* 153, 171.

[74] See n 55 (2019) 11 *Journal of Media Law* 142, 155.

[75] See n 43 (2021) 13 *Journal of Media Law* 153, 178.

ally be entitled to anonymity until the point of charge. This consensus emerged in reaction to increased societal knowledge of the severe harm unwanted publicity of criminal suspicion can cause. This consensus, however, is by no means unanimous as the academic debate above has shown. Moreover, the recent victories for those who champion the pre-charge anonymity through the courts may also prove to be short lived. In December 2021, the Government published a consultation document outlining its proposals to reform the Human Rights Act 1998. It proposed that there should be strengthened protections for the right to freedom of expression and that 'courts should only grant relief impinging on [this right] where there are exceptional reasons.'[76] The Government articulated a preference for 'a presumption in favour of upholding the right to freedom of expression, subject to exceptional countervailing grounds clearly spelt out by Parliament.'[77]

Following the ruling of the UKSC in *Bloomberg v ZXC*, the Ministry of Justice hinted that the domestic courts' development of the misuse of private information tort to include anonymity for suspects might be in the crosshairs of government reform plans. In response to the judgment, a 'government spokesperson' reportedly told *The Guardian* that the Government was keen to safeguard freedom of the press and would 'study the implications of the judgment carefully.'[78]

The Government introduced the Bill of Rights Bill on 22 June 2022. The Bill would repeal and replace the Human Rights Act 1998, although some provisions are retained. Despite an overwhelming majority of respondents of its consultation on human rights reform indicating that a proposal to strengthen freedom of expression was not needed, the Government included such reforms as part of the Bill without explanation.[79]

In the months leading up to the publication of the Bill, the Society of Editors expressed concerns that press freedoms had been 'significantly weakened over the years by the emerging development of the tort of misuse of private information'.[80] Against this backdrop, a new provision, seemingly designed to protect free speech from 'creeping judicial-made privacy law',[81] is set out in clause 4(1) as follows:

> When determining a question which has arisen in connection with the right to freedom of speech, a court must give great weight to the importance of protecting the right.[82]

The Bill of Rights Bill aims to recalibrate the balance struck between freedom of expression and privacy rights in such a manner that will prioritise the former.

[76] *Human Rights Act Reform: A Modern Bill of Rights: A consultation to reform the Human Rights Act 1998* (Ministry of Justice, 2021), para 213.

[77] ibid, para 215.

[78] J Waterson, 'Privacy laws could be rolled back, UK government sources suggest' *The Guardian* (19 February 2022).

[79] See *Human Rights Act Reform: A Modern Bill of Rights, Consultation Response* (Ministry of Justice, 2022).

[80] M Fouzder, 'What will Dominic Raab's bill of rights look like?' (*Law Gazette*, 25 March 2022).

[81] ibid, where these comments were attributed to the sponsor of the Bill of Rights Bill, Dominic Raab MP.

[82] Bill of Rights Bill HC Bill (2022–23) [117], cl 4(1).

Clause 4 leaves the rule that suspects have a prima facie pre-charge 'reasonable expectation of privacy' over information that they are subject to criminal process untouched. However, clause 4 seems to place an obligation on courts to give 'great weight' to the interests of the press and other groups under Article 10 ECHR in its 'stage two' analysis where the suspects privacy rights are 'balanced' against the Article 10 rights of the publisher.

Much has happened in British politics between June and December 2022, the time of writing. Without retracing all that history here, Dominic Raab MP, the Secretary of State for Justice who sponsored the Bill under Boris Johnson's premiership, was relieved of his office for the duration of Liz Truss MP's ill-fated period as Prime Minister between 6 September and 25 October 2022 and, during this time, it appeared that the Bill would not proceed to a second reading. Upon succeeding Truss as Prime Minister, Rishi Sunak MP has reinstated Raab. However, it remains unclear when, if ever, the Bill will proceed to its second reading as it has reportedly been 'deprioritised' over concerns it could be blocked by the House of Lords, stalling the progress of other Bills.[83] Meanwhile, there have been some developments indicating the potential for a movement towards enhanced anonymity for suspects. A Private Members' Bill to protect the anonymity of suspects was presented to Parliament in June 2022 by Sir Christopher Chope, the Conservative MP for Christchurch. The second reading for this Bill is scheduled to take place in March 2023, but the Bill has yet to receive any explicit government support. The idea of protecting suspect anonymity seems to enjoy general support from the Home Secretary, though. In October 2022, in her first stint in the role, the recently reinstated Suella Braverman MP indicated to a meeting of the young conservatives that she wished to examine the possibility of giving anonymity to criminal suspects before charge.[84] This issue may yet expose a fissure within the governing party, which currently has no clear position on whether it is the press or criminal suspects that need greater protection through law reform in this area.

4. A Proposal for Criminal Law Reform

Irrespective of whether we see the misuse of private information tort fettered through the Bill of Rights Bill, the preceding analysis indicates that individuals subject to criminal suspicion should, subject to limited exceptions, remain anonymous until the point of charge. It is submitted that a statutory automatic reporting restriction on the publication of identifying particulars of criminal suspects, and

[83] A Allegretti, 'Sunak's next U-turn may be to ditch Raab's bill of rights' *The Guardian* (8 December 2022). *Editor's Note: Dominic Raab MP was in due course replaced by Alex Chalk MP in April 2023 and a Bill of Rights now seems highly unlikely in the time left to the current government..*

[84] R Syal, 'Suella Braverman to consider giving anonymity to suspected criminals' *The Guardian* (3 October 2022).

the creation of a strict liability offence for breach, could remedy many of the deficiencies in the legal framework, increase legal certainty, and strike a fair balance between the competing principles and fundamental rights at stake. To make good this claim, this section of the analysis will first explicate what form such a statutory protection might take before considering and addressing potential objections to such a wide reaching and general protection. A statutory reporting restriction would break new ground in terms of offering encompassing anonymity protection to criminal suspects. However, the concept of a reporting restriction to protect suspects' anonymity is not alien to English law.[85] Drawing on the drafting of similar reporting restrictions, the proposed automatic restriction could take the following form:

1. Restriction on the publication of identifying particulars of a criminal suspect

(1) No matter relating to a person shall be included in any publication if it is likely to lead to members of the public to identify him as the subject of a criminal investigation.

(2) Subsection (1) does not apply after the earliest time when any of the following events occurs—

(a) the person is charged with a criminal offence in relation to that investigation, or a prosecution is otherwise commenced.

(b) the person is issued a diversionary caution, or a community caution in relation to the matter investigated

(3) In this section 'publication' includes any speech, writing, relevant programme or other communication in whatever form, which is addressed to the public at large or any section of the public, but does not include an indictment or other document prepared for use in particular legal proceedings.

(4) For the purposes of this section, a person is 'the subject of a criminal investigation' if he is arrested, searched, questioned under police caution, or otherwise investigated by a representative of a state agency with a view to it being ascertained whether he should be charged with a criminal offence.

(5) A representative of a state agency may dispense to any extent with the restriction imposed under subsection (1) insofar as to do so is necessary to apprehend a person unlawfully at large or wanted in connection with a criminal offence.

(6) Any person may make an application to a magistrates' court for an order dispensing with the restrictions imposed by subsection (1).

(7) A court may by order dispense to any specified extent with the restriction imposed under subsection (1) above if it is satisfied that to do so is strictly necessary—

(a) in the public interest; or

(b) to avoid injustice.

[85] See section 2 above. Recently, in Northern Ireland, the Justice (Sexual Offences and Trafficking Victims) Act 2022, s 12 created anonymity protections for suspects in certain sexual offence investigations.

(8) The court's power under subsection (7) above may be exercised by a single justice

(9) A court shall not exercise its power under subsection (7) above without—

- (a) affording the parties to the proceedings an opportunity to make representations; and
- (b) taking into account any representations which are duly made.

(10) The restriction in subsection (1) also ceases to apply if—

- (a) the person who is the subject of the investigation includes a matter in a publication, or
- (b) another person includes a matter in a publication with the consent of the person who is the subject of the investigation.

2. Offence of breach of restriction on publication

(1) Any person who includes in a publication material in breach of section 1(1) above is guilty of an offence.

(2) Where a person is charged with an offence under section 2, it is a defence for the person to prove that at the time of publication the person was not aware, and neither suspected nor had reason to suspect, that the publication included the matter in question.

The draft statutory provision addresses several of the deficiencies in the regulatory framework governing the publication of the identity of criminal suspects. First, the provision hardens further into law the growing judicial and political consensus that the fact of an individual's involvement as the subject of a criminal investigation should not be publicly disseminated save in exceptional circumstances. Currently, the discretion of police and publishers to disclose is not subject to prospective rules of law that provide adequate guidance as to the circumstances in which publication might be justified. The framework of protections for criminal suspects as it is currently constituted offers little by way of consistent protection generally, nor *ex ante* guidance on the limits of the rights of publishers. The guidance that does exist has proven ineffective in preventing 'jigsaw identification', and identification outside of large media outlets. As with similar reporting restrictions that protect other groups, the draft provision encourages publishers to be mindful of whether the dissemination of personal information is likely to lead to the identification of an individual as part of a criminal process, taking due account of how different types of personal information might be 'pieced together' even if the name of a criminal suspect is not disseminated.

The remedies for wrongful identification under the current framework are, as a matter of empirical reality, distributed unevenly. Whereas tort law has been a successful mechanism for celebrities and powerful businessmen to win sizeable sums in damages for the reputational harm caused by the sensationalist reporting of major media organisations, it has proven less effective at deterring the 'feeding frenzy' of online identification and smears that can follow involvement in a criminal process in less high-profile cases, where the publishers are often a disorganised band of social media users.[86] The creation of a criminal offence would provide a stronger deterrent to malicious and harmful publication practices, and one that is of universal application.

The statutory publication restriction is not susceptible to Moreham's concerns that suspects might win damages for harm to reputations tainted as a result of their involvement in criminal acts. The focus of the statutory restriction is on calling to account the actions of publishers that are contrary to the public interest, and not on vindicating the conduct of, or compensating, particular individuals. At the point that a newspaper or online vigilante publicly identifies an individual as the object of criminal suspicion, the wrongfulness of the conduct in that moment turns on the potential harm to that individual, his or her relatives and friends, the administration of justice, and the existence of any countervailing justifications, and not on whether the targeted individual is eventually found guilty.

As we have seen, charge is generally accepted as a defensible point at which a suspect's identity may be revealed because of the significant change in the level of evidence-based suspicion of guilt, and the more pressing demands of open justice as a case progresses to trial.[87] This is because, where an individual has been charged, the state has taken the decision to formally prosecute the individual based on evidence that is, in the view of an independent prosecutor, at least: capable of being put into an admissible format for presentation in court, reliable, and credible.[88]

Section 1(2) also outlines that the reporting restriction will apply until the point of criminal charge or of a non-conviction disposal which is issued to an adult suspect as an alternative to formal prosecution. Section 1(2) is drafted in terms that incorporate the reforms of the out of court disposal framework contained in the Police, Crime, Sentencing and Courts Act 2022, Pt 6. This streamlines the range of available cautions, warnings and penalty notices into a two-tier framework of diversionary and community cautions. Both of these cautions can be given to a person aged 18 or over in respect of an offence, provided that there is sufficient evidence to charge the individual with the offence, the individual admits to having committed the offence; and consents to being given the caution.[89] Consequently, the reforms proposed here also preserve the heightened anonymity protections

[86] For an example of how, in the absence of targeted legal protections, rituals of shaming and stigmatisation of criminal suspects can proliferate online, see J Purshouse, '"Paedophile Hunters", Criminal Procedure, and Fundamental Human Rights' (2020) 47 *Journal of Law and Society* 384.

[87] See n 43 (2021) 13 *Journal of Media Law* 153, 155.

[88] For full details of the relevant tests that must be satisfied before a suspect is charged with a criminal offence, see *Code for Crown Prosecutors* (2018) 3.1–5.11. A joint inspection by HMIC (now HMICFRS) and HMCPSI showed that in 91.9% of the cases examined, the decision to charge an individual complied with the Code for Crown Prosecutors. See: HMIC/HMCPSI, *Joint Inspection of the Provision of Charging Decisions* (2015) 27.

[89] Police, Crime, Sentencing and Courts Act 2022, Pt 6, ss 99 and 108.

that apply to youths subject to criminal process, even where the state has taken the decision to subject a youth to formal prosecution.[90]

The proposed statutory offence also makes important accommodations to safeguard free expression and the role of the press in keeping the activities of states' agents in administering criminal justice open to public scrutiny. Much like the misuse of private information tort, the provision does not prohibit publishers from reporting information as to the result of their own investigations into wrongdoing, nor from publishing details surrounding the underlying facts of a criminal investigation, which do not result in the identification of an individual as the subject of a criminal process.[91]

One risk with any movement towards greater anonymity protections is that this may have a chilling effect on complainants, or even result in individuals being prosecuted for sharing their own experiences of victimisation. Whilst it is conceded that this risk could materialise under proposed legislative framework, there are several reasons for which this risk should, on balance, be tolerated in the face of the important reasons for protecting anonymity at the earliest stages of a criminal process outlined above. Given that the offence only applies to publishing personal information likely to lead the public at large to identify the alleged perpetrator as the subject of a criminal investigation before charge, it is a limited constraint, which does not prevent complainants publishing all material relating to their experiences, nor from talking about their experiences to friends or a therapist. A similar risk is already tolerated in English law. Section 1(1) of the Sexual Offences (Amendment) Act 1992 entitles complainants in certain sexual offence cases to lifelong anonymity, and breach of this automatic anonymity provision (outside of limited exceptions[92]) is a criminal offence. The effect of this provision is such that anyone who has been the subject of a false allegation could find themselves prohibited from naming their accuser unless and until that person is subject to separate proceedings in relation to their dishonesty.[93]

In the interests of ensuring that the media can report on 'whistleblowers' and expose corrupt practices by law enforcement agencies, section 1(10) also provides protections for individuals to waive their right to anonymity and section 1(6)–(8) allows for the restriction to be lifted on application to a single judge, if to do so is necessary in the public interest or to avoid injustice. As with similar reporting restrictions, section 2(2) creates a defence for publishers who are not aware, and neither suspected nor had reason to suspect, that the publication included material subject to the automatic restriction in section 1. The offence put forward here

[90] The more significant harms that might attach to the naming of youths subject to criminal process are recognised in international law under the so-called 'Beijing Rules'. See The UN Standard Minimum Rules for the Administration of Juvenile Justice 1985.

[91] This follows a similar model to that applied in Germany, where the identity of suspects is subject to stringent protection. See M Bohlander, 'Open justice or open season? Should the media report the names of suspects and defendants?' (2010) 74 *Journal of Criminal Law* 321.

[92] See Sexual Offences (Amendment) Act 1992, s 3.

[93] ibid, s 1(4) and *R v Jemma Beale* [2017] EWCA 1012 (Crim).

bears similarities to the structure of strict liability provisions in the Contempt of Court Act 1981. Notably, in interpreting the scope of these provisions, the courts have been prepared to place a degree of responsibility on would-be publishers to discover whether there are relevant reporting restrictions in place before publishing.[94]

One recurrent objection to any anonymity protection of this kind is that it may have a prohibitive effect on criminal investigations, and particularly that it could discourage other potential victims or witnesses from coming forward to report offences.[95] Whilst the provisions in section 1(6)–(8) address this concern to some extent, there is a need for great caution here. As was observed by Sir Richard Henriques in his review of Operation Midland, once a suspect is identified in the press, 'all subsequent complainants are exposed to the assertion that they have been influenced to make their allegation by what they have read in the press or in social media'.[96] Further complaints in a case where anonymity has prevailed are not amenable to this line of attack and are thus more likely to be believed. Whilst Henriques accepted that, in certain cases, it may be necessary to appeal for witnesses, he suggested that such occasions should be controlled by application to a court to guard against 'the use of publicity as "flypaper", namely releasing details of a suspect in the hope that others will come forward to support an insubstantial initial allegation'.[97]

Ordinarily, where there is sufficient evidence to justify the intrusions occasioned by using a suspect's identity as 'flypaper', the threshold for charging the suspect should have been met, which triggers the loss of anonymity in any event. The high threshold of 'strict necessity' in section 1(7) above serves as a constraint on law enforcement or media over-use of the single justice procedure in section 1(6)–(8), in recognition that the anonymity right of suspects should be protected unless there is truly exceptional reason for publication.

5. Conclusion

The laws and guidance which regulate the conduct of criminal justice agencies and publishers have developed through a series incremental and context-specific protections, which provide some protection to some suspects, but do not address consistent issues around 'jigsaw identification', police breaches of their own guidance, and a lack of meaningful deterrence for ad hoc publication by less organised groups or individuals (typically online), who are much less likely than large media outlets to be sued in civil courts. Even the protections that the courts have devel-

[94] See *Attorney General v Yaxley-Lennon* [2019] EWHC 1791 (QB).
[95] *Key issues for the 2015 Parliament* (House of Commons Library, 2015) 102.
[96] See n 24, para 1.66.
[97] See n 24, para 1.70.

oped through incremental extension of the misuse of private information tort may yet be weakened through broader statutory reforms, which aim to reset the balance between freedom of speech and privacy firmly in favour of the former.

This chapter sought to show that, despite the Government's preference for stronger free speech protections, there has been growing recognition among lawmakers and criminal justice practitioners that suspects should typically be entitled to remain anonymous until the point that they are charged with a criminal offence. This 'right to anonymity' is grounded in the lasting reputational damage that the individual is likely to suffer through being publicly identified as the subject of state suspicion, whatever the eventual outcome of the case. However, the legal framework provides inconsistent protection to suspects, and overlaps itself in prolix ways.

This chapter proposed the creation of a statutory reporting restriction and a criminal offence for any breach of this restriction. The proposed offence also makes accommodations to safeguard the fundamental rights of publishers, true victims and the value of open justice. It is hoped that Parliament will act to place the protection of suspects' anonymity on a statutory footing. This will ensure that those subject to a criminal investigation are no longer subject to gratuitous publicity before the state has so much as mounted a credible case against them, nor the attendant reputational damage that inevitably follows.

Comment on Chapter 8

The Proposal for a Statutory Right to Anonymity for Criminal Suspects Pre-Charge

MONICA STEVENSON* AND MATTHEW DYSON**

This chapter responds to Dr Purshouse's proposal for a statutory right to anonymity for *all* criminal suspects pre-charge. The proposal takes the form of a prohibition on state agencies investigating criminal offences from publishing information which would identify an individual as a suspect unless certain conditions have been met. It is, in effect, a default rule, with what appear to be quite wide ways to circumvent it. Such legislative change would confer a privacy right on any person accused of or being investigated for a criminal offence before formal charges are brought. It would also make it a criminal offence for someone to act in a way which breached this right, for example by naming that person online.

There are good reasons for suspect anonymity prior to charge in some situations. The argument for a default ban on identifying material also has value. As Purshouse notes, English law has tried wider protections before, and removed them for various reasons, most notably in regard to those accused of sexual offences. The challenges appear to be how to craft the ban, and how to enforce it. Whilst it seems unarguable that unfounded criminal allegations can be unfair and cause serious hurt and reputational damage, an automatic privacy right for *all* persons accused of *any* crime pre-charge is both ambitious and far-reaching in scope. Further, such change has serious implications for the notion of open justice, relations between media and police; and challenges triggered by complex criminal investigations, not least those played out under the glare of the public and media spotlight.

In this response, we will be focusing more on some of the practical issues thrown up by such a privacy right for criminal suspects pre-charge. We also want to identify some likely challenges in the application and enforcement of such a

* Barrister (Criminal) 25 Bedford Row.
** Professor of Civil and Criminal Law, Faculty of Law, University of Oxford; Global Professor of Law, London Law Programme at the University of Notre Dame in England; Associate Member of 6KBW College Hill.

law. We begin by considering in brief terms some broad issues which come with the proposal (section 1) and then identify particular details which might require further attention (section 2).

1. Anonymity for Criminal Suspects Pre-Charge

Perhaps the first point to consider is to what extent such a move fits into the direction of travel of approaches in this area now. For a start, the police themselves might welcome this move, at least if they are already cautious about naming suspects. As Purshouse notes, when it comes to the naming of criminal suspects, the College of Policing has issued Media Relations Guidance. The version currently in force was first published on 24 May 2017 and most recently updated on 27 July 2022.[1] The most relevant part states that:

> Respecting suspects' rights to privacy: Suspects should not be identified to the media (by disclosing names or other identifying information) prior to the point of charge, except where justified by clear circumstances, such as a threat to life, the prevention or detection of crime, or a matter of public interest and confidence.[2]

Interestingly, in the early part of 2023 some draft media guidance was issued by the College of Policing which included a change in semantics that was read as giving police forces a discretion about whether to name someone *charged* with an offence. The suggested re-formulation proposed replacing 'should' name those charged with a crime to 'can be named'. The media outcry which ensued illustrates the delicate interplay between police and media when it comes to the reporting of crime, as well as the importance of open justice in a democracy. One journalistic note of caution opined that: 'A wall of silence around police activity would mark an alarming shift towards a system of secret justice. Anyone could be picked up for questioning and no one would know – a routine practice in oppressive and authoritarian states. Police could operate with impunity'.[3]

The proposals were seemingly shared with news outlets but have now been withdrawn following the backlash, and the original paper is not available on 'Policing Guidance' or the 'Research' section of the APP's website.[4] Whilst this proposed change to media guidance concerned the naming of persons *after* charge, some of the same concerns apply when it comes to anonymity of criminal suspects

[1] College of Policing, Latest changes – media relations (webpage showing changes to guidance over time: www.college.police.uk/app/engagement-and-communication/media-relations/changes).

[2] College of Policing, *Media relations* (2022) 4.

[3] F Gibb, 'Suella Braverman's idea is dangerous: justice depends on naming names' *The Sunday Times* (9 October, 2022).

[4] W Turvill, 'Police U-turn to say suspects "should be named" on charge after Press Gazette story prompts backlash' *Press Gazette* (27 March 2023); J Phillips, 'Police must reject rules which withhold names of suspects – media chiefs' *Evening Standard* (22 March 2023).

pre-charge, not least the risk that such privacy can result in less scrutiny of decisions taken by agents of the state, such as the police or CPS.

Moreover, the proposal for a right to anonymity for *all* suspects of crime, irrespective of the nature or severity of the allegation, requires consideration of whether such a right is capable of being enjoyed by all persons to whom it applies. The scope of the proposal would create a wide spectrum, covering everyone from the petty shoplifter on a local estate to the high-profile celebrity charged with historic sexual assaults. A critical consideration is the danger that an anonymity law of this kind would be observed by trained journalists and responsible media outlets but ignored by some members of the public (not least those operating anonymously online). The difficulties in enforcing such a law – particularly on social media platforms – could see the emergence of another two-tier system, whereby criminal suspects are not identified by responsible media outlets but can be identified via a cursory search of the internet. Until such time as control of social media platforms is improved, there remains a real risk that anonymity for *criminal suspects* pre-charge would be observed by responsible media alone. The publication of accurate information and accountability in authorship, remain preferable to speculation on social media.

This is clearly a live issue. Further recent evidence came in *WFZ v and The British Broadcasting Corporation*[5] in June 2023, which concerned an application to restrain (until trial) intended publication by the BBC of information regarding a claimant under investigation for serious sexual offences. The High Court noted the difference between unsubstantiated rumour on social media as compared with reporting by an established media outlet. Collins Rice J stated that whilst there had been speculation on social media about the claimant's identity, permitting his identification by an established media organisation such as the BBC would '… undoubtedly be a substantial game-changer'.[6] The judgment identified some of the likely repercussions of the BBC naming the claimant before charging decisions had been made. These included '… an uncontrolled explosion of personal comment and speculation on the allegations themselves, in both mainstream media and especially online, of which the Claimant would be the epicentre and which he would be powerless to stem or withstand.'[7] The fact that there were multiple complainants and possibility of mixed charging decisions could, it was said, '… open up the immediate prospect that the proposed publication will place into the public domain a quantity of material which may not bear directly on the issues raised by any charges that are brought, but which would still amount to "bad character" material in relation to those charges.'[8] In addition to this, defence witnesses, it was said, may be daunted by the publicity and discouraged from coming forward.

[5] [2023] EWHC 1618 (KB).
[6] ibid, [52].
[7] ibid, [56].
[8] ibid, [63].

The BBC proposal was held to be unusual, and ultimately, problematic. It was

> … a departure from what the decided authorities describe as the "uniform general practice" of the police, and the mainstream media, of not publicly identifying an individual arrested in relation to serious criminal allegations before a charging decision has been made. It has itself been following that practice in this case up until now. A uniform general practice is, however, not a legal rule. It is what the law has to say about the practice, the reasons for it, and most importantly its relevance or otherwise to the particular facts and circumstances of this case, that is the necessary focus of these proceedings.[9]

WFZ considers the prejudice that can flow from media coverage of allegations before charging decisions have been made, whilst also illustrating how such risks are greater for high-profile celebrities. On the particular facts, the injunction was granted, restraining publication of the BBC's report in a form which identifies the applicant or enables him to be identified as the subject of active criminal proceedings. That gave a choice to the BBC: 'publish its report now without identifying the Claimant, or to await charging decisions (either way) when a fully informed and balanced decision can be taken about the competing interests that might then be engaged.'[10]

2. Drafting and Implications

We now turn to look at the specific draft proposal in Purshouse's chapter. That provision is the result of careful consideration, built in part of provisions already in English law. Some drafting suggestions are made in the version below, followed by some specific queries. Text expressed through a strikethrough is text that has been deleted, text in bold has been added, and text in italics has been moved.

1. Restriction on the publication of identifying particulars of a criminal suspect

(1) No matter relating to a person ~~shall~~ **may** be ~~included in any publication~~ **published** if it is likely to lead to members of the public to identify ~~him~~ that person as the subject of a criminal investigation.

(2) Subsection (1) ~~does not apply after the earliest time when any of the following events occurs~~ **ceases to apply if**:

(a) the person concerned is charged with a criminal offence or cautioned by the police in relation to the criminal investigation, or a prosecution is otherwise commenced; or

(b) The person concerned voluntarily publishes or consents to the publication of the information.

[9] ibid, [39].
[10] ibid, [90].

(3) In this section 'publication' includes any speech, writing, relevant programme or other communication in whatever form, which is addressed to the public ~~at large~~ or any section of the public, but does not include an indictment or other document prepared for use in particular legal proceedings.

(4) For the purposes of this section, a person is 'the subject of a criminal investigation' if **that person** is arrested, **that person's property is searched**, **that person is** questioned under police caution, or otherwise investigated by a representative of a state agency with a view to it being ascertained whether **that person** should be charged with a criminal offence.

(5) A representative of a state agency may dispense to any extent with the restriction imposed under subsection (1) insofar as to do so is necessary to apprehend a person unlawfully at large or wanted in connection with a criminal offence.

(6) Any person may make an application to a magistrates' court for an order dispensing with the restriction imposed by subsection (1). *A court, including a single justice, may by order dispense to any extent with the restriction imposed under subsection (1)* ~~above~~ *if:*

(a) it is satisfied that to do so is strictly necessary—

i. in the public interest; or

ii. to avoid injustice; ***and***

(b) it has afforded the parties to the proceedings an opportunity to make representations and taken into account any representations duly made.

2. Offence of breach of restriction on publication

(1) A~~ny~~ person who ~~includes in a publication~~ **publishes** material in breach of section 1(1) is guilty of an offence.

(2) Where a person is charged with an offence under ~~section 2~~ **this section**, it is a defence for the person to prove that at the time of publication the person was not aware, and neither suspected nor had reason to suspect, that the publication included the matter in question.

Whose Conduct does the Provision Cover?

This provision does not appear to apply to investigations by non-state agencies, such as quite common prosecutors like the RSPCA, or other less frequent private prosecutors (see section 1(4) where none of the definitions apply to a private prosecutor: 'arrested, he or his property is searched, he is questioned under police caution, or otherwise investigated by a representative of a state agency'). That might provide further reasons for the prosecution to be pushed into the private sphere, a trend which is already of some concern. It might also be an incentive for the state to rely on investigation, in the non-technical sense, conducted by a non-state agency and then to take over the prosecution. But to do otherwise, and to apply the prohibition to investigations conducted by non-state actors might be difficult, without requiring that the person(s) involved in publication knew about the non-state actors' investigations.

What must the State Show to Establish Public Interest?

What are the thresholds for the state to decide that disclosure is in the public interest 'insofar as to do so is necessary to apprehend a person unlawfully at large or wanted in connection with a criminal offence' under section 1(5)? What are the mechanisms for review of such a decision, judicial review? It seems quite possible that no review would be brought swiftly enough, since there would be no need to notify the individual concerned (there would be for the application to dispense with the restriction). It is striking that the state agency would not need permission from a court, but any other person would. A state agency might apply to a magistrates' court, perhaps, to protect against a possible claim for damages for any loss flowing from the publication.

What Conduct would Amount to the Breach of a Suspects' Right to Anonymity Pre-Charge?

If one considers the Sexual Offences (Amendment) Act 1992, which grants anonymity to *complainants* of sexual offences, analogous wording for a system of anonymity for criminal suspects would be along the following lines:

> Where an allegation has been made that someone has committed a criminal offence, no matter relating to that person may be included in any publication if it is likely to lead members of the public to identify that person as the person who is the subject of the allegation.

In *Marie O'Riordan v DPP*,[11] the High Court noted that the phrase 'likely to lead to identification' had been considered by Dame Elizabeth Butler-Sloss in *Attorney General v Greater Manchester Newspapers Limited* in the following way:

> The use of the word 'likely' in the order is not to be equated with statistical probability that it will lead to the identification of the boys or their whereabouts, but to the real risk, the real danger, the real chance that it may lead to that dangerous situation.[12]

Any act said to breach the anonymity of a suspect would therefore need to involve conduct which gave rise to a real risk or danger that they may be identified (as opposed to mere possibility).

Need the Allegation be True?

Is the prohibition triggered by identification which is in fact not true? Put another way, is 'identify' only operative where the person concerned really is the subject

[11] [2005] EWHC (Admin) 1240.
[12] *The Times* (7 December 2001).

of such an identification? The relevant text, 'if it is likely to lead to members of the public to identify that person as the subject of a criminal investigation': seems to suggest that an identification in error would still be an identification. That could mean that publishing information which is likely to make members of the public identify a person as being under investigation, when that person is not, would breach the prohibition. It would also likely be a criminal offence unless the narrow defence applies. It is not clear that criminalising *risking* making others think (wrongly) that you are a suspect is necessarily warranted.

What Fault is Required?

The offence is strict liability, which is a significant infringement of the autonomy of individuals. There is a defence of not knowing of the matter being included, or having no suspicion or reasonable grounds for suspecting it. That is a very narrow way out, and a defence, so the burden would be on the defendant to show one or more of those negatives. At the very least the state should have to prove negligence on the part of the publisher, but better yet, prove a positive state of at least suspicion, or the net of criminal liability is drawn very wide. Doing so would not diminish the prohibition.

What Statutory Defences should be Available to a Person Accused of having Breached a Suspects' Right to Pre-Charge Anonymity?

The defence itself is also somewhat vague, the mental state being about the fact that 'the publication included the matter in question'. That might include not knowing about the information, how likely the information was to identify the person concerned, that the person concerned was under investigation, or the form or stage of the investigation. An ambiguous defence should be interpreted in favour of the defendant, which might perhaps help to keep it wide.

At present, there is no general defence in the Sexual Offences (Amendment) Act 1992 to the charge of having breached a complainant's right to anonymity. Would a criminal offence of breaching a suspect's anonymity pre-charge be similarly lacking? Or should it include a potential defence, given the potential factual scenarios in which such breaches might occur? For example, should the statute import a defence of acting with 'good reason', 'reasonable excuse' and/or 'lawful authority'? Potential defences of this kind would see a person accused of such a breach being permitted to justify their conduct grounds to be considered by a judge or jury (depending on the tribunal). Investigative journalism could in some cases be strongly inhibited by laws preventing publication of details that risk identifying a criminal suspect. Similarly, a whistleblower within an organisation or company, may be fettered in naming the problem or individual concerned, if there is a risk of criminal sanction.

What Consequences should there be for Committing such a Breach?

The sanction for breaching a complainant's right to anonymity (again, under the Sexual Offences (Amendment) Act 1992) is currently a fine of up to £5,000. Would there be any basis for applying different sentencing powers to breaches with respect to the anonymity of criminal *suspects*? If disclosing the identity of criminal suspects was an offence, the volume of such breaches is difficult to predict. Would a fine be much of a deterrence? And what would be the public cost in prosecuting and enforcing such breaches?

One point worth considering further is the form of the obligation, and the means to enforce it. There is clearly a criminal offence created. It might be a summary offence, triable either way, or indictable only, and with a range or possible penalties and potential gateway conditions, such as the consent of the Attorney General (which is needed to institute a prosecution for any breach of a complainant's anonymity under the 1992 Act[13]). There is also the possibility of a criminal compensation order under sections 133–146 of the Sentencing Act 2020 for losses caused by a breach of the prohibition. Those orders provide compensation but do so on slightly different and potentially wider terms than civil liability. There need not be an underlying civil liability, and the rules of causation are wider, for example.[14]

A further area for consideration is the ability of any criminal *suspect* to lodge a complaint about a breach of their right to anonymity. Remedies under tort law (the misuse of private information) are said to be the preserve of wealthy individuals. Is there a risk that any law relating to a *suspects' right to anonymity* would be rigorously enforced only by the same people, especially if considerable expense were required to identify the authors of online disclosures? Affluent individuals could and would instruct legal teams to detect and raise such breaches with the police. Less savvy or powerful individuals entitled to the same statutory right may not know or be able to do the same, creating a distorted picture of anonymity breaches across the jurisdiction. If the *enforcement* of a statutory right to anonymity for *criminal suspects* proved arbitrary in application – with some police forces not having the inclination, time or resources to investigate such breaches, unless and until prompted – this could create a law that would not be equal in application.

Indeed, as Purshouse demonstrates, consideration of this area must include the options open to suspects in civil proceedings. To what extent would these avenues co-exist? Criminal justice has tended to work faster than civil justice, but this situation might be different; it is the disclosure of being a suspect which is

[13] Section 5(4) states: 'Proceedings for an offence under this section shall not be instituted except by or with the consent of the Attorney General [if the offence is alleged to have been committed in England and Wales or of the Attorney General for Northern Ireland if the offence is alleged to have been committed in Northern Ireland.'

[14] See generally, M Dyson, *Explaining Tort and Crime* (CUP, 2022) ch 6.

the starting point of the civil claim, and this might, by a long time, precede a criminal trial let alone its conclusion. Craig and Phillipson think that the problem, such as it is, of a suspect gaining remedies in civil law before later being found guilty (which might then suggest that the information regarding the arrest was not so worthy of protection after all) can be avoided in practice.[15] One of their alternatives, that the civil claim might be suspended until any relevant prosecution has been completed, used to be the default rule in English law for all felony prosecutions.[16] But it is a little unclear how that stay would work under existing rules; it might require a new rule.

The current law is now governed by a Practice Direction within the Civil Procedure Rules.[17] It makes clear that in an application for the stay of civil proceedings pending the determination of related criminal prosecution: any party to the civil or criminal proceedings may make the application; every other civil party must be made a respondent in the application; the application must give grounds for and estimate the duration of the stay and finally that it was not necessary for the prosecutor or defendant in the criminal proceedings to be joined as a party to the civil case.[18] But the key point is that the stay is granted in respect of the risk of prejudice of the criminal proceedings, not on the integrity of the civil claim.[19] It is not clear that that power could be used here. The alternative is to rely on the general powers of a civil court to stay an action, as covered in, for example, CPR 3.1(f). The question then seems to be whether the defendant might successfully argue that the stay should be granted because the claimant was the subject of a criminal prosecution on the same facts. If the defendant were later convicted, the conviction would be admissible in the later civil claim by virtue of section 11 of the Civil Evidence Act 1968, and for the purposes of a defamation claim, the conviction would be conclusive under section 13. It would be admissible, or if appropriate, conclusive, about the facts on which it must have been founded.

Of course, even if it were permissible as a matter of formal rules, there are reasons why the later criminal prosecution might be affected by the stayed civil claim. If the claim had not reached judgment, there might be an argument that any party to the civil claim might be less effective as a witness in the criminal prosecution given the party's interest in the outcome of the civil claim.

Finally, we might consider whether sealing a judgment, and putting any remedy on ice until after any criminal prosecution, might be suitable. This might have

[15] R Craig and G Phillipson, 'Privacy, reputation and anonymity until charge: *ZXC* goes to the Supreme Court' (2021) 13 *Journal of Media Law* 152.

[16] See in detail, M Dyson, *Explaining Tort and Crime* (CUP, 2022) ch 7.

[17] Practice Direction – Applications (2001) P.D. 23, [11A.1–11A.4].

[18] On occasion judges have even taken the Civil Procedure Rules as a reason to be aware of criminal law issues in the cases before them: eg, *Secretary of State for Trade and Industry v Crane* [2001] 2 BCLC 222 (HC), 226–227 (Ferris J).

[19] See, eg, *V. C* [2002] CP Rep 8 (CA), [24]–[44]. Witnesses not co-operating while the criminal cases are pending has not been enough: *Secretary of State for Health v Norton Healthcare Ltd* [2003] All ER (D) 419. For defendants not co-operating, see *Balfron Trustees Ltd v Peterson and others (No 2)* (2001) All England Official Transcripts (1997–2008), [17]–[36], esp. [33]–[36].

advantages, though it does seem more laborious and thus potentially inefficient. It would seem to require quite detailed and special rules, including provisions for interest and on which body would make the final decision.

But this discussion only serves to highlight the difficulty of reconciling rights of privacy, confidence and the forms of protection society should give to them. In the proposal made by Purshouse, no mention is made of civil liability for the breach of the suspect's protection by the prohibition. Another possible implication of creating a *right* in statutory form would be the possibility that the tort of breach of statutory duty might then apply. The claimant would have to show that despite not mentioning civil liability, the Act meant to impose it. If successful, there would be no defence of not knowing, suspecting or having reasonable grounds to suspect, the investigation or the identification. For civil liability, the prohibition in section 1(1) would be breached, even though no criminal offence might be committed. Such possible tort liability might usefully be anticipated in the legislation.

The Legal Test for Media or Individual Applying to Lift a Suspects' Right to Anonymity?

Purshouse proposes that a complainant's right to anonymity can be lifted where a party applies to the court and argues that it presents an 'unreasonable restriction on the reporting of the trial and is in the public interest for it to be lifted.'[20] The arguments for lifting at least in part hinge on the defendant's right to a fair trial enshrined in Article 6 of the European Convention on Human Rights. Consideration would need to be given to legitimate reasons that may compel the exposing of a criminal suspect pre-charge. In some cases, the media may make such an application but it would and should be open to individuals to do the same. Opposition to such applications and arguments in favour of preserving anonymity would also be relevant.

3. Conclusions

This proposal has implications for the notion of open justice and interplay between the police and the media, both of whom perform a different yet valuable function within any democracy. In considering this proposed reform, it pays to ask whether such a law is in fact enforceable, or whether it could end up creating more problems than it solves. There is an underlying question about how much can the criminal law shroud its proceedings in secrecy to protect individuals from the moral failings of the mob. Will a prohibition like this make the charging step

[20] Sexual Offences (Amendment) Act 1992, ss 3(1) and (2).

itself seem more demonstrative of guilt, on the basis that before charge there was anonymity? There are enough non-guilty pleas in this jurisdiction, of the order of 30 per cent,[21] and much higher for offences like serious sex offences, that it would be inappropriate to assume that a person who is being made to plead is in fact guilty. That might, or might not, be different in some legal systems where the conviction rate is up to 99 per cent.[22] Given the clear evidence that being a suspect can harm a person's standing in the community, one answer is clearly holding back that allegation from the public until it comes to a sufficiently certain point, such as the point of charge (or later). But such a reform would need monitoring, and potentially improving over time, to make sure that the inappropriate censure was not simply being delayed, and perhaps, magnified.

[21] The precise number varies across years, and it depends slightly in which court, as guilty pleas are more common in the magistrates' court. 70% is the post- and pre-pandemic figure: *Criminal court statistics quarterly: October to December 2022* (Ministry of Justice, 2023) Section 3. The year before, the annual figure from the CPS recorded 76% of all pleas being pleas of guilty to all charges in the magistrates' court in 2021–2, and 72% in the Crown Court: *Crown Prosecution Service, Annual Report and Accounts 2021–2022* (HC 487, 2022) 44 and 45.

[22] As is said to be the case in China, for example: www.chinajusticeobserver.com/a/what-is-the-conviction-rate-in-china.

9

Challenges in Decriminalising Simple Drug Possession

DOUGLAS HUSAK*

Several novel ideas were presented at the Conference hosted by Criminal Law Reform Now in September 2021. One important idea which caught my attention was a 'modest' proposal by Alex Stevens, Niamh Eastwood and Kirstie Douse[1] to decriminalise the possession of drugs (without intent to distribute) in the United Kingdom, by the simple measure of repealing the relevant subsections of the Misuse of Drugs Act 1971. I concurred wholeheartedly with the sentiments behind their proposal and have advocated them myself in the United States for nearly 40 years of my professional life.[2] Indeed, several legal philosophers (not only myself) have been calling for this sensible reform for years.[3] I predict that future generations will ask 'what took you so long?' when they learn that the mere possession (and use) of a substance was once a criminal offence for which literally millions of individuals in the United Kingdom and the United States were arrested, prosecuted and punished. However, I have over the years come to be somewhat less confident about the merits of this proposal. Since I was unable to express all of my reservations about its potential pitfalls at the Conference, I am delighted to have the opportunity to do so briefly in this volume. Concerns over predicting future behaviour and how best to present the risks and possible advantages to sceptics are likely to be applicable to many proposals to decriminalise all sorts of behaviour, including prostitution.[4]

* Douglas Husak, Distinguished Professor of Philosophy and Law, Rutgers University, USA.

[1] Later references to the authors of the proposal are to these three persons, whose works are likely already to be familiar to many of those who take an interest in this area. I should add that many of my comments are applicable to other proposed reforms in this difficult area too, and that is one reason why I am pleased to record my reflections here.

[2] D Husak, *Drugs and Rights* (CUP, 1992).

[3] See E Nadelmann, 'Drug Prohibition in the United States: Costs, Consequences, and Alternatives' (1989) 245 *Science* 939; D Richards, *Sex, Drugs, Death and the Law* (Rowman & Littlefield, 1982).

[4] See T Palmer 'Decriminalisation of Prostitution', ch 2 in this volume.

1. The Merits of the Simple Proposal to Decriminalise

Before I describe five pitfalls in campaigning for decriminalisation of drug possession, I should say that I applaud the caution of the author's proposal. They propose decriminalisation for simple possession – and nothing further. 'First things first' – in this case, stopping the countless harms we know are caused by arrest and punishment (including imprisonment) for mere possession or use, and consequent criminal records. At this juncture, it is too ambitious to go further in one swoop and to outline a scheme for controlling drug markets as well. Such caution might be advisable in other areas where criminalisation has a long history based upon supposed harms, despite being lacking in demonstrable justification.

In so restricting themselves, the authors were keenly aware that many progressives (or 'radicals') will respond that the failure to legalise drug markets will frustrate some of the important goals they seek to achieve: black markets will continue to thrive, tax revenue will be lost, and supplies of drugs will continue to be unnecessarily dangerous because they will remain unregulated. Moreover, the recent prevalence of fentanyl (which no one foresaw even a decade ago) makes the absence of regulations governing the distribution of opiates more worrisome than ever throughout the United States (and especially in Scotland in the United Kingdom). To my mind, however, the construction of a regime to govern drug manufacture and sale is far more complex and controversial than the simpler step which the authors advocated. In the United States and elsewhere, questions of licensing, quality control, optimal rates of taxation, regulations of purchases, locations of outlets; and a host of additional issues have proved to be far more difficult to navigate. Once possession and use have been decriminalised, and we have ample experience assessing the results, these other problems can and should be tackled. In the meantime, however, no sufficient reason justifies the state in continuing to punish persons for merely possessing and/or using a drug. As the authors persuasively indicated, this simple change will eradicate the most direct harms of drug criminalisation: those of arrest, punishment, and the consequences of a criminal record for offenders. Although Stevens, Eastwood and Douse were not explicit on this matter, I gathered, or perhaps hoped to think, that they would also recommend that the criminal convictions of previous offenders should be overturned and their records expunged – a welcome step recently implemented by President Biden for federal drug possession offences in the United States.

In one respect, it should be noted that many critics would charge that the authors' proposal is *not* modest, in the sense that their proposal is not limited to any particular drugs – although I would not concur with this criticism either. It is true that in all but one state throughout the United States, only cannabis has been decriminalised. Oregon is the sole state to have gone as far as the authors recommend, and I comment further on its mixed experience below. As a matter of justice, however, it is hard to see why some drugs but not others should be criminal to use and possess. Each drug is different from others and poses unique challenges. But the alleged contrast between 'hard' and 'soft' drugs has always been more a matter of prejudice than of pharmacological fact.[5] Still, I anticipate that this aspect of the authors' proposal will encounter quite a bit of resistance – but again, not from me.

I also approve of the authors' unwillingness to make suggestions for increasing the capacity for diverting people to education or treatment. Many liberal reformers reflexively gravitate to treatment as a substitute for penal sanctions. As the authors recognise, the majority of people who use controlled drugs have no more need for education or treatment than the usual consumers of licit drugs such as alcohol and tobacco. They should have added that the treatment industry has not had overwhelming success with the persons whose consumption it has sought to curb. Relapse rates should make us reluctant to view treatment as the obvious panacea for the harms of drug addiction, let alone for those of simple drug use. Perhaps treatment regimes will improve. At present, however, I agree that plans to expand the availability of treatment must be evaluated on their own merits and should not be coupled with plans to decriminalise.

The defence of decriminalisation constructed by the authors omitted many of its advantages, although I would imagine that they are fully aware of them. In particular, several decriminalisation models would be a colossal boon to Central and South American countries, where the *real* drug war has long been waged. We naturally tend to focus on the consequences of drug prohibition in our home countries, but the more significant costs are abroad.

2. Pitfalls of Decriminalisation

Since I endorsed virtually all aspects of the authors' proposal, I felt somewhat sheepish about expressing my few reservations. I suspect that the authors, distinguished veterans of drug policy debates, are cognisant of the five worries I subsequently recount, and that time was too short at the Conference to address them fairly. But these reservations may nonetheless be worth stating, minor though they are. That is, *I* say that they are minor because even if I am correct about each of them, I do not believe they outweigh the enormous advantages of the authors' proposal. But others may think differently about their importance and would-be reformers must be prepared to meet a wide range of concerns and objections.

Implementation

First, the authors had little to say about our limited experience in implementing their proposal. Outcomes have not been as encouraging as many reformers had

[5] See D Nutt et al, 'Development of a Rational Scale to Assess the Harm of Drugs of Potential Misuse' (2007) 369 *The Lancet* 1047.

hoped. The single most trenchant example is the State of Oregon, where a majority of 58 per cent of voters decided in 2020 to decriminalise the possession of small amounts of all drugs. Today, instead of facing arrest, persons who use opiates or other substances are issued a citation, similar to a speeding ticket, which allows for a fine of $100. The fine is waived if the user calls a hotline and has a health assessment.

Opinions about this ongoing experiment differ widely, although no one contends that the results have been uniformly positive.[6] Advocates remind us of the injustice and ineffectiveness of employing the criminal justice system to combat the dangers of drugs. Although no one was imprisoned solely for drug use by 2020, arrests were frequent and the ensuing criminal record made obtaining a job or a house more difficult. Moreover, racial disparities were common; black Oregonians were 2.5 times more likely than whites to be convicted of possession. In short, arrest and punishment did not seem to be a sensible policy.

Since decriminalisation became effective in February 2021, however, it is increasingly difficult to pronounce the experiment as successful.[7] Trying to get people into health facilities through citations has proved to be fruitless, as most users simply ignore the fine. From the 4,000 citations issued in Oregon in the first two years of the policy, fewer than 200 people called the hotline and fewer than 40 were interested in treatment. The cost to taxpayers has been about $7,000 per call. Moreover, as I have indicated, no treatment regime has emerged as clearly successful. In any event, it remains unknown how the new policy has actually affected the incidence of drug use, since rates of addiction increased during the pandemic throughout the country as a whole. But overdose deaths in Oregon almost doubled between 2019 and 2021, compared with a national rise of 50 per cent. They show no signs of abating in 2023.

What has gone wrong? Clearly, Oregon dismantled a flawed system to deal with addiction, but had no careful plan about what would replace it. To be fair, viable solutions are far from obvious, and few observers are calling for a return to the failed policies of old. Before generalising too swiftly from the plights of street addicts, we should remind ourselves that not all users are addicts, and casual, problem-free drug users were once caught in the web of criminal justice along with those who could not control their consumption. But the horrors of addiction can be very real and can be seen on the streets of Portland every day. In a free society, many consumers make bad choices and lose control when experimenting with highly addictive substances. Perhaps most significantly, heroin and pharmaceuticals are disappearing from the market. Most addicts today use fentanyl, which few commentators foresaw flooding the streets even a decade ago. Fentanyl

[6] Much of the evidence about Oregon is drawn from 'The Oregon Experiment' (*The Economist*, 15 April 2023).

[7] See J Hinch, 'What Happened When Oregon Decriminalized Hard Drugs' (*The Atlantic*, 19 July 2023).

is extremely potent, and, most importantly, is incredibly cheap. Even the poorest addict finds it easier than ever to pay for a fix.

Supporters of Oregon's policy had hope that peer mentors – former addicts – could encourage users to get clean. They were allocated extra funding in the same ballot measure in 2020. But even though possession was decriminalised three months after voting, it took another 20 months for the funding to roll out fully. And the extra money often goes to other services, such as to needle exchanges and subsidised housing. Primarily through the widespread use of naloxone, Oregon has had modest success keeping existing addicts alive. Unfortunately, 'harm-reduction' approaches have been less able to induce them to quit or to dissuade persons from becoming addicts in the first place. Unless these latter goals are achieved, efforts to combat addiction will remain stalled. Advocates urge that more time is needed before the policy turns the corner, but patience is growing thin.

The other source of experimental evidence comes from Portugal, which became the first country to decriminalise the possession of all drugs for personal use in 2001. But the evidence from Portugal is inconclusive as well; although rates of opiate use fell after the new policy became effective, they were already going down prior to 2001 and continued their downward trend.[8] Portugal's prevalence of high-risk opioid use is lower than that of France and Italy. In any event, Portugal's policy is different from that of Oregon, as offenders are taken to a police station and made to go before a 'dissuasion commission' at the Ministry of Health. Repeat offenders face punishment, like being banned from bars, or made to perform community service. These incentives are lacking in Oregon. At first, fully 80 per cent of Portuguese addicts choose to begin treatment, but police are less inclined to refer addicts to dissuasion commissions today, because many addicts have appeared previously to no avail.[9] Again, treatment is no panacea. The fundamental question is whether a drug policy that involves jail time is more harmful to society than decriminalisation. Clearly the evils of addiction are more visible when states do not resort to jail, but it is hard to say they have lessened overall. Although reasonable minds differ about this matter, I concur with the authors that the use of criminal penalties is the worse option.[10]

Although Oregon remains the only state to have attempted the decriminalisation of all drugs, its uneven results have not discouraged others from trying it. Bills to decriminalise possession have been introduced in nine states of the USA, including Massachusetts, New York and Washington. In Canada, British Columbia has unveiled its own decriminalisation scheme. Further experimental evidence may well be available soon, and both friends and foes of various drug initiatives would be wise to draw from it.

[8] See H Laqueur, 'Uses and Abuses of Drug Decriminalization in Portugal' (2015) 40 *Law & Social Inquiry* 746.

[9] A Faiola and C Fernandes Martins, 'Once Hailed for Decriminalizing Drugs, Portugal is Now Having Doubts' *The Washington Post* (7 July 2023).

[10] M Szalavitz, 'Portugal Has Succeeded Where We've Failed With Addiction' *The New York Times* (29 August 2023).

Collateral Impacts

My second reservation is that the consequences of the authors' approach are bound to extend well beyond its impact on drug use and drug-related harms. Let me explain. The authors pointed out that their proposal would limit existing police powers to stop and search, presently authorised under section 23 of the Misuse of Drugs Act 1971. The foregoing section currently empowers constables to search persons or vehicles and to seize substances if they have 'reasonable grounds to suspect that any person is in possession of a controlled drug in contravention of this Act'. Since drugs for personal use would no longer be 'in contravention of this Act,' this police power would cease to exist. The authors allege that this change represents a 'strong advantage' of their proposal, 'as it would limit the harms imposed by disproportionate and ineffective stop and search practices.' Perhaps so. They are not alone in portraying the large number of stops and searches conducted during the height of the drug war as an unmitigated evil.

Apparently, then, the authors did not believe that the resulting disability would have a significant impact on the power of police to detect and prevent serious crime. But quite a few law enforcement officials in the United States deny (albeit frequently off the record) that their primary objective in enforcing drug proscriptions *is* in fact to reduce drug use. Instead, they allege that their ability to use drug laws as a pretext to stop, question and frisk has been a substantial factor in the dramatic decrease in violent crime from (roughly) 1992 to 2020.[11] Nearly everyone agrees that this power had been grossly misused in many jurisdictions, as some cities in the United States came to resemble police states. But without the power the authors propose to withdraw, the police will have fewer opportunities to seize the guns used in serious crimes, and they are bound to find other pretexts to attain their objectives. If so, the cost savings of decriminalisation will turn out to be exaggerated.[12]

To be sure, criminologists hotly dispute the crime-control effects of the police powers made available by drug proscriptions, although the current rise in violent crime is very real and must be brought under control. The centrality of crime as a political issue among contemporary voters does not create an atmosphere conducive to the adoption of the proposal the authors defend. Once the streets are made safer, the public is likely to be more receptive to liberal reforms in the substantive criminal law. Admittedly, even if my worry is trenchant, the fact that guns are much less common in the UK makes my point less salient. Police in the UK have far less reason to remove weapons from the streets than their counterparts in the US (although knives remain a concern). My larger claim, however, is that

[11] R Kelly, *Vigilance* (Hachette Books, 2015); D Husak, 'Drug Proscriptions as Proxy Crimes' (2017) 36 *Law and Philosophy* 345.

[12] D Husak, 'Police and Racial Discrimination: Throwing out the Baby with the Bath Water' in M Gardner and M Weber (eds), *The Ethics of Policing and Imprisonment* (Palgrave Macmillan, 2018) 87.

the criminalisation of drug possession may have a few societal advantages almost wholly unrelated to its effect on drug use itself.

Medicinal Drugs

Next, what are the implications of the authors' proposal for the fate of the system of medicinal drugs, presently available only through prescription by a licensed physician? At the Conference this was not clear to me, but different reformers might have different stances here. Some may reason that if it is lawful to possess and use heroin and cocaine, for example, how can it continue to be unlawful to possess and use (without a prescription) drugs such as anabolic steroids, Prozac and antibiotics? But others will be less sanguine about allowing persons to use such drugs without first obtaining a prescription.[13] Consumers have not distinguished themselves by the wisdom of their purchases of the items sold in so-called 'health stores' throughout the United States. Would the legal freedom to use and possess any and all medicinal drugs be a benefit the authors would endorse along with their advocacy of lawful recreational substances? I am sceptical. But if not, then what do they say about it? Reformers need to think about the different reasons why medicinal and performance-enhancing drugs are controlled.

Related Drugs Offences

Fourth, the authors' modest proposal retains Misuse of Drugs Act 1971, subsection 5(3), which makes it 'an offence to possess [controlled] substances with intent to supply them to another person.' As I am sure they are aware, this 'intent to supply' exception to their general scheme opens a huge can of worms. Under the authors' plan, users will presumably continue to obtain drugs in the same way they do at present – primarily through their network of drug-using friends. When the opportunity arises, many users purchase drugs for their mates as well as for themselves. Thus, many and perhaps most users eventually distribute; legally, the line between the 'simple possession' or the 'mere user' and that of 'dealing' or the 'drug supplier' is not remotely sharp. And depending on how the term 'intent to supply' is construed, a host who purchases enough drugs to share with attendees at his party may still be eligible for criminal punishment. As a result, the enforcement of this 'intent to supply' exception is likely to replicate many of the harms to users the authors are so keen to avoid.

Unfortunately, there is no easy way to solve the problem the authors leave unaddressed in the absence of a system to govern manufacture and distribution. Hopefully the sensible exercise of police and prosecutorial discretion will alleviate

[13] See J Flanigan, *Pharmaceutical Freedom* (OUP, 2017).

many of the unfair hardships that could be created by retaining the 'intent to supply' exception. But a legislative solution would be preferable – if one could be found.

Increase in Drug Use

Finally, I believed that the authors downplayed too greatly the possibility that decriminalisation will increase use. I suspect that many advocates of decriminalisation of possession will tend to do this, or to overstate the 'conservative' critiques concerning the possibilities of increased use. But like crime in general, trends in the incidence of drug use have proved notoriously hard to predict. Many factors cause the use of a given drug to go up or down, and no expert has an especially good track record in anticipating them. For almost any product that persons want to consume (including alcohol and tobacco), cost and availability are key factors in stimulating use. We simply do not know how the absence of criminal penalties for possession and use will affect cost and availability and thus would need a crystal ball to predict its impact on consumption. I read the empirical evidence about this matter to be considerably mixed and uncertain. At least, I am not confident that anyone can properly assert that decriminalisation should reduce the harms of criminalisation without also increasing drug use.

Why are so many would-be reformers seemingly certain about the impact of decriminalisation on rates of consumption? They seem to reason from the premise that criminalisation is in any event ineffective in deterring use. That much is true: the threat of punishment produces little deterrence in this domain, largely because its infliction is so sporadic. Users know that detection is unlikely. But deterrence may not be the primary mechanism by which criminalisation affects behaviour. The criminal law also has an important expressive effect, and opponents of decriminalisation are bound to charge that it 'sends the wrong message.' In some populations, at least, the use of some drugs is stigmatised, and stigma creates a powerful incentive against use. Some reformers admit that criminalisation creates stigma – indeed it might be one of their many objections to it, but if criminalisation contributes to the stigma that is a barrier to treatment, then reformers should also acknowledge the likely role of criminalisation in reinforcing the stigma that might in some cases act as a barrier to the initial use. As usual the matter is complicated. Criminalisation also causes a significant 'forbidden fruit' effect that probably stimulates use. How decriminalisation will affect the stigma or the allure of (some) drugs is nearly impossible to gauge. Different populations are likely to respond differently.

My own concern is that would-be reformers should have to own this uncertainty. The worry is that they will not persuade anyone that there is no risk of an increase in drug use, and then any such perceived risk might be thought to be too great to justify decriminalisation. It might be argued that the precautionary principle applies; we should not risk reform because of the uncertainty of its effects. Better to explain why the risk, to the extent that it might exist, *is* worth taking.

We should also not be quick to reject the so-called 'gateway' hypothesis by which the use of less dangerous drugs increases the likelihood that more dangerous drugs will be used. In particular we should not repeat the canard that 'most of us drank water before alcohol, and our mother's milk before that and that yet we do not conclude that water and breast milk increase the risk of alcohol use.' Because I encounter this rhetorical point so frequently among drug reformers, it may be important to address it head-on. The fact that an overwhelming majority of (so-called) hard drug users begin with cannabis (and/or alcohol) is a *salient* fact about them; the fact they also drank water is not. A salient fact, on my account, is one that any good explanation of drug use cannot afford to neglect.

At the risk of stressing the obvious, allow me to provide a (fanciful) analogy. Quite a few researchers have studied the psychological and social factors that contribute to creating serial murderers. Suppose a researcher were to discover an astounding fact: nearly all serial murderers had changed their religion shortly before they went on their killing spree. Attempts to explain this remarkable fact would occupy a central place in attempts to understand the motivations of serial killers. It would be baffling if someone attempted to downplay the relevance of this surprising discovery by pointing out that nearly all serial killers had slept in a bed before committing their crimes. The overwhelming majority of bed-sleepers do not become serial murderers, but if an extraordinarily high percentage of serial killers had recently changed their religion, researchers should take note and try to explain what it is about this conversion that makes them more prone (than those who have not changed their religion) to commit mass killings. And so it is with the (so-called) gateway effect.

The precise mechanism by which 'soft' drugs lead to 'hard' drugs among so many users of the latter is a matter of enormous debate. Almost certainly, no single mechanism exists, but here is one of several possibilities: if someone is first introduced to cannabis by a friend (which is the typical pathway), and comes to enjoy the experience, her friend is likely to have credibility if he assures her that she is likely to enjoy cocaine too. In my judgment, the gateway hypothesis is clearly true; the trick is to explain and accommodate it rather than to neglect it.

No reliable *long-term* studies of the effects of decriminalisation on use can be found. And the long-term substitution effects, where users decrease their consumption of some drugs while increasing their consumption of others, are unknown as well. How will the fact that persons may use the heretofore illegal substance of their choice alter their consumption of, say, alcohol? Rates of consumption are affected by time and place restrictions as well as by the policies of private sector institutions rather than by a change in law. Will corporate employers continue to test for drugs and sanction employees who fail to pass? No one can be sure, and the paths of the UK and US may diverge on this matter. To complicate the reliability of forecasts further, the inevitable appearance of new drugs is bound to change the calculus. The sudden appearance of substances unknown a generation ago has a way of confounding even the most astute predictions.

3. Concluding Thoughts

Given these reservations and uncertainties, one might wonder why I continue to endorse decriminalisation of drug use with such enthusiasm? I offer two answers. First, I believe that a more defensible position, in conformity with the 'harm reduction' perspective which the authors at the Conference also adopted, is to argue that any harms caused by a long-term increase in drug use are likely to be offset by a decrease in the harms caused by criminalisation itself. In short, more use need not translate to more harm. It is better, I think, to be more explicit about this matter. The spectre of increased drug use has long been cited as the chief obstacle to reform, and reformers should confront this worry directly: greater use, *if* it happens, is *not* fatal to the rationale for decriminalisation. Any increase in use is likely to be an acceptable cost if we aspire to reap the several advantages of decriminalisation that would-be reformers, including the proposers at the Conference, document so well.

Second, I am not inclined to make the case for decriminalisation to be so dependent on empirical conjectures. To my mind, the better framework posits *rights* that our current system of criminalisation routinely violates. Rights, by their very nature, are worth protecting even if the consequences of so doing turn out to be somewhat worse. For example, since consumers in a free society have a right to eat whatever they please, the fact that they make bad decisions in grocery stores should not tempt states to attach criminal penalties to fatty foods. To be sure, we should not stand on rights at *all* costs, that is, even if the heavens should fall. But a cogent defence of the right to control our consciousness through the substances we ingest and the activities we perform should not be hostage to the sort of cost-benefit or harm-reduction calculus that applies when rights are not at stake. It is true that politicians are often unmoved by appeals to rights. In my experience as a drug reformer, however, deontological arguments (which I do not equate with being 'libertarian') have proved surprisingly effective in persuading fair-minded sceptics.

I have spent a fair amount of time expressing my five misgivings. Thus, I reiterate that my reservations are relatively minor, and are perhaps little more than quibbles that can be solved (or mitigated) with ingenuity. Most importantly, they should not be construed to conceal our far more fundamental points of agreement. Decriminalisation of drug possession is long overdue, and it is wise for this to be the first reform before any others are considered. But being so long overdue, we should not underestimate the range of objections to it, nor should we risk failure by overstating our arguments and assertions.

10

Dynamics and Drivers for Change in the Criminal Justice System

STEPHEN WOOLER*

This chapter offers a high-level review of what I perceive to be the most significant changes affecting the fairness and effectiveness of the criminal justice system over the past 50 years. It therefore differs from previous chapters which have focused on reform of the substantive and procedural law. It is about the system within which that law is applied – exploring changes and reform to the mechanisms of justice. Those changes range across organisation and structures, cultural, governance, financial, political and public expectations.

The most visible of these is perhaps the shift from a locally based system to a national/central system. Taking it *as an example*, one can point to some benefits but there are also unanswered questions whether it has achieved greater efficiency within the CJS; and whether it has generated governance arrangements that properly balance the competing interests of the different stakeholders in the criminal justice system. It calls into question the government's continuing commitment to the principle of local justice. The magistracy has more than halved in numbers in the last 20 years with half of the magistrates' courts being closed altogether in the last ten years. The unified crown court was established in 1972 against a backlog of cases, but nothing like the 62,800 recorded in Ministry of Justice management information for quarter 3 of 2022 – the most recent available. The Institute of Government analysis[1] of that management information showed that even before the legal profession's industrial action, the criminal courts were still not operating as efficiently as before the pandemic. That failure did not reflect a lack of spending

* Following practice at the criminal and common law bar, Stephen joined the office of the Director of Public Prosecutions in 1973, rising to become Assistant Director of Public Prosecutions in 1982. He was seconded to the Law Officers' Department in 1983 and was instrumental in establishing first the Crown Prosecution Service and then the Serious Fraud Office. In 1987 he became Chief Crown Prosecutor in London before returning to the Law Officers' Department as Deputy Legal Secretary where he served until 1999 when he became HM Chief Inspector of the Crown Prosecution Service. He was made a Companion of the Order of the Bath in the Queen's Birthday Honours 2005.

[1] Institute of Government, *Performance Tracker 2022/23* (Spring Update, 2023) ch 9.

or resources but a less efficient service. When adjusted for complexity, the backlog is twice as large as before COVID-19 – and falling slowly. Consequently, victims are witing for justice for longer than at any time on record.

Another *example* is the increasing involvement of politicians – disproportionate even allowing for their legitimate interest in the formation of criminal justice policy and in legislative and other means of implementing it. Although direct involvement by political ministers in initiatives to raise numbers of convictions for particular types of offence may be viewed as a response to public concerns (eg, the Street Crime initiative under the Blair administration and the Rape Review initiative spear-headed by the Deputy Prime Minister), the undoubted pressure on investigators and prosecutors has the potential to compromise the objectivity of decision-making. Political intervention in individual cases now seems tolerated. The personal appearance by the then Attorney General in the Court of Appeal to urge the judges to increase the sentences passed on three youths for the manslaughter of a police officer on the grounds that the experienced trial judge should have ignored sentencing guidelines to pass a more severe sentence received a strong rebuff.[2] There have been several instances of Lord Chancellors intervening to discourage the Parole Board from allowing the release of prisoners. Other changes have been less direct but cumulatively have significant impact on the culture within the criminal justice system. For example, amendments to the Parole Rules by the Secretary of State for Justice that had the effect of prohibiting prison or probation staff from making recommendations in favour of release or removal to open conditions. They were struck down by the Administrative Court as unlawful.[3]

My aim has been to identify trends – from a practitioner rather than academic point of view – and at the same time to bring the perspective of an insider. Called to the Bar more than 50 years ago and having been involved with some of the changes, I have had the luxury of observing how things done at the outset of my career have panned out. The criminal justice system has a habit of confounding predictions and all too often expectations are disappointed; when one comes to analyse dynamics, a major challenge is working out what is cause and what is effect.

If this chapter does no more than generate better understanding and awareness of centralisation and the other factors thereby stimulating critical scrutiny and possibly research, it will have succeeded.

My starting point has been the massive organisational changes and associated consequences for management and governance of the criminal justice system.

[2] *Long Bowes and Cole* [2020] EWCA Crim 1729, [84], per Dame Victoria Sharp P: 'That is, to say the least, an unusual submission. It involves the proposition that in the circumstances of this case, a sentence within the guideline offence range was not within the range properly open to the judge, who was instead required to pass a sentence outside that range. We think it regrettable that, in advancing that submission, the structure and ambit of the guideline were not addressed. Nor was any sufficient explanation given why it is contended that the judge was not merely entitled to depart from the guideline but positively required to do so.'

[3] *Secretary of State for Justice ex parte Bailey and Morris* [2023] EWHC 821.

They spanned a period that also saw the inexorable rise up the political agenda of law and order from the mid-1990s. It was propelled mainly by rising crime figures. A 'richer mix of cases' coming through the system – to use a term beloved by bureaucrats – also added to pressures on a system already reeling from a series of cases that had severely dented public confidence in the criminal justice system. They included high-profile miscarriages of justice[4] and an apparent inability to handle the increasing number of complex fraud cases.[5] It culminated in the determination of New Labour to overhaul and join up the criminal justice system; and to manage it from the centre against a set of objectives and associated performance targets for each of the component agencies. That determination rather begged the crucial question: can the CJS ever be properly managed as a single system?

This chapter also considers the impact of these developments on procedural and cultural issues. Other drivers have been public finances as well as changes in public attitudes and expectations. Each is considered individually as well as in the context of the others to see how they impact on each other. Whilst it is easy to trace the steady shift of the CJS over a period of 50 years from fragmentation to unified structures, it is less easy to answer the big questions they pose: have we built ineffective impersonal monoliths that are simply not amenable to central management and yet divorced from local communities? Can the current sense of crisis and apparent lack of confidence in the CJS be attributed to these changes? If so, to what extent? The only valid conclusion may be that 'one size does not fit all'!

But there is another, perhaps paradoxical point to be made. Alongside the greater political interest in criminal justice, and the tendency to produce figures and targets that come with centralisation, still there is no joined up sense of a criminal justice system. One would struggle to say which ministry has responsibility for the system as a whole. This goes beyond the familiar points that the Home Office retains responsibility for the police and matters of national security whilst the Ministry of Justice has responsibility for the prisons, the judiciary, and the court structure, whilst the Attorney General has the power to refer certain cases or issues to the appeal courts and superintends the Crown Prosecution Service. It also goes beyond the consequent uncertainties as to which arm of the executive should prevail in cases of overlapping responsibilities (a simple example being out of court disposals which would affect both police and prosecutors). The bigger point is that criminal justice policy is now made on the initiative of sponsoring departments, and no figure appears to have overall oversight or the ability to object to new schemes on the basis that they create inconsistencies with other parts of the system. So, centralisation without an overall fulcrum.

[4] *Report of the Royal Commission on Criminal Justice* (Cm2263, 1994) was a direct response in particular to the quashing of the convictions of the Maguire Seven (referred by the Home Secretary to the Court of Appeal following an interim report by Sir John May published in July 1990) and those of the Birmingham Six.

[5] Cases relating to the Maxwells, BCCI, Blue Arrow and Roger Levitt were all problematic.

1. Changes from Local to National Structure

The main components of the criminal justice 'system' – although Sir Robin Auld would dispute that description[6] – are the police, who investigate and initiate most proceedings, the CPS and other prosecuting authorities, the courts, probation service and prisons. All have been subject to major change. Prosecution, courts and probation have become national services whereas prisons (national for much longer) remain under national control but with some institutions being run privately. Policing is moving in the same direction. The following sections explore the changes on each agency.

Higher Courts

When I was called to Bar in 1969, hotchpotch was the order of the day and Dr Beeching, famed for his railway axe, was at work in the higher courts.[7] The two-tier system of Assizes and Quarter Sessions areas was fragmented. Assizes worked on a county basis with High Court judges travelling on circuits to each Assize town whilst Quarter Sessions generally sat in the seat of each county and county borough, and in numerous non-county boroughs (mainly, but not exclusively, ancient boroughs), which were entitled to hold their own quarter sessions. One small county (eg, Bedfordshire) could be served by three higher courts: Assizes; Borough Quarter Sessions; and County Quarter Sessions. Local authorities were responsible for providing accommodation and funding. Arrangements became particularly complex in urban areas and massive backlogs prevailed (déjà vu). The establishment of the Crown Court unified[8] the structure and initially built on the local arrangements, but central government tends to be less sensitive to local needs, especially when there is an opportunity to reduce costs. For example, Bedfordshire no longer has a higher court and nor does neighbouring city of Milton Keynes; that scenario is by no means unique.

Based on its performance over the last two decades, the Crown Court cannot be regarded as delivering anything approaching efficient and effective justice. Lack of resources means that fewer courtrooms and sitting days are available: participants including the judiciary and court staff are universally disillusioned – and while this was being first penned, the criminal bar was taking industrial action.

A study on the Western Circuit, 'This Doesn't Look Like Justice',[9] noted that nationally the start to finish gap, time elapsing between an offence and the end of

[6] He dismissed criminal justice as 'no system worthy of the name': Sir R Auld, *Review of the Criminal Courts of England and Wales* (2021) 8.1.

[7] Lord Chancellor's Office, *The Royal Commission on Assizes and Quarter Sessions, 1966–1969* (LCO 7).

[8] The Crown Court is a single national court sitting in multiple locations. Initially this included the vast majority of existing locations but many were whittled away.

[9] K Brunner QC, A Midgley and H Rust (2020).

a case in the Crown Court, rocketed from 392 days in 2010 to 525 days in 2019.[10] The main cause identified was the progressive cuts in the number of sitting days funded – according to the report, sitting days in the Crown Court were cut by 15 per cent from 97,400 in 2018/19, to 82,300 in 2019/20 (later increased by a relatively insignificant 700 days). The practical outcomes were stark; witnesses in some courts having to wait almost two years after the alleged offence before they give evidence; trials taking days longer than they should as judges juggle other hearings so that three-day trials became spread over four or five days. More and more trials and other hearings were being adjourned or moved to other courts – sometimes 80 or 100 miles away – at the last minute. Delays, adjournments, and moving trials mean distress to witnesses, causing them to withdraw support for the prosecution, and bring financial hardship to advocates.

The indictment is a powerful one. Although based on the Western Circuit experience, the report was considered representative of the situation nationally. Moreover, the scenario described pre-dated the COVID-19 pandemic which further exacerbated the situation but had the beneficial side-effect of galvanising the government into some action. The then Parliamentary Under Secretary of State for Justice (James Cartlidge MP) told the House of Commons on 9 November 2021 that he was:

> … pleased to say that the spending review provides an extra £477 million for the criminal justice system, which will allow us to reduce Crown Court backlogs caused by the pandemic from 60,000 today to an estimated 53,000 by March 2025.

A few days later the Lord Chief Justice was quick to concede to the Justice Select Committee that such reduction was 'not much'.

More recently the Institute of Government[11] has confirmed further deterioration with a Quarter 3 2022 backlog of 62,800 with an explanation that the 'complexity adjustment' raises the figure to over 80,000 – making the true backlog more than twice as large as before the pandemic.

Although such poor performance was not an inevitable outcome of creating a unified court, it was reasonably predictable since central government is accustomed to working within rigid and uniform structures (especially as regards finance) that are less sensitive to the softer benefits of the localised system including civic pride and the greater impact of justice which is seen to be locally administered. Achieving meaningful and sustained improvement in the administration of criminal justice will inevitably be a lengthy process. Only time will tell whether the immediate post-COVID-19 government focus on the criminal justice system will be maintained. But what are the dynamics for that? Courts are now run by HM Courts and Tribunals Service, an executive agency of government. Critics would point to the vice-like grip of HMT on the budget of HMCTS as a major factor.

[10] MoJ, *Pivot Table Analytical Tool for England and Wales* (Criminal Court Statistics publication, 2019).

[11] Institute of Government (n 1).

However, the temptation to hark back to the days when justice was a matter of civic pride should be resisted: the same vice-like grip now extends to local authorities.

Magistrates' Courts

A similar picture emerges. Prior to 2005, magistrates' courts' committees (MCCs) had overall responsibility for management of the magistrates' courts service within their areas in England & Wales albeit under the loose oversight of (initially) the |Home Office. In 1992, the Lord Chancellor's Department assumed that responsibility and following the Police and Magistrates' Courts Act 1994 was able through a series of arranged (shotgun) marriages and mergers to reduce their number from 105 in 1997 to 42. These amalgamations were accompanied by a move to confine a number of benches within individual MCC areas to a single justices' clerk and the placing by central government of limits on MCC budgets. Further governance change occurred by virtue of the Courts Act 2003 when, on 1 April 2005, responsibility for the 42 remaining magistrates' courts committees and the Court Service (responsible for the County Courts and Crown Court) passed to Her Majesty's Courts Service which, on 1 April 2011, merged with the Tribunals Service to form Her Majesty's Courts and Tribunals Service. Local justice had effectively disappeared. For example, with the amalgamation of court areas. Buckinghamshire has one magistrates' court and is served by one bench of magistrates covering the whole of Thames Valley (albeit nominally assigned) and there is a Justices' Clerk based for South East England!! Thereafter, the Lord Chancellor's Advisory Committees exist only to provide bodies to sit on selection panels and ask centrally prescribed questions and mark individual candidates to a centrally prescribed regime but with no further input. There is no longer any significant local input into courts' management; and magistrates are viewed simply as unpaid staff. Local benches are no longer trusted to deal with misconduct. Managers at local level within HMCTS have little discretion and just about any form of local initiative – for example trying to improve diversity amongst applicants – requires central approval.

So where does this leave the lay magistracy – the ultimate symbol of local justice? Very much in decline is the short answer; the number of lay magistrates stood at around 30,000 when Sir Robin Auld delivered his Review of the Criminal Courts in 2001 and has since been in constant decline. Numbers of lay magistrates decreased 43 per cent from 25,170 on 1 April 2012 to 14,348 by 1 April 2019. There was a further fall to 12,651 by 2021. This reduction in headcount was officially attributed to falling workloads in the magistrates' courts after the abolition of committal proceedings in 2017. That attribution is suspect, and the true reasons probably lie elsewhere. The House of Commons library statistics showed that between 2010 and 2019, 162 of the 323 magistrates' courts in England and Wales had shut – a loss of 50.2 per cent of the estate. By 2022, that figure had risen to 167 and those closures were additional to the 125 magistrates' courts closed between 1997 and 2009.[12]

Particular concerns have been raised about the single justice procedure under which a defendant may be tried by one justice instead of two or three. The change was imposed on magistrates. At the outset the Chair of the Magistrates' Association said:

> Whilst the Single Justice Procedure has some potential advantages in terms of making the justice system more efficient, there is a trade-off between efficiency and openness, as cases are not happening in a public forum.
>
> The Magistrates' Association raised our concerns when the Single Justice Procedure was first introduced; these have not been satisfactorily addressed by HM Courts and Tribunals Service or the Ministry of Justice. There is a danger that unless they are, public confidence in the justice system may be damaged.[13]

It is therefore unlikely that the procedure would have been widely adopted had it been a matter for local discretion.

Concerns were exacerbated by its extensive use in dealing with alleged breach of COVID-19 regulations. According to Ministry of Justice figures cited by the Independent, 4,400 defendants were prosecuted and 3,500 convicted for offences relating to COVID-19 in 2020. By the end of September, more than 1,000 of those cases had been dealt with through the Single Justice Procedure and analysis suggests that the number later rose to at least 2,000.

The Crown Prosecution Service reviewed all 1,800 COVID-19 cases that were heard in open court between March 2020 and March 2021.

It found that all charges under the Coronavirus Act and one in five under the Health Protection Regulations were wrong. If the same rate is applied to the Single Justice Procedure cases the CPS did not review, at least 400 miscarriages of justice may have occurred. It subsequently emerged that several of those convicted under the single justice procedure for their participation in a vigil on Clapham Common to mark the death of Sarah Everard had been unaware that proceedings had been commenced against them; and the convictions had to be set aside.[14]

The Times 10 June 2021 described the magistrates' courts as being 'in a state of disarray' with practitioners describing new procedures, notably the single justice procedure, as likely to cause substantial numbers of miscarriages of justice. One practitioner commented: 'Fairness has been sacrificed on the altar of efficiency'.

[12] James Cartlidge MP (Parliamentary Under-secretary of State for Justice) HC Deb, 10 February 2022.

[13] L Dearden, 'Miscarriages of justice under coronavirus laws "going unchallenged" as court hearings bypassed' *Independent* (31 May 2021).

[14] L Dearden, 'Sarah Everard vigil attendees prosecuted 'without knowing it' despite High Court ruling police actions unlawful' *Independent* (26 July 2022).

Prosecutions – Crown Prosecution Service (CPS)

The CPS was established in 1986 following the Philips Royal Commission[15] recommendation to establish an independent prosecution service to be responsible for prosecutions previously instituted by the police. Again, 'hotchpotch' is apposite to describe the pre-existing arrangements whereby the police might lack objectivity in assessing the evidence yet any legal advisors would act under instructions if their view did not prevail. Philips was robustly against a nationally organised service recommending 'a locally based service with some national features'.[16] In rejecting arguments in favour of a single national service, it said:

> We believe it to be hazardous to argue from the experience of other jurisdictions, that a national prosecution service would be workable in England and Wales. We know of no common law jurisdiction in which the equivalent of a national prosecution system of the type we are discussing covers an area with anything approaching the population of England and Wales (although some are geographically much larger) or deals with a crime load of anything like the same order of magnitude.[17]

Despite that, the government went ahead and created the CPS as a single national service, albeit initially with a local structure of 31 areas. Professor Rock's Official History of the Criminal Justice System examines the decision which was influenced in equal measure by serious concerns about the likely impartiality of prosecution decision-making if left in local hands and the natural centralising tendency of national government and Parliament.[18]

That structure did not survive long – regions first being superimposed and then the number of areas was reduced under the Directorship of Barbara Mills to 13. Amidst widespread concern about the performance of the CPS, the incoming Labour government in 1997 established the Glidewell Review with terms of reference reflecting its CJS manifesto commitment to a locally based criminal justice system based on 42 areas linked directly to police force areas.[19] Glidewell endorsed the proposal that CPS areas be aligned to police forces and recommended a much-devolved structure. A much smaller headquarters would oversee the service responding to information from the new independent inspection arrangements he proposed. Glidewell's final plea was that a CPS which had been through a troubled period should be allowed a period of stability. But it was not to be. The 1997 emphasis on localism seemed to wane in the face of Labour's wider cross-government centralisation. A programme of mergers followed and accelerated with the austerity around 2008, bringing extensive mergers and wholesale closure of offices.

But that is only part of the picture. Contrary to widely held belief, the CPS is *not* a universal prosecutor. It is a creature of statute whose primary duty is to review

[15] Sir C Philips, *Royal Commission on Criminal Justice* (Cmnd 809, 1985).
[16] ibid, para 7.25.
[17] ibid.
[18] P Rock, *The Official History of Criminal Justice in England and Wales* (2 Vols, Routledge, 2018/2020).
[19] Rt. Hon. Sir Iain Glidewell, *The Review of the Crown Prosecution Service* (Cm 3972, 1998).

and prosecute criminal cases initiated by the police (and following a merger with the Revenue and Customs Prosecutions Office) HMRC – and a number of other investigative bodies specified through the Attorney General's power to assign functions.[20] There are a plethora of other prosecuting bodies ranging from the Health and Safety Executive, local authorities in relation to trading standards, public health and planning enforcement through charities such as the RSPCA[21] in relation to animal welfare, the Care Quality Commission and the Financial Conduct Authority; and the number continues to grow.

The position as regards non-police prosecutions was considered by the Philips Royal Commission[22] which noted their haphazard nature but signalled a disinclination towards significant change to the broader structure of prosecution arrangements. At paragraphs 7.40 to 7.45, it made it clear that its proposals should cover not just prosecutions initiated by the 'civil police' – those forces maintained under the auspices of the Home Office – but those by other specialist forces such as the British Transport Police. However, it concluded at paragraph 7.44 that the role of the new service should not extend to prosecutions brought by all agencies. Its reasoning was two-fold: the resources likely to be required and the variety of agencies involved together with their different ways of working and their differing approaches to the use of prosecution as part of enforcement.

The law in England & Wales also confers on any individual an almost unfettered liberty to institute criminal proceedings – commonly known as 'private prosecutions' although, once instituted they are, in law, no different to any other prosecution. The Philips Royal Commission was sceptical as to the value and justification of private prosecutions.[23] Nonetheless, it fell short of proposing complete curtailment and instead advocated more[24] stringent filters for the commencement of private prosecutions to guard against the risk of malicious, vexatious and utterly unreasonable prosecutions and the associated harm to those subject to the allegations. That proposal was never implemented.

It is a paradox that, although mainstream prosecutions – which are also a substantial majority – are highly centralised, the overall prosecution arrangements are fragmented and unregulated to the extent there is no Minister or other office holder with responsibility/authority over all prosecuting agencies or for establishing a framework within which they operate.[25] It reflects the government focus on

[20] The Prosecution of Offences Act 1985, s 3(2)(g).

[21] Although the RSPCA is not a public body, the extent of its prosecution activity and the de facto reliance by public authorities on it to undertake the majority of animal welfare prosecutions requires that, in the view of the author, it be treated as a prosecuting body.

[22] *Royal Commission on Criminal Justice* (n 15).

[23] ibid, para 7.50: 'Criminal sanctions are imposed for the benefit of society as a whole, on its behalf and at its expense. We do not think that private citizens should have an unlimited right of access to the criminal process to remedy wrongs for which other measures might be more appropriate.'

[24] Over and above the requirements in specific cases to seek consent from either the DPP or the Attorney General, and the uncertainty about reimbursement of costs.

[25] HM Attorney General has a statutory duty to superintend the DPP and SFO but no responsibility for prosecutions generally or the framework of the criminal justice system.

the interests of the central agencies to the exclusion of other legitimate interests. This has implications for the governance of the criminal justice system overall which are considered later.

Probation Services

Probation has been formally available since 1907 through a set of area-based services interacting at arm's length with central government. The National Probation Service was established in its current form by the Criminal Justice and Courts Services Act 2000 in April 2001. However, since 2007 there have been three major upheavals. The Offender Management Act 2007 sought to integrate prison and probation services. The National Probation Service became part of His Majesty's Prison and Probation Service (HMPPS), which transferred to the Ministry of Justice from the Home Office on 9 May 2007. It comprises 42 probation areas coterminous with police force area boundaries, served by 35 probation trusts. Trusts are funded by HMPPS and employ all staff except the chief officer; they are accountable to their boards (comprising up to 15 members appointed by the Secretary of State) for day-to-day operations and financial management, and to HMPPS via a Regional Offender Manager. Local authorities were divested of responsibility. Probation services would be delivered by commissioning of probation trusts and other organisations in accordance with an annual plan and delivered according to a new set of national standards.

Further radical change (the Grayling Reforms) came about in 2014. Under those reforms, the work of the probation sector was divided between a public sector organisation, the National Probation Service (NPS) which retained responsibility for managing high-risk criminals, and 21 private companies, known as community rehabilitation companies (CRCs), responsible for the supervision of 150,000 low to medium-risk offenders. The changes were criticised at the time and proved unsuccessful both in terms of effectiveness/public confidence and financially. According to a *Guardian* report on 28 June 2021, the government had to bail out the private providers, by more than £500million.

June 2021 saw the reversal of the Grayling reforms and reunification of probation functions. However, their success has yet to be demonstrated. The same report quoted HM Chief Inspector of Probation warning that any cash investment would have to be sustained to correct the mistakes of the past notes:

> There are no magic bullets here: structural change needs to be backed by sustained investment for there to be true improvement. Real transformation is a long-term commitment, and unification is just the beginning of that journey.

Policing

Change here has been more subtle. The number of forces remains unchanged since mergers in 1974; an attempt in 2006/2007 to force further mergers without resort to Parliament was unsuccessful. However, major changes to governance followed through the establishment of the Policing College and replacement of police authorities with elected Police and Crime Commissioners (PCCs). The latter creates a form of democratic accountability but introduces a political dimension since candidates stand under established political party colours supported by party machines. Lord Blair (Commissioner of the Metropolitan Police 2005–08) wrote of the police service: 'Its governance in the form of police and crime commissioners is a solution in search of a problem'.[26]

Finance is now heavily dependent on central government to an extent that renders the concept of local policing illusory. The majority of funding comes from central government although PCCs do have limited revenue raising powers through a council tax precept. The limit is set by central government although it may be raised by a few percentage points (usually around 2 per cent) if the PCC secures authority through a local referendum.

2. Direct Implications of Centralisation

It is noteworthy that such a comprehensive if rather piecemeal shift from local to national structures was not underpinned by any clear strategy. Apart from perhaps a general belief that central unified structures offer better consistency and efficiency, no overarching justification has been advanced by government; nor was any co-ordination around decisions about different aspects of the system apparent. One problem is that once the centralisation is accepted as a matter of faith as saving money (and perhaps promoting consistency) then, considering also the tightening of budgets across central government, further developments are likely to be made with an eye on saving money; and the further decision-makers are from the effect of those savings 'on the ground', the more readily such decisions will be taken.

For example, the underlying concept of an independent prosecution service was that all proceedings except the most minor would be subject to review by a qualified lawyer and even the most minor would be reviewed before proceeding as a contest. Amendments to the 1985 legislation watered that down by permitting designated staff who were not legally qualified to undertake the majority of magistrates' courts work (including handling bail applications) except trials. As mentioned above in relation to the courts, the single justice procedure has reinforced that watering down of safeguards for citizens yet further with the CPS being bypassed in a large tranche of casework.

Indeed, the process of centralisation inevitably shifted costs to central departments (who were then moved to reduce them). The running of the courts, probation service and in many cases prosecuting solicitors' departments (before

[26] Letter to *The Times* (13 August 2022).

their absorption into the CPS) had all historically been substantially funded by local authorities. Changes to the prosecution costs regime associated with the creation of the Crown Court and subsequent inception of the CPS offer a good example of the shift of costs. The cost of prosecutions originally fell initially on the relevant police force (or other prosecutor) although the Costs in Criminal Cases Act 1952 enabled prosecutors to recover their costs in relation to indictable cases (whether in the summary or higher courts) through orders (made on an individual case basis) for the costs to be paid out of local funds. It was the relevant County or Borough that bore the costs. The Courts Act 1971 established the Crown Court and transferred that burden to central funds. From a Treasury perspective, this made it difficult to control the cost of the new exposure even though the costs were assessed by the 'proper officer' in accordance with centrally made regulations. Whether or not enthusiastic about the creation of another national service (CPS), the Treasury certainly welcomed Part II of the Prosecution of Offences Act 1985. It introduced changes both of principle and of practice. The CPS was to be funded directly by parliamentary Vote,[27] and awards of costs from central funds in its favour were not therefore required. The Bill also put other public authority prosecutors in the same position, while retaining the power of the courts to award private prosecutors their costs from central funds. Thus, a significant block of public expenditure was brought within budgets more easily controlled by the Treasury. But this resulted in cuts. The CPS had to cut the costs of instructing counsel and that in due course provided the platform for the Treasury (through the departmental Vote system) to constrain fees for all publicly funded criminal work over a long period of time. The Legal Aid Agency was subject to similar budgetary constraints. That was the longer-term background to the aforementioned industrial action by the Criminal bar, which at one time would have been beyond contemplation.

By the time the probation service had become a national organisation, practically the whole cost of the criminal justice system had fallen to central government and was therefore subject to Treasury control. It therefore competed for funds much more directly with other central government responsibilities such as health and defence.

The process of centralisation also had implications for Ministers who became more directly accountable for operational matters. The creation of executive agencies was perceived as a means of distancing departments from operational matters but never really achieved that. Moreover, whatever the theory, Ministers find it very difficult in practice to stand back from the operational – the instinct of

[27] A Vote is in effect a departmental budget. The term is used because Parliament has to authorise all public expenditure through a system of Supply and Appropriation Bills. The resultant Acts give authority for the Government to use the expenditure requested in the estimates and to be issued with money from the Consolidated Fund (the Government's bank account). In addition, they also place limits on the purpose for which the money may be spent by setting out the services particular budgets are to be used for.

politicians is to intervene in high profile or controversial issues, whether to take the credit or promise a solution. Inexorably expectations are raised, and they get further sucked in. It becomes a vicious circle: the more that ministers hold themselves out as accountable for; the more they feel they must control.

It also affected their relationships with inspectorates which had been created to report on locally delivered services – initially, police, prisons,[28] probation and magistrates' courts. Then there was the addition of HM Crown Prosecution Service Inspectorate in 2000 following a decision by the incoming Labour government in 1997 that the service should return to a more local structure. It is one thing to report objectively on a local service for which a Minister does not have direct accountability; and another (and more difficult) thing to report that the performance delivered by his/her own department is below standard.

The character of the central departments changed radically – and not just in a machinery of government sense. Whereas bodies such as the Lord Chancellor's Department (later the Department for Constitutional Affairs and then the Ministry of Justice) and Home Office historically were accustomed to making policy to be implemented through local structures for policing, probation and the magistrates' courts, their role increasingly became one of delivery.

This brings us to our next theme; that with centralisation comes extra political interest in criminal justice, but it is too easily shaped by headlines and events; and it is all too easy to identify this as a marked trend over the last 50 years.

Criminal Justice Rises on the Political Agenda

From the mid to late 1990s the criminal justice ministers in the Conservative administration began a move towards more collaborative working amongst the agencies. But that was only one of several important drivers. Rising crime rates were even more significant. The increases were sufficient in the early 1990s to cause a sea-change in public opinion such that the Royal Commission (Runciman) established in March 1991 as a response to serious miscarriages of justice (including the Maguire Seven[29] and Birmingham Six) became instead one focused equally if not more on impediments to successful prosecutions. It was later described as a re-balancing! Symbolic legislation brought forward under the Home Secretaryship of Michael Howard began to qualify the right to silence with the prosecution being able to adduce evidence in court where a defendant had chosen not to give

A Supply and Appropriation Bill includes a schedule containing the substantive content of the estimates that have been approved by the House.

[28] Although HM Prisons Inspectorate was only established in its present form by the Criminal Justice Act 1982, the Prison Commission established under the Prison Act 1877 was a statutory board to administer and inspect prisons in England and Wales in accordance with the general or special directions of the Secretary of State (the Home Secretary).

[29] A family with republican sympathies alleged to have operated a bomb factory for IRA active service units.

evidence in order to undermine any explanation by the defence, and the historic words of the police caution had to be amended.[30]

That process was to gather momentum. 1997 saw Tony Blair steal the Tory clothes with his 'Tough on crime; tough on the causes of crime' manifesto mantra. A second theme was 'joined up government'; it applied across the board and not just to criminal justice. But in fact, the government-wide approach did not fit very comfortably with the criminal justice aspect of Labour's manifesto with its emphasis on local justice areas, and in the event, attention became diverted from long term issues and change. The focus was the delivery of a plethora of short-term initiatives mandated often from the Prime Minister's Office and directed at short term political targets which could not be missed. The Street Crimes Initiative driven by Tony Blair personally in 2002 was prompted by increasing incidences of street robberies. Under the initiative, all police forces had targets for detection and arrest with prosecutors and courts being required to put in place special arrangements for fast-tracking those cases. Courts were encouraged to deal severely with offenders. Results were reported weekly to 10 Downing Street who co-ordinated publicity. The initiative lasted for well over a year under the Prime Minister's personal command and undoubtedly had a short-term effect – often at the expense of other priorities and through some judicious massaging of statistics.

The targeting of persistent young offenders (PYOs) followed. Although those and other initiatives had joint working as a central theme, the fact that they were so politically driven undoubtedly worried many of those within the criminal justice system accustomed to a more apolitical approach. Despite the soundness of the underlying purpose of those initiatives, many practitioners had reservations about the criminal justice processes being harnessed for the overt purpose of delivering political kudos. That was especially so at a time when government emphasis was supposedly on rebalancing the criminal justice system – but notably in favour of victims and witnesses.

Trying to Re-Set the System: Diagnosis by Sir Robin Auld

This had developed against the background of a wide-ranging review by Sir Robin Auld who was appointed to report on the criminal courts of England & Wales; he did so in October 2001 which was later than expected. Insiders speculated that he had slowed down the process to avoid perceptions that he had been used and the purpose of establishing the review had been that its findings should be the central plank of the Labour manifesto policy for the 2001 election. His work was thorough, and his 300 proposals included the creation of a 3-tier unified court structure with individual cases being tried at a level appropriate to their seriousness; and the court itself having discretion whether jury trial would be appropriate.

[30] For criticism, see H Quirk, 'The Case for Restoring the Right of Silence' in JJ Child and RA Duff (eds), *Criminal Law Reform Now: Proposals and Critique* (Vol 1, Hart, 2019) ch 9.

Auld's analysis of the criminal justice system quickly identifies two key drivers: public expectations (feeding into public confidence) and politics. As to the former, he notes that the overarching aims and principles of criminal justice can be simply stated,[31] but he adds that he:

> … cannot here, by a process of analysis or assignment of priorities, draw on them to provide an over-all approach or answer to the many practical questions posed in the Review. *Different priorities apply in different contexts and circumstances.*[32]

He points to the different interests that must be balanced. Auld seems to recognise how things may change commenting: 'we should not expect too much of the criminal justice system, the courts in particular, as a medium for curing the ills of society.'[33]

A contemporaneous example of the difficult interface between expectations and public confidence as drivers may be seen in proposals advanced in relation to certain type of offence that are notoriously difficult to prosecute (sexual offences and fraud come to mind) where proposals by some commentators have bordered on undermining the presumption of innocence.

As to politics, Auld comments:

> It would be naïve to suggest that politics should be removed from the forces driving change in the criminal justice system. As for any other field of public concern, politicians have a legitimate interest in the formation of criminal justice policy and in legislative and other means of implementing it. However, the criminal justice system and the public's confidence in it are damaged if, as has happened all too often in recent years, insufficiently considered legislative reforms are hurried through in seeming response to political pressures or for quick political advantage. I take it as a legitimate starting point that there should be some mechanism of objective and informed assessment between the rawness of political enthusiasms of the moment and the transformation of their products into law. More is needed than the present unofficial, often perfunctory and late consultation with the higher judiciary, coupled with the absence of any consultation for the purpose with the Criminal Justice Consultative Council.[34]

That might be code for 'Stop making policy on the back of envelopes.' Yet who can forget the momentous morning a couple of years later when the criminal justice

[31] Even though 'simple', Auld did not state them shortly (n 6). The best formulation is still Rule 1.1 of the Criminal procedure Rules: The overriding objective 1.1. – (1) The overriding objective of this procedural code is that criminal cases be dealt with justly. (2) Dealing with a criminal case justly includes – (a) acquitting the innocent and convicting the guilty; (b) dealing with the prosecution and the defence fairly; (c) recognising the rights of a defendant, particularly those under Article 6 of the European Convention on Human Rights; (d) respecting the interests of witnesses, victims and jurors and keeping them informed of the progress of the case; (e) dealing with the case efficiently and expeditiously; (f) ensuring that appropriate information is available to the court when bail and sentence are considered; and (g) dealing with the case in ways that take into account – (i) the gravity of the offence alleged, (ii) the complexity of what is in issue, (iii) the severity of the consequences for the defendant and others affected, and (iv) the needs of other cases.

[32] Auld (n 6), ch 1, para 10 (my emphasis).

[33] ibid, ch 1, para 9.

[34] ibid, ch 1, para 34.

world woke up to learn that the post of Lord Chancellor was to be abolished with immediate effect?! Immediate backtracking was inevitable as lawyers pointed out to No.10 that it left nobody to exercise the literally hundreds of powers vested in the officeholder.

Chapter 8 of the report addressed structural issues and opened with the assessment:

> The word 'system' in the expression 'criminal justice system' is misleading. There is no 'system' worthy of the name, only a criminal justice process to which a number of different Government departments and agencies and others make separate and sometimes conflicting contributions.[35]

Apart from some adjustments as between Home Office and Ministry of Justice, the position appears to remain much the same today. As to the impact, Auld sums up the position:

> Each of the departments and of the various agencies has aims, policies and budgets broadly directed to the common end of reducing crime and the fair and efficient administration of criminal justice, but which, in their application, often conflict. These operational conflicts are inter-departmental and interagency, but they also occur within different managerial or geographical divisions of the same department or agency. They are, no doubt, the stuff of any large organisation or group of organisations, different parts of which endeavour to contribute in their own ways to a common end. Human nature is such that departmental loyalties engender sectional interests and, sometimes, mutual distrust. But where they arise in the administration of criminal justice, sharpened by firm budgetary and spending constraints, they can cause much harm – including injustice, distress, expense and inconvenience to defendants, witnesses, victims, jurors, legal practitioners and others involved in the process – and much inefficiency and wastefulness in the 'system' as a whole.[36]

Fast forward to the 2020s and one finds 'This Doesn't Look Like Justice' coming to very similar conclusions.

Mention has already been made the series of 'public service agreements' across government that linked funding to the relevant objectives. Although the Criminal Justice Strategic Board (forerunner to the National Criminal Justice Board) was created to maintain oversight of the system and promote a collaborative approach to addressing its challenges, it remained for individual ministers to set the objectives and associated performance framework for the individual agencies – a particularly difficult task in relation to the criminal justice system. Even if it was possible to identify 'right' numbers of arrests, prosecutions and convictions, they would not be suitable targets for a prosecuting authority let alone the courts service. So, objectives were couched in general terms around protecting the public and just outcomes whilst the performance regime looked at those outcomes in terms of proportions of cases discontinued and those successfully

[35] ibid, ch 8, para 1.
[36] ibid, ch 8, para 9.

prosecuted and how effectively they went through the court process. It was the responsibility of Local Criminal Justice Boards to develop and implement a strategy for delivery at local level. The challenge is best appreciated by reference to Auld's equally dismal assessment of criminal justice at local level:

> But, sadly, this 'working together', or 'joined-up government' as it is called, is not achieving results commensurate with all the enthusiasm and effort put into it. There is little overall planning or direction, as distinct from pooling ideas, plans and schemes for co-ordination. There are a multiplicity of inter-departmental and inter-agency bodies at national and local levels. Mostly they have no authority or operational function. Sometimes they are uncertain of their role and/or of their relationship one with another. Often, they have overlapping memberships and terms of reference, and spend much time reporting to each other on the same or similar issues. In addition, some members of these bodies, particularly at local level, have no authority to commit those whom they represent to whatever collective recommendations or decisions that might otherwise be made.[37]

His proposed solution was a move to central joint direction and local joint management. Departments would pool their authority under a Criminal Justice Board with a broad base of membership including non-executive members with experience of high-level management of large and complex organisations outside the criminal justice system. At local level the emphasis was empowerment. The concept may have been good and indeed even reminiscent of what the Philips Royal Commission had recommended (in vain) for prosecution arrangements – a local service with national elements.

However, it was a big ask not least because of the set ways of the centre. After consideration of the Auld report, the government published 'Cutting crime, delivering justice – A strategic plan for criminal justice 2004–2008'.[38] A government commitment to bring an additional 150,000 offenders to justice raised eyebrows with some questioning whether there could be a 'right' number of prosecutions. Its wider goal was even more ambitious: by 2008 to provide a service that as a matter of everyday routine:

- is visible and responsive to law abiding citizens;
- is sensitive to the needs of the victim, ensuring that victims are supported and that their voices are heard;
- operates fairly, protecting the innocent and pursuing the guilty;
- is joined up in a modern and efficient process that works;
- applies appropriate punishments, focused on tackling the causes of offending, and makes sure they are completed; and
- exploits the potential of modern IT to improve the experience of all users.

[37] ibid, ch 8, para 12.
[38] Home Office, (Cm6288, 2004).

Although Auld's recommendations for discrete reforms were welcomed, especially where offenders could be brought to book (for example, the abolition of double jeopardy in certain serious cases where new and compelling evidence emerged after the defendant had been acquitted by jury), government never successfully created the mechanisms necessary for delivering such a demanding national strategy. Indeed, the widespread dismay and lack of confidence in the criminal justice system at present suggests little or no progress since then.

Part of the response included the creation of an Office of Criminal Justice Reform (OCJR). It was short-lived, largely because it lacked a clear position and authority within the machinery of government. Its main role was to service the Criminal Justice Strategic Board and to bring about delivery of national policies. However, it remained for individual ministers (negotiating with HMT and No.10) to set the objectives and associated performance framework for the individual agencies. OCJR did not have its own minister. On many matters, it had to work through influence rather than authority – especially in the areas of policing and the courts. It is little wonder that it floundered.

Inspectorates

The government policy driven by HMT was to brigade all inspectorates together to align with the four main public expenditure blocs: health and adult social care; local government and administration; education (including children in care); and criminal justice (police, courts, probation, prisons and prosecutions). Views were mixed amongst chief inspectors as to the merits of a single criminal justice inspectorate (as opposed to collaborative working) but all were united in resisting the proposal for inspectorates to report to OCJR (as opposed to criminal justice ministers). A new dynamic had entered the scene since the proposal would have involved the proposed single inspectorate reporting to the national managers of the system to be inspected. Although it might have avoided the awkwardness of inspectorates delivering critical reports to ministers about their own organisations, what price independence? In the event, the legislation was voted down in a late ambush in the House of Lords by peers associated with prisons and policing. The tension between independent inspection and national criminal justice agencies was highlighted by the sudden decision in 2009 to abolish HM Inspectorate of Courts Administration. Created in 2003, it had absorbed the work of the former HM Magistrates Courts Inspectorate after those courts had been merged into the Courts Service but also been responsible for inspection of the administration of the Crown Court – a role never really welcomed within the higher courts.

3. Tensions within Departments

It follows then that, given Auld's findings, we have to be careful about speaking of the centralisation of the criminal justice system. It is more accurate to say that the major constituent parts of the system have been gathered into central government agencies. It does not follow that the system itself is centrally led; or that there is any single ministry which has full ownership of the system such that anomalies or inconsistencies can be addressed in a neutral way. Changes might often be undertaken by criminal justice departments on a unilateral basis with little regard to alignment, and others might or might not know about them in advance. So increasingly, policy is made by sponsoring departments who may or may not receive full scrutiny from outside. This means that the working relationships between different agencies become ever more important and that the interests of those who are not represented within any government agency are at risk of being ignored, unless perhaps campaign groups are especially alert to bring them to the attention of the media.

The roles of those advising them have also changed. My personal experience was that, although sometimes irreverently dubbed as 'mandarins', senior Home Office officials responsible for the criminal justice system usually had great experience and brought to policy development a degree of detachment and intellectual rigour. They were not responsible for delivery and their arms-length relationships with all the key players gave them understanding but less direct interest. Proposals put to ministers were based on careful analysis of the facts and the problems, identification of options with pros and cons and measured judgement of a kind not permitted by contemporary pressures. Such processes seemed to deliver more balanced decision-making that took more account of wider societal issues and those of other stakeholders outside the main criminal justice agencies such as police and prosecution etc. But where advisers are rather more aware of targets to be met or promises they have to keep, it is that bit harder to give what might be known to be unwelcome advice.

4. Conflicting Objectives

The transition to this current state of affairs, to my mind, has its roots in the introduction in 1982 of the government's Financial Management Initiative (FMI) – part of government's general strategy for improving Civil Service efficiency. Its central objective was to promote in each department an organisation and a system in which managers at all levels would have:

(a) a clear view of their objectives; and means to assess, and wherever possible measure, outputs or performance in relation to those objectives;
(b) well-defined responsibility for making the best use of their resources, including a critical scrutiny of output and value for money; and
(c) the information (particularly about costs), the training and the access to expert advice which they needed to exercise their responsibilities effectively.

Whilst laudable as a general approach, the emphasis on departmental objectives and resources was not conducive to the development of a cohesive criminal justice system. The criminal justice system differs from most large organisations (both public and private sector) where the component parts can work in natural harmony towards a single set of objectives. The various players all serve different purposes and are not always mutually supportive. In practice, departmental interests and budgets easily get in the way of solutions which may be best for the criminal justice system. One obvious turf war has concerned the decision to charge suspects. CPS dissatisfaction with the quality of files submitted by the police to substantiate charges prompted it to press (successfully) for transfer of the decision to initiate proceedings (which had remained vested in the police) to the CPS in a large proportion of cases so that charges would not be authorised until the case was complete. This was never popular with police and proved prohibitively costly and impractical as well as introducing substantial pre-charge delay – causing the arrangements to be steadily scaled back to the point where, as a result of continual delays in the CPS, some senior police officers are suggesting that the decision to charge should be theirs alone.

Two other examples have always jarred with me: the custody time limits regime and prosecution disclosure arrangements.

Custody time limits (CTLs) were introduced by the Prosecution of Offences Act 1985 because ministers (Home Office ministers in particular) believed that an equivalent of the Scottish 110-day rule would obviate delays and reduce the numbers of unconvicted people in custody.[39] However, the scheme is dependent upon large amounts of administrative work by the prosecution who may well not have all the data/information necessary to manage it. A damaging series of custody time limit failures in the early 2000s inflicted serious reputational damage on the CPS. Most applications for extensions are necessary because either the defence is not ready, or the case cannot be listed in time because of court availability. On occasion, a defendant may wish to defer trial so that the chosen representative can be available. The complications are endless – CTLs attach not to cases but to individual charges; and one case may have several defendants each with several different time limits if the charges are preferred at different times. Individuals can have several cases pending, but their custody/bail status may differ. If an individual is granted conditional bail but cannot meet the conditions s/he may remain in custody without the prosecutor being aware. Or they may be arrested for breach of bail conditions and spend time in custody before again being released but with time having started to run again during the custody period. In short, a nightmare. Logic suggested at the outset that the courts would be best placed to manage custody time limits in individual cases.

[39] This longstanding rule is currently found in the Scotland procedure Act 1995, s 65(4), as amended by the Criminal Justice (Scotland) Act 2016, s 65(4). The effect of the amendment is that the accused person must be liberated after 110 days, if no first diet has been held, and 140 days if such a diet has been held, unless the trial begins within that period. This is subject to a power of the courts to extend the period in certain circumstances.

The Home Office (whose Bill the 1985 Act was) wanted time limits; the Lord Chancellor's Department (LCD) was content to adopt the proposal provided that the courts would not be responsible for monitoring time limits and making any necessary applications to extend. LCD and had greater clout than the yet to be established CPS. It is hard to believe that something more satisfactory could not have been devised. Chickens came home to roost and the absurdity of this position was underlined in September 2022 when His Honour Judge Pringle sitting at Oxford Crown Court was required to consider whether the absence of defence representation because of industrial action by the Criminal Bar Association amounted to a 'good and sufficient reason' for extending custody time limits in circumstances where it was common ground that the prosecution had conducted the case 'with all due diligence and expedition'. He ruled that it did not and directed the release on bail of four defendants charged with murder although that ruling was the subject of a successful application for judicial review.

The prosecution disclosure regime introduced by section 3 of the Criminal Procedure and Investigations Act 1996, following recommendations by the Runciman Royal Commission, is again founded on sound principle. But the number of cases ending in disaster (good cases collapsing and wrongful convictions) through disclosure failings remains worrying – and countless inspection reports as well as external reviews have failed to solve the problem. The usual prescription is better systems, technology and compliance. Perhaps the time has come for a more radical look – in particular at whether the responsibilities within the regime are sensibly allocated. Their division remains to a large extent as at the outset. The police were concerned that they should not have to copy all unused material for the CPS (digital software was nowhere on the horizon); and the CPS was equally determined that it could not afford for its lawyers to read all the material. So, apart from a core of documents routinely provided, disclosure officers are required to summarise all other documents and provide an assessment whether they meet the disclosure test. The summary is supposed to be sufficient to enable the CPS to take properly informed disclosure decisions. The problems are many: first, it can take longer to summarise a document than to copy it; second, police officers are not always masters of the written word and the quality/completeness of summaries is problematic; third, the process is undertaken at an early stage when the issues in the case may not be clear, and the officer cannot really know the likely issues to assess what may be relevant. These initial problems are compounded by the number of CPS lawyers through whose hands a case may pass. Bearing in mind the duty of continuing review, the only person properly placed to take an informed disclosure decision is likely to be the trial advocate – and that may come at a relatively late stage and go back to the quality of the summary. The likelihood of the necessary radical re-think necessary is reduced by the agency perspective and focus on budget implications. Relieving police officers of tasks they are ill-equipped to undertake through greater lawyer involvement would undoubtedly require adjustments of budgets across the agencies. But where are the players who can take such a holistic view?

5. Governance Arrangements – Balancing or Skewing the System?

It is difficult to detect a culture of governance in which decision-makers detach themselves sufficiently from the policies/party lines and budgets of their individual agencies to look critically at proposals and address the important questions: what is best for the integrity of the criminal justice system as a whole and its underlying objectives? Different players of course have different clout. As I finished my term as Chief Inspector of HM Crown Prosecution Service Inspectorate, I was conscious of real cultural change such that the overarching aim of all agencies seemed to be the creation of processes designed to remove cases from the courts system and, where that could not be achieved, to elicit the maximum number of guilty pleas at the earliest possible time with minimum investigation and consideration. Where proposals are advanced to streamline processes, there is often no obvious player who ensures that they remain fair and offer sufficient safeguards to accused persons.

In the absence of a responsible minister who can take holistic views, one might hope that the National Criminal Justice Board would act as a champion of the underlying values of the criminal justice system, say, in the face of cost-cutting proposals which dilute the safeguards for accused persons. The current composition of the Board makes for interesting reading – a galaxy of Ministers, senior judges, heads of national agencies and senior civil servants. The Chair of the Bar Council and President of the Law Society are invited to attend but are not part of the Board. But this composition is not such as to create a major focus on the users of the criminal justice system, a matter to which each will bring their own institutional perspective. It is not clear, for example, how effective such structures might be in evaluating the impact of proposed changes, or the impact of legal aid arrangements on defence practitioners and on those defendants who cannot afford counsel. The position is mirrored in the composition of the Criminal Rules Committee whose minutes record an attendance which again focuses on the perspectives of the criminal justice agencies despite the attendance of some external members.

Years later the process continues, and the Judicial Review and Courts Act 2022 contains a raft of measures to keep cases out of court – automatic online conviction and penalty for certain summary offences; the guilty plea in writing procedure – usually associated with cases sufficiently minor to be dealt with by summons – extended to proceedings following police charge; and the extension of single justice procedure to corporations. One can see why justice was described as having been 'sacrificed on the altar of efficiency'. Unfortunately, it is the sort of efficiency that produces poor quality products.

Just for good measure, section 45 of the same Act put the final nail into the coffin of local justice by abolishing all local justice areas so as to create a unified magistrates' court. Local justice areas had replaced the petty sessional divisions on which magistrates' courts had for long been founded.

Weak governance has contributed in other ways too. This included the fixed penalty notices, extensively used by police with levels now increased. As noted already these were used extensively for alleged breaches of lockdown rules in circumstances where police themselves often did not understand law/guidance. There has also been an undue reliance on the Single Justice Process, discussed above. Additionally, regarding legislation, two major concerns must be quality and balance.

Despite Auld's warnings the ensuing years saw numerous examples of legislation which was enacted but never implemented or in some cases repealed without any commencement. In addition, current structures do make proposals for substantive legislation much more susceptible to influence by law enforcement agencies. In April 2021 Sir Jonathan Jones QC (former Treasury Solicitor) gave evidence to the House of commons Justice Select Committee about the government's use of law as regards the response to COVID-19. He started by deprecating the government's tendency to legislate at extremely short notice invoking emergency powers under public health legislation. But he commented more widely saying: 'bad legislative habits had become ingrained and the rule of law would be at risk if people could not find the law that applied to them.' He added that 'the police needed to understand the difference between policies announced by ministers at press conferences and laws made under the authority of Parliament'.

But perhaps as good an example as any as to the way in which policies are influenced by lobbying departments, in the absence of anyone with overall responsibility for the criminal justice system, has been the lack of response to the difficulties caused by private prosecutions. By definition (at least, so far as the term refers to individuals and private companies) no ministerial department has an interest in these, and there is no champion anywhere in government for the interests of defendants. Thus, despite disquiet on a number of fronts about the behaviour of some private prosecutors over the last ten years (during which they have become increasingly more prominent) the lack of interest was deafening and if it changes at all, it will only be as a result of the well-publicised revelation of the scandalous practices of Post Office Ltd. It was the Justice Select Committee of Parliament, rather than the Ministry of Justice, which first reacted to the likelihood that dozens and maybe hundreds of convictions would need to be overturned and considered possible safeguards against abuse. When the Committee sent a list of recommendations, including safeguards against future abuse, it was telling that the Ministry's first reaction was to embrace only those which would save money (by drastically capping the amount of costs that may be recovered by prosecutors from central funds) and to insist that other measures were not needed or needed careful consideration.

6. Key Questions and Concluding Thoughts …

Some 50 years in the criminal justice system will inevitably have created some unconscious bias towards how things were done. When developing this chapter, I have tried to keep three key questions in mind:

- Have the degree of centralisation within the agencies and the other drivers of change identified achieved greater efficiency and effectiveness within those agencies individually?
- Has the degree of centralisation, together with related changes, enabled greater efficiency and effectiveness across the criminal justice system as a whole?
- Do the governance arrangements properly balance the competing interests of the different CJS stakeholders?
- Has the degree of centralisation facilitated the increased politicisation of the CJS?

Setting aside the bias of age, it remains difficult to answer any of the first three questions in the affirmative. The fourth is a resounding 'yes'. The drivers and dynamics are many and complicated, but the dominant ones have been the financial grip of the Treasury and associated culture changes – facilitated by the concentration of responsibility at the centre; and the political encroachment that has also resulted.

There is no easy fix. Proper funding is vital, but money alone will not solve the problems, rebuild confidence and attract practitioners back. There needs to be a change of culture in the way the criminal justice is run and managed including greater willingness by those at the centre to look critically at the quality of the service actually being delivered. Particularly in relation to the treatment of victims, there is often a wide gulf between policy and what is actually capable of being delivered at local level. Ministers and senior officials seem to be in denial. Perhaps they should reflect on the conclusion of a heavy-weight Royal Commission that a nationally managed prosecution service would not be workable. Inevitably it is even more difficult to manage the entire criminal justice system on a national basis.

Whether or not that is accepted, perhaps the most important lesson to be learned from this potted history is the need to separate policy making from delivery.

Nor is turning back the clock an option. Local government as a whole is now so constrained with its funding also being so tightly controlled by central government. Most resources now come in the form of central grants with tight caps on the raising of revenue through council tax. So, the impact of returning services to local authorities might be limited for the simple reason that they would be able to do only what government funded them to do. There are some aspects of criminal justice that do need to be handled at a national level – the investigation and prosecution of terrorism and the response to fraud are prime examples. Some jurisdictions do have two-tier structures and that is a course that could usefully be and should be explored further.

But the key message is that one size certainly does not fit all and a wholly centralised system seems both unwieldy and inflexible as well as detracting from the traditional ethos of the justice system.

Postscript

During final editing of this chapter, a critical report by the Public Accounts Committee[40] reinforced doubts whether the scale and complexity of criminal justice agencies makes them amenable to successful central management and how individual agencies continue ploughing their own furrows without holistic strategy or a single minister with responsibility for the system.

The Courts and Tribunals Reform programme was a project that in 2014 promised a 'single integrated system which would allow electronic case management' was planned to allow access to all parties to a case – including the CPS which already had its own case management system. It was described by one commentator as 'selling off courts to buy computers'.[41]

In 2018, the PAC described the £1.2 billion project as 'hugely ambitious and on a scale which has never been attempted anywhere before'.[42] The pressure to deliver quickly and make savings was limiting HMCTS's ability to consult meaningfully with stakeholders. It risked driving forward changes before it fully understood their impact on users and the justice system more widely. There was no guarantee of real savings as opposed to shunting costs to other parts of the justice system. Four years into the project, it lacked a sufficiently well-developed plan of what it was trying to achieve!!

The 2023 report is similarly bleak. Completion is now expected in 2025 with £1.1 billion spent and just £120m remaining. The criticisms remain:

> HMCTS's approach to implementing the common platform has remained detached from the needs of those who use the courts system.
>
> It has not done enough to listen and respond to users' concerns, leaving staff and courts to suffer the consequences. HMCTS's lack of data and research means that it has a limited understanding of whether reformed services are delivering the expected benefits, the total cost of its reforms to the taxpayer or the impact on other services.[43]

The PAC chair, Dame Meg Hillier MP records being told by the government that the complexity of managing some of these reforms was like 'redesigning the jet engine while it is in flight'.[44]

[40] *Progress on the courts and tribunals reform programme* (HOC1002, 2023).
[41] J Rozenberg, 'Court reform: the verdict' (*A Lawyer Writes*, 2023).
[42] *Transforming courts and tribunals* (2018).
[43] Public Accounts Committee (n 40).
[44] ibid, ch 1, para 12.

INDEX

www.ingramcontent.com/pod-product-compliance
Ingram Content Group UK Ltd.
Pitfield, Milton Keynes, MK11 3LW, UK
UKHW020236290926
15470UKWH00002B/574

9 781509 959181